W9-CRB-530

INSIGHT GUIDES

Created and Directed by Hans Höfer

PeRU

Edited and Produced by Tony Perrottet
Update Editor: Andrew Eames
Photography by Eduardo Gil and others

Editorial Director: Brian Bell

Houghton Mifflin

APA PUBLICATIONS

Perrottet

Höfer

Dempsey

von Hagen

Reid

This is a thoroughly revised and updated edition of one of Insight's most alluring South American titles. Since the first edition, edited by regional editor **Tony Perrottet**, fans of the country have had a frustrating time. Of the three key landscapes of the breathtaking Sierra, arid coastlands and lush Amazonian basin, the mountains have long been a main attraction. But it was in the mountains that Shining Path guerillas were at their most active, producing enough horror stories to keep tourists away.

But that frustration has eased. Now that the Shining Path is a spent force and its leader is in prison, parts of Peru that were closed are once again back on the travelers' map, with a new edition of this book to take account of these changes and set you on your way.

The riches of Peru are manifold. Is it Machu Picchu, Cuzco, the Nazca Lines, Lake Titicaca, or the Amazon that appeals? Are you interested in the Incas, the Indians or the colonising Spanish? Or perhaps your enthusiasm is for the dazzling birdlife of the tropical jungle? It's all in these pages.

Such a complex destination lends itself perfectly to the approach taken by the 200-title award-winning Insight Guides series, created in 1970 by **Hans Hofer**, founder of Apa Publications and still the company's driving force. Each book encourages readers to celebrate the essence of the place rather than try to tailor it to their expectations, and is edited in the belief that, without insight into a people's character and culture, travel can narrow the mind rather than broaden it.

The books are carefully structured: the first section covers a destination's history, and then analyses its culture in a series of magazine-style essays. The main Places section provides a comprehensive run-down on the things worth seeing and doing, with a little bit of gossip thrown in for good measure. Finally, a fact-packed listings section contains all the information you will need on travel, hotels, shops, restaurants and opening times. Complementing the text, remarkable photography sets out to communicate directly and provocatively life as it is lived by the locals.

The team behind the original *Insight Guide: Peru* was put together by Tony Perrottet, who is based in New York. Australian-born Perrottet studied history at Sydney University before turning to journalism. Lured by tales of relatives who had worked on the sheep farms of southern Patagonia, he explored South America from tip to toe. Later he revisited many individual nations for Apa, assembling an impressive list of books.

For *Insight Guide: Peru* Perrottet swiftly enlisted the support of **Mary Dempsey**, who had previously contributed to *Insight Guide: South America* and went on to contribute to several other titles. Dempsey, born in Toronto, settled in Lima in the 1980s, and used her experience to write in this book on subjects as diverse as Peruvian cuisine, Cuzco, Arequipa, the North and Lake Titicaca.

Chosen to write the chapter on pre- and colonial history was **Adriana von Hagen**, the daughter of one of Peru's most famous archaeologists. Von Hagen lives in Lima and works for the prestigious business journal *Andean Report*.

British-born journalist **Mike Reid** contributed the chapters on Peru's new

Frost

Smith

MacQuire

Wagenhauser

democracy, Mario Vargas Llosa, Lima and on Huallaga, the coca valley. Reid is Lima correspondent for the BBC.

Also well-known to Peru enthusiasts is **Peter Frost**, author of *Exploring Cuzco*. After living for many years in the Inca capital, it was appropriate that Frost should write about Inca society and Machu Picchu.

The chapter on Peruvian society was originally shaped by US-born journalist **Michael L Smith**, who was a correspondent for the *Washington Post* in Lima, and has written a book about Shining Path.

Compiling the chapter Daily Life in the Andes was American artist and writer **Julia Meyerson**, who spent several years living amongst the Quechua. The adventure was described in her book, *Tambo: Life in an Andean Village*.

Also a veteran of tribal living is **Kim MacQuarrie**, anthropologist, jungle guide and freelance writer. He has written a book about the Nahua, a remote tribe in the Manu National Park, and in this book writes about the Amazon Indians and the Amazon jungle.

Several other specialists are at work here. Anthropologist **Lynn Meisch** contributed the section on Cuzco fiestas. Naturalists **Barry Walker** and **Katherine Renton** contributed the sections on Sierra wildlife and Amazonian birdwatching respectively. Sections on trekking and rafting were put together by **Betsy Wagenhauser**, then at the South American Explorer's Club in Lima. **Simon Strong** wrote about Lima's Oasis of Hope, while **Lesley Thelander** used her experience in the travel industry to put together the Travel Tips section.

Finally, the section on the Quest for Lost Cities was written by anthropologist and adventurer **Robert Randall**, who ran a hotel in Ollantaytambo,

making regular expeditions into the jungle, before his tragic death in 1990.

More than 15 photographers contributed their work, with the Argentinian **Eduardo Gil** most prolific amongst them. Gil studied sociology and trained as a pilot before turning to photography. Peru-born **Heinz Plenge** is well-known nationally for his newspaper and magazine work.

The superb nature photography comes from Liechtenstein-based **Andre Bartschi**. **John Maier**, a US photographer living in Rio, added a series of shots from his latest assignment in Peru. Mountain photographer **Jim Bartle** provided material from the Callejon de Huayllas, while priest and photographer **Victor Campos Rios** sent work from his home city of Cajamarca.

Gil

The updating work on this new edition was carried out by two key figures, original author **Mary Dempsey** and newcomer **Simon Elgar**, who has taken over from Betsy Wagenhauser at the South American Explorer's Club. Between them, they effectively rewrote several chapters where much had changed (Discovery and Desecration, Democracy and Crisis, Changing Face of Society, Adventure in the Andes' as well as making extensive corrections elsewhere. Dempsey added a new chapter on the city of Ayacucho, an architectural gem which is now open again to visitors. New photography came primarily from specialist South American photographer **Sue Cunningham**, and the new Travel Tips was revised by Apa's German office. The project was co-ordinated by **Andrew Eames**.

CONTENTS

Places

Maps

TRAVEL TIPS

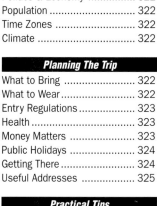
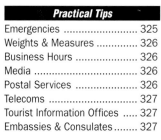
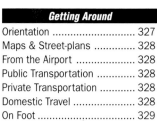
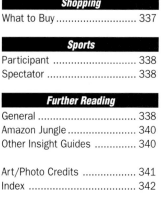

WELCOME TO PERU

Despite its rugged and often inhospitable landscape, Peru ranks amongst the world's great centers of ancient civilization. The sun-worshipping Incas are only the most famous in a long line of highly-developed cultures that thrived thousands of years before the arrival of Europeans. Their remains fascinate travelers and archaeologists alike. Along with the stunning Inca ruins near Cuzco and the "lost city" of Machu Picchu, Peru is home to the Nazca lines etched on its coastal deserts, Colla burial *chullpas* near Lake Titicaca, the enormous adobe city of Chan Chan and the recently-discovered Moche burial site of the Lord of Sipán. These cultures left no written records, just mysterious works in gold, silver and stone.

But ancient ruins are only a fraction of the story. Peru is the classic Andean republic, and, although the traditional American world was shattered by the bloody Spanish Conquest in the 1530s, the legacy of ancient cultures is very much alive. Roughly half of Peru's 22-million population are of pure Indian origin: often living in remote mountain villages, they still speak the Quechua or Aymará tongue of their ancestors, and many of their beliefs and customs are a mixture of traditional Andean ways and the culture imposed by the Spanish *conquistadores*.

Peru is also one of the most spectacular countries on earth. Its variety is astonishing: scientists have ascertained that of 103 possible ecological zones, Peru has 83 crowded into its borders. As a result, the country has virtually every possible physical attraction. The Peruvian Andes have become a mecca for trekkers and mountain climbers. Over half of Peru is part of the Amazon jungle. And the coastal strip is one of the world's driest deserts.

Meanwhile, Peru's often chaotic modern reality is an essential part of the experience. In Jean Renoir's 1953 film *The Golden Coach*, a troupe of Italian actors arrives in 18th-century Lima to be greeted with the question: "What do you think of the New World?" The chief actor looks around at the provincial square and replies politely: "It will be nice when it's finished." Many people have a similar reaction today. Peru is a nation still in the process of being formed – coping not only with the demands of economic development in the 20th century, but also the cultural divisions that began with the Spanish Conquest over 450 years ago. Peru remains one of the world's great travel destinations.

Preceding pages: expert horse rider of Trujillo (North); sumptuous tapestries from Cuzco; Mount Huascarán in the Callejón de Huaylas; Machu Picchu; in the foothills of the Andes. Left, girl from Arequipa.

LAND OF VOLCANOES

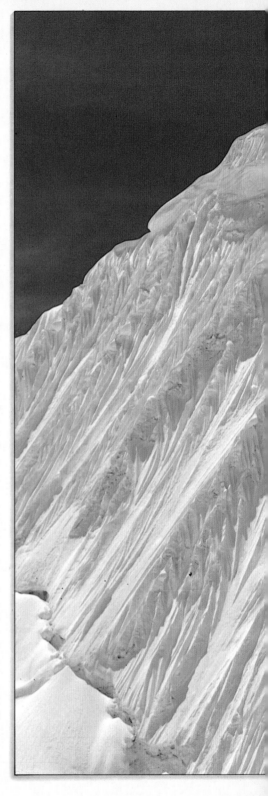

Ask Peruvians about their country and they will cut it into geographical slices – desert coast, highlands and jungle – proudly noting theirs is South America's only nation with all three. That geography, challenging to humans, sometimes even insurmountable, has given Peru its so varied legacy of ethnic cultures, foods, music and folklore.

Within that framework, Peruvians use the superlative to describe the country's offerings. They include Lake Titicaca, the world's highest navigable lake at 3,856 meters (12,725 feet) above sea level, and Mount Huascarán, Peru's highest Andean peak and South America's second tallest mountain at 6,768 meters (22,334 feet). The Amazon River, the world's mightiest, and its namesake rainforest make up much of Peru. Here, too, runs the world's highest single-gauge rail line cutting over the Andes, the globe's deepest canyon (the Colca outside Arequipa) and Cuzco, capital of the Inca empire.

Settled among those wonders – both natural and man-made – are 22 million Peruvians, 6½ million of whom are crowded into Lima. About 45 percent of the nation's residents are Indians, 37 percent are *mestizos* (mixed white and Indian), 15 percent are of European extract and 3 percent are either descendants of black slaves brought to work the mines or Japanese and Chinese immigrants. Spanish and Quechua are the offical languages. An estimated 92 percent of the country's residents are Roman Catholic although the religious rites they practice still bear traces of the pre-Christian religions the Indians once followed.

Barren beaches: The Spanish conquistadors' first glimpse of what is now Peru was along its 2,500-km (1,500-mile) coastal desert – one of the world's driest in this, the continent's third largest country after Brazil and Argentina. Visitors familiar with South America's Caribbean coast find Peru's sandy beaches unsettling, with their harsh backdrop of dunes or cactus-covered cliffs. But when conquistador Pizarro arrived the coast

Preceding pages: the dense Amazon rainforest. **Right**, snowy Mount Alpamayo in the Cordillera Blanca near Huaráz.

was less desolate; the Indians had sophisticated irrigation systems and fields of vegetables and grains flourished in the desert. The northern desert where Pizarro landed with his men was, in part, mangrove swamps.

On the southern coast, Chile's appropriation of some of this desert land more than a century ago in the bloody War of the Pacific meant the loss of a hidden treasure – tracts rich in the nitrates sought for fertilizers. Still, the coast has brought wealth to Peru despite its inhospitable landscape and dearth of water. (Only a cup of measurable precipitation every two years is recorded in some areas.) And fish are plentiful in the coastal waters, making Peru one of the world's foremost exporters of anchovies.

In fact, it is this frigid, fish-bearing current that keeps rain from the desert separating the ocean and the Andes. So little moisture accumulates above the cold Humboldt current running along the hot coast that ocean winds heading toward the mountains rarely carry condensation. What they do bring to the land, however, is a thick, dense fog that causes havoc with air traffic and covers Lima for half the year with a gloomy mist known as *garua*. The exception to this rainless period are the freak showers when El Niño, a warm current traveling from the equator, comes too close to the coast.

Mountainous heart: But it is the highlands that are most associated with Peru. Here Quechua-speaking women weave, condors soar above the Andes and wild vegetation camouflages Inca ruins. Although breathtaking to look at, the Sierra seems brutally inhospitable: the thin, cold air here combines with rugged landscape to make the Andes an obstacle to transportation, communication and development.

Nevertheless, nearly half of Peru's population is scattered across the Sierra, on poor rocky land where alpacas and llamas graze while subsistence crops are eked out of terrace farms used since Inca times.

Although the Incas found a way to survive in the Andes, cutting terrace farms into steep hillsides, building aqueducts that astound modern hydraulic engineers and erecting massive forts and cities in isolated valleys, they met a formidable foe in the jungle – the region even they could not successfully pen-

Left, Terraces in the Colca Valley near Arequipa.

etrate. Three-fifths of Peru is jungle, divided into the hot, steamy low Amazon and the so-called high jungle, or *ceja de la selva* (eyebrow of the jungle). The latter is the area where the mountains meet the Amazon, a subtropical patch where Peru's coffee and 60 percent of the world's coca crop is grown.

Peru has set itself aside from its neighbors by aggressively protecting the rainforest through legislation and by designating virgin areas as national parks. Extending from the Andean foothills east of Cuzco into the low jungle is Manu National Park, boasting one of the world's most impressive concentrations of wildlife; more than 500 bird species alone have been spotted from the park's research station.

A few hours by river from Puerto Maldonado is another protected area, the Tambopata Wildlife Reserve with more than 1,110 butterfly species and a number of insects found only there.

Land of volcanoes: Nature as much as man has dealt this country cruel blows. Peru straddles the Cadena del Fuego, or Chain of Fire – a volcanic line over a geologic fault running the length of the continent. The line passes Peru along its coast, cutting directly through Arequipa which, over the centuries, has borne the brunt of the seismic damage.

In the Sierra, quake damage is aggravated by the breaching of highland lakes, pulling tons of water and mud on to small towns and burying their residents alive. The world's worst recorded disaster of this type occurred in 1970 in Yungay, near Huaráz. Tremors opened the banks of a lake over the city and 18,000 people were washed into a chasm. The ghastly site is marked by the tops of three palm trees – once on the city's Plaza de Armas – protruding from the earth.

The broad range of weather conditions from one part of the country to another leaves labels such as "winter" and "summer" of little practical use. Lima residents refer to summer as their hot sunny months (December to April) and winter as the rest of the year when the fog sets in. In the Sierra, winter is the months of rain (October to May). Snow is uncommon in inhabited highland areas even though the highest of Peru's Andean peaks are snow-covered year round. The jungle, meanwhile, is hot and humid all year.

Right, The barren coastal desert.

Civilization in the Andes has long been equated with the Incas. Impressive accounts by 16th-century Spanish chroniclers told of fabled Inca wealth, and the architectural achievements of the Incas, inevitably compared to the feats of the Romans, featured in almost every account of Peru. But archaeologists working on the Peruvian coast and highlands have now shown that the origins of Peruvian civilization reach back four millennia, 3,000 years before the Incas emerged from their highland realm to forge Tahuantinsuyu, their enormous empire of the four quarters of the world (*see page 48*).

It was not until the turn of this century when scientific archaeology was first carried out in Peru, that the true antiquity of Peruvian civilization began to emerge. No-one imagined at the time that civilization in the New World could be as ancient as that of the Old World. New data emerging from Peru, however, shows that the earliest monumental architecture is roughly contemporary with the pyramids of Egypt and predates the large-scale constructions of the Olmec in Mesoamerica by over a thousand years.

The beginnings of civilization: Peru's harsh environment hardly seems the place to spawn such achievements. Along the coast, some 50 river valleys slice through the desert, creating fertile oases interspersed by arid expanses of sand. Between 2500–1800 BC, a time known to archaeologists as the Cotton Preceramic, small communities thrived along the coast, harvesting the rich Pacific Ocean for its bounty of shellfish, fish and marine mammals. On river floodplains they cultivated cotton and gourds and hunted for deer. In the *lomas*, lush belts of fog vegetation located a few miles inland, they gathered wild plants. Before the introduction of true weaving, they created twinned and looped textiles of cotton and sedge, some decorated with intricate designs that attest to technological and aesthetic skills.

Towards the end of the Cotton Preceramic,

larger settlements, such as that of Paraiso just north of Lima, covered 58 hectares (143 acres). Over 100,000 tons of quarried stone were used here to build monumental platforms. At the site of Aspero in the Supe Valley, 145 km (90 miles) north of Lima, the largest mound, built of rubble and stone blocks, is 10 meters (33 feet) high and measures 30 by 40 meters (98 by 131 feet) at its base. Both these centers were surrounded by sprawling residential areas containing burials and thick midden, or refuse, deposits.

Some time around 1800 BC, at the beginning of what is known as the Initial Period, these fishing communities began to move inland. Although the majority of sites documented from this time average only 20 km (12 miles) from the coast, they were far enough up-valley to tap the rivers and construct irrigation canals, substantially increasing the ancient Peruvians' subsistence base. Evidence from the middens indicates that in addition to cotton and gourds they grew squash, peppers, lima and kidney beans, peanuts and avocado, supplementing their diet with marine products. Maize, which would become an Andean staple, was introduced

Preceding pages: the historic library in San Francisco Church, Lima. <u>Left</u>, gold figurine at the Brüning Museum. <u>Right</u>, Moche lord unearthed at Sipán.

somewhat later, possibly from Mesoamerica where it was first domesticated.

Two further revolutionary inventions belong to this period: the introduction of simple weavings and pottery.

Sierra cultures: The emergence of complex society on the coast was paralleled by developments in the highlands, where archaeologists have documented the rise of ceremonial architecture at sites such as Huaricoto in the Callejón de Huaylas, 250 km (155 miles) northeast of Lima. Unfortunately, preservation of organic matter is not as good in the highlands as it is on the arid coast, and the archaeological record for this area is not as complete. Nonetheless, excavations at Hua-

Pampa de las Llamas. Located 18 km (11 miles) inland, the complex once covered an area of 2.5 square km (1 square mile) dominated by two mounds. The 27-meter (90-feet) high pyramid of Moxeke, excavated earlier this century, was decorated with awesome adobe friezes of snarling felines and human attendants, which are painted red, blue and white. The temple facade has been reconstructed at Lima's recently-opened Museo de la Nacíon.

Facing Moxeke lies Huaca, or Mound A, which once stood almost 6 meters (20 feet) high and measured 135 by 135 meters (450 by 450 feet). Here, access to storage areas was controlled by wooden doorways and the

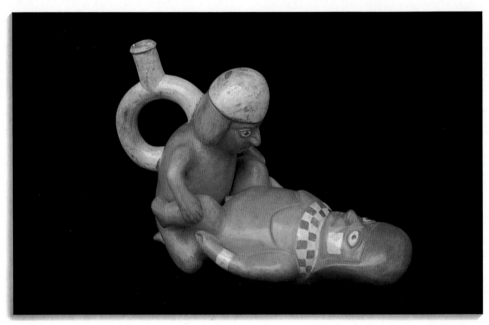

ricoto have unearthed ceremonial structures with firepits, where offerings were burned. Llamas were already domesticated by this time, serving as beasts of burden and providing an important food source. Llama caravans carried highland produce – potatoes and other Andean tubers and grains – to the coast in exchange for goods from the warm coastal valleys: dried fish and shellfish, seaweed, salt, cotton, peppers and coca leaves. The guinea pig, an Andean delicacy, was probably also domesticated about this time.

In the Casma Valley, 275 km (170 miles) north of Lima, large Initial Period settlements flourished at sites such as Moxeke-

images of two fanged felines guard one of two entrances to the complex.

These architectural monuments, with U-shaped platforms and sunken circular courtyards, have been documented from sites just south of Lima to the Moche or Trujillo valley, 595 km (370 miles) north of Lima. Near Trujillo stands the Huaca de los Reyes, which also contained elaborate adobe friezes of felines, once painted red, yellow and cream. The arms of the U-shaped temple point upriver, towards the Andes and the source of water. Then, as now, water was valuable on the rainless coast, and a constant preoccupation of ancient, and modern, Peruvians.

Sometime toward the end of the Initial Period, around 900 BC, archaeologists believe increasing warfare led to the construction of sites such as Cerro Sechin, also in the Casma Valley. Here a macabre procession of victorious warriors and their dismembered carved victims commemorate a battle on stone monoliths surrounding an earlier adobe temple.

The Early Horizon: In the highlands, construction began around 800 BC at the ceremonial center of Chavín de Huantar in the Callejón de Conchucos, southeast of the Callejón de Huaylas. Perhaps one of the most famous sites in ancient Peru, the site of Chavín was believed until recently to be the

Coastal sites contemporary with the florescence of the Chavín temple were perhaps branch shrines of a powerful Chavín oracle. Painted cotton textiles found at Karwa, near the Bay of Paracas on the south coast, for example, depict deities reminiscent of those carved on stone slabs at Chavín de Huantar. Located midway between the coast and the jungle lowlands, Chavín iconography even incorporated jungle fauna into its elaborate system. The Tello Obelisk, on view at Lima's National Museum of Anthropology and Archaeology, features a fierce caiman.

The spread of the Chavín cult brought with it innovations in textile and metallurgy technology. Weavings found buried with mum-

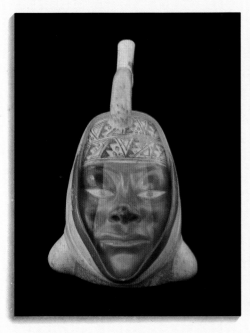

inspiration for the related art style that spread throughout much of coastal and highland Peru. It is often referred to as the Early Horizon (800 BC–AD 0). Research over the past 20 years has shown that Initial Period developments on the coast (U-shaped temples, circular sunken courtyards, stirrup-spout ceramics, and an elaborate iconography featuring fanged felines and snarling gods) culminated at Chavín, and did not originate there as some have thought.

Left, erotic Moche drinking vessel. **Above**, carved Moche gourd. **Above right**, drinking vessel of the Moche culture.

my bundles at Paracas and dated to about 400 BC are perhaps the finest cloth ever produced in ancient Peru. This was followed by the Necropolis phase, named after the hundreds of mummy bundles buried in stone-lined pits. Almost every technique known to the Andean weaver had been invented by this time. Evidence for a far-flung trade network is also visible at Paracas: obsidian from the highland region of Huancavelica to the southeast, cameloid fiber, probably alpaca, also from the highlands, and feathers of tropical birds used to adorn fans, which probably came from the jungle.

Traces for the use of cameloid fiber in

north coast weavings, again probably alpaca, also appear at this time.

Metalworking techniques such as soldering, sweat welding, repoussé and gold-silver alloys were first used by ancient Peruvian smiths during the Early Horizon. Only the Moche were to add to the repertoire of metalworking techniques a few centuries later.

Birth of new cultures: The decline of Chavín influence led to the emergence of regional culture in river valleys on the coast and in highland valleys during a time known as the Early Intermediate Period (AD 0–600). In the Nazca Valley, weavers and potters followed the Paracas Necropolis tradition, but instead of producing painted and incised pottery

Although there is plenty of evidence to tie these ancient markings to their Nazca creators, writers such as Erich von Daniken would like to attribute their construction to visitors from outer space. Other theories, such as that they formed part of an astronomical calendar, have gained little acceptance among archaeologists. A more recent theory suggests that the geoglyphs were linked to mountain worship and fertility. Indeed, many of the animal images can be tied to Andean fertility concepts and some of the lines point to the mountains in the distance, the source of valuable water.

The ancient Nazca lived in settlements dispersed around the Nazca drainage. They

they began to make slip-decorated ceramics which were painted with a variety of mineral pigments.

On an arid plain north of the modern city of Nazca, the ancient Nazca people etched giant images on the desert by brushing away the surface soil and revealing the lighter colored soil beneath. Images of birds, some measuring 60 meters (200 feet) across, predominate, but they also drew killer whales, a monkey (90 meters/300 feet across), and a spider (45 meters/150 feet long). All these animals feature on Nazca ceramics. The straight lines and trapezoids were built a few hundred years later.

worshipped their gods at the ceremonial center of Cahuachi, downriver from the modern city of Nazca.

On Peru's north coast, the Moche people flourished in the Moche or Trujillo Valley, known in ancient times as Chimor. From their early capital at the Pyramids of the Sun and the Moon, south of the modern city of Trujillo, the Moche held sway over 400 km (250 miles) of desert coast. The Pyramid of the Sun, one of the most imposing adobe structures ever built in the New World, was constructed of over 100 million bricks. They built irrigation canals, aqueducts and field systems that stretched for miles, even connecting neighboring valleys, and cultivated maize, beans, squash, peanuts and peppers. From their totora reed boats they fished and hunted for sea lions and captured deer along the rivers. They kept domesticated dogs and traded for luxury goods such as turquoise from northwestern Argentina, lapis lazuli from Chile and exotic seashells from the Gulf of Guayaquil, today Ecuador.

Masterful sculptors: Famed for their ceramics, Moche potters created realistic portrait heads and fine line drawings of gruesome blood-letting ceremonies. Perhaps the most imaginative and skilled metalsmiths in ancient Peru, they perfected an electrochemical-plating technique that gilded copper objects.

che kingdom came to an end. Torrential rains produced by the El Niño phenomenon, when the warm waters of the Ecuadorian current replace the cold waters of the Humboldt current, brought about massive destruction to irrigation canals, causing famine. In 1982–83 such rains flooded large areas and destroyed crops in much of northern Peru.

With the fall of Moche in the north and the decline of Nazca to the south, a powerful southern highland kingdom exerted its architectural and artistic influence over large areas of Peru between AD 600–1000. The capital of this empire was Wari, a large urban center near the modern city of Ayacucho. Archaeologists have excavated Wari sites

The discovery in 1987 of the tomb of a Moche lord at Sipán, near the modern city of Chiclayo almost 800 km (500 miles) north of Lima, has provided a wealth of new data on the ancient Moche, including evidence that most valleys under Moche influence had a powerful lord of their own. Discoveries at Sipán even link its metalwork to similar pieces looted from the site of Loma Negra near Piura, on Peru's far north coast.

Sometime between AD 650–700 the Mo-

near Cuzco at Piquillacta, Cajamarquilla near Lima and Marca Huamachuco in the highlands east of Trujillo.

The Wari style is strongly reminiscent of ceramics and sculpture from the Bolivian altiplano site of Tiahuanaco, which flourished between 200 BC–AD 1200. Situated at the southern end of Lake Titicaca at 3850 meters (12,600 feet) above sea level, Tiahuanaco was the highest urban settlement in the New World. The ancient people of Tiahuanaco employed an ingenious cultivation system that archaeologists estimate could have sustained a city of 40,000 people.

Tiahuanaco farmers cultivated potatoes,

Left, sun design in the Gold Museum of Lima. **Above**, mask found in the Lambayeque Valley of northern Peru.

oca and *olluco* (Andean tubers) as well as *quinoa* and *cañiwa* (Andean grains) on raised fields known as *camellones*. They dug canals fed by the lake and heaped up the soil from the canals to construct raised fields some 10 meters (33 feet) wide.

During the day the sun heated the water in the canals, and at night the water radiated its warmth to protect the crops from frost. Recent experiments revealed that crops grown on these raised fields produced harvests seven times higher than the average yield.

With the decline of Wari influence, regional cultures again flourished in the coastal valleys. In the north the Lambayeque or Sican culture centered at Batan Grande, 48 km (30

miles) north of Chiclayo. Here, elaborate burials, some containing scores of gold and silver vessels, point to Batan Grande as an important metalworking center.

But Batan Grande also appears to have been abandoned in about AD 1100, flooded by torrential rains caused by El Niño. The remnants of Batan Grande's population moved a few miles south to Túcume, a center of 26 large, flat-topped adobe pyramids and numerous smaller structures. The largest complex of monumental adobe architecture in the New World, Túcume and the Lambayeque Valley were conquered by the Chimú a few centuries later.

Adobe City: In Trujillo construction had already begun at Chan Chan, the Chimú capital near the ancient Moche capital at the Pyramids of the Sun and the Moon. The earliest constructions at Chan Chan probably date back to AD 800 and the center was continuously occupied by the Chimú dynasty until it fell to the powerful Inca armies in about 1464.

The largest kingdom to rule Peru before the rise of the Incas, the Chimú realm stretched 965 km (600 miles) along the coast, from the Chillon Valley in the south to Tumbes on the Ecuadorian border to the north. This time is known archaeologically as the Late Intermediate Period (AD 1000–1476).

Seventeenth-century Spanish chroniclers recorded a Chimú origin myth that told of the Chimú dynasty's legendary founder Tacaynamu. It relates how he arrived on a balsa wood raft, but it is thought that details of this life are largely mythical, although he probably existed. The legend spoke of 10 Chimú kings, who ruled for about 140 years, placing the date of the founding to the first half of the 14th century.

Curiously, there are ten rectangular compounds at Chan Chan, each one corresponding to a Chimú monarch. Each compound served as the realm's administrative center as well as the reigning monarch's palace, royal storehouse, and, on the king's death, his mausoleum. The succeeding monarch built a new compound for himself and the deceased ruler's compound was kept up by his family and loyal retainers.

The surrounding population, estimated to have numbered 50,000 people, was composed almost entirely of weavers, potters and metalsmiths who supplied the royal storehouses. These craftsmen lived in and around the royal compounds in crowded, small-roomed dwellings.

Today the sprawling mudbrick capital of Chan Chan is a bewildering labyrinth of ruined adobe walls, some still standing 7.5 meters (25 feet) high and stretching for 60 meters (200 feet). At its height in 1450 the city covered 23 square kilometers (9 square miles). Remains of adobe friezes of fish and birds still can be seen adorning some of the compound walls.

Above left, mummy found in Paracas. **Right**, the Tello obelisk from the Chavín culture.

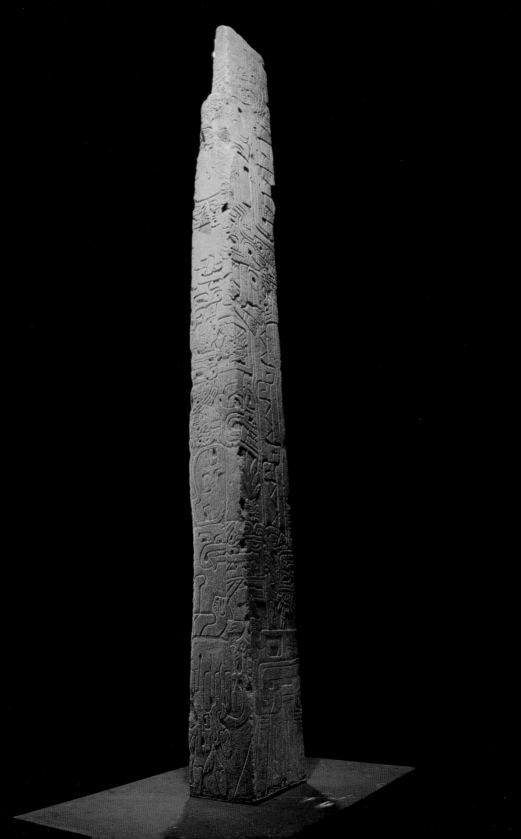

DISCOVERY AND DESECRATION

Police in northern Peru thought they were on a routine raid when they burst into the house of an out-of-work mechanic near the port of Chiclayo and confiscated a bag of booty he'd nabbed from an ancient Indian grave. After all, antiquities looting had been common-place there since the Spanish Conquest and the occasional raids were for show more than anything else.

But what the officers found when they opened the bag set off a chain of events that shook the scientific world and sent anthropologists and scholars rushing off to rewrite the history of the Americas. During moonlight digging at a 2,000-year-old pyramid near the 30-family village of Sipán in 1987, the mechanic and nine of his pals had stumbled onto a cache of splendrous gold and silver artifacts.

Walter Alva, the curator of the Brüning Archaeological Museum in nearby Lambayeque, was astonished by what awaited him when he arrived to catalog the confiscated artifacts. He watched officers unwrap a hammered sheet of gold fashioned into a face with lapis lazuli eyes, a treasure worth tens of thousands of dollars on the black market. Two jaguar masks with conch shell fangs, gold ear ornaments inlaid with turquoise, warrior amulets and oversized gold and silver peanuts joined the treasures pulled from the rice sack. The shaken Alva knew thieves had accomplished what archaeologists had never been able to do: they had found a royal tomb of the ancient Moches.

Revelations: Not since Harvard's Hiram Bingham stumbled onto the lost city of Machu Picchu in 1911 and Peruvian Julio C. Tello uncovered the first Paracas funeral bundle on the Pacific coast 18 years later have scientists been so enthusiastic about obtaining new information on ancient Indian cultures that thrived centuries before the arrival of the conquistadors.

Alva, now chief archaeologist at an excavation in Sipán, describes the Moches as one of the most developed civilizations in the centuries before the Inca empire appeared,

Left, Norwegian explorer Thor Heyerdahl with an oar found at Túcume.

boasting earthquake-resistant architecture that rivaled that of the Incas, weaving that may have been the finest in ancient Peru, pottery that puts all but the Maya to shame and metallurgy techniques that the Europeans wouldn't develop for another 200 years. Buried sponges and shells from what is now Ecuador and minerals from the distant highlands revealed the Moches' far-flung trade routes. Even the gold they worked might have come from outside their valley.

Archaeologists at the Sipán pyramid – officially known as Huaca Rajada – have located at least eight Moche graves, most of them the gold- and silver-laden burial chambers of royalty. The first was an 1,800-

funerary offerings. The most amazing find proved to be a three-dimensional ear ornament showing a man gripping a war club in one hand and a shield in the other. One of the most valuable pieces of pre-Columbian jewelry ever excavated, this miniature figure was an exact replica, in gold and turquoise, of the buried lord. The tomb of this royal chieftain, the Peruvian equivalent of Tutankhamun, was described by the National Geographic Society as the richest burial vault ever discovered in the Americas.

As excavations continued in 1988 and 1989, archaeologists opened the tomb of the "Old Lord of Sipán," buried more than a century before the Moche civilization began

year-old tomb of a nobleman scientist dubbed the "Lord of Sipán". The man, believed to be a regional governor who also held military and religious rank, was buried with three concubines, a child, a dog and four guards or soldiers. Normally, the 1,150 pieces of funerary pottery that accompanied the robust man to his afterlife would have been sufficient evidence of his high rank. But this tomb contained something more: gold and silver in astonishing quantities.

Buried riches: A two-foot wide headdress of copper, solid gold ear spools bedecked in turquoise, silver nose rings and a gold necklace of owl-shaped beads counted among the

the 200 years of prosperity that ended in AD 400 when alternating floods and droughts caused food shortages and incursions by highland Indians brought down the kingdom. The Old Lord was dubbed "Spiderman" because of an oversized gold arachnid necklace found with his remains. Then came a third tomb, that of the "Priest" buried in a wooden coffin surrounded by immense quantities of gold and silver and a coterie of servants and animals.

More on the Moches: More important than the dazzling treasures recovered from the excavation was the new information gleaned about the Moches, once thought to be an obscure regional civilization notable only for its realistic pottery. Scholars now sketch a picture of finely dressed Moche lords who relished the trappings of their class, including specially trained falcons for their hunting expeditions.

Moche artisans electroplated gold on to copper and painstakingly crafted gold and turquoise royal jewelry, weavers turned cotton into fine cloth that was dyed and decorated for the priests, and potters created molds for the ceramic vessels from which the priests drank the blood of conquered Moche enemies. Serfs lived in adobe huts with thatched palm roofs, raised llamas, ducks and guinea pigs, and toiled in vegetable, grain and cotton fields; advanced water canal systems allowed the Moches to tap into rivers and irrigate the arid coastal valley where rain is still rare today.

The Lambayeque Valley where the Moches lived was dotted with urban centers supporting tens of thousands of people. Local markets were bursting with goods catering particularly to the tastes of the upper class. The Moches adhered to strict codes of social conduct and their feudal lords commanded personal militias.

The Sipán discovery also sparked an unprecedented effort to stop looting in Peru, rumored land of forgotten cities of gold and a place where poverty heightens the lure of buried riches. So determined are Peruvian *huaqueros,* the Quechua Indian language term for looters, they once diverted a river to gain access to a pre-Hispanic pyramid. In the 1960s, they drove a bulldozer to one archaeological site and plowed several days a week for five years, leaving a wake of dirt and broken ceramics.

When well-diggers in a shanty town outside Lima accidentally uncovered 600-year-old skeletons in the early 1990s, they scavenged marketable artifacts, giving no thought to reporting the find. At that site, and thousands of others where notable pre-Columbian cultures like the Inca, Chimú, Nazca and Paracas flourished, pottery shards and centuries-old pieces of bones now blanket the ground, reminders of the illicit incursions that have robbed scientists of information about Peru's long-lost kingdoms. Archaeol-

ogists say some sites are pocked with as many as 100,000 holes, marking many centuries of looting.

Heyerdahl's project: The notable exception may be the Túcume, a more than 900-year-old collection of 26 pyramids being excavated under the direction of Norwegian explorer Thor Heyerdahl, best known for his daredevil voyage from Peru to Polynesia on the balsa raft *Kon-Tiki* in 1947. First built around AD 1100 by people of the Lambayeque culture, and later used by the Chimús and Incas, Túcume has eluded looters. That's because, centuries ago, the Spanish told superstitious locals that the devil haunted the spot. So ingrained was the belief that Heyerdahl had

to find a local witch doctor to perform a special purification ceremony before the local community allowed the dig to begin in 1987.

Although he has recorded numerous graves containing silver figurines and textiles worked in tropical feathers, Heyerdahl showed most enthusiasm over artifacts that supported his long-held theory that ancient Americans were capable of long-distance navigation and, in fact, were the first settlers in Polynesia – not Asians, as is generally held. As evidence of this theory he recovered a wooden oar and stumbled upon a balsa raft frieze on a long section of wall at the site.

Left, gold mask found at Sipán. Right, excavating at the Sipán dig.

For professional plunderers, the Promised Land lies among the river valleys of arid northern Peru. Here, in one of the world's driest deserts punctuated with irrigated rice, cotton and sugar cane fields, hills of tan dirt hide adobe temples, pyramids such as Huaca Rajada and Túcume and even sometimes whole buried cities.

One by one, these ancient sites are being ravaged by midnight scavengers who, burning wood for warmth and sipping sugar cane liquor for fortitude against the spirits of the dead, randomly plunge shovels into what were once palace walls, funeral chambers and sacred rooms, erasing mankind's history in a search for riches.

The lucrative looting trail is a complicated labyrinth, starting with *campesinos* who rob ancient sites and leading to private collectors and even prestigious museums in North America, Europe and Japan.

Efforts to trace the stolen items and launch court battles for their repatriation have been time-consuming, expensive and only mildly successful. So, in an unprecedented program watched by governments across the continent, Peru's elite police corps – normally assigned to track down terrorists – have joined Walter Alva in a campaign to stop the plunder in northern Peru.

Anti-looting campaign: Alva's anti-looting plan targets villagers who rob ancient sites, rewards black market informers and uses public education campaigns to halt antiquities smuggling – a multi-billion dollar underground industry rivaled globally only by drug and arms trafficking. Although police agree that the most difficult part of the program is identifying the local black market kingpins, they are infiltrating local smuggling operations and following the tips of informants. But much of their work involves routine stops at ancient sites, to look for signs of fresh digging, and raids on the homes of known grave robbers.

As many as 300 pre-hispanic artifacts have been recovered in a single raid. Once officers found 200 people digging at a single site. When police recover artifacts or encounter villagers sacking sites, they not only arrest the perpetrators, they lecture the lawbreakers on the shame of "robbing their grandfathers' graves."

The police raids are complemented by aerial surveillance. Archaeologists board Air Force flights over the Lambayeque Valley every month, working with maps as they chart mounds that may conceal ancient complexes and sites where looters are working or human destruction is obvious.

Although optimistic, the police are facing opponents who have bottomless pockets. The most successful grave robbers have walkie-talkies, radio-equipped trucks and paid lookouts who, peering from the tops of hills in the otherwise flat desert, can spot police cars coming from miles away. Although looters once rarely carried guns, firearms are showing up with more frequency. Even Alva packed a .38-caliber pistol for a short time after a high-profile trafficker threatened his life.

Proponents of the effort claim it has posted measurable success. Peruvian *campesinos* are beginning to turn in looters. The Moches and other ancient cultures now figure prominently in Peru's public school curricula and thousands of students annually are bused to Sipán to see the graves and talk with archaeologists eager to regale them with the evils of grave robbing. Many of the anti-looting supporters have rallied behind a plan to use ancient sites to lure tourists – and community-building tourism revenues – to the area. Most use Chiclayo, 40 minutes from Sipán, as their base.

Intrepid travelers who make their way to the Sipán excavation in cabs, or in travel agency buses equipped with bilingual guides, can watch archaeologists clean sand from tombs under excavation. Tourists can see looters' holes as they wander along dusty paths at Sipán, a rural site banked by a 30-meter (100-foot) high eroded hill that hides an adobe pyramid once connected by a ramp to the lower pyramid-shaped ceremonial temple under excavation.

They can view the reconstructed royal tomb of the "Lord of Sipán" and make a quick stop at the dig's on-site museum before heading down the road to Túcume. Then it's another 16 km (10 miles) to the town of Lambayeque and its Brüning Archaeological Museum, one of Peru's best archaeological museums and the place where the best Sipán discoveries are displayed in a high-security gallery.

Right, The "Lord of Sipán" as he was found. There is now a reconstructed tomb on the site.

THE INCAS

Peru's pre-Hispanic history is a long one filled with the marvels of ancient Indian civilizations that fed multitudes by irrigating deserts, who wove textiles so fine they cannot be reproduced even today and who built adobe cities that have survived millennia of earthquakes. Some, like the Chimú, Moche, Chancay, Nazca, Wari and Chavín, left behind traces that have allowed archaeologists and Andean scholars to reconstruct pieces of their societies. Other may always remain nameless and obscure. However, no group is as well-known, or perhaps as astounding, as the Incas – the magnificent culture the Spanish conquistadors found dominating much of the continent.

Nearly 800 years ago, the Inca nation appeared in Peru as a small regional culture in the central highlands. Like the Chimú, Chancay, Ica and other groups that thrived elsewhere in the region at the same time, they exerted local autonomy over large population centers and had distinct styles of textiles and pottery. But in the early 1400s, under the reign of Pachacuti, the Incas began an expansion – one of the greatest and fastest that has ever been recorded.

In little more than 50 years, the Inca domination was extended to as far north as what is now Colombia and south to present-day Chile. Indian groups that resisted were summarily vanquished and relocated as punishment. Others, through peaceful negotiations, joined the kingdom with little loss of regional control provided they added Inti, the Sun, as their supreme god and paid homage to the Inca leaders.

As each regional culture fell, Inca teachers, weavers, builders and metallurgists studied the conquered peoples' textiles techniques, architecture, gold-working, irrigation, pottery and healing methods. As a result, the Incas quickly accumulated massive quantities of information in advance of their own. By the time the Spanish arrived, Cuzco was a magnificent urban gem, storehouses of food throughout the empire had eliminated hunger, irrigated deserts and terraced moun-

tainsides produced bountiful crops, and Inca military might was legendary.

Although the accuracy of Spanish chronicles are suspect and the Incas themselves left no written word or codices, scholars, anthropologists and archaeologists have pieced together fragments of what certainly was a magnificent world.

A strict world order: Inca society was clearly hierarchical and highly structured, but it was not necessarily tyrannical and repressive. Everyone had a place and a part to play. Life

wasn't easy, but food and resources were stored and distributed so that all were fed and clothed. There was no private property, and everything was communally organized. It may have been a society in which the majority accepted their role without feeling aggrieved or exploited.

The Inca polity was a pyramid, with the ruling Inca emperor and his *coya*, or queen, at the apex. Under him stood the Inca nobility, the "Capac Incas," supposedly the true descendants of Manco Capac, the founding Inca, and belonging to some 10 or 12 *panacas*, or royal houses. Each Inca emperor founded a *panaca* when he ascended to power,

<u>Left</u>, Inca burial *chullpa* at Sillustani, near Lake Titicaca.

and the current ruler's was therefore the only *panaca* headed by a living man. The other *panacas* centered their lives and cult around the mummified remains of a former Inca emperor.

The city of Cuzco was filled with the huge palaces constructed by Inca rulers to house their *panaca*: that is, their personal retinue, their descendants via many wives and concubines, and, finally, their own mummy. This mummy was attended to as royally after the death of the ruler, as during his lifetime. It was consulted through seers and mediums on all important matters. It received daily offerings of food and drink, and at certain festivals it was taken out on its royal litter,

and paraded around Cuzco. Other nobility were also mummified after their deaths, and kept in lesser shrines. At one annual festival the royal mummies were carried about the countryside, revisiting the favorite places of their lifetimes.

The *panacas* of Cuzco existed together with a similar number of *ayllus* – large kinship groups – of lesser nobility, the so-called "Incas-by-privilege", who were early inhabitants of the Cuzco region, pre-dating the Incas. They held lands, ritual and economic functions, and many other aspects of life in common. The *panacas* and noble *ayllus* belonged to two moieties, Upper and Lower

Cuzco, whose relationship was both competitive and complementary.

Below these groups stood the regional nobility, who were not Incas at all, but held aristocratic privileges along with intricate blood relationships and reciprocal obligations to the ruling caste. Everyone in the empire was bonded to the whole by these sorts of connections, except for one large, amorphous group called *yanakuna*. They were a domestic class, primarily serving the *panacas*. They served without receiving formal reciprocal benefits, and although they could reach a high status, their loyalty was usually negotiable. Many of them defected to the Spaniards after Atahualpa's capture.

The privileges of power: The Inca nobility reserved many privileges to themselves, granting them selectively to outsiders. Polygamy was common, but exclusively aristocratic. Likewise, chewing coca leaves and wearing *vicuña* wool were privileges of the ruling caste. Noble males wore huge, gold ornate ear plugs in their pierced ears. Their beautifully woven tunics carried heraldic symbols called *tokapu*. All citizens wore the clothes and hairstyle fitting their station and ethnic group. The streets of Cuzco were colorful, for hundreds of groups were represented in the city, each with its own distinctive costume.

Scores of local languages existed, but the lingua franca of the empire was Quechua, a language spoken today from northern Ecuador to southern Bolivia. The origins of the language are obscure, but the Incas are believed to have acquired it from some other group. The nobles also used a private language, possibly a "high" chivalric dialect with elements of both Quechua and the Aymara language of the Titicaca region.

The ruling lords were fond of hunting. A royal hunt was a spectacular affair, involving thousands of beaters who encircled a vast area of land and drove all the animals into the center. The animals were not slaughtered indiscriminately, but culled. Young females of most species were released for future reproduction.

The myth of power within the Inca state held that the emperor was a divine being unlike ordinary mortals, descended from the Sun via his founding ancestor, Manco Capac. He gave voice to the desires and intentions of this powerful deity. Some Spanish chroniclers claimed that this was a cynical deception, foisted on the people.

The Sun may have become the supreme Inca deity after the rise of the ninth emperor, Pachacuti; before that, the supreme deity of the Incas was Viracocha, an almighty creator god also worshipped by other cultures.

Inca religion was not confined to the Sun and Viracocha. Cuzco's great temple, the Coricancha, or Court of Gold, contained shrines to the Moon, Lightning, the Pleiades, Venus, and the Rainbow. Moreover, there were shrines to scores of local deities – idols or sacred relics brought to Cuzco by the innumerable tribes and regions incorporated by the Incas. They did not attempt to erase

Coricancha like the spokes of a wheel. This conceptual system of sacred geography, known as the *ceque* system, was closely linked to the ritual and economic life of Cuzco. The *panacas* and *ayllus* had care of individual *huacas*, and groups of *ceque* lines. Additionally, the *ceques* delimited landholdings, assigning rights and responsibilities to Cuzco's immensely complex irrigation and flood-control system.

Holy concubines: Also important in Inca worship were the *acllas*, or chosen women. The Spanish drew a simplistic parallel between them and the Roman vestal virgins, labelling them Virgins of the Sun. Some may have been virgin devotees of certain deities,

local religions, they simply included them in an ever-expanding pantheon.

Besides the local and celestial deities there were the *apus* – usually the spirits of great mountains – and the *huacas*. These were stones, rock outcrops, caves, grottoes, springs, waterfalls, believed to contain spirit powers. More than 300 *huacas* existed around Cuzco, many of them housing the mummies of lesser nobility, and all of them connected by imagined lines that radiated from Cuzco's

Far left, Inca administrators cross a bridge (from the chronicle of Waman Puma). **Above**, the famous 12-angled stone in Cuzco.

but chastity was not a major preoccupation of the Incas, and young people were not expected to be sexually modest until they were married. The acllas were a motley group, selected from throughout the empire for their talents and beauty. Many were concubines of the Inca, some were destined to become wives of selected nobility, others served the main temple, producing weavings and foods whose destination was the sacrificial fires of the Coricancha. It's also likely that some belonged to a caste of astronomer-priestesses associated with the cult of the Moon, whose divine incarnation was the *coya*, sister and principal wife of the emperor.

The young Inca nobles were educated by *amautas*, scholars who transmitted the knowledge of the culture, often in the form of mnemonic songs and verses. Music and poetry were respected arts among the nobility, and so perhaps was painting. There was an immense "national gallery" called Puquin Cancha, containing paintings of individuals and scenes from Inca history, which was destroyed either during Pizarro's conquest, or the civil war that preceded it.

The Inca calendar featured an array of important festivals, which marked annual stages of life and the agricultural calendar. The summer and winter solstices were probably the two greatest celebrations, held with numerous sub-festivals. The Capac Raymi summer solstice, for example, also featured the coming-of-age celebrations for the new crop of young nobles. The males underwent severe trials, including ritual battles, and a death-defying foot race. Another great ceremony was *Sitwa*, in early September, when all foreigners had to leave Cuzco, and the Incas engaged in a huge ritual of purification, casting out sickness and bad spirits.

Cuzco itself was a holy city, as well as the administrative capital of the empire. It was the centre of Tahuantinsuyu – the four quarters of the world. The great royal roads to the four *suyus* began at the city's main square. Here all things came together. Here soil from every province was ritually mingled with the soil of Cuzco.

The four suyus corresponded roughly to the cardinal points. The northern quarter was the Chinchaysuyu – northern Peru and modern Ecuador. The south was the Collasuyu – Lake Titicaca, modern Bolivia and Chile. The Antisuyu was the wild Amazon forest to the east. The Contisuyu was the region west of Cuzco, much of it also wild and rugged country, but including the south and central Peruvian coast.

A rural empire: The Tahuantinsuyu was not significantly urbanized. There was the great complex of Chimú, on the north coast, and of course Cuzco. And there were a few large administrative centers along the spine of the Andes, housing a mainly transient population, which mustered and distributed the resources of entire regions. But most of the population lived in small rural communities scattered across the land.

The complex organization of the Inca state rested on a foundation of efficient agriculture. Everyone from the highest to the lowest was involved to some degree in working the land. Even the emperor ritually tilled the soil with a golden foot-plow, to inaugurate the new planting season, and it is notable that virtually any Inca ruin one visits, no matter what its original function, is surrounded and penetrated by agricultural terraces and irrigation channels. Fields of corn stood in the very heart of Cuzco.

Corn was their prestige crop. The great irrigated terracing systems whose ruins we see today were mainly devoted to its cultivation. Other Inca staples were potatoes and some other indigenous Andean root crops,

plus beans, quinoa and amaranth. The tremendous altitude range of the tropical Andes allowed the Incas to enjoy a great variety of foods, but it also required them to develop many localized crop strains for particular microclimates. This they did, with typical thoroughness, at several experimental agriculture centers, whose ruins survive today.

The Incas' great food surpluses enabled them to divert labor to many different enterprises. They created a vast road network, so expertly laid that much of it survives today, despite centuries of neglect. They built astonishing structures of stone so finely worked and of blocks so large that they required staggering amounts of time and effort. They used thousands of artisans to produce ornaments of gold and silver, pottery and fine textiles. And they raised great armies, able to march thousands of miles without carrying any provisions, so extensive was the network of storehouses.

The system which made these works possible was called *mita*. It was a kind of community tax, paid in labor. Every community sent some of its able-bodied young men and women for a limited period into the service of the state. The period varied according to the hardship of the work – mines, for example, were a tough assignment, and accordingly brief. Working in a state pottery was

easier, and correspondingly longer. Some communities – such as the famous one which rebuilt the Apurimac suspension bridge each year – rendered their *mita* in a specific task. One Inca-by-privilege *ayllu* provided the emperor with inspectors of roads, another with inspectors of bridges, and one ayllu even supplied the state with spies!

The life of a transient *mita* worker was rewarded by institutional generosity and punctuated by public festivals of spectacular drunkenness. Peasants who were otherwise

Left, working in the fields during a *mita* (Waman Puma). Above, Inca funeral garb.

tied to their villages for life mingled with groups from exotic locations worlds away, and caught a glimpse of the dazzling world of the Inca nobility. It was probably the most exciting time of their lives. Later the Spanish took over this institution and turned it into a nightmare of slavery and early death.

Binding the Andes to Cuzco: Another, less benign institution was the *mitmaq*. Loyal Quechuas were sent to distant, newly incorporated provinces whose inhabitants were proving troublesome, in order to pacify and "Inca-ize" the region; the recalcitrant ones displaced by the first group were moved to the Inca heartland where they were surrounded by loyal Quechuas.

About every 10 km (6 miles) along the great skein of roads that knit the empire together stood a *tambo*, a kind of lodge with storage facilities for goods in transit, and communal quarters for large groups of people. Closer together were the little huts which served as relay stations for the *chasquis*, the message-runners, who could allegedly cover the 2,400 km (1,500 miles) between Quito and Cuzco in five days.

Every major bridge and tambo had its *quipucamayoc*, an individual who recorded everything that moved along the road. Their instrument was the *quipu*, a strand of cord attached to color-coded strings, each carrying a series of knots tied so as to indicate a digital value. The *quipucamayocs* were the accountants of the empire. *Quipus* possibly served also as a cumbersome means of sending messages, certain types of knot being assigned a syllable value, so that a row of knots made a word.

Crimes of property were rare, and the Spanish "Viracocha" aura dimmed when it was learned that they not only stole from the Peruvians – which, though bizarre, made a kind of sense – but also from each other. Under the Incas, stealing was regarded as an aberration and dealt with ruthlessly when it occurred. Offenders suffered loss of privileges, with public humiliation and perhaps physical punishment. Serious or repeated crimes were punished by death, the victim being thrown off a cliff or imprisoned with poisonous snakes and dangerous animals.

A combination of techniques sustained the growth of the Inca empire. Military conquest played a part, but so did skillful diplomacy; some of the most important territories may have been allied confederates rather than subordinate domains. The glue holding the empire together was the practice of reciprocity: ritual generosity and favors to local rulers on a huge scale, in exchange for loyalty, labor and military levies, women for the Inca nobility, products special to the region, and so on. The emperor maintained fabulous stores of goods to meet his ritual obligations and create new alliances.

The Incas possibly were not imperialist in our usual sense, at the outset. There was an ancient Andean tradition of cultural influences, spreading out by means of trade and pilgrimage from important religious centers, such as Chavín, and later Tiahuanaco. It's likely that Cuzco started in this way, too; later the Incas extended their sway in southern Peru by means of reciprocal agreements and blood alliances.

The path to power: Then came the pivotal war of survival against the Chancas, a powerful group from the north. The historical existence of the Chancas has never been confirmed by archaeology, but the Inca version current at the time of the Conquest states that the man who would take the title Pachacuti – "transformer of the world" – defeated the invading Chancas at the very gates of Cuzco. Subsequently he transformed Inca culture from the roots up, and launched the career of expansion which would be continued by his son and grandson. As the Incas extended further and further from their center, they confronted groups with ideas and identities increasingly different from their own. Thus, continued expansion increasingly required the use of force.

By the time of the Spanish invasion, Pachacuti's grandson, Huayna-Capac, was far from his homeland, fighting almost continuously in the mountains along what is now the northern frontier of Ecuador with Colombia.

Quito, the base from which these campaigns were launched, had become a *de facto* second capital, and a northern aristocracy without roots in Cuzco had formed. On the death of Huayna-Capac the two groups fell into violent conflict, and the disastrous civil war between Huascar and Atahualpa was the result (*see page 53*).

Many groups that the Incas had conquered, such as the Huanca from the Mantaro Valley of Peru's central highlands, resented and resisted Inca domination. They had to be held in place by the threat of force, and later they happily deserted the Incas to fight alongside the Spanish.

When the Incas used military force they used it generously. Many an opponent surrendered without a fight when he saw the size of the army sent against him. If it came to a trial of arms, the Incas still preferred to cut off an enemy's water supply, or starve him into submission, rather than confront him directly in battle.

War and warriorhood was an important part of Andean life from early times. Yet it surely cannot have been of paramount value to the Incas. If it had, then military tactics and technology would have been at the peak of

their achievements, whereas in fact their weapons and methods of warfare were extremely primitive – far inferior to their attainments in administration, architecture, agriculture and engineering – and had not evolved since the earliest times of Andean culture. They fought with clubs, stones and all-wooden spears. Even the bow and arrow, though known to them, was not widely used in battle. The gulf between their fighting capacity and that of the steely Spanish conquistadors was tragically wide.

Artists in stone: Like other peoples of the New World, the Incas had not discovered how to smelt iron ores. Their use of other metals was, however, quite sophisticated. They had mastered many techniques for working gold and silver, and created bronze alloys of varying types for different uses.

The finest bronze was too soft to be much use for working stone, however. Stoneworking was a major activity, involving staggering amounts of time and care. Modern research shows that their finely fitted stones were primarily cut and shaped using hammer-stones of harder rock. This process was laborious, but not as slow as we might imagine. Their vast manpower and their evident reverence for stone enabled them to persevere through the decades and even through the generations it took to complete such

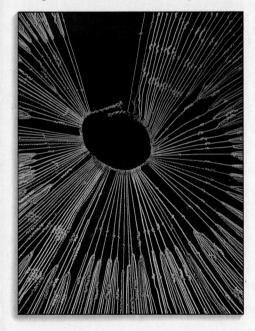

astounding structures as Machu Picchu and Sacsayhuaman.

How they moved and fitted the stones remains a mystery. Rollers and pulleys have been proposed, yet no theory explains how the combined efforts of 2,500 men – the number believed necessary to haul the largest stones up the ramp at Ollantaytambo – were simultaneously applied to a single stone. As for fitting, a common suggestion is simply trial and error: stones were set and then removed; high spots were marked, as a den-

Left, a *chasqui*, Inca message-runner (Waman Puma). **Above**, a *quipu*, used for records.

tist marks a filling; adjoining faces were then smoothed, and the process repeated, until the stones fitted together with astounding perfection. It sounds plausible – until one sees the stones; boulders so colossal that the mere thought of lifting them makes one nervous. A recent theory proposes that the cut stone profiles were matched by a large-scale version of the method we use today for duplicating door keys. Then again, some people explain the whole mystery in a single word: extraterrestrials.

Whether or not the Incas had access to lasers and intergalactic travel, they evidently had not discovered the wheel, or a form of writing. Andean terrain is the most vertical on earth, and the Incas' only draft animal was the small, lightly built llama, who sinks to his knees under a load exceeding 45 kg (100lb). So the absence of a wheel is understandable.

Thus, lacking the first reasons to devise a wheel, the Incas never discovered its other uses, such as the potter's wheel. They did, however, inherit the distaff spindle for spinning thread, which has been used in the Andes for millennia.

Another invention the Incas lacked was the arch, an important engineering device in the Old World. Instead, to span great gaps, they built sturdy suspension bridges. Their trademark workaday structural shape was the trapezoidal aperture. This shape – tapering upwards, with a stone or wooden lintel across the top – will take a fair amount of weight from above. All four walls of almost every Inca building also leaned slightly inwards, making them very stable. This technique, combined with the brilliantly interlocking joins of their stonework, made their buildings almost earthquake-proof – a useful feature in Peru.

The absence of some form of writing is harder to explain. The *tokapu* textile symbols and the *quipus* were the closest they came. Quechua is full of ambiguities, puns, juxtapositions and multiple meanings, relying heavily on context for its true sense; it is the language style of an oral culture, but whether this is the cause or effect of not having any written language it is impossible to say. And although the Incas might have lacked certain things we would consider essential, this did not prevent their creating a sophisticated civilization, whose echoes still reverberate through the Andes.

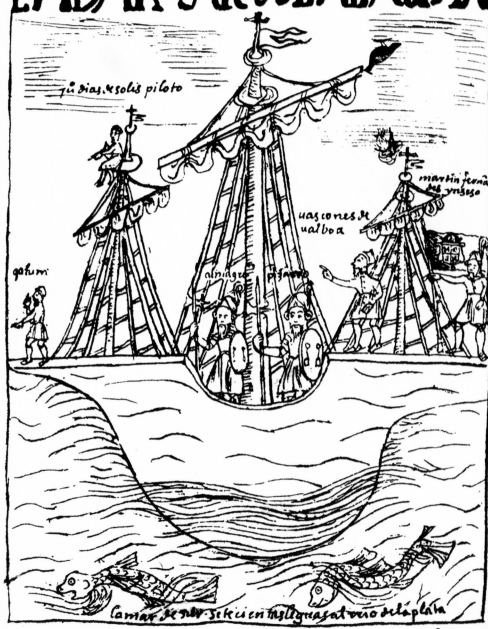

CONQVISTA
EMBARCAROSE ALAS INDIAS

iu dias de solis piloto

martin fernandes yngueso

uascones de ualboa

almagro pisaro

gofum

la mar de nr se sesis en mil leguas al oro dela plata

la mar

On September 24, 1532, a motley collection of Spanish *conquistadores* appeared at the fringes of the Inca empire, at that time the largest and most powerful that South America had ever known. In the months to come, these 62 horsemen and 106 foot soldiers commanded by an illiterate pig farmer named Francisco Pizarro would march to the heart of Peru and brutally seize control of the Inca throne. Within a decade, a glittering Andean world would be firmly in the grip of the Spaniards, its glories stripped and people virtually enslaved.

Few historical events are as dramatic or cruel as the conquest of Peru. Although only a handful in number, the invading Spaniards had on their side an astonishing streak of good luck, complete technological superiority and a lack of principle that would have made Machiavelli shudder. Apparently experiencing no other emotions than greed and fear, they were repeatedly able to trick their way into the confidence of the Incas only to betray them. By the time the Incas realized the ruthlessness of their foes, it was too late.

The invasion of America: Cautiously marching into Peru's coastal desert, Pizarro and his men were in the front ranks of Spain's explosion into the New World. It had been only four decades earlier, in 1492, that Christopher Columbus had landed in the West Indies – the same year that Castile drove the last Moors from European soil. The violent energies of Spanish soldiers were soon directed across the Atlantic: in 1519, Hernando Cortés, with 500 men and 16 horses, conquered the fabulously wealthy Aztec empire in Mexico. Panama was settled and conquistadors were soon looking at the newly-found Pacific Ocean as a route to further riches.

Although the existence of Peru was still no more than a rumor, three Spaniards in Panama formed a partnership to conquer it. Francisco Pizarro and Diego de Almagro were already relatively wealthy soldiers from Spain's barren Extremadura; the third was an ambitious

priest named Hernando de Luque. They led two expeditions down the west coast of South America before stumbling on the Inca city of Tumbes in modern-day Ecuador. Intoxicated by the prospect of conquering a new Mexico, Pizarro went back to Spain and recruited a band of adventurers and cutthroats from his home town Trujillo.

By the time Pizarro returned to Tumbes in 1532 with his 168 men, it was in ruins. In a stroke of fortune that would determine the fate of Peru, the Spaniards had found the Inca

empire in an unparalleled crisis, weakened for the first time by a bitter civil war. Several years earlier, a virulent disease – probably smallpox, spreading like wildfire from European settlements in the Caribbean amongst the Amerindians – had struck down the supreme Inca Huayna-Capac and his probable heir. Two sons had been left untouched by the plague: Huascar, in the capital city of Cuzco, and Atahualpa, heading the imperial army at Quito. In the civil war that followed, Atahualpa's troops were victorious, but the empire was rocked by the struggle.

When Pizarro landed, Atahualpa had only just learned that he was undisputed Inca. He

Left, the *conquistadores* leave Spain for the New world (Waman Puma). **Above**, portrait of Inca leader Atahualpa.

was heading in triumph south from Quito to the capital when news arrived that a group of tall, bearded men had entered his lands. As luck would have it, Atahualpa was camped not far from the Spaniards' route of march. The Inca decided that he would meet the strangers himself.

Into the Andes: Pizarro and his force turned away from the barren coast to climb the rough road into the Andes. Although exhausted by the thin, high-altitude air, the conquistadors marveled at the first signs of the Inca civilization: steep valleys were lined with rich terraces of maize; shepherds stood by with flocks of ungainly llamas; and powerful stone fortresses overlooked the Spaniards' path. But the Inca warriors watched the advancing strangers impassively: Atahualpa had given orders that they should not be hindered.

Finally Pizarro came to the town of Cajamarca. Stretching into the valley beyond were the tents of the Inca's army and entourage. One chronicler recorded the Spaniards' awe at the sight: "Nothing like this had been seen in the Indies up to then. It filled all us Spaniards with fear and confusion. But it was not appropriate to show any fear, far less to turn back. For had they sensed any weakness in us, the very Indians we were bringing with us would have killed us." Pizarro entered the near-deserted town and sent his brother Hernando with a group of horsemen to meet Atahualpa.

The Inca received the envoys with all the pomp and splendor of his magnificent court. When permitted to speak, the Spaniards used a translator to convey that Pizarro "loved (the Inca) dearly" and wished him to visit. Atahualpa agreed to meet in Cajamarca the following day.

Only that night did the Spaniards fully appreciate what they had got themselves into. Pizarro had no definite plan, and the conquistadors heatedly debated what should be done. They were several days' march into an obviously huge empire. Outside, the camp fires of the Indian army lit up the surrounding hillsides "like a brilliantly star-studded sky." They were terrified, but the lust for gold was stronger than fear.

The capture of the Inca: Next morning, the Spaniards prepared an ambush. Hidden in Cajamarca's main square, the Spaniards waited tensely all morning without any sign

of movement in Atahualpa's camp. Many began to suspect that their treacherous plan had been detected and they would all be slaughtered outright – one conquistador later recalled: "I saw many Spaniards urinate, without noticing it, out of sheer terror." It was not until nearly sundown, after Pizarro had once again sent envoys to promise that "no harm or insult would come to him," that the Inca decided to pay his visit.

The Incas arrived in full ceremonial regalia. "All the Indians wore large gold and silver discs like crowns on their heads," one observer wrote. Atahualpa himself wore a collar of heavy emeralds and was borne on a silver litter by 80 blue-clad nobles. Sur-

rounding him were "five or six thousand" men with battle axes and slings. But the Inca Atahualpa found no Spaniards in the square. He called out impatiently, "Where are they?"

Friar Vicente de Valverde emerged from the darkness with a translator and copy of the Bible. What happens next is confused by the chroniclers, but has been pieced together by John Hemming in his classic *Conquest of the Incas*. It appears that Valverde began to explain his role as a priest. Atahualpa asked to look at the Bible, never having seen a book. "He leafed through [the Bible] admiring its form and layout. But after examining it he threw it angrily down amongst his men, his face a deep crimson." This "sacrilege" was all that the Spaniards needed to justify their actions. Valverde ran away from Atahualpa, screaming, "Come out! Come out, Christians! Come at these enemy dogs who reject the things of God!"

Pizarro gave his signal. Cannons blasted and the Spanish spilled into the plaza with their battle cry of "Santiago!" Cavalry crashed into the horrified Indian ranks and began a wholesale slaughter: the Indians "were so filled with fear that they climbed on top of one another – to such an extent that they formed mounds and suffocated one another."

Retreat had been blocked, and none of the entourage escaped alive. Pizarro himself

The Inca empire, already divided by the civil war, was now without its absolute leader. Atahualpa issued orders from captivity on the instructions of the Spanish, and the stunned Incas could only obey.

The conquistadors took whatever they wanted from the surrounding camp. Inca soldiers looked on as Hernando de Soto demanded men as porters, women as slaves, llamas for food – and, naturally, as much gold, silver and jewelry as his squadron could carry. Atahualpa saw immediately that the Spaniards were interested in nothing but precious metal and assumed they must eat it. He offered a ransom for his freedom: a room of 88 cubic meters in size would be filled

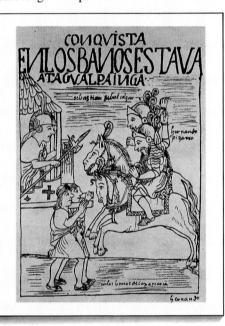

hacked a path straight for the Inca and grabbed his arm. He suffered the only wound to befall the Spanish troops: a blood-crazed conquistador went to stab the Inca but Pizarro deflected the blow, cutting his hand. Atahualpa was rushed away from the carnage and locked, ironically enough, into the Temple of the Sun.

The royal prisoner: The Spanish could hardly believe their luck in capturing Atahualpa.

<u>Left</u>, contemporary portrait of Francisco Pizarro. <u>Above</u>, the Spaniards surprise Atahualpa (Waman Puma). <u>Above right</u>, the Inca taken hostage (Waman Puma).

once over with gold and twice with silver.

The Spaniards were amazed at the offer and Pizarro hastened to agree – summoning a secretary to record the details as a formal pledge and give a stamp of legality to the deal. In return, Pizarro promised to restore Atahualpa to Quito. It was a blatant lie, of course, one that served the conquistadors' purpose brilliantly: the whole Inca empire was mobilized to supply them with booty. Llama trains from Quito to Lake Titicaca were soon starting out, loaded down with precious statues, bowls, jugs and dishes.

Waiting for this treasure's arrival, the Spaniards became impressed by their royal prisoner. One of Pizarro's men later wrote that "Atahualpa was a man of 30 years of age, of good appearance and manner, although somewhat thick-set... He spoke with much gravity, as a great ruler." The Inca possessed an incisive intellect, grasped Spanish customs quickly, learned the secrets of writing and rules of chess. During all this time, Atahualpa's servants and wives maintained the royal rituals, bringing the Inca his cloaks of vampire bat skin and burning everything he touched or wore.

Abuse and murder: Meanwhile, a small group of Spaniards went to Jauja, where Atahualpa's greatest general Chalcuchima was stationed. Unfortunately, the general obeyed Atahualpa's instructions that he should accompany the Spaniards back to Cajamarca, giving Pizarro the only other man that might have led a coordinated resistance to his invasion. Having treated the general well until his arrival at Cajamarca, they tortured him for information about gold and set about burning him at the stake. He was released "with his legs and arms burned and his tendons shrivelled."

Atahualpa began to realize that he had made a mistake in cooperating with the invaders and that they had no intention of releasing him or leaving his empire. In mid-April 1533, Pizarro's partner Diego de Almagro arrived from Panama with 150 Spanish reinforcements, before leaving again for Spain with news of the Conquest and booty for King Charles V. The influx of treasure into Cajamarca turned it into a Wild West town and made the Spanish bolder. Pizarro put a chain around Atahualpa's neck to ensure that he would not escape, but rumors began that Inca forces were massing to rescue their leader.

Many Spaniards became convinced that they were in danger so long as Atahualpa remained alive. Others still saw the value of the Inca as a prisoner, and argued that it would be difficult to justify an execution. Chroniclers record that a Nicaraguan Indian was captured who claimed to have seen an Inca army marching on Cajamarca. Pizarro panicked and called an emergency council. It was obvious that the Inca could no longer be counted on to support Spanish rule. The council quickly decided that he should die.

Pizarro's secretary coldly recorded the sordid proceedings. The Inca was "brought out of his prison...and was tied to a stake. The friar (Valverde) was, in the meantime, consoling and instructing him through an interpreter in the articles of our Christian faith... The Inca was moved by these arguments and requested baptism... His exhortations did him much good. For although he had been sentenced to be burned alive, he was in fact garrotted by a piece of rope that was tied around his neck."

News of the execution horrified Atahualpa's supporters, the Quitans, especially when it was learned that no Inca column was in fact advancing on the city. When news arrived in Europe, educated opinion was equally appalled. Even Spain's Emperor Charles V

was upset with the execution, realizing that it offended the divine right of kings upon which his own rule was based. But by then the Crown's share of booty was steadily arriving from Peru and such scruples would have to be overlooked. The priceless art and sculpture of the great Inca empire went straight to the smelters of Seville.

Onwards into the heartland: In August 1538, the Spaniards marched on to Cuzco. It seems an astonishingly audacious project, but it is important to realize that a large part of the Inca empire's population, especially around the southern Sierra, openly welcomed the news of Atahualpa's death. To those who had backed his brother Huascar in the civil war, Atahualpa was a usurper and his Quitan troops an enemy occupying force. And many tribes still bore resentments at the Inca yoke. Pizarro was now ready to pose as the liberator of the Andes.

At Jauja, a contingent of Atahualpa's Quitan army tried to make a stand. The Spanish cavalry charged and routed them immediately. This first armed clash of the Conquest revealed a pattern that would be repeated: The native foot soldiers were no match for the mounted and well-armored Spaniards. Horses gave the conquistadors mobility and allowed them to strike downwards upon their opponents' heads and shoulders, while the

strange animals also created fear and confusion amongst the Incas. The Spaniards' steel armor was almost impenetrable to the natives' bronze hand-axes, clubs and maces. And Pizarro's conquistadors were some of the most experienced fighters Europe had to offer. Again and again the invaders would use their technological advantage to press home victories against apparently overwhelming odds.

Pizarro founded Jauja as the new Peruvian

Left, Atahualpa asks Pizarro whether the Spaniards eat gold (Waman Puma). Above, the Inca taken to execution.

"capital" and pressed on. What followed was a desperate race to cross the several rope bridges spanning the Andean gorges before the Quitans could destroy them. On one occasion the Indians attempted an ambush, and managed to kill several Spaniards in hand-to-hand battle. Pizarro decided that the captured general Chalcuchima had planned the attack and ordered him to be burned alive. But the attack had been to no avail: there was a final pitched battle in the pass before Cuzco and the Quitans' morale broke. They slipped away from the Urubamba Valley under cover of night and left the Inca capital to the invaders.

Dividing up the spoils: Pizarro and his men marched unopposed into the nerve-center of the Inca world, the "navel of the universe," Cuzco. "The city is the greatest and finest ever seen in this country or anywhere in the Indies," Pizarro wrote back to Charles V. "We can assure Your Majesty that it is so beautiful and has such fine buildings that it would be remarkable even in Spain." But the invaders barely had time to marvel at the precise Inca masonry and channels of water running through every street before installing themselves in various Inca palaces and starting on the serious business of pillaging the city.

The historian Leon-Portilla describes the conquistadors' frenzy in the gold-laden Coricancha, the Temple of the Sun: "Struggling and fighting among each other, each trying to get his hands on the lion's share, the soldiers in their coats of mail trampled on jewels and images and pounded the gold utensils with hammers to reduce them to a more portable size... They tossed all the temple's gold into a melting pot to turn it into bars: the laminae that covered the walls, the marvelous representations of trees, birds, and other objects in the garden."

Pizarro realized that his small force would not survive a true popular uprising, and so attempted to keep the looting of Cuzco relatively orderly – at least until reinforcements arrived. He offered his men allotments of natives, called *encomiendas*, to induce them to stay on as colonists. After "founding" the city in the name of the Spanish king, Pizarro then rode back to the barren coast of Peru and created his colonial capital, facing the sea: modern-day Lima.

By this time Pizarro had also accepted the

offer of a 20-year-old native prince named Manco, one of Huayna-Capac's sons, to become the new Inca. Manco wanted the Spaniards to restore him to his father's crown, and the conquistadors were happy to have him as a puppet leader in the southern Sierra. He lived in Cuzco while two groups of Spaniards headed towards Quito to take on the retreating imperial army that remained loyal to Atahualpa's memory.

The reality of conquest: While Pizarro was founding Lima in 1534 and 1535, Cuzco under Manco's nominal rule seemed tranquil enough. But it wasn't very long before the puppet Inca began to see the Spanish so-called "liberators" in their true colors. The

to begin a rebellion. Unknown to the Spaniards, vast numbers of native soldiers were mobilized and Manco slipped away from Cuzco into the mountains. The great rebellion had begun.

Incas on the offensive: Manco's troops quickly took Sacsayhuaman, the great fortress overlooking Cuzco whose massive stone blocks still awe visitors today. Chroniclers record that the Inca force was about 100,000 warriors against the Spaniards' 80 cavalry and 110 foot soldiers, commanded by Francisco Pizarro's brother, Hernando. The defences were bolstered by large contingents of native forces, but the outlook was grim: Cuzco was surrounded and, for all the

conquistadors' greed and brutality grew with their confidence: they were obviously in Peru to stay.

Manco was distressed to see the Inca world crumbling before his eyes. The natives of Cuzco refused to obey him, while many of his subject tribes began to assert their independence. The swelling ranks of Spaniards began forcing Indians into press-gangs, extorting gold from nobles and raping Inca women. They harassed Manco for treasure, took his wife and pillaged his house.

Finally Manco decided that he could tolerate no more: he summoned a secret meeting of loyal chiefs and announced his intention

defenders knew, they may have been the last Spanish outpost in Peru.

The Inca attack finally began with slingshot stones, made red-hot in camp fires, hailing down onto Cuzco's thatched roofs, setting them alight. But the roof of the building where the main body of Spaniards was hiding remained untouched.

Priests would later claim that the Virgin Mother herself had come down to douse the flames, but eyewitnesses suggest that Negro slaves stationed with buckets of water had a more practical hand in the job. Even so, Manco's forces had captured most of the city. The Spaniards decided on a desperate plan: to counterattack the strategic fortress of Sacsayhuaman.

Another Pizarro brother, Pedro, led 50 horsemen in a charge straight at the native lines. Despite their overwhelmingly superior numbers, the Incas still did not have a weapon that could seriously injure the Spanish cavalry. Although Juan Pizarro was killed by a stone dropped on to his head, the conquistadors forced their way onto a safe position on the hill opposite Sacsayhuaman. They prepared a night attack using medieval European siege tactics, and took the outer terrace of the fortress.

An Inca noble swore to fight to the death in defence of the inner towers. He is said to

impossible to take. Fighting continued with extraordinary cruelty. Captured Spaniards had their heads and feet cut off. Indian prisoners were impaled or had their hands removed in Cuzco's main square.

The rebellion was more successful in other parts of the empire. Francisco Pizarro organized several relief expeditions from Lima, but by now the Incas had learned to use geography against the Spanish cavalry. One group of 70 mounted conquistadors were caught in a narrow gorge by a hail of rocks from above. Almost all were killed, and the remainder captured. Another force of 60 men under Diego Pizarro was trapped in a similar fashion: their heads were sent to

have knocked down any Spaniard who climbed on to the rampart and killed any Indian who attempted to retreat. Finally, when the Spanish attack was proving irresistible, the noble flung himself from the parapets in a spectacular suicide.

The Spanish hold on: The capture of Sacsayhuaman was the key to Cuzco's defence. Although the city remained surrounded for another three months, the Incas found it

Far left, the Incas rebel against the Spanish (Waman Puma). **Left**, the siege of Cuzco. **Above**, the fortress of Sacsayhuaman, where the greatest battle of the rebellion took place.

Manco Inca. Now the victorious Indians marched on to Lima.

The attack on the town came from three sides, but in these flat, open coastal plains, the Spanish cavalry proved invincible once again. A determined charge routed the main Indian force and the Inca's commanding general was cut down in his tracks.

Meanwhile the Spaniards went on to the offensive in Cuzco, with an attack on Manco in the terraced fortress of Ollantytambo. Archers from the Amazon jungle kept the conquistadors at bay, while Indians used weapons captured from the Spaniards to drive home an attack. Manco himself was seen at the crest of the fortress riding a captured horse and directing troops with a lance. The conquistadors beat a hasty retreat and the siege dragged on. But the tide had turned in the rebellion.

Reconquering Peru: Spanish governors from other parts of the Americas were quick to come to Pizarro's aid. Reinforcements soon arrived from Mexico and Nicaragua, while Diego de Almagro returned with troops from a failed expedition to Chile. When Almagro relieved Cuzco in April 1537, Manco Inca decided that his cause was lost and retreated with his forces into the remote Vilcabamba Valley. The Spaniards chased him as far as the Vitcos, but became distracted by looting.

friends plunged Peru into civil war. No sooner had the Inca fled than the three surviving Pizarro brothers united against Diego de Almagro. Now Spaniard was pitted against Spaniard on Andean battlefields. The Pizarrist faction eventually defeated Almagro outside Cuzco and ordered that the general be garrotted.

Victory and revenge: At 63 years of age, Francisco Pizarro was at the peak of his bloodstained career. He was undisputed governor of a Peru which, although Manco Inca still occasionally harassed Spanish travelers from his jungle hideaway, was firmly under control. He possessed fabulous wealth and had been made a Marquis by the Spanish

The Inca escaped under cover of darkness, carried in the arms of 20 fast runners.

The Spaniards would have time to regret their greed: far inside the sub-tropical valley, behind an almost impenetrable series of narrow gorges and suspension bridges, Manco created an Inca court-in-exile that would survive in various forms for another 35 years.

But by now there was a new twist to the complicated politics of the Conquest that would distract the Spaniards: Almagro and Ferdinand Pizarro, the original partners who had arranged the invasion, had not agreed on how the empire should be divided between them. The plotting between the two former

Crown. But on Sunday, June 26, 1541, Pizarro's past caught up with him: he was surprised in his Lima palace by a group of 20 supporters of the murdered partner Diego de Almagro. The architect of the Conquest was able to kill one of his attackers before being hacked to death. His corpse was thrown in a secret grave. Pizarro's ally Bishop Vicente de Valverde – who had first shown the Bible to Atahualpa – tried to escape to Panama, but the ship was wrecked off the island of Puna, where cannibalistic natives devoured the hypocritical cleric.

The wretched deaths of Pizarro and de Valverde seem a fitting end to the first stage of the Conquest. But the era that was born was no less brutal. Now that most of the easily grabbed Inca treasures had been taken and distributed, the Spanish began to exploit the population mercilessly. The 480 conquistadors who had been given natives as encomiendas became the new elite of the colony, extorting grain, livestock and labour. The rituals of conquest were becoming institutionalized, and the "black legend" of Spanish cruelty would mark Peru for centuries to come.

The last Incas: Manco Inca maintained his court in Vitcos for several years, teaching his troops Spanish fighting techniques to keep up a guerrilla war. He escaped another Spanish attack led by Gonzalo Pizarro, this time by diving into a river, swimming across and disappearing into the jungle. (In frustration, Pizarro took the Inca's wife, raped and beat her before having her shot to death by arrows. As a final touch, the corpse was floated down the Yucay River so that Manco could see it.)

Manco's fatal mistake was to spare a group of pro-Almagro conquistadors who fled to Vilcabamba. The refugees grew bored and – with typical logic – realized that they would be pardoned if they murdered the Inca. The Spaniards were playing horseshoe quoits with their host Manco when they fell on him and stabbed him repeatedly. All paid with their lives for the treachery but the Inca leader was irreplaceable: with his death, resistance to the Spanish all but collapsed.

While Peru was sinking into colonial degradation, Manco Inca's son Titu Cusi maintained the court. The Spanish understood that, as long as any legitimate royal figure stayed free, there would always be some faint hope for the Indians. Long negotiations were aimed at drawing the Inca out to live in Cuzco, without avail.

Then, in 1569, two Augustinian friars entered the secret Inca nation and attempted to convert the Inca to Christianity. When Titu Cusi became ill, one friar prepared a healing potion to save him. Unfortunately, the Inca dropped dead as soon as he drank it. One friar was killed immediately by the horrified troops and the other dragged for three days by a rope driven through a hole behind his jaw, before

being dispatched with a mace to the skull.

This "martyrdom" gave the Spanish a pretext to invade Vilcabamba yet again. This time the conquistadors gathered an irresistible force. The new Inca Tupac Amaru put up a spirited defence against the invading column, but the Spaniards captured Vitcos and then Vilcabamba. Once again, the Inca tried to escape into the thick Amazon jungle, but this time progress was slowed by the Inca's wife on the verge of giving birth, and a local chief betrayed the party's movements. Finally a pursuing team of Spaniards saw a camp fire in the rainforest and pounced on the Inca, capturing him and bringing him back to Cuzco with a golden chain behind his neck.

The final humiliation of the ancient Inca empire was at hand. Native generals were tried and hanged. The Inca Tupac Amaru was put on trial for murdering the two Spanish priests. Despite appeals from Spanish liberals and native nobles, the Inca was condemned to be beheaded. On the scaffold, the Inca told his people that he had become a Christian and that the Inca religion was a sham. His head was placed on a pole, but because Indians gathered around it and seemed to be worshipping, it was removed and the Inca's body burned. Four decades after the Spanish arrived in Cajamarca, the last Inca had finally been killed.

Left, the Spaniards turn on one another. **Above right**, the capture of Tupac Amaru (Waman Puma).

THE QUEST FOR LOST CITIES

When the Admiral Christopher Columbus first approached the coast of South America, he believed that he had come to the place where the sun rose on the day of the creation. The earth, he wrote, was like a "round ball, and on one part of it something like a woman's breast" rose up toward heaven. The Earthly Paradise was located on the nipple of this breast, and the breast itself was to be found on the equator of the South American continent. Columbus was also convinced that the tribe of Amazon warrior women of classical antiquity lived somewhere in this same region.

Dragons and mermaids: Although Columbus's mind had become somewhat unhinged at the time that he wrote about these matters, his ideas did not seem fantastic to most Europeans. So many true wonders were soon reported by the explorers and conquerors of the Americas that the line between reality and fantasy was completely blurred. Large land iguanas were confused with medieval dragons, and underwater manatees with breasts merged into mythical mermaids. The innocent natives, "as naked as the day they were born," were proof that the Garden of Eden was to be found in the vicinity. And the fierce women warriors of the Carib tribes were obviously related to the Amazons.

However, although such marvels were cause for speculation, they held no intrinsic interest for the more materially-minded *conquistadores*. None of the ancient texts mentioned gold mines in Paradise, and the Spanish crown cared little for mermaids. But once the royal coffers began to bulge with the riches of the conquered Aztec and Inca nations, the belief in the existence of the Earthly Paradise took on another dimension.

If such empires existed, why should there not be another golden city hidden somewhere in the vast rainforests of South America? If the Terrestrial Paradise consisted of something more than lost innocence and spiritual serenity – if it happened also to contain untold riches to take home – it therefore really became something worth discov-

Right, watching the dawn on a recent expedition.

ering. And, of course, quickly conquering.

Thus the Garden of Eden – located, according to Columbus, on the nipple of the breast of the world – was the teat at which a strange, semi-mythical golden beast was suckled. Once weaned, this beast would undergo many incarnations and be responsible for the deaths of thousands of men and women. In the 16th century it would be transformed into a chimera known as El Dorado, "The Golden One."

By the 17th century it would become Paititi, the last refuge of the Incas who had taken with them all of the gold they had hidden from the Spaniards. And in the late 1900s it would merge with Vilcabamba, the city which

present-day Colombia made sure that the quests would continue when they told Spaniards about a tribal chieftain who, in an annual ritual, anointed himself in gold dust and then plunged into a lake. It is likely that this ceremony had actually taken place in a lake near modern Bogotá, but the destruction of the Muisca culture assured that it would not occur again. However, the plunge into the lake was the baptism which gave the beast its first name – El Dorado, the Golden Man.

As this legend spread throughout Spanish America, El Dorado became "The Golden City." There was no lack of men and women willing to risk their lives and endure enor-

the rebellious Incas had actually occupied and which had been "lost" since its conquest by the Spaniards in 1571.

Today the golden beast, in its manifestation as Paititi, still haunts the fevered imaginations of the explorers of South America – particularly in Peru. In the course of the search for it, hundreds of minor "lost cities" have been found, but the beast itself continues to elude its seekers. And it continues to devour the lives of those who would hunt it.

Death in the jungle: No sooner had the Inca empire been destroyed than *conquistadores* began setting off into the Amazon, searching for the Lost City. The Muisca Indians of

mous hardships on the hunt. A typical expedition was led in 1540 by Gonzalo Pizarro, half-brother of the conqueror of the Incas. He left Quito with no fewer than 220 horses and 5,000 live pigs for food. A year and a half later, he returned with fewer than 100 diseased Spaniards. However, 50 of his men under the command of Francisco de Orellana had built a ship and made the first descent of the river that would be called the Amazon – because an Indian captive had told them that a tribe of Amazon women lived near the river.

The beast itself would survive in other forms, and over the centuries hundreds of expeditions set off after it – most of them disastrous. Its fascination has lasted into the 20th century, making world-famous two modern explorers in South America, Colonel Percy Fawcett and Hiram Bingham.

A modern obsession: Percy Fawcett was a British army officer who came to South America in 1906, contracted by the Bolivian and Brazilian government to help define their jungle borders. But his real interest was in tracking down a golden city that, according to an 18th-century Portuguese document, had been found in Brazil by a group of adventurers. Fawcett also possessed a stone idol of supposed Brazilian origin which, according to the psychics whom he con-

he sent a message back to his wife which ended with the words: "You need have no fear of any failure." Then he and his party "disappeared," mysteriously swallowed up by the beast.

However, that was not the end of the story. Over the years various explorers reported that they had either met Fawcett or had heard rumors of his whereabouts. According to some of the tales, he was living with a group of Indians, while Jack had married one of the tribal women who had given birth to a white, blue-eyed son. A number of expeditions set out in search of him, but all were finally unsuccessful. And this was perhaps the strangest metamorphosis of the golden beast:

sulted, had actually come from the lost continent of Atlantis. The idol contained mysterious inscriptions which he claimed were identical to some strange scribbling at the end of the Portuguese document.

Armed with this conclusive proof of the existence of the Atlantean city, Fawcett plunged into the "green hell" of the Amazon in search of it. On his second expedition in 1925, on which he was accompanied by his son Jack and a man named Raleigh Rimell,

Left, early explorers became obsessed with tales of El Dorado. **Above**, a 19th-century expedition near Cuzco.

for Colonel Percy Fawcett had himself become the beast he had stalked!

Success in Peru: The golden beast, however, is only semi-mythical, and not all of its mutations have been chimerical. In 1536 the Incas rebelled against the Spaniards and then withdrew to Vilcabamba in the jungles to the northeast of Cuzco. There they remained for 35 years before they were finally defeated. Vilcabamba itself was rapidly consumed by the forest, but as such it became one of the beast's real manifestations – known as "The Lost City of the Incas."

There was little interest in discovering the whereabouts of Vilcabamba until the latter half of the 19th century when there was a revival of enthusiasm for American archaeology; and it was this beast that Hiram Bingham was tracking when he "discovered" Machu Picchu. Bingham and his party left the Inca village of Ollantaytambo on muleback one morning in 1911 and, following a recently dynamited road down the Urubamba canyon, they arrived in the evening at a small hut. Bingham was told by the owner, Melchor Arteaga, that there were some fairly good ruins on the ridge above.

The next morning Arteaga took him up a path where he met two farmers who had been cultivating the Inca terraces. A photo taken at the time even shows the famous Intihua-

aces with tiles in imitation of the architecture of the Spanish conquerors.

Still, Espíritu Pampa is only one of many Inca ruins in the region, and in 1976 the Peruvian archaeologist Edmundo Guillén claimed another site as the true Vilcabamba. Other explorers think that neither identification is correct and the real city is yet to be found. The controversy thus promises to continue for a long while – especially as more explorations turn up more ruins.

In 1985 Savoy uncovered another pre-Inca site in the jungles of northern Peru which he claims covers 310 sq. km (120 sq. miles) and consists of over 20,000 structures. Called Gran Vilaya, it may turn out to be the largest single

tana Stone in the midst of a cornfield. The entire demanding journey had lasted just one and a half days.

To give Bingham credit, he did continue on to find many other Inca sites under far more arduous circumstances. He even came across some ruins in a place called Espíritu Pampa, but he did not bother to investigate. In the 1960s, however, another American, Gene Savoy, did explore the area and declared this site to be the true Vilcabamba. The most convincing evidence to support his claim is the existence of piles of roof tiles – since a 16th-century chronicle affirms that the Incas roofed one of the Vilcabamba pal-

complex of ruins to have been found in South America. In the same year, the University of Colorado announced the discovery of another "lost" city – Gran Pajatén. But this time the beast had outdone itself in chicanery – for the UC scholars had failed to mention that these ruins had been described by Savoy in 1965 and that they had been excavated in 1966 by the Peruvian archaeologist Duccio Bonavía.

However, all of these are just appendages of the beast. The truly romantic explorer is still after its heart – Paititi.

Above, the railroad comes to Peru – but there were still discoveries to be made.

The legend of Paititi: With the destruction of the Inca empire, the chameleon-like chimera underwent yet another metamorphosis, this time into Paititi – and as such the golden beast clings tenaciously to life to this day. According to the legend, a group of disaffected Incas fled into the jungle, taking with them thousands of llamas loaded with gold. Anyone who enters the rainforests to the east of Cuzco will come across countless tales of Paititi. The most common is that of a peasant who follows the trail of a lost animal for several days into the cloudforest. Disorientated, he stumbles through the fog, falls asleep and awakens to find himself in Paititi. Inevitably, one of the Incas gives him a golden ear of corn to take home with him. But he is never again able to find the site.

Is this manifestation of the beast mythical or real? According to documents from the late 16th and early 17th centuries, a son of the Inca Huayna-Capac discovered a small range of mountains in the jungle, conquered its peoples and populated it.

He cultivated its rich soil, mined its vast gold veins and built temples. He then sent a delegation to Cuzco to inform the Inca of the land, but because he was jealous of his holdings, he warned them to say nothing of the gold. They were to tell the Inca, *"Paytiti"* ("That place is just lead"). However, when they arrived in Cuzco they found the Spaniards already there. They thus returned to Paititi, taking with them many Inca nobles, gold and hundreds of llamas.

All of this could be simple legend, of course, but according to one early testimony, the Incas of Paititi had communication with Cuzco. And in 1602, when Melchor Carlos Inca (a grandson of Huayna Capac) was sent back to Spain, it was said that many Incas never before seen in Cuzco arrived from Paititi to wish him well. But if the beast is real, where is its lair? The documents indicate habitats as far distant as the forests of northern Bolivia and western Brazil but the beast has taken most of its victims in the high jungles to the east of Cuzco.

In the cat's lair: There are two other possible explanations for the name "Paititi." "Titi" is also the Agmara word for a wild mountain cat, and many legends state that the lost city is guarded by pumas or jaguars. However, most of the those who have hunted the cat in the forested slopes east of Cuzco would probably agree with the Guarani approximation – for in this jungle language, "Piatitti" means "sadness, affliction, anguish."

In 1970 an American journalist named Bob Nichols set off with two Frenchmen – Serge Debru, a photographer, and Geraud Puel, a sociologist – up the Shinkikibeni River into the Pantiacolla Mountains. Coming across a massive rockface covered with ancient petroglyphs, they followed a stone road until it was lost and then proceeded up the canyon. They were never heard from again, but a Japanese adventurer, Yoshiharo Sekino, later met a group of Machiguenga Indians who claimed to have killed them. The Machiguengas are also said to be guardians of Paititi.

Petroglyphs are common in the forests of the region; and Father Juan Carlos Polentini, an Argentinian priest who has searched for the golden beast for 13 years, has found some which he claims to be a map to the lost city. In his book, *Por las rutas de Paititi*, he recounts a tale told him by an old man of three young men who found Paititi near a lake on top of a mountain called Apu Katinti (or Qatini). Starving and weak, they were only able to cut off a finger of a golden idol; and one of them died and was buried up there. According to the old man, who was 92 at the time, he himself had gone up the mountain and found the gravestone carved with a cross and the man's initials.

Not much credence should be given to this tale, but a group of Paititi-seeking friends recently found a stone etched with a cross and letters on Apu Katinti. They also arrived at the lake, but were unable to climb to the top and found no sign of ruins (later they were to find out that another explorer, Gregory Deyermenjian, had actually made it to the peak – but he also discovered no ruins).

Over the years a number of people have stumbled upon many small ruins and followed many Inca roads which lose themselves in the impenetrable forests, but they have yet to find any golden idols.

Does Paititi exist? Those who have stalked the golden beast can answer with an unqualified yes. It prowls somewhere in the jungles of the soul of the seeker, animating one's dreams with its growls and stirring one's heart with its musky scent. And if the actual Paititi were ever to be discovered, we seekers would soon have to invent another.

The chaotic years of early colonial administration suddenly changed with the arrival in 1569 of Francisco de Toledo, Peru's fifth viceroy. A brutal but efficient ruler, Toledo consolidated Spain's command over the former Inca empire. After finally crushing the rebel bastion of Vilcabamba, he set about ordering every aspect of Indian life.

Spain's iron fist: The effects of Toledo's decrees were to alter the face of the Andes for ever. One of Toledo's most drastic measures was the establishment of *reducciones*, forced resettlements of peoples into Spanish-style towns complete with a central plaza, church, municipality and prison, the symbols of Spanish authority. *Reducciones* facilitated the collection of tribute from the Indians and their conversion to Christianity.

The new viceroy also secured the *encomienda* system, whereby Indians provided labor and tribute to an *encomendero*, their trustee. The premise of the *encomienda* was completely alien to the Andean way of life, a system based on reciprocity and redistribution. In addition, the large tracts of land that formed the *encomiendas* ignored the Andean concept of verticality, whereby an ethnic group living near, say, Lake Titicaca, had access to land and produce – cotton, fish, hot peppers (*aji*) – from the warm coastal valleys. Under the colonial order, people were bound to tribute payments that went in only one direction: from tribute payer to local ethnic lord (*curaca*), and thence to *encomendero*. Indians provided their Spanish masters with cloth, llamas, maize, wheat (first introduced by the Spanish and cultivated almost exclusively for Spanish consumption), *aji*, dried fish, wild birds, beans, potatoes and coca leaves.

No longer did the state provide the necessary raw materials for people to carry out their tribute obligations. In Inca times, for example, a married woman had to provide the state with one woven garment per year. The fiber-cotton or alpaca was provided from the state storehouses. Under colonial administration, however, the textile tribute was due

every four months and weavers had to provide their own raw materials.

One group of tributaries serving an *encomienda* in Conchucos, near the city of Huanuco in the north-central highlands, had to provide their *encomendero* annually with 2,500 pesos of gold or its equivalent in silver; the harvest of over 1,500 hectares (3,700 acres) in wheat, maize, barley and potatoes; 30 sheep, 12 kilos of candle wax; and 15 pairs of grouse every four months. In addition, they also had to give their master 20 eggs every Friday throughout the year and 25 donkey-loads of salt annually, 10 of which went to the viceroy.

Because the *encomendero* lived in town and rarely traveled, the curacas were instrumental in the collection of tribute. Swept up by the colonial administration, the curacas, terrorized by the Spanish, in turn terrorized the Indians into fulfilling their tribute obligations. Some *curacas* also used their position of power to abuse the Indians. They quickly learned Spanish and borrowed the trappings of colonial nobility, dressing in Spanish-style clothing, carrying firearms and riding on horseback.

Squeezing Peru dry: Spanish colonial economy was essentially based on plunder. The treasures of Cuzco had already been distributed, but there were other sources. In the north coast city of Trujillo, named after Pizarro's birthplace in Spain, the Spanish crown granted licenses for the pillage of the ancient *huacas* (mud brick temples).

Once the Spanish had exhausted pre-Columbian tombs as a source of plunder, they turned to mines, a quest that led to the discovery in 1545 of Potosí. Today a bleak mining city in the Bolivian highlands at 4,070 meters (13,349 feet) above sea level, in its heyday Potosí was the richest and largest city in the world. At the time of Toledo, Potosí boasted a population of 150,000 people, more than that of contemporary Naples or Milan. Potosí's silver filled the coffers of Spanish royalty with the necessary cash to finance battles across Europe. Its coat of arms read: "I am rich Potosí, treasure of the world and envy of Kings."

But the discovery of Potosí brought with it

<u>Left</u>: **Indian nobles kept Inca trappings even in the 17th century.**

renewed hardship for the Indians. In 1574 Toledo legalized the mine *mita*, the traditional Inca system of enforced labor on a rotational basis. It was another example of an Andean institution twisted to suit Spanish needs: the Indians worked but received nothing in return. Although Toledo tried to limit the distance people had to travel and the amount of time they spent at Potosí, his ordinances were largely ignored.

Thousands died on the long, forced march to Potosí. The annual *mita* from Chucuito consisted of 2,200 Indians and their families, altogether more than 7,000 people. Each Indian took eight to 10 llamas as pack animals and alpacas for food to nourish him and

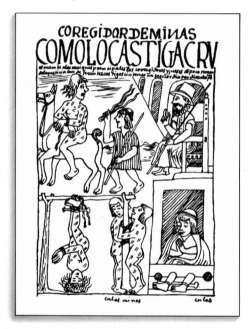

his family on the two-month, 480-km (300-mile) journey. Many would never return. Two out of every three Indians sent to Potosí died as a result of the appalling working conditions, where miners were forced to remain below ground for six-day stretches.

Even more horrific were the nearby mercury mines in Huancavelica – one of which, Santa Barbara, soon became known as the "mine of death." Thousands of Indians from neighboring provinces died in the mines, asphyxiated by lethal fumes of cinnabar (sulphide of mercury), arsenic, arsenic anhydride and mercury.

Coca was initially condemned by the Span-

ish Church, until it realized that Indians could not survive the brutal mining *mita* without it. The leaf was soon touted by the Spanish as a cure-all to ward off hunger, thirst and fatigue. The trade was organized and controlled: thousands of highland Indians, unadapted to life in the torrid jungle, died working the coca fields. Llama caravans carried coca leaf from Cuzco, the center of production, to Potosí, 1,000 km (621 miles) away, where in only one year, 95,000 basketfuls of coca leaf were consumed. The church reaped the benefits of the lucrative trade, collecting a tithe on each full basket.

Because of coca's connections to Andean religion, some authorities tried to limit the production of this "diabolical herb." But too many fortunes were made from the trade. "There are those in Spain who became rich from this coca, buying it up and reselling it and trading it in the markets of the Indians," wrote Spanish chronicler and soldier Pedro de Cieza de Leon, who traveled throughout Peru in the 1540s. "Without coca there would be no Peru," noted another contemporary observer. This terse statement on 16th century coca production has a familiar if not sinister ring almost 500 years later, with the multi-billion dollar cocaine industry now threatening the stability of Andean nations.

Toledo also created the *mita de obrajes*, or textile workshops. Hundreds of Indians, working under factory conditions, wove for their Spanish masters, producing cloth for local consumption and export.

Toledo fought to limit the wealth of the *encomiendas* by ensuring they reverted to the crown after a couple of generations and replacing them with *corregimientos*. By the mid-1600s, the similarly-run *corregimientos*, headed by crown-appointed *corregidores*, or co-regents, also collected tribute and provided Indians for the *obraje* and mine *mitas*. Poorly-paid *corregidores* supplemented their incomes by extorting the Indians.

Christians on the march: The early 1600s saw a far-flung campaign against idolatry, spurred on by a revival of native religion in 1565. The renewed religious zeal of the Spanish church led to a push to stamp out native religion once and for all. The church crusade also produced volumes of valuable dictionaries and accounts that are still being studied by historians today. Priests visited outlying provinces, collecting information on cults and torturing villagers to reveal the whereabouts of idols and *huacas*.

But in many ways, the Catholic campaign only served to entrench native beliefs even deeper. Rather than taking over, Christianity formed only a thin veneer over traditional cults and beliefs, many of which still exist today. This syncretism, in which traditional beliefs dominate, led to the replacement of Andean pilgrimage centers and festivals by other superficially Catholic ones. Many are still in use. Modern-day Copacabana on the Bolivian shores of Lake Titicaca, for example, is nothing more than a Catholic church built over an important Andean shrine venerated by peoples around the lake in Inca times.

By the early 1700s the colonial system was firmly established throughout the Andes. It was a system based on the exploitation of the Indian and marked by rampant corruption and extortion by Spanish officials.

At its height, the viceroyalty of Peru was 15 times the size of Spain and for two centuries ruled from Panama to Argentina. The South American mines, exhausted by almost two centuries of exploitation, eventually began to languish and output declined. But colonials in Peru flourished: Spain decreed that all trade from South America should pass through Lima first, ensuring a massive flow of taxes. Lima became the opulent "City of Kings," crammed with magnificent churches and mansions.

Spain, meanwhile, saw the replacement of the Hapsburg dynasty by the Bourbons, who reigned until Napoleon occupied Madrid in 1808. Efforts by various Bourbon monarchs to improve the colonial economy and stem corruption were to little avail. The colonial system, by now well-established, had acquired its own momentum.

Indian uprising: During the 18th century, unrestricted exploitation sparked off various Indian rebellions from Quito to La Paz. The most serious of these was the uprising instigated by José Gabriel Condorcanqui, also known as Tupac Amaru II.

Tupac Amaru claimed to be descended from Tupac Amaru I, the renegade Inca emperor killed by the Viceroy Toledo. Born in Tinta, south of Cuzco, Tupac Amaru studied in Cuzco at a school for Indians of

noble birth. After the death of his father, he inherited the title of curaca. It was never Tupac Amaru's intention to rid Peru of the Spanish yoke. Rather, he fought against the tyranny of the *corregidores*, and in his letters to crown officials spoke of the miserable conditions at the *haciendas*, mines, *obrajes* and coca plantations. Increasingly, he lobbied for Indian rights, demanding that the mine *mita* be lifted and the power of the *corregidores* limited.

One evening in 1780 he invited Tinta's hated *corregidor*, Antonio Arriaga, to dinner. After the meal, Arriaga was taken prisoner and later hanged in Tinta's public square. It was the start of a public revolt. The rebel-

lion spread throughout the Peruvian highlands and Spanish reinforcements were sent from Lima to quell the uprising. At a decisive battle in Checacupe in 1781, the Spanish dispersed Tupac Amaru's men and captured the rebel leader and his wife.

The crown spared no one. First, Tupac Amaru was forced to witness the execution of his family. He was then drawn and quartered, like his ancestor before him, in Cuzco's public square. The survivors of Inca nobility were sent to Spain, where Charles III had them imprisoned.

As a result of the rebellion, French nobleman and Viceroy Teodoro de Croix (1784–

LAS TAPADAS

Friction between Peru's Spanish-born residents and its upper-class *mestizos* did more than spark the independence revolution. It also bred a rivalry between women from the two camps and gave Lima its most scandalous fashion.

The Spanish ladies enticed men in traditional fashion with their tiny waists, by waving elaborate fans and by moving sveltely next to the shorter, darker and plumper Limeñas. Not to be outdone, the *mestizas* (women of mixed parentage) created an alluring look of their own by covering their faces with an Arab veil – except for one eye that peeked out. They were the *tapadas* or "covered ones."

Although veiled, the *tapadas* were not entirely modest. Their skirts were hiked shamelessly up to show feet which were tinier than those of their Spanish rivals. Simultaneously, the *tapadas* dropped their necklines, knowing the fair-skinned Spaniards would remain covered under Lima's strong sun (how fashions have changed: now the locals cover up, and the fair skins try to get as dark as possible).

When the European women squeezed their middles even more, the thick-waisted *mestizas* scrimped on the fabric encircling their ample hips. As a result, skirts in the 1700s became so tight that the Lima *mestizas* could take only the tiniest of steps as they promenaded slowly down the street.

But one part of this costume remained constant throughout these changes: the veil hiding all but an eye, with which a great deal could be said and done.

"This costume so alters a woman – even her voice since her mouth is covered – that unless she is very tall or very short, lame, hunchbacked or otherwise conspicuous, she is impossible to recognize," French feminist Flora Tristan wrote about the *tapadas*. "I am sure it needs little imagination to appreciate the consequences of this time-honored practice which is sanctioned or at least tolerated by law."

The *tapadas* spent their afternoons strolling and the "consequences" of their tantalizing fashion ranged from sinful trysts to playful flirting – sometimes even catching out their own unknowing husbands.

So scandalous was the behaviour the costume permitted that the archbishop attempted to condemn it, but the *tapadas* conspired and refused to serve their husbands, attend their families or carry out church duties while the sanction was in effect.

Conspiracy, in fact, was endemic at the time and many *tapadas* used their afternoon walks to pass notes anonymously and messages to organizers of the revolution, thus playing an important part in the formation of the nation.

The site for this romantic and political intrigue was the Paseo de Aguas – a walkway of reflecting pools and gardens which was built for one particular woman who inspired one of South America's most famous romances.

By stealing a viceroy's heart, *mestiza* Micaela Villegas placed herself firmly in history and legend. Count Amat y Juniet built her Lima's finest house, bought her a gold and silver coach and, although in his sixties, fathered her only child. Their love inspired Jacques Offenbach's 1968 opera, *La Perichole*.

Villegas was known as "La Perrichola," Amat's mispronunciation of the "half-breed bitch" epithet he threw at her during a heated argument. Despite the moniker, Amat adored the actress who had caught his eye on a Lima stage.

A Cristal beer factory now stands where La Perrichola's opulent mansion once gleamed so regally, but Paseo de Aguas – built so the couple would have a spot of their own to stroll – survives in the Rimac district north of the river, behind the Presidential Palace and next to the Convento de Los Descalzos. The latter is worth visiting in itself for its collection of paintings from local schools.

The Perrichola story has a sad ending. Inconsolable when her aged lover was ordered back to Spain (where, in his eighties, he married one of his nieces), La Perrichola vowed she would never love again, gave her wealth to the poor, and entered a convent. ∎

90) began to institute long overdue reforms. He set up a special *audiencia*, or royal court, in Cuzco to deal with Indian legal claims. Meanwhile in Spain, Charles III ordered that trade and commerce be opened up, allowing other American ports to trade with Spain and foreigners. He banned the *repartimiento*, the forced sale of shabby goods to Indians at inflated prices, and ended the corrupt *corregimiento* system. In additional Charles III ordered that the viceroyalty be divided into seven intendencies under direct royal rule, paving the way for the regionalism that would break South America into its present patchwork of republics.

Not all members of the Spanish govern-

over 1,000 drawings, plans and maps in ink and watercolor bound in nine volumes and covering antiquities, flora and fauna, customs, music, and costumes of northern Peru. The cleric is also considered by many to be the grandfather of Peruvian archaeology: he collected some 600 pre-Columbian textiles and ceramics for shipment to the king, who founded a "Cabinet of Natural History and of Antiquities" in Madrid.

The push for independence: On the eve of Napoleon's march on the Iberian peninsula, Spain's hold on its colonies was already waning. When Napoleon forced Charles IV to abdicate in favor of Ferdinand VII, and then placed his brother on the Spanish throne,

ment and clergy exploited the Indians. One clergyman of the time, Don Baltasar Jaime Martinez de Compañon y Bujanda, stands out. Appointed Bishop of Trujillo in 1779, Martinez de Compañon spent his years traveling around a vast diocese covering the northern third of Peru. In a letter to Charles III dated 1786 he described the "wretchedness" he saw everywhere. Fascinated by natural history and colonial life, Martinez de Compañon and his team of artists produced

<u>Left</u>, scandalous fashion of "the covered ones".
<u>Above</u>, Simón Bolívar takes on Spanish forces in the Peruvian Sierra.

South America rebelled. Declarations of independence in Upper Peru (Bolivia) and Quito in 1809 were followed by uprisings in the Peruvian cities of Huanuco and Cuzco. But freedom from Spain was not so easy: royalist troops regained control in many parts of the continent and bloody wars were waged for the next 15 years. And many Peruvians supported the colonial system, since Lima was still its wealthy administrative capital. Peru became the strongest bastion of pro-Spanish feeling, and other independent countries could not feel secure until it, too, was liberated.

After the Argentine general José de San

Martín's successful invasion of Chile in 1818, a rebel navy commanded by the colorful British admiral Lord Cochrane sailed from the Chilean port of Valparaíso and landed in Paracas, on Peru's south coast. The following year the armada attacked Lima, dispersing royalist troops who fled to the central and southern highlands. Meanwhile, on Peru's north coast, the cities of Trujillo, Lambayeque, Piura and Cajamarca declared their independence.

General San Martín entered Lima in 1821, proclaiming independence for all of Peru on July 28.

San Martín's first move was to abolish the dreaded Indian tribute, the mine *mita* and

historians Henry E. Dobyns and Paul L. Doughty, "is one of those Latin American nations whose national politics have been plagued ever since independence by a futile quest for a functional substitute for a king."

In the tumultuous months following Peru's declaration of independence, the monarchical plan was scuttled following the election of a parliament. The seven viceregal intendencies became departments headed by a prefect, modelled on the French plan.

In 1822 San Martín sailed to Guayaquil, Ecuador, where he met with Venezuelan statesman and fellow independence-seeker Simón Bolívar. San Martín sought troops for Peru to rout out the last Spanish royalist

encomiendas. The children of black slaves were freed. He even went so far as to ban the term "Indian" and for the first time proclaimed the descendants of the Incas to be citizens of Peru.

But this was all too much for a conservative elite still immersed in its colonial ways. San Martín and the leaders of Lima opted for a monarchy to replace Spanish rule and at one stage actually searched for a prince in Europe to rule the former Spanish colony.

Peru was not prepared for self-rule. The descendants of the Spanish *conquistadores* and colonial administrators thrived in Peru, dependent on the motherland. "Peru," write

forces holed-up in the Andes and offered Peru's leadership to Bolívar.

Bolívar, however, advocated republicanism during his brief presidency of Peru between 1824 and 1826. He commanded troops at the Battle of Junín in 1824, but it was not until the decisive Battle of Ayacucho later that year that rebels headed by Venezuelan general José de Sucre finally crushed royalist troops commanded by Viceroy José de la Serna while Arequipa, whose strong regional streak had sparked off uprisings before, advocated independence from Peru.

Freedom and chaos: Bolívar's departure for Colombia in 1826 created a power vacuum and the congress elected José de la Mar president. Between 1821 and 1826, eight men had governed Peru, establishing the pattern of *coups d'états* and instability that characterizes the country to this day.

San Martín's promises to abolish the Indian tribute, *mita,* servitude and even to recognize Quechua as an official language, were never followed through. The wars of independence had left the countryside ravaged, crops unattended and food scarce. Instead of granting Indians equal status as citizens of a republican Peru, an all-out assault began on Indian land-holdings. The next 50 years would set patterns for the mistreatment of Indians that lasted well into the 20th century.

By 1830 Peru discovered a new resource that replaced minerals as the country's main export: guano. The rich piles of bird droppings deposited on Peru's off-shore islands were much sought after in industrial Europe as fertilizer and fetched enormous prices. The first guano contract was negotiated with Britain in 1840. Indians worked in appalling conditions at the guano stations, where ammonia fumes shriveled the skin and often caused blindness. In 1854 traders even staged a raid on Easter Island off the coast of Chile, kidnapping hundreds of Easter Islanders to work the guano deposits. Most died, decimating the island's tiny population.

The industry became so important that, by

Between 1825 and 1865, 35 presidents governed Peru, many of whom were military officers. Chaos reigned in Lima and the countryside. Charles Darwin, a witness of early republican years, recalled: "Lima, the city of Kings, must formerly have been a splendid town." But he found it in a "wretched state of decay; the streets are nearly unpaved, and heaps of filth are piled up in all directions, where the black *gallinazos* (vultures) pick up bits of carrion."

Left, missionaries head into the Amazon basin. Above, defending Lima from Chilean attack in the War of the Pacific.

1849, Peru's economy was almost entirely in the hands of the London-based firm of Anthony Gibbs and Sons and the Montane Company of Paris, who shared exclusive guano marketing rights. There were a few other sources of income: large cotton and sugar estates developed on the coast and in 1849 Peru began to import Chinese labor to work the fields. At the same time, the government encouraged migration from Europe.

In 1865 Spain tried to gain a foothold in its former colony and occupied the Chincha guano islands, in response to what it considered unfair treatment of a group of Basque immigrants. A year later president Mariano

Prado declared war on Spain and in 1866 the Spanish navy bombarded Callao, but were unable to capture it. As a result of the Spanish attack, Peru decided to revamp its fleet, buying up arms and munitions in Europe and borrowing heavily on its future guano income. Using the guano concession as a guarantee, Peru acquired the *Huascar* and *Independencia* warships in Britain, and owed its creditors the vast sum of 20 million pesos.

The guano boom also initiated an era of railroad construction. President José Balta signed contracts for eight major lines, including Arequipa-Puno, completed in 1876, Callao-La Oroya, completed in 1878, and Juliaca-Cuzco, completed in 1909. US rail-

concession to nitrate of soda and borax deposits in the province of Tarapaca. Bolivia levied a tax on the concessionaires, but Chile refused to pay. Although Peru sought to resolve the conflict peacefully, Chile declared war on the two countries in 1879.

Despite some successes, Peru and Bolivia's armed forces proved to be woefully unprepared for the war. Chilean troops occupied southern Peru and then bombarded Callao, occupying Lima and cutting off the capital from the hinterland. The troops plundered Lima's national library, taking valuable books and manuscripts. When President Prado left for Europe in search of support, Nicolas de Piérola seized power. Following

road entrepreneur Henry Meiggs, nicknamed the "Yankee Pizarro", won the bid for the Callao-La Oroya line, a engineering feat of tunnels and bridges that began at sea level and rose over 5,000 meters (16,400 feet) to the mining town of La Oroya. Travelers can still take this spectacular route to Huancayo.

The bubble bursts: Peru financed its railroad construction with a 60 million soles loan from the French firm of Dreyfus, the leading guano trader. But in 1877 the second Mariano Prado regime was unable to pay back its British creditors and Peru was plunged into bankruptcy.

Meanwhile, Chile had obtained a Bolivian

the peace treaty of 1883, Peru ceded Tarapaca to Chile. Bolivia remains landlocked to this day.

The war with Chile brought eco-nomic chaos. Desperate for funds, it reinstituted the Indian tribute and levied a tax on salt. Three years after the peace treaty, British bondholders started up debt negotiations. The negotiating team, headed by a son of W.R. Grace who had business interests in the country, cancelled Peru's debt in exchange for 66 years of control of the major railroads and two million tons of guano. The bond-holders set up the Peruvian Corporation in 1890 to manage their Peruvian interests.

By 1900, US interests were replacing British in controlling the Peruvian economy. Mining once again became pre-eminent. North American investors set up the Cerro de Pasco Mining Company, soon controlling all of the mines in the central sierra, and in 1922 a smelter at La Oroya began belching fumes of arsenic, lead and zinc into the atmosphere, ravaging the countryside. Fishmeal began being exported from Peru's abundant anchovy schools, while some industry grew in Lima and other urban centers.

These workers in the mines, coastal factories and urban sweatshops began hesitantly to form unions. But it was in the north coast, where laborers in the sugar haciendas began to organize, that a new class consciousness found political expression. In 1924, while exiled in Mexico, a popular activist named Victor Raul Haya de la Torre formed the Alianza Popular Revolucionaria Americana (APRA), with a loose platform based on anti-imperialism and nationalization that attracted members of the middle class feeling left out by the oligarchical rule.

Haya was allowed back into Peru to contest the 1931 elections, but was defeated in what Apristas denounced as a fraud. Party faithful rose up in rebellion in the northern city of Trujillo, killing some 60 military officers they had taken captive. The army retook the city and executed over 1,000 Apristas in the ancient ruins of Chan Chan.

Urban drift: For the next 50 years, APRA was kept out of power as Peru oscillated between conservative and military governments. (During one such rule in the late 40s, Haya was forced into hiding in the Colombian embassy in Lima for over eight years). In that time, Peru's manufacturing industry grew and hundreds of thousands left the countryside for Lima.

Pressure for land reform and some redistribution of wealth grew. The first government of Fernando Belaunde (1963–68), who promised some cautious progressive measures, was a failure: after widespread disgust at tax concessions given to the International Petroleum Company (a subsidiary of Standard Oil of New Jersey), yet another military coup occurred. Belaunde was marched out of the

Presidential Palace in his pyjamas and on to an airplane and exile. But General Juan Velasco, who headed the new junta, was not typical of military rulers. He went on to champion many of the most radical APRA reforms that Haya himself had given up as impossible.

Velasco's measures drastically changed Peru. They included a sweeping agrarian reform, expropriating vast land-holdings and turning family-run estates into cooperatives overnight. The petrol, mining and fishing industries were nationalized at a stroke. Food for the urban population was subsidized by the state. And, in a profound symbolic gesture, Peru was recognized as a bilingual

country, with Quechua as the second language. Unfortunately, the "Peruvian revolution" ran up against the 1973 oil crisis.

The economy deteriorated and the military split into factions. In 1975, Morales Bermudez staged a bloodless coup against Velasco, who died of an illness soon afterwards. The coup provoked no popular protests, but Velasco's funeral train was followed by the largest crowd that Lima had ever seen.

Despite a series of economic plans, the new military government proved that it was incapable of running Peru. Debt was soaring, inflation out of control. Democratic elections were scheduled once again for 1980.

<u>Left</u>, the 1956 inauguration of President Manuel Prado. <u>Above right</u>, General Juan Velasco, who began wide-ranging reforms in the late 1960s.

The 1980s proved to be a period of immense difficulties for Peru – a downward spiral of economic crisis and political violence which many predicted would lead to total collapse. However despite a brief period of authoritarian rule in 1992–93, the country's fragile democracy has re-emerged on a wave of new hope, economic growth and a measure of political stability.

Democracy returns: The 1980s began hopefully with the restoration of constitutional rule and signs of economic progress. The election in 1980 was Peru's first with universal suffrage. Voters awarded Fernando Belaúnde a second term in power, by a comfortable margin, 12 years after he had been ejected from the Presidential Palace by army tanks. He took over a country very different from the one he had hurriedly left.

Though Belaúnde was quick to restore democratic freedom, including freedom of the press and municipal elections, by 1983 his government was facing serious problems. Some of the causes were external: after Mexico's default unshered in a Latin American debt crisis, foreign loans to the region dried up and Peru found itself thrust back into the arms of the International Monetary fund and a new austerity program. A particularly strong El Niño (the rogue warm current that periodically disrupts Peru's climate) brought severe flooding to the north coast and drought to the southern Andes. The result of all this was rising inflation, a persistent budget deficit and a sharp recession.

Andean rebellion: But these familiar problems were compounded by a new development. The 1980 elections had seen the debut of the Maoist Sendero Luminoso (Shining Path) guerrilla movement. In its first armed action, Sendero dynamited a polling station in the remote Andean village of Chuschi. As the decade wore on, Sendero cast an everlonger shadow over Peruvian democracy.

Formed as a radical splinter party in the mid-1970s, Sendero was the brainchild of a group of obscure provincial intellectuals

Left, the imprisoned Abimael Guzman, leader of Sendero Luminoso. **Right**, supplicants waiting in García's APRA office.

gathered at the University of San Cristóbal de Huamanga in Ayacucho. Under the leadership of Abimael Guzman, a former philosophy lecturer known to his followers as "President Gonzalo," Sendero went underground and prepared for a Mao-style "prolonged popular war to surround the cities from the countryside" against the state and capitalist society. By exploiting rural grievances, Guzman argued, Sendero could foment a communist-style revolution. Its initial actions involved bomb attacks against state

property and the killing of landlords and officials in and around Ayacucho, in the central-southern Andes at the center of the poorest and most neglected area of Peru.

The Belaúnde government made two serious mistakes in handling Sendero. First, the President ignored it, allowing the guerrillas to consolidate a political presence in the Indian farming communities of Ayacucho. Then, when he did send in a police counter-insurgency battalion followed by the armed forces, he allowed them to act with indiscriminate violence against the Quechua-speaking Indian population. Human rights organizations blamed the security forces for the "disappearance" of almost 2,000 people during this period. Hundreds more were massacred in villages.

Youthful president: The 1985 elections gave Peru grounds for hope once again. Under the fresh and energetic leadership of Alan García, the populist-nationalist APRA (American Popular Revolutionary Alliance), Peru's oldest and best-organized political party with roots in the extensive lower middle class, had emerged from a period of decline. With outstanding campaign oratory and a populist promise to be "President of all Peruvians," the tall, good-looking García seized the middle-ground of politics and became, at the age of 35, South America's youngest president.

serves and the country was effectively bankrupt and in the iron grip of a deep recession.

Worsening problems: García's government limped through to the end of its term amid mounting chaos. Inflation ranged between 30 percent and 60 percent a month. Living standards plunged. Poverty increased. Government tax revenue slumped to less than 4 percent of national income. State investment shrank to zero, key state industries such as oil and electricity were bankrupted, and the upkeep of roads and other infrastructure was badly neglected.

Meanwhile the guerrilla movement led by Sendero began to consolidate *de facto* control over much larger areas. These included

García made a swift and positive impact. He announced a unilateral cut in payments on Peru's foreign debt, and stopped payments to the IMF, whose policy prescriptions he denounced as "imperialist." García used the money saved to inflate the economy, which grew by a fifth in two years.

However, this boom was consumer-led and the administration's free-spending policies, coupled with García's unwillingness to court unpopularity with tough anti-inflationary measures opened the way for Peru's isolation from the international credit community. By the late 1980s the Central Bank had totally run out of foreign currency re-

the Upper Huallaga Valley, where booming demand for cocaine in the United States and later in Western Europe had created Peru's only growth industry of the 1980s – the cultivation of coca, the ancestral Andean shrub from whose leaves cocaine is derived. By 1990, there were up to 200,000 hectares of coca in Peru, more than half the world's supply. A US-sponsored and designed anti-drug program focused on forcible eradication of coca crops, causing resentment among those farmers that helped Sendero to gain control over the valley. But Sendero also made important mistakes: its killings of trade union, peasant and community leaders turned new sections of the population against it. In the shanty towns of Lima and in Puno, for example, it faced organized opposition from the church and the democratic left.

Under García, a third of the country came to be under a permanent state of emergency and military control. Human rights violations continued, and a shadowy extreme right paramilitary group, apparently linked to the security forces, claimed responsibility for killings of students and leftist sympathisers.

"Fuji-shock": The 1990 election campaign was dominated by the economy. Mario Vargas Llosa stood as the candidate for a reorganized right-of-center alliance, preaching a radical free-market program. With the left cutting Vargas Llosa's vote to 27 percent. In a run-off ballot, Fujimori won by a mile.

Fujimori inherited a potent cocktail of intractable problems: urban poverty, economic stagnation, widespread political and judicial corruption, ant the increasingly lethal insurgency of Sendero Luminoso.

One of his first acts on the economic front was to adopt many of the neo-liberal causes espoused by Vargas Llosa. "Fuji-shock" as the process was called, enacted some of the most drastic and far-reaching reforms to be seen in Latin America in order to bring Peru back into the fold of the international economy. A whole series of rigid measures were brought into play, including slashing public

splitting in 1989 and APRA discredited by its record in government, he faced little opposition. But the poor majority appeared to see Vargas Llosa as a class warrior for the rich and they distrusted the politicians around him who had governed under Belaúnde. In the final month of the campaign, a remarkable snowballing protest vote gathered behind Alberto Fujimori, a little-known former university rector of Japanese descent who was making his political debut as an independent. Fujimori surged into second place,

Left, on the trail of the Shining Path. Above, a youthful Fujimori celebrates his 1990 victory.

spending and state employment, and increasing taxation. He also initiated a series of large-scale privatisations, and state industries were sold off at low prices in order to attract foreign investment. The effects of these reforms created problems of their own as unemployment shot up, hyperinflation took control and salaries effectively dropped.

Nonetheless, the benefits of Fuji-shock came to be seen by the end of 1992 when the economy began to record slight growth and prices stabilized somewhat. In 1993 direct foreign investment increased by 22 percent to $400 million and by 1994 economic growth was the highest in South America.

Continued war against Sendero: Elsewhere, Fujimori's authoritarian instincts, which had won him the sobriquet of "The Emperor," led him in April 1992 to suspend the constitution, dissolve congress and arrest prominent opposition politicians. In addition, he declared war on Sendero – by this time the struggle had claimed more than 25,000 lives. Fujimori justified the *autogolpe* (self-coup), by claiming that a corrupt congress and judiciary was unable fully to fight terrorism.

Soon the army was being accused of employing similar tactics to those of the terrorists, and the security forces were able to act without the appearance of democratic restraint. But this position was quickly vindi-

cated in September 1992 when they captured Abimael Guzman and three high-ranking members of Sendero's "Central Committee" in a suburban house in Lima. The messianic Maoist, a shadowy figure seldom photographed, was paraded before television cameras and turned out to be a tubby, bespectacled 57-year-old with a graying beard. Riding on this success, Fujimori held elections for a new legislative congress in November 1992, in which his supporters won a clear majority in the new Constitutional Democratic Congress.

In his counter-insurgency efforts, Fujimori continued to have some success. The July 1992 Ley de Arrepentimiento (Repentance Law) provided for amnesties and lenient treatment for those guerrillas who gave themselves up, on condition that they cooperated with the authorities by giving information on the identities and whereabouts of other terrorists.

However, a real turning point in the fight against Sendero was reached in October 1993 when Guzman was displayed in front of the media signing two letters requesting "peace talks" with the government, and a cessation of hostilities, at least until conditions were more suited to change.

This, in conjunction with the Repentance Law, led to thousands of rebels surrendering between 1992 and the end of 1994 when the Law expired. Whilst other Senderistas remained committed to a hard-line continuance of the armed struggle under the control of a new leader, "Comrade Feliciano," there is no doubt that Sendero's power base was hugely undermined by the "defection" of so many of its numbers.

In the run-up to the 1995 general election, Fujimori ran into an unforseen problem when his wife Susana Higuchi came forward to denounce corruption in congress, and announced that she would be running for president against her husband. Amidst allegations of fraud, Susana was eventually barred from running for the presidency and divorce proceedings were initiated.

The effects of this upon Fujimori appear limited, as he entered the election race against strong opposition from former United Nations secretary general Javier Peréz de Cuellar. In April 1995, against all predictions that it would be a closely fought election, Fujimori won a second term in office, gaining nearly two-thirds of the popular vote, with his Cambio '90 Nueva Mayoria party achieving a slight majority in Congress.

Hopes that such success would lead to a liberalization of the Fujimori administration have thus far been unrealized. In fact, developments have included the passing of the Ley de Amnistía (Amnesty Law) which provides for pardons for members of the armed forces previously convicted of human-rights abuses. Similarly, a new bill makes it harder for other political parties to take part in municipal elections.

Left, the rule of law personified.

PERU'S HIGH-PROFILE NOVELIST

Mario Vargas Llosa is Peru's best-known intellectual and novelist, the author of works such as *The War of the End of the World* and *Aunt Julia and the Scriptwriter*. Possessed of a precocious literary talent, he first emerged as a hot property in international publishing in the 1960s, a youthful prodigy of the "boom" in Latin American fiction.

He has not been content to remain simply his country's chronicler. Though the continent's intellectuals have rarely shunned politics, few have sought such an active political role as Vargas. But the novelist's bid to become President of his country in 1990 ended in a failure as resounding as his literary success.

Vargas Llosa, the author of 10 novels and three plays and a prolific essayist, was born in Arequipa into a middle- class family in 1936. His parents were estranged, and he scarcely knew his family until he was 10.

He went to school in the northern city of Piura and the Military College in Lima. Both were to provide material for books. His first novel, translated as *The Time of the Hero* and set in the Military College, is a taut exploration of adolescence lived in a closed, authoritarian world. The military authorities responded by burning copies of the book on a public bonfire.

Vargas Llosa is a meticulous and sophisticated stylist, a conscious craftsman of words. For many of his countrymen, his greatest novel remains *Conversation in the Cathedral* – a complex, multi-layered tableau of power and its perversions, set mainly in Lima in the 1950s during the dictatorship of General Odria. But Vargas Llosa himself prefers *The War of the End of the World,* his 1981 historical novel about a fanatical backwoods rebellion in turn-of-the-century Brazil.

"Peru is for me a kind of incurable disease," he has written, "and my feeling for her is intense, bitter, and full of the violence that characterizes passion." But to express that passion in writing, he

Mario Vargas Llosa: as intense as his works.

chose to live in Europe for 16 years, returning to Peru mainly for summer vacations to his impressive house, on a cliff overlooking the Pacific Ocean in Barranco, Lima.

As a student at Lima's San Marcos University, he briefly joined the Communist Party. He remained a man of the left for almost two decades before gradually mutating into a supporter of the radical Right, an admirer of British Prime Minister Margaret Thatcher and a bitter detractor of the Cuban revolution which he once defended. Vargas himself identifies a common thread in his apparently differing political positions: an on-going concern for freedom of expression.

Vargas's plunge into active politics began when he led a public campaign in opposition to President Garcia's bid to nationalise the country's private banks. Out of this came, initially, a political movement which was called "Libertad" (Freedom), and then a presidential candidacy for the right-of-center Democratic Front. Vargas used this platform to expound a radical free market economic program that included the promise to sell-off all of Peru's state companies.

It was a strange role for someone who had once boldly declared that "when politics invades... the writer dies."

But this was not the only apparent paradox. "I left my books because I think there is a real, immediate possibility of changing the history of Peru," he told his final campaign rally.

Uttered by a character in one of his novels, this statement might be intended to reveal the kind of dangerous, messianic obsession that is a favourite Vargas Llosa theme.

Though Vargas Llosa has written so penetratingly about his country, the campaign suggested that he lacked an understanding of the aspirations and perceptions of ordinary Peruvians. They turned their backs on him, and an early lead in the opinion polls was wiped out as political unknown Alberto Fujimori gained a surprised victory.

In turn, Vargas Llosa can now be seen to have rejected the Peru that rejected him. In 1994 he elected to receive Spanish citizenship, and his 1993 account of his political experiences, *A Fish in the Water*, is a bitter diatribe from a man who obviously feels let down by his country. ∎

Back in 1949 a group of intellectuals intent on forging a new national identity ventured into Peru's Andean provinces to discover the truth behind the stereotypes of the indigenous interior. In an Ayacucho workshop they found the impish Don Joaquín Lopéz Antay crafting *sanmarkos*, which are three-dimensional wooden boxes filled with brightly painted miniature saints and used for branding rituals. The style's roots lay in the portable shrines brought to Peru by the conquistadors.

Intrigued by what they saw, the intellectuals encouraged Don Joaquín to develop his medium but change his subject matter. He started to introduce the ebb and flow of life into the boxes: drunken fiestas in the streets, the bustle of markets, the repression of crowded jails, and the festive processions of Nativity and Easter, thereby creating something distinctly Peruvian. The intellectuals named this new piece of folk art a *retablo*, or altarpiece.

This encounter between the modernizer and the traditional was repeated up and down the Andes over five decades in the latter half of the 20th century. The new art forms, music, literature and thirst for knowledge that resulted have become typical of the new and unique identity of Peru.

Divided society: Since pre-Columbian times Peruvians have been divided by nature. From the arid deserts of the coast, the Andean Sierra rises up to 6,000 meters (19,700 feet) and more above sea level. The highlands comprise about a quarter of Peru's territory, but are home to about half of Peru's population. For the modern nation-state, this mountain mass poses major problems for development and integration into a single society. The huge natural barrier severely limits the penetration of motorized transport and telecommunications while frequent earthquakes and landslides further complicate the already arduous terrain.

The result is dramatic regional diversity, and considerable inequalities in services and living standards. Health, education and law enforcement programs are unevenly distributed across Peru. The social anthropologist John Murra described the Andes as an archipelago, or series of island-like pockets of isolated communities.

Many worlds: At first sight, Peruvian culture may seen brutally divided between indigenous and colonial societies – the mountains and the city. Elite white creoles trace their bloodlines back to the Spanish Con-

quest of 1536. Like the generations before them, most live in Lima, the old colonial capital that still boasts a statue of the chief invader Pizarro in its main square. They enjoy the cultural legacy of colonialism and their eyes are firmly fixed on Miami: North American mass culture, from Reebok to Disneyland, is part of their children's upbringing. Hence, a European visitor will feel a comfortable familiarity in Lima's cafés and supermarkets.

On the other side, rural communities now also aspire to ownership of televisions and blue jeans but this comes into conflict with their traditional cultural values. Heirs to awe-

Preceding pages: riotous fiesta in Cuzco; rich Limeños in bar; skateboard riders in Lima. Left, flowers for sale in Chiclayo. Above right, chic and shocked.

inspiring pre-Columbian cultures, the people of the Andes are maintaining the traditional practices of their ancestors in a rapidly changing world. Their livelihood continues to be based on family-owned fields or *chakras* which are farmed by hand or with the help of draft animals.

The social organization of communities in the Andes differs greatly from that of Europeanized creole culture. Work, marriage and land-ownership are centered around a complex extended family organization called the *ayllu* in Quechua which dates back to at least Inca times. One of the main functions of *ayllus* is to organize reciprocal work exchange. This often takes the form of group

The Andes have two large ethnolinguistic groups: the larger of the two speaks Quechua, the language of the Inca empire; the smaller group speaks Aymará and is settled around Lake Titicaca and also in neighboring Bolivia. The Quechua language is far from uniform and someone speaking the dialect of Huancayo may not be understood by a Quechua-speaker from Cuzco because of regional differences.

Beyond these global distinctions, other complexities arise. There are "white" ethnic groups, like the Morochucos of Pampa Cangallo (Ayacucho) who have light-colored eyes and hair, speak Quechua and see themselves as *campesinos* (traditional farmers).

projects like roof-raising or potato harvesting which are coupled with festive meals and plentiful *chicha* (homemade corn beer).

Complex mix: Over the past 400 years, there has been a long process of inter-cultural mixing, creating the *mestizo* of part-Amerindian, part-European heritage. Today the majority of Peruvians would fall into this category, and in Peru you can become *mestizo* not only by birth but also by choice. Anyone assuming Western dress in the rural hinterlands is usually referred to as *mestizo* or sometimes *cholo*. Peruvian social divisions can thus be said to be not so much racially as culturally defined.

The *misti*, the dominant social class in the Andes, may speak Quechua and share other cultural traits but enjoy access to education and the luxuries of the modernization. Meanwhile, in the Amazon jungle, there are at least 53 ethnolinguistic groups (*see "Tribes of the Amazon" on page 107*), although only around 5 percent of Peru's population lives in the *Selva* (the humid, tropical region east of the Andes of the jungle).

Due to its New World history, Peru also enjoys a rich cultural diversity. Up to the 19th century, landowners brought in African blacks to serve as slaves on their *haciendas* and frequently used them to repress the local

Indians. Between 1850 and 1920, Chinese and Japanese laborers provided the hands and backs to build railways over the Andes and farm the land when there was a scarcity of labor.

Until the 20th century, the hold of Peru's oligarchy was based on exclusive control of the nation's best land resources, especially the fertile highland valleys which they managed from Lima. A symbol of this class was the Club Nacional, an exclusive private club located on Plaza San Martín in downtown Lima. In its high-vaulted dining rooms and smoking parlors, these elites plotted to overthrow uncomfortable reformist governments that did not serve their interests between

nessmen and political reformers of the 20th century including Mario Vargas Llosa, Hernando De Soto and Javier Peréz de Cuellar. These were the men who believed in universal rights and progress and wanted to extend them equally to the nation's indigenous people and *mestizos.*

The Andes are still a refuge for Peru's underprivileged Quechua and Aymará-speakers, with approximately 5,000 peasant communities located throughout the Andean Sierra. These communities are based on a non-industrial agricultural economy, and families supplement their incomes with cottage industries including the distinctive handicrafts, foodstuffs (such as bread, cheese

1900 and the land reforms of 1962. Today, the sons of the plotters no longer frequent the Club Nacional, leaving it to dozing old men. The businessmen and bankers who now form Peru's more entrepreneurial ruling class do not sit around planning political schemes but concentrate on maximizing profits in an unstable economy.

This same privileged class also boasts many great intellectuals, progressive busi-

Far left, young dancers in Trujillo (The north); left, praying before a grave. Above, pipe-playing on Taquile Island; above right, soccer player in the slums of Lima.

and honey) and other similarly labor-intensive activities.

A large majority of highland people live a marginal and impoverished existence and are removed from the modern benefits of the national economy. While retaining a fierce loyalty to their ancestral heritage, so well known to the outside world through their bright homespun costumes, the poor of the Andes are nevertheless equally eager to share in the luxuries of a "modern" lifestyle which includes education, electricity, sewage and running potable water. But rather than improving, the economic status of these communities is deteriorating, leading to massive urban migration to the shanty towns of the coastal cities.

The most difficult social terrain to define in Peru is the middle class. Up to the 1960s, it was the poor cousin of the oligarchy, providing clerks, merchants and civil servants to service the dominant class. Once modernization started in earnest in the 1970s, the middle class grew into its own, both in Lima and in provincial cities. This growth was due to the diversification of the economy and to the expansion of the Peruvian state, both as a purveyor of public services and as an entrepreneur. Its composition is more defined by education and social values than by ethnic origins. As the impact of economic

Peruvian nationalism even in the most remote communities.

These social changes were matched by political changes. A military regime under Army General Juan Alvarado Velasco broke the stereotypes of Latin American strong-arm governments. The military enacted progressive programs by expropriating large land-holdings, nationalizing foreign companies and asserting a more independent foreign policy. This approach, at times demagogical, at times nationalistic, marked a change in attitudes. The *campesinos* and shantytown residents began to challenge creole leadership.

The Ayacuchan artist mentioned at the

fluctuations have shown, however, the middle class is also vulnerable because it depends on disposable income, which has been eroded by inflation.

Decade of change: In the 1970s, several trends began to break down the isolation of much of Peru. Roads penetrating into the Sierra and the Amazon Basin started to link up the hinterland with Lima and important coastal markets.

Mass communication began to reach out to new audiences. In 1970, the Peruvian football team's participation in that year's World Cup, which was broadcast nationally on radio and television, promoted a sense of

beginning of this chapter, Don Joaquín, might be seen as a symbol of the changes at work in Peru. In 1975, he was awarded a National Art Prize for his innovation and creativity in shaping folk art and the *retablo*. This decision was promptly criticized by many mainstream urban art critics and artists who couldn't see why folk art should be given the same status as the "fine arts."

But the story didn't stop there. A new generation of image-makers, like Florentino Jimenez, gave the *retablos* new dimensions. He started working themes that asked broader questions, such as: where does the Andean peasant fit into national history and identity?

He made massive *retablos* which portrayed national events – for instance, the battles for political independence from Spain. He also narrated events from local history, such as protest marches.

This shift in theme and content would not have been possible without the explosion of public education in the latter half of the 20th century. *Campesinos* and their recently migrated cousins in the cities struggled and sacrificed to gain an education – not just the three Rs, but even university degrees – so that they could gain access to status and income. But schooling represents a great lifestyle change for *campesinos* as children traditionally work on the farm and tend live-

equivalent to gaining full citizenship and a ticket to progress. Education in the highlands is opening new horizons.

Growth of a monster: In the 1960s and 1970s, Lima seemed like a promised land to Peru's rural poor. An invasion of migrants from places like Ayaviri, Bambamarca and Huaráz gradually filled the coastal city with a huge Andean population. In the 1980s, the capital was flooded by refugees from the central Sierra fleeing the brutal civil war.

Urban authorities were unable to satisfy the basic needs of these newly urban migrants, and thus the multitude of *pueblos jovenes* or shanty towns surrounding Lima came into being, as there simply was no

stock. It also represents a new and difficult expense. Thousands of poor rural communities built one-room schools with dirt floors, benches and painted blackboards. The communities bore the costs and labor to construct and maintain these schools and also support their teachers. The added household expenses of school uniforms and supplies with the loss of child labor further complicates rural education programs. Still, the sharpest students are sent off to the cities to finish their schooling, and learning to read and write can be

Left, enjoying a glass of *chicha*. **Above**, a rather more formal meal.

place within the city for all these people to go (*see "Lima's Oasis of Hope" on page 172*). A symbol of this cultural influx is the vibrant *Chicha* music of Lima which mixes the traditions of Andean and creole music to express the melancholy realities of urban life.

Today, the capital has come to represent all that went wrong with Peruvian development. One city now concentrates most of the country's capital, services and other resources, but they are grossly inadequate to sustain its 8 million inhabitants. Lima also concentrates an inordinate amount of political control and the belated attempt to decentralize power into the hands of novice regional governments initiated by President García has thus far proved to be ineffective. Indeed, under Fujimori, regional poles of development such as those centered in the cities of Trujillo, Cuzco, Iquitos and Arequipa have failed to flourish as resources are directed at the capital.

Haphazard development: Westerners often take for granted the virtues of the 20th century. In Peru, democracy, urbanization, industrialization, consumer markets, the mass media and accelerated technological innovation are an inflammable mixture. The forced march of modernization has crammed huge behavioral changes into the span of a generation. In developed countries, these

lifestyle of the central Sierra from modernizing pressures from outside.

Even the Roman Catholic Church, a pillar of the old order, has changed tremendously in recent decades, with consequences for Peru's predominantly Catholic population. The idea was to make the church relevant to a temporal world, which in Peru meant reaching outside the traditional pastures. The archbishop of Lima moved out of his palatial residence on the Plaza de Armas to a modest neighborhood. Not only are Masses said in Spanish, but also in Quechua, Aymará and other dialects. The National Bishops' conference issued communiques that challenged politicians to reduce poverty, injustice and

changes took place over 300 years. In Peru, the leap in expectations, frustrations and sensitivity to injustice has far outrun the capacity of the government and other institutions to deliver.

This lesson was driven home with a vengeance in the 1980s. The Peruvian economy proved unable to sustain living standards acquired during the preceding three decades. At the same time, forces like the Shining Path guerrilla insurgency in the Andes and drug trafficking in the Amazon began to threaten the state. Indeed, one of the purported concerns of the Shining Path movement was to protect the traditional Andean

inequality. Although not all of the hierarchy and faithful are convinced that the church should play a political role in changing the country, its language and methods have been irrevocably altered.

A slower transformation is to be found in the role of women in Peruvian society. Traditionally, women in pre-Conquest, Andean Peru had rights and obligations on a more equal footing with men than was to be found in the colonial era. Property was owned by both women and men and could be passed down from both mothers and fathers. Unlike later creole society, one's female lineage and heritage was important to individual identity. Although the rights of women have been eroded throughout the post-Conquest years, there have been changes – more women now go to university and hold down professional careers than before; within local communities women are assuming leadership roles and taking back control of their lives. Role models such as Martha Chavéz, President of Congress, ethnohistorian María Rostworowski and linguist and congresswoman Martha Hildebrand are inspiring a whole new generation.

Responding to the new order: A striking feature of contemporary Peruvian society is the massive scale of the informal economy. The decay of the national economy has led to

ket structure is thriving and chaotic. This is epitomized by the so-called "*combi-culture*" which resulted when large-scale government layoffs led to an explosion of independent *combi* (minibus) and taxi drivers attempting to replace lost state jobs. Cars and *combis* would be bought with severance pay and launched into direct competition with existing transport services.

And examples like this are found not only throughout the marketplace but also all over the country, as Peruvians call upon their ability to adapt to an ever-changing socio-economic climate. Driven by economic need it may be, but the informal economy is indicative of a willingness to utilize traditional

an elaboration of traditional market street trade and bartering at market stalls is an integral part of daily life. *Ambulantes* (street vendors) can be found on every corner selling a huge variety of goods from fresh coconut to sandals made of used tires and fluorescent light bulbs.

In the absence of a centralized infrastructure, approximately 40 percent of the nation's population work in the informal economy. The visual impact of Peru's mar-

strengths of organizational skills, hard work and inventiveness to acquire a share of the nation's wealth.

Despite decades of political upheaval and social unrest, Peru can now be seen to be entering a more stable phase in its history. An increasing level of governmental consistency and growing economic strength has led to growing confidence from within – a belief in a renewed and unified country overcoming the shackles of a turbulent past.

Like the image-makers of Ayacucho, Peruvian society as a whole is moving into the modern world, but with a proper sense of national history.

Left, a model suburb of Lima (*see Lima's "Oasis of Hope" on page 172*). **Above,** enjoying a beer in Lima's Cordano bar and restaurant.

DAILY LIFE IN THE ANDES

The route to most villages in the Andes is a narrow, graded-earth road, in the winter baked concrete-solid under the fierce dry-season sun, in the summer awash with torrents of rain, slick with mud, narrowed or closed by rock-slides. These roads wind tortuously through the mountains, making complicated switchbacks up and down their flanks or following deep river valleys. The vehicles that ply them, the means of transportation readily available and affordable to most of the inhabitants of those villages, are sometimes small, rattle-trap buses, retired from service on proper roads somewhere else and consigned to end their days traveling perilous mountain routes; or, more often, heavy, several-ton trucks with wooden sides and a gate and ladder at the back, which carry everything from grains and potatoes, destined for markets in the cities, to livestock and people.

The villages at the ends of these roads of the Peruvian Andes are inhabited for the most part by the Quechua, descendants of the population once ruled by the Inca, whose empire encompassed at its height an area from what is now Ecuador south to Chile and east to Bolivia. In the ensuing centuries, the resilient Quechua have adapted to the cultures superimposed upon their own, adopting elements that were forced upon them, like the ardent though shrewdly flexible Catholicism of their conquerors, and also those that were useful to them, like the Old World livestock and crops the Spanish introduced to the Americas.

They took the European dress of the period of the Conquest which, in most places and in a derivative form, is still worn to this day. And more recently they have accepted such amenities as running water (in some places) and aluminium pots and pans, radios, record players, and flashlights.

Nevertheless, today, although the accoutrements are different, the fundamental outlines of Quechua life remain remarkably as they were in the 16th century, resembling life in a medieval European village more

<u>Left</u>, Colorful *campesino* market.

than any modern way of life we might be familiar with.

Harsh agricultural world: Life in the village is simple and hard, based on subsistence agriculture and pastoralism. Most villages are only marginally connected to the national cash economy through the production of some crops for sale in city markets, and so, as they have done since the inception of agriculture in the Andes, each family must produce during the growing season the food it will live on for the entire year – and enough to sustain it through a bad year if the crops should ever fail. Amenities are few. Only the larger towns have electricity or even generators. Some villages now have a system of

for a Quechua woman – and men sit on earthen benches built against the walls of the house. The family's possessions consist of their clothing, their pots and pans and cooking and eating utensils, simple agricultural implements and a few other tools, their house and land and animals and usually, and most prized, a radio. The radio is their sole connection to the rest of the world, a connection perhaps most valued in years when the World Cup soccer tournament is played.

The Quechua inhabit the entire range of altitudes in the complex vertical ecology of the Andes that will sustain human life, from the lushest, subtropical river valleys to the high, desolate *puna*. Each village exists within

drinkable water, so that there may be taps outside houses or at selected points throughout the village where cold mountain water can be drawn (sparing people a several-times-daily trek to a spring or stream to fetch water). The houses are of adobe bricks or, in some places, of stone, with packed-earth floors and thatched or tiled roofs, the open rafters inside always blackened and sooty from years of smoke from the cooking fire in a hearth in the corner. There is no furniture save perhaps a couple of rudimentary stools, though a more affluent family may have a bed, or a table; women sit, or more often, squat, on the floor – a characteristic posture

a sort of micro-climate that affords it a certain range of crops – perhaps tropical fruits such as lemons, limes, oranges, avocados and chilis and a variety of vegetables both familiar and exotic.

High-altitude living: The character of each village is in large part determined by the potential of the land it controls. For a village in the high *puna*, the economy consists mainly of the cultivation of potatoes and high-altitude grains and of herding – mainly of llamas, sheep, a few goats and perhaps a few cattle. There is little arable land to be conserved and it might be widely dispersed amongst various settlements of small houses of one or two joined or detached rooms, sometimes with a second-story storeroom, built often of stone and roofed with a heavy thatch of *puna* grasses. Among the houses might be corrals for the animals, ringed by fences of stacked stone. Around the perimeter of the village will be small potato fields, their ridges and furrows giving them the appearance of corduroy patches on the smooth fabric of short tough *puna* grasses.

Other towns in this range reveal a markedly different plan. These were the *reducciones* ("reductions") created by the Spanish in the 1570s as they gathered together the native population living in scattered settlements throughout a particular region, for purposes of control and taxation, forced conversion to Catholicism, and, in general, "civilization." The *reducciones* were laid out according to a plan prescribed by Viceroy Francisco de Toledo, the Spanish king's representative in Peru, after a four-year tour of the highlands to determine what means would be necessary to govern the new country: they were to be founded in this most temperate zone – deemed to be the most healthy – neither too high nor too low in altitude, near a good source of water; they were to have perpendicular streets laid out on an orderly grid, a town plaza, prison, house for the local governor, and, of course, a church. Finally, each family's house or compound was to have a door on to the street, so that they could be easily seen and policed.

The populations of many *reducciones* are today much smaller than they were at the time of their initial settlement, for many of the inhabitants have drifted back to their native communities and land, a migration which began in some cases soon after the towns were created and has continued for 400 years. But the straight, roughly-cobbled streets remain, and the broad public plazas, and, sometimes, in some little town in the middle of nowhere, you will find a magnificent old rambling adobe church, its tiled roof sagging, its gloomy interior still brightened by a great altar of tarnished silver or flaking gilt, its walls still adorned by enormous paintings, their ornate frames warped and their images darkened to obscurity by the years.

Left, drinking up at a fiesta. **Above**, woman with llamas.

The Andean cycle: The activities of nearly every member of nearly every family are determined throughout the year, and indeed, throughout their lives, by the needs of the crops. The agricultural cycle begins, in villages in this middle range, in August and September, when the Andean winter – a succession of warm, cloudless days and stunningly clear and frigid nights – just begins to draw to a close. The crops are planted generally from low altitude to high altitude, and harvested in reverse order.

Summer, the growing season, is also the rainy season. During these months, the fields are hoed and weeded, and the earth of fallowed fields is turned in preparation for

the coming year's crops, often under most unpleasant conditions – in rain, hail and mud. In May, when the rains have ended, the potatoes are harvested. The village's communally-held potato lands lie in the *puna*, often two or three hours' walk from the village, and the harvest is a tedious and time-consuming labor, so each family packs up the essentials of its household – food and pots and serving and eating utensils, bedding and perhaps even the chicken – and, leaving behind someone, an older child perhaps, to pasture the sheep and cows, moves to the fields until the harvest is completed. They live during that time in a tiny, temporary hut, much like a form of camping. The grains and beans are then cut and allowed to dry for threshing; the corn is harvested in June. After the grains are threshed, the community turns to the dry-season activities of weaving and building and repairing the damage done by the rain, and to the wholehearted celebration of the numerous Catholic religious festivals that fall during these months.

Twenty-four hours in the village: The day begins when, in the darkness well before the first cock's crow, someone stirs and perhaps turns on the radio. In the south central highlands around Cuzco, it will be tuned to Radio Tawantinsuyu, a station based in that city whose disc-jockeys broadcast their programs

consists of *mate* with bread or with *mote* – boiled dried corn, one of the elemental dishes of Quechua cuisine. As her sleepy family eats this simple meal, she begins to prepare the next: *almuerzo*, or "lunch," which will be taken at an hour when most of *us* would be having breakfast.

Almuerzo – usually a rich soup of potatoes and other vegetables, served with boiled potatoes and perhaps a hot pepper sauce and hearty glass of *chicha*, a homemade corn beer – is served before the men set out for their day's work. The man of the household is assisted in his work by his sons and grandsons, and by other men – often *compadres*, the godfathers of his children – who owe him

in Quechua and Quechua-Spanish. In the dark the day's first strains of *wayno* and *marinera*, the "country music" of Peru, are heard. The woman of the family rises from her bed, a pallet of heavy, handwoven woolen blankets laid over a pile of sheepskins on the earthen floor of the adobe hut, or, in more fortunate households, on a spare wooden bed-frame with a mattress fashioned of bundles of spilt reeds. She moves over to the hearth and stirs up the embers of yesterday's fire, adds a few sticks of firewood, fetches water and puts on a kettle for *mate*, which here means a heavily-sugared herbal infusion like tea. Breakfast, at or before dawn,

a day's work in exchange for a day he has spent helping them in their fields. The entire complement of laborers gathers in the woman's kitchen to be fortified with as many bowls of soup and glasses of *chicha* as they can be persuaded to consume. They will work steadily all day, pausing only occasionally for *chicha* and once for a meal, which the woman will bring later, in the hope of completing the job in one day.

As they leave the house, the woman begins cooking her third meal of the day, a bountiful meal, considerably more complex in its preparation, of two or three dishes, with meat and potatoes and *mote*, because this meal is a gesture of gratitude toward the men assisting her husband. At the same time, she tends to the children and animals, feeding children, chickens and pigs, and milking the cow before it is led to pasture by one of the children, along with the sheep. Depending on the task being performed in her husband's fields, she may be assisted in her kitchen by the wives of the men working with her husband, or only by her daughters and small children, sometimes a dubious benefit.

By midday, she packs the meal into a carrying cloth with plates and spoons, and sometimes a bottle or two of cane liquor for the men, and sets out herself for the fields, sometimes accompanied by another woman

another cup or two of *chicha* and the last of the *trago*, everything is gathered up and they begin the walk home. The group meets up in the deepening shadows with the children driving home the cattle and herds of sheep and goats. At home, the small children drowse in their parents' or their siblings' laps as the adults have another cup of *chicha* warmed over the fire, perhaps another class of *trago*, maybe only a cup of *mate*; and eventually the fire is allowed to die, the pallets are laid out, and everyone settles for the night into well-earned sleep.

Days of celebration: But on other days, the villagers' primary obligation will be not work but the hearty celebration of one of the nu-

or two who carry a share of the burden, sometimes trailing small children if she hasn't left them in the care of an older child, her mother, a sister, or a *comadre*.

At the side of the field, she will serve the fruits of her efforts. The men pause in their work to eat, to drink *chicha* and a few tiny glasses of cane liquor, called *trago*. As the men plow or hoe the last rows of the field, the women may help, though more often they sit and watch, talking among themselves and sipping *chicha*. At the end of the day, after

Left, a heavy load, Taquile Island. **Above**, grinding maize on the Uros Islands.

merous Catholic religious festivals that fall throughout the year. Each village celebrates a series of Catholic saints' days – that of its patron saint certainly, and those of other saints significant to the village for one reason or another – and certain other signal dates in the religious calendar: Christmas and Carnival and Easter, the Day of the Holy Cross, and All Souls' Day, the Day of the Dead. Those which fall during the months of the dry season, when the most critical and urgent work of the year – the work upon which simple survival depends – is done, are approached with special abandon.

While the basic religious formulas pertaining to at least the most significant of these holidays are generally observed in some fashion – Masses spoken and attended, vigils kept, the processions of the images of saints followed piously through the plaza or streets of the village – each of these festivals has taken on, in the Andes, a distinctly Quechua flavor. Around each there has developed a whole separate complex of ceremony which seems to have little to do with Spanish Catholicism, and much more to do, perhaps, with Andean traditions of worship and religious observance which long pre-date the Spanish Conquest.

Every festival – as well as birthdays and anniversaries of various events, weddings,

baptisms and christenings – is also celebrated by the sometimes overwhelming exercise of the characteristic, near-compulsive, Andean hospitality, resulting in the serving of great quantities of food and copious drink. The point here is to serve your guests more and richer food than they would normally eat, and literally to force them to get very drunk and to dance (much to the consternation of any representative of the official church hierarchy who may be present).

Cultural mix: In short, contemporary Quechua culture is a result of syncretism, a thorough blending of the ideologies of two very different cultures – Quechua and Spanish. While pictures of saints may adorn the walls of adobe huts, and nearly everyone in the villages has learned and may remember at least some of the words of common Catholic prayers in Quechua, people pay homage and turn as often or more often for guidance and healing to the traditional powers of the Andes – the mountains and the earth.

One ironic example of the intimate coexistence of Quechua and Catholic custom exists in the contemporary Quechua rituals of marriage. The ultimate goal of the process is a proper Catholic wedding in a church, registered in the parish log-books, but the Quechua take a distinctly un-Catholic route to get there. An alliance between a young couple is arranged by their parents, based on the expressed interest of the two young people. From this point, the couple enter into a period called *sirvinakuy* – the word means, in Quechua, "to serve each other" – during which each helps his or her potential in-laws with the work of their households, the young woman her mother-in-law, the young man his father-in-law, a test of their suitability and readiness for marriage. During this time also, the young couple sleep together under the roof of one set of parents or the other.

The couple will not marry until a child is conceived, demonstrating the reproductive viability of the union, and may not even then – a wedding, to be sponsored (and paid for) by the parents and godparents of the couple, is an elaborate and expensive affair, and may be put off for years, although the couple must be officially married before their children can be baptised. And though the Quechua practice of this system of trial marriage is commonly known, among the clergy as well as everyone else, the issue is generally studiously avoided when the couple finally arrive at the church, often with children in tow, to be married.

How to celebrate: A festival such as the Day of the Virgin of the Nativity, in one village, might include an array of events: playing host to the visiting images of patron saints from the churches and chapels of other villages, daily Masses and processions, led by a priest, throughout the week-long celebration – some holidays are celebrated until the *octava*, the "eighth day," though sometimes the celebration wanes before then as the will to drink and dance falters from simple exhaustion. There may be bullfights, and soccer tournaments between regional village teams, all performed in the shadows of enormous altars the men of the village have erected in the plaza, made of eucalyptus poles adorned with complex configurations of painted wooden panels, banners and small mirrored boxes containing miniature images of saints.

For other festivals, there are bands of musicians, local or hired from the nearest city, playing instruments ranging from brass and accordions and drums to native flutes, violins, the little Andean mandolin, the *charango*, the body of which is the shell of an armadillo, and the Andean harp with its great half-conical sounding box.

sanitario, a rural doctor. At night there might be bonfires in front of the altars in the plaza, tended all night long as people dance in their light, with music giving the night an unaccustomed life and *chicha* flowing freely until the celebrants stagger home to collapse into bed. The festival might also attract vendors from the cities and other nearby towns who come to offer for sale everything from clothing to candy to small manufactured goods such as barrettes, sewing needles, toys and balloons.

The villagers themselves may claim a space among the vendors at the edges of the plaza to sell *chicha* and prepared food and produce, so that the village enjoys for the dura-

Or the music may be provided by scratchy 45-rpm records of *waynos* and *marineras*, played on little, portable, battery-operated phonographs, the kind you find now only in nursery schools, turned up to full volume, the words of the songs and even the tunes rendered unrecognizable by distortion. There may be troupes of dancers in costumes which transform their wearers into entities and personages from every era of Andean history – characters ranging from the *ukuku* or Andean spectacled bear, to the soldier and the

Far left, boy in the Sierra. **Above**, celebrating their Inca heritage at Sacsayhuaman.

tion of the festivities the benefits of its own open-air market.

Feasting, drinking and dancing also goes on in the households – especially those of the *carguyugs,* the men who have accepted and fulfilled the responsibility for some element of the public celebrations. The hospitality and generosity of the host family is another ritual gesture of gratitude for whatever small or large part another has played. The village is transformed. Everywhere, the holiday reigns: work is temporarily abandoned, and everyone revels in the respite from the weighty responsibilities of everyday life and survival.

"I say truly to Your Highness that these people are the most insolent that I have seen in all the time that I have traveled in the Indies and engaged in their conquest."
– Captain Hernando de Benavente on the Jivaro Indians, March 25, 1550, to the Royal Audiencia of Spain.

It was Francisco Orellana, a Spanish conquistador in Gonzalo Pizarro's expedition, who first got close to Peru's Amazon Indians and ultimately became the first European to float 3,500 km (2,200 miles) down the Amazon river.

Four years after Francisco Pizarro had brought the Inca empire to its knees, in 1540 the elder Pizarro dispatched his younger brother Gonzalo to seek out rumors of an empire of gold to the east – the enduring legend of El Dorado. Leaving what is now Quito, Ecuador, with a vast expedition that included over 200 Spaniards, 4,000 Indian slaves, horses and flocks of llamas and pigs, the conquistadors headed over the Andes and down through the cloud forest before constructing a boat and floating down what is now the Napo river.

It wasn't long before they came upon the inhabitants of this mysterious, dripping world. He later recalled: "We saw coming up the river a great many canoes, all equipped for fighting, gaily colored, and the men with their shields on, which are made out of the shell-like skins of lizards and the hides of manatees and of tapirs... they were coming on with a great yell, playing on many drums and wooden trumpets, threatening us as if they were going to devour us."

Unlike the younger Pizarro, Orellana was anthropologically astute. Separating from Gonzalo's party which would later return to Quito, Orellana learned several Indian dialects as he descended, kept his men from killing them, and questioned the Indians at length. Eventually, after a voyage of nine months, Orellana and his men sailed from the mouth of the Amazon and returned to Peru via Panama. One and a half years after the expedition had begun, Gonzalo Pizarro

Left, Yagua Indian near Iquitos.

and a ragged crew stumbled into Quito. Only 80 of the original 4,200 men had survived.

Feared jungle warriors: The Amazon Indians have long played a part in Peruvian history. According to Inca oral history, hordes of fierce jungle Indians were said to have climbed into the Andes and to have sacked the Inca capital of Cuzco several times. Indeed, the Inca fortress of Pisac is thought to have been an outpost protecting the capital from the attack of the feared jungle tribes living to the east. The Incas themselves referred to the eastern quarter of their 4,500-km (2,800-mile) long empire as *Antisuyo*, and to the Indians who inhabited its jungles as the *Antis*; it is from the latter word that the name Andes derives.

When not warring, trade was routinely carried out between the Incas and the Antis, the former trading cloths, manufactured goods and bronze axes in return for gold, feathers, exotic fruits, woods and other jungle products. After the empire was sacked by the Spaniards one of the last Inca kings, Manco Capac, fled from Cuzco and established a new capital deep in the jungle in Vilcabamba (the lost capital was rediscovered in 1964 by the American explorer Gene Savoy). Manco Capac was aided by legions of loyal jungle warriors who were deadly with bow and arrow.

After the collapse of the Incas, the jungle was largely abandoned by the Spaniards, who concentrated instead on mining wealth from the more tractable peasants in the Andes and on the coast. The few expeditions mounted into the jungle generally met with disaster. In a few cases, such as among the fierce, head-shrinking Jivaro Indians living in northern Peru, the Spaniards did establish jungle towns and attempted to tax the Indians' increasing quantities of gold. In 1599, however, the Jivaros staged a massive revolt, burning and sacking the cities and slaughtering an estimated 20,000 to 30,000 men, women and children. They then captured the Spanish governor who happened to be on a tax-collecting mission at the time.

"They stripped him naked, tied his hands and feet; and while some amused themselves with him, delivering a thousand castigations and jests, the others set up a large forge in the courtyard, where they melted the gold. When it was ready in the crucibles, they opened his mouth with a bone, saying that they wanted to see if for once he had enough gold. They poured it little by little, and then forced it down with another bone; and bursting his bowels with the torture, all raised a clamor and laughter."

In southern Peru, the Spaniards didn't fare much better. An expedition mounted to explore the Madre de Díos and Manu rivers encountered numerous hostile Indians. A second Spanish expedition was then launched, after convincing the authorities that the first had no legal right to conquer

time of the Spanish contract, had fewer than 2 million 50 years later. The same pattern was repeated in the jungle, beginning in the zone of greatest contact – the Amazon and its major tributaries – and gradually working its way into deeper parts of the forest.

Slave raiding, which started on Brazil's coast in the 16th century, gradually worked its way further into the Upper Amazon and Peru. Within a hundred years of Orellana's descent, the "teeming Indians" that had once infested the Amazon's banks were nowhere to be seen. Indian tribes that hadn't been captured or wiped out by disease simply retreated further into the jungle's interior.

The biggest incursion into Peru's Ama-

new empires. When they met, the two groups nearly annihilated each other, whereupon the ever watchful Indians massacred all but two of the survivors.

Decimated by disease: From then on for Peru's Indians, however, it was all downhill. As elsewhere, their greatest nemesis was not so much the Spaniards as it was the introduction of European diseases. Having crossed the Bering Strait out of Asia anywhere from 10,000 to 40,000 years ago, the New World Indians' immunological systems were totally unprepared for European pathogens. The Inca empire, for example, which is thought to have had about 7 million Indians at the

zon, however, didn't occur until the rubber boom exploded in the late 19th century. Almost overnight, the most isolated jungle rivers and streams were overrun by rubber tappers who carried the latest Winchester carbines. Rubber trees were few and far between – hence rubber tapping demanded intensive labor. Entire Indian villages were therefore sacked to capture Indian slaves. In the case of especially hostile tribes, *correrias*, or armed raids, were carried out in which villages and Indians were surrounded and slaughtered by the employees of the great rubber barons. Whole areas of the Amazon were thus wiped clear of native populations in a matter of decades. In 1912, however, the rubber market began to collapse and this time, almost overnight, the rubber tappers withdrew. Haltingly, the remaining tribes were left alone except for occasional missionaries. In the 1960s, as the peasants in the Andes became more numerous, Peru's government – burdened by hordes of peasants moving into the coastal cities and unwilling to enact land reform in the Sierra – chose the easier alternative and began encouraging these peasants to move into the vast, unsettled Amazon which makes up two-thirds of the country. A north-south marginal highway was bulldozed through the jungle to encourage settlement and soon impoverished

southeastern jungle). Today the majority of Peru's 200,000 Amazon Indians exist in varying stages of acculturation.

Indian cultures: Although in the 16th century there was considerable discussion in Europe as to whether the New World Indians were indeed "the sons of Adam and Eve" and hence deserving of the rights of real human beings, in 1512 a Papal Bull decreed that Amazonian Indians possessed souls. In later centuries scientists such as Wallace, Bates, Humboldt and Agassiz visited the Amazon and eventually anthropologists began living with different tribes and recording a bewildering variety of cultures. Today it is generally recognized that the culture of any human

Peruvians began to pour in. The extraction of hardwood trees – mahogany, cedar and caoba – repeated the pattern of the rubber boom as peons bankrolled by wealthy patrons once again moved into the virgin forest looking for quick extractable wealth. Gradually, one by one, isolated Indian tribes were contacted by missionaries, woodworkers and/or oil drillers. Although there were some 40 uncontacted tribes in the Peruvian Amazon at the turn of this century, today there are only two or three of these tribes left (all in the

Left, two generations. <u>Above</u>, Yaminahua Indians in Manu National Park.

group is strongly influenced by its environment. Thus, while incredibly diverse, because of their unique environment Amazon tribes have many features in common.

While certain areas on the Peruvian coast and mountains encouraged and supported permanent settlement and, later, statehood by virtue of stream valleys that renewed their soil (much as the Nile river did in Egypt), the Amazon jungle is characterized in contrast as having extremely poor soils and game animals that, while diverse, are few and far between.

As a result, the typical Amazon village on the *terra firme* – the immense lands between the large rivers – are typically small (25 to 100 people), mobile and widely spaced out as a result of the jungle's low bioproductivity and the quick exhaustion of the land. In addition, *terra firme* tribes almost universally practiced warfare and contraception or infanticide techniques in order to keep their populations down. Thus, the Jivaro Indians' penchant for head-shrinking was simply a variation on trophy-head taking and warfare patterns widely practiced throughout the Amazon.

But tribes on the *varzea* – the more limited floodplain areas where the soil is renewed annually – did not fight among themselves and instead had permanent villages ranging into the thousands of inhabitants. Although battles were sometimes fought with the *terra firme* tribes in order to take slaves to work in *varzea* fields, population control did not exist. The necessity of carefully monitoring seasonal planting patterns and river fluctuations gave rise to temples, priests, complex rule and food storage. And although the *varzea* tribes were the first hit by contact and disease, Orellana's men reported numerous *varzea* tribes and towns with temples and roads that led off into the interior.

Given their similar habitat, the Amazon tribes had other features in common. Almost invariably, they viewed their forest and the animals in it as sacred and imbued with spirits. Most Peruvian tribes took one or more hallucinogenic drugs such as *Avahuasca*, the "Vine of Death," which allowed them to see and interact with the powerful spiritual world. The forest was their provider – their mother – and was not to be abused. Even today, most scientists concede that no one understands the jungle better than the remaining Indians. For thousands of years they have lived in the jungle harmoniously, and while they do not possess our own overwhelmingly more powerful technology, they also do not possess our almost complete lack of understanding and our irreverence for this most complex habitat on earth.

A people left in limbo: Currently there are some 200,000 native Indians in the Peruvian Amazon who are divided into 53 different ethnic groups and speaking languages from 12 different linguistic families. Some groups, such as the Toyeri in southern Peru, are composed of only a handful of surviving families. Others, such as the Machiguenga

and Campa, living in the jungles east of Machu Picchu and who are thought to have been the allies of the Incas, number in the tens of thousands.

Unlike Brazil, which has a governmental entity (FUNAI) to regulate Indian affairs, jungle Indians in Peru have little governmental support. Legislation allowing Indian communities to possess land was only finally passed in 1974. Over 30 native organizations have sprung up in the last two decades as different Indian groups have gradually realized that only by putting aside historical enmities and organizing themselves can their rights be defended or secured.

Despite increasing organization, however,

Peru's Amazon Indians continue to exist in a social and legal limbo. At best they are seen as a hindrance to a government whose goal is to "develop" the Amazon. Enormous pressure on the part of the national society, missionaries and the education system encourages Indians to reject their own culture and become deracinated Peruvian citizens. The US protestant missionary group, the Summer Institute of Linguistics (SIL), has a large airbase just outside the jungle town of Pucallpa and has worked with dozens of tribes since 1946.

Although the SIL has nursed a number of recently-contacted tribes through contact-induced epidemics, they and a host of other missionaries have had an enormous acculturative impact. In a very real sense, because of the Peruvian government's historical lack of interest, foreign missionary groups have been relegated the job of contacting and integrating Peru's jungle Indians into the national culture.

Some cultures, however, seem to withstand or assimilate acculturation better than others. The numerous Shipibo Indians living in central Peru along the Ucayali river have – despite long historical contact – maintained much of their traditional culture. They even operate a Shipibo-owned cooperative store (Moroti Shobo in Yarinacocha, just

effect on native cultures, especially if poorly handled. Certain tour groups in Iquitos advertising visits to "wild Amazon Indians," for instance, use completely acculturated tribes which strip down and put on costumes to play the part of "savages." Other companies have been known actually to fly tourists out specially to visit relatively unacculturated Indians.

Courtesy for visitors: The Indians' lack of immunity to common colds and other diseases, along with their culture's relatively fragile nature, however, make such practices questionable. When visiting any native community, therefore, the tourist should always ask first before taking photos, should offer

outside of Pucallpa), where they sell and export their exceptionally high-quality weavings and pottery to museums and collectors all over the world. In 1990 the Ashanika Indians, living on the Ene river, went on the warpath when the Maoist Shining Path guerrillas killed their chief, shooting and expelling all guerrillas from their territory. Other tribes, however, have less resistance to change and have lost their cultures within a very few generations.

Tourism can sometimes have an adverse

small presents such as fishing hooks or fishing line in return, and should, when buying, pay a good price directly to the Indians themselves for their handmade traditional crafts.

For most Indians, however, culture change is inevitable. As one anthropologist working in Peru's Amazon phrased it, "The Indians cannot be expected to remain 'pristine' and thus live somewhere where they are caged in by 'white' wardens in parks. They are very curious about our world and it is inevitable that they will change. Their culture doesn't die, however, rather it reformulates itself so that it can better deal with the outside world."

Left, Yagua children. **Above**, preparing for a ritual in the southeast.

Long before the Incas, Peru was a land of craftspeople. Fine weaving found in the funeral bundles at Paracas, gold pieces worked by the Chimú Indians in northern Peru and startlingly realistic Moche ceramics pay testimony to a people for whom work done with the hands was always important. Specially chosen women in the Inca empire dedicated their lives to such tasks as weaving delicate capes from exotic bird feathers. And metallurgy was a high-status job before the Spanish arrived in the New World.

Fortunately, those artistic traditions did not die with the European conquest and today there are few places in Peru where handicrafts – some little changed from those done hundreds of years ago, others modified for the tourists – cannot be found.

Ancient artefacts: For Indian cultures with no written word, handicrafts played multiple roles. Moche ceremonial cups were not simply for drinking, they told stories – depicting everything from festivities to daily events. Through these finely detailed ceramics archaeologists have identified the diseases afflicting the Moches, discovered the Indians punished thieves by amputating their hands (then fitted the reformed criminals with prosthetic limbs) and determined that they practiced rudimentary birth control. Likewise, the patterns on clothes woven in the highlands have unraveled some of the secrets of how the Aymará Indians lived.

Designs in some clothes told the status of the wearer, others were used only for special fiestas and still others had woven into them motifs that were important to the community. (Nowadays those designs carry airplanes and other modern inventions that have changed the lives of the Indians.) After the Spanish conquest, handicrafts began to fuse the old and new ways as Indian wood carvers whittled statues of virgins dressed like *campesinos* or angels with Indian faces.

Some handicrafts are found all over the country, but in different colors and designs, such as the popular wall hangings displayed in outdoor markets. Other items come from only one community or region. The decorative gilt-edged mirrors sold in Peru generally originate in Cajamarca. Authentic Pucara bulls are crafted in Pupuja, near Puno. Real Yagua Indian jewelry comes only from the jungle area near Iquitos. But, like Peru's residents who migrate from far-flung areas of the nation to the capital, artisan work from all over the country can be picked up in Lima.

The biggest selection of handicrafts in Lima is available at the **Mercado Arte-**

sanal, a group of Indian markets in the 10th block of Avenida La Marina between downtown and the airport. Some of these goods, especially the Christmas tree ornaments and *arpilleras* – embroidery and appliqued scenes – are produced by Mothers Clubs cooperatives in Lima's shantytowns. At these markets, visitors can find gold- and silver-trimmed wine glasses, carved leather bookbags, handknit wools of all kinds, blowguns from the jungle, ceramics carrying both modern and antique designs and jewelry. At the Mercado Artesanal, bargaining is traditional and the bill may be comparable to what might be paid in Cuzco, Pisac or the

Preceding pages: weavings of the Nazca culture. Left, ancient craft, modern view. Right, traditional weaving technique.

jungle. At the cooperatively run **Artesanías del Peru**, Avenida Jorge Basadre 610 in San Isidro, the selection is smaller but the items are all of highest quality. Almost as intriguing as the finely displayed collection of everything from woven pillow covers and colorful wood carvings of toucans to pewter mugs and delicate silver and turquoise jewelry is the neo-colonial style house in which the shop is located. Artesanías del Peru, which has handicrafts from all over the country, has sister stores in Arequipa at Avenida General Moran 120, and in Iquitos at Putumayo 128. Arrangements can be made here for shipping articles overseas and the prices – although not negotiable – are quite attractive.

scene, in blindingly brilliant gold, perfect in detail down to the tiniest butterfly perched on a plant. Worked in gold were objects and animals common to the Indian life: llamas, corn stalks, flowers, birds. What remains in the Mujica Gold Museum in Lima and the Brüning Archaeological Museum in Lambayeque is but a fraction of the gold, silver and copper work that once existed.

Today, gold and silver items, ranging from silver trimmed crystal glasses to fruit bowls and candelabras, are available from a number of boutiques in Lima. The oldest and best-known stores are on Jirón de la Unión: **Casa Welsch** at Jirón de la Unión 498, **Murguia** a block down at number 553 and **Johari** at

Lima's upscale Miraflores neighborhood is a goldmine of handicraft boutiques. Hand-knit sweaters of llama and alpaca in modern styles, and carved wood and leather furniture, grace store windows. These shops are also the best place to find antique paintings, traditional silver and jewelry.

Sweat of the sun: Just as Chile has its lapis lazuli and Colombia its emeralds, the item most associated with Peru is gold, with silver and copper running close seconds. The 16th-century chronicles by Garcilaso de la Vega tell of the Europeans' first glimpse into the courtyard of Koricancha, the Temple of the Sun in Cuzco. Before them was a lifesized

851. A fine selection of gold and silver is also available at **Cabuchon** on Libertadores 532 in the suburb of San Isidro. For the best in gold and silver jewelry in both stylized and traditional Inca designs, stop by H. Stern. This outlet for fine quality jewelry has stores in most of the South American capitals; in Peru its locations are in the Hotel Sheraton, Hotel Bolívar, Hotel Cesar's Miraflores, Jorge Chavez Airport in Lima and the Museo de Oro (Gold Museum) in Lima.

Jewelry made from out-of-circulation Peruvian coins is sold at Plaza San Martín in Lima and around the Plaza de Armas in Cuzco; the most popular are earrings, necklaces and bracelets made from leather and sol coins bearing the image of a llama. These informal jewelry-makers also sell necklaces and earrings made from Peruvian turquoise and hand-painted ceramic. But Peru's best quality hand-painted ceramic jewelry is designed by the Association of Artisans of **Pisac Virgen del Carmen** in Pisac, about an hour outside Cuzco.

Woven tales: Although much of today's *artesanía* is more practical than illustrative and is geared toward tourists, some still tells stories. Delicately woven belts sold in the Sunday market at Huancayo carry designs of trains, a tribute to the metal monster that connected that isolated highland city to the rest of the country. (The wide belts are worn for decoration and to give support to the women who trudge the highlands with their children on their backs.) Colors in the textiles and knitted goods on Taquile, the distinctive weavers' island in Lake Titicaca, can indicate the wearer's marital status or community standing. Some colors are used only on certain holidays. Legend has it that the rainbow Kuyichi, angered by the Taquile Indians, took away their color and left them in a world of grays and browns. But the

Indians used their fingers to weave color back into their lives.

The Taquile items can be purchased from the cooperative on the island. Knitted items are available from a number of shops in Cuzco and some of the best bargains (although the quality is hit and miss) come from the women selling their wares in the arcade around the Plaza de Armas in that city. Be wary of assurances by these unlicensed vendors about whether the item is wool, llama or alpaca as they are likely to upgrade the fiber to assure a sale; stop at some of the upscale shops and feel the difference between the wools from the three animals before starting your shopping. Also beware of the rare un-scrupulous merchants who claim to be selling anything made from vicuñas. It is nearly certain to be untrue and, if the item actually does contain vicuña fibers, then it has been made in violation of international law.

Wool cloth purported to be "antique" usually is not. The damp highland climate does not allow wool to last indefinitely and many weavers now intentionally use dark colors and ancient designs to give the impression the textile has been around for centuries. These cloths are no more antique than are the rustic-looking dolls that some sellers claim come from ancient graves.

Without a doubt, knits and weaves are the

Left, tapestries for sale at Pisac (near Cuzco). **Above**, elaborate carving.

most popular purchases of visitors. Highland markets – including the weekend market in Pisac outside Cuzco – abound with alpaca sweaters, llama rugs, small woolen bags called *chuspas* used to carry coca for chewing, blankets and cotton cloth. In Cajamarca, Indian women in layered skirts called *polleras* walk down the streets with drop spindles dangling from their fingers. And in some communities even the men weave.

Tourists find that the quality of woven items ranges from crude wools still embedded with flecks of thistle to fine modern designs found in Lima's upscale boutiques. Often they use brilliant dyes made from seeds, herbs and vegetables. When an agree-

ment can be worked out with the United Nations, Peru may even begin marketing vicuña fabric, under strict guidelines to limit the amount of fur shaven from the protected animals. Cloths can come from the Andean highlands, particularly Cuzco, Puno and Cajamarca, or from as far away as the jungle where Conibo and Shipibo Indians weave cotton with designs of serpents and, since missionaries entered the rainforest, Christian crosses.

For those who do not visit the jungle, crafts from that region of the country can still be obtained. In the Lima suburb of Miraflores, the **Antisuyo** store on Tacna 460 specializes

in rainforest handicrafts. The South American Explorers Club (Av. Republica de Portugal 146) also sells a variety of items from the jungle.

Not all weavers handle cloth; from frigid Puno to the hot desert near Chiclayo, Peru is proud of its basket weavers. On Lake Titicaca, tortora reed baskets and miniature boat souvenirs are produced by the Indians who themselves live in reed huts on reed islands. In the north, basket weaving started in fishing communities where the finished works stored fish, rice and fruits. In the port of Huanchaco, the fishing boats themselves are woven from reed; tourists can purchase miniature versions. In the Amazon, Indians weave hammocks. The northern coastal region is also known for its finely woven straw hats, similar to Panama hats, known as *jipijapas*. These hats and white cotton ponchos make up the traditional dress of the northern cowboys, or *chalanes*.

Erotic pottery: Contemporary ceramics in Peru, while plentiful, do not live up to the tradition of ancient cultures such as the Moche, whose erotic *huacos* – or pottery – still startle observers by graphically depicting marital relations, contraceptive methods and death allegories. The finest pottery techniques died with the Spanish Conquest, but ceramics are still an important craft. Modern-day pottery ranges from simple baked clay dishes found at open-air markets to the stylized work produced at the Aylambo workshops outside Cajamarca. (*See "The North" on page 285.*)

Shipibo women in the Amazon jungle mix tree ash with clay to form their thin pottery decorated with delicate lines and glazed with tree resin, which they bake in rudimentary ovens dug in the earth, while *naïf* clay churches painted with designs of corn and flowers come from Ayacucho (boasting the greatest number of churches per city block than anywhere else in the country). Tawaq, a workshop started by a group of ceramics artisans in Quinua outside Ayacucho, has expanded and now involves most of the residents of that small village. Their pottery is polished with river stones and painted with hen feathers.

Pucara bulls, actually made down the road from Pucara in the town of Pupuja, have changed over the years to accommodate tourists' tastes. These clay bulls from near Lake

Titicaca are now colorful and ornate, unlike the dull pink and brown clay bulls first used in annual branding festivals; those bulls had small hollows where oils were burned in offerings to the gods. The bulls are an example of how a legacy of the Spanish – the fearful bull that awed the Indians – has been incorporated into native crafts. The best examples of these can be purchased in Cuzco and Puno.

When the Spanish reached Peru, they found skilled craftsmen working gold and silver into finely turned jewelry and adornments. This tradition has not been lost, as evidenced by the intricate gold filigree produced in Catacaos outside Piura in the northern desert.

Face of Society" on page 91.) Smaller nowadays and tucked into a decorated wooden box or the hollow of a reed, these are busy scenes – often religious in nature – that may be solemn or comical depending on the artist's mood. The figures in wood, plaster or clay overflow from the scenes showing religious processions, rollicking fiestas complete with a snoozing drunk, disruptive children and wayward animals or even artisans making hats or weaving cloth. Superb *retablos* fashioned of hollow gourds are a specialty in Ayacucho. Wooden *retablos* may be found in most outdoor markets but the most delicate *retablos* – carved from the white and gray Huamanga stone some call "Peru's

These complicated pieces, which try an artist's patience and imagination, dangle from the ears of the townswomen who claim gold shines even brighter under the desert sun. These are the big, drooping earrings that women dancing the *marinera* wear. In San Jeronimo, near Huancayo in the central highlands, silver filigree is tooled into peacocks, fighting cocks and doves.

Religious scenes: Nearly as detailed as the filigree are the colorful *retablos*, originally small portable altars. (*See "The Changing*

marble" – are found only in boutiques and cooperatives, such as Artesanías del Peru. Actually a type of soapstone, Huamanga is carved into anything from matchbook-sized Nativity scenes to oversized chess sets – with figures of Incas and llamas replacing the traditional kings and knights. Much of what appears to be marble in Peru's churches is actually Huamanga stone.

Beyond Lima and Cuzco, the best places to purchase crafts are usually cooperatives or outdoor markets. Depending on the town, the markets may last only from predawn to mid-morning once a week, or they may go on for days at a time.

Far left, master goldworker. **Above**, a selection of silver jewelry.

HAUNTING SOUNDS OF THE SIERRA

How many times have I told you, my heart,
"Do not want, do not love!"
But always you answer me,
"I can't, I can't."

One day, oppressed by sorrow,
Alone, I asked my heart,
"Why are you so sad and dejected,
finding no happiness in anything?

"Don't you hear the laughter of the mountains,
and smell the perfume of the flowers?
The song of the rivers,
the play of the fishes?"

Again, it cries,
"Happiness no longer exists for me,
I lost all feeling long ago,
My dead heart is already buried."

—Peruvian *wayno* from *Huaynos del Cuzco*

Many of us became acquainted with Andean music (whether to this day we are aware of it or not) in the late 1960s when Paul Simon and Art Garfunkel released a recording called *"El Condor Pasa,"* accompanied by a group called Los Incas. Its English lyrics were new to the song, but the melody was ancient, a traditional Andean folksong of haunting native tonalities. Los Incas, who later called themselves Urubamba, were in the vanguard of a movement to preserve this element of the indigenous culture of the Andes, to present it proudly to the world beyond the borders of its native countries. And so now, this music is played by the *conjuntos folklóricos* who perform in settings – either dimly lit restaurants in fine hotels or on a stage in Paris – which the indigenous people, for whom this music is a part of daily life, can probably scarcely conceive.

It can also be heard on the street corners played by native musicians who, often because of some disability, must depend on their talents – sometimes extraordinary – and other people's appreciation of them to gain themselves a meagre living. And it can be heard far from the nightlife of the cities, in the villages where a less well-rehearsed group

of musicians may gather to accompany the private celebration of a wedding or the public performance of a costumed dance during a festival, or where a lone shepherd, perhaps a young boy, might play a melancholy song on his *quena* on the mountainside where he pastures his family's animals.

Ancient musical tradition: The instruments, forms of the songs, and lyrics have constituted a linked tradition of oral poetry in a culture which until recently has had no written language. Its roots lie deep in Peru's pre-Columbian history. In the ruins and ancient

graveyards on the Peruvian coast you can still find small broken clay panpipes and whistle-like flutes which play pentatonic or diatonic scales, and sometimes other exotic scales which defy description by Western musical notation. They were tossed aside by *huaqueros* (robbers) in search of the fine textiles and pottery buried in the graves. The Incas inherited from the cultures before them an astonishing variety of wind instruments, including flutes and panpipes of all types and sizes. Inca musicians also played conch shell trumpets and drums made from the skin of the Andean puma.

To this ensemble the Spanish introduced

strings, which native musicians readily adopted, inventing new, uniquely Andean instruments such as the *charango* (a tiny guitar scarcely the size of a violin, the body of which is the shell of an armadillo) and the Andean harp with its great, boat-like, half-conical sounding-box.

These, essentially, are the instruments which are played today – joined occasionally by a violin or accordion – though the drums now are more likely covered with goat skin than puma skin, and the eerie, wind-like call of the conch shell trumpet may be heard only in the most traditional villages, deep in the mountains, at certain times of the year.

The effect is magical, utterly characteristic the result that each has its own reedy voice.

The panpipes, called *antaras* or *zamponas*, vary also, from a few inches long to several feet, from one set of four or five pipes to three or four joined sets of eight or 10 pipes each, each of a different octave, to be played, of course, by a single musician with an astonishing dexterity. *Antaras* and *zamponas* are played by blowing across the end of the pipes, a technique which gives a breathy sound, which may be as high-pitched as a bird call or almost as deep as the voice of a bassoon. They are often played in a kind of complex duet, with musicians alternating single notes of a quick, smooth-flowing melody, never missing a beat.

tic of the Andes, evocative of high, windy passes, of the breeze blowing through the reeds of Lake Titicaca, of the dwarfing immensity of the mountains on a clear, bright, winter day. The *quenas* are notched, end-blown flutes with a fingering style similar to that of a recorder. *Quenas* were often made of llama bone, but are now most often carved of wood. They play a pentatonic scale which, to ears trained to a European musical tradition, has a distinctly melancholy tone to it. *Quenas* vary in size and thus in pitch, with

An ensemble of *quenas* and *zamponas* weaves a rich tapestry of windy pentatonic harmony. Into this fabric is woven, like golden threads, the bright, quick sound of the *charango* – which may be strummed or plucked, but is most often strummed in an intricate rhythm of inconceivable velocity – and the voice of the harp.

The Andean harp has 36 strings spanning five octaves of the diatonic scale, though it, too, is usually played in a pentatonic mode. Its deep sounding-box gives it a full, rich sound and a powerful bass voice, so that a bass line is usually played by the left hand while a melody or harmony is plucked by the

Left and <u>above</u>, musicians play Andean tunes in the Hotel Bolívar, Lima.

right. Percussion is provided by a simple, deep-voiced frame drum – a *tambor* or a *bombo* – played with a stick with a soft, hide-covered head, or by an even simpler instrument called the *caja*, which is, as its name implies, a wooden box with a sound hole for reverberation, upon which one sits to thump out a rhythm with the hands. The instrument is actually a little more sophisticated than it may appear, and a skilfull *caja* player can elicit a remarkable range of tone.

This is the basic ensemble, though, of course, infinite variations occur offstage. In the villages, for example, the group may consist of any available musicians playing whatever instruments they happen to have.

these names only that of the *yaravi* or *haravi* seems to have survived in common usage, but nevertheless the lineage of contemporary Andean music can be traced back to at least the 17th century, and probably to pre-Columbian origins, perhaps the songs named by Waman Puma.

Folklore renaissance: The traditional music, which has survived in relatively pristine form among native musicians and in the past few decades enjoyed its renaissance as folklore, has also evolved, naturally, a parallel, popular form. Today this is not only performed in the *chicherias* or cantinas frequented by both urban and rural Quechua speakers, but is recorded in sound studios on

The native Peruvian chronicler, Felipe Waman Puma de Ayala, in his massive descriptive history of life under Inca and then Spanish rule (*Nueva Cronica y Buen Gobierno*, which he began about 1576 and completed in 1615), listed the names of a number of song forms, which are the ancestors of contemporary Andean music: the *yaravi*, the *taqui*, the *llamaya* – a shepherd's song, the *pachaca harahuayo*, the *aimarana*, the *huanca*, the *cachiva*, and the *huauco*.

Many of these he attributed to particular characters or activities – like the shepherd's song, or songs for victory in war or a successful harvest or for working in the fields. Of

phonograph records and cassette tapes, and played on the radio.

The recording artists, like North American or European musicians and vocalists, are known to everyone – at least to everyone of a certain social stratum – and their careers followed attentively; they come into and fall out of fashion much like any groups one hears anywhere in the world.

The primary form of popular music which has evolved from those traditional forms is the *wayno* (or *huayno* in its Spanish spelling, and pronounced "wino"), which constitutes a rich complex of poetry, music and dance. The *wayno* is a rural music, like bluegrass, for example in the United States, and each region of the country has developed its own characteristic variations.

Music has always accompanied nearly all aspects of Quechua life – as Waman Puma's list suggests – from the most mundane activities to the most solemn ritual and the most abandoned celebration.

The Quechua people live, in a way, to dance: all new clothing – new shoes, a new skirt – is said to be "for dancing"; and the *wayno* is fundamentally music for dancing. It is typically played in 2/4 time with an insistent and infectious rhythm; the dance is usually performed by couples, their hands joined, with much stamping of the feet to

ed in the waters… Perhaps, if God approves, we shall one day meet and be together forever. Remembering your smiling eyes, I feel faint; remembering your playful eyes, I am near death…" (translated by Christopher Dilke in *Letter to a King*, E.P. Dutton, 1978). Waman Puma's example of the *yaravi* reveals much the same themes.

The modern *wayno* is clearly a direct descendant of the songs of Waman Puma's day. Melodramatic as they may be, however, anthologies of lyrics disclose a sophistication of poetic form and of poetic voice, ranging from tragic to ironic to comic, which is remarkable in a completely unwritten, completely oral, tradition. *Waynos* to this

cries of "*Más fuerza! Más fuerza!*" ("Harder! Harder!").

But the *wayno* is also a literary form, representative of a tradition of oral poetry which goes back at least to the time of the Incas. The *wayno* is essentially a love song, but a melancholy and melodramatic one: a song of love found and lost or rejected, a song of rivalry and abandonment and separation and wandering in strange lands far from home. Waman Puma offered the words of a song he called a *huanca*: "You were a lie and an illusion, like everything which is reflect-

day are learned and preserved in the social context itself, transmitted informally and most often anonymously, from musician to musician, in the setting of private celebrations or great religious festivals in every village of the Peruvian Sierra.

Certainly, they will continue to evolve: today, an urbanized form of this fundamentally rural music is developing, in which the traditional naturalistic motifs are being replaced by abstract terms more universally understood. But, in light of its history, it seems pretty safe to guess that this music will survive for nearly as long as the Andes themselves.

Left, an Andean ensemble. **Above**, Andean harp.

THE ANCIENT ART OF PERUVIAN CUISINE

An Indian tale describes the dismemberment of the god Pachacamac. His teeth were changed into grains of corn and his genitals into yucca and sweet potatoes, providing the earth with food. Another legend tells of an Inca noble who fell into a well while walking. His father, the sun god, looked down sadly on his imprisoned son. The tears of gold that fell from the father's eyes reached the earth, irrigated it and made the fields flourish. The grains of corn that grew were said to be the golden tears of the sun god.

Food and its importance are intrinsic parts of Peruvian culture and history. The legends of the ancient Indian civilizations highlight the food products that were most important in the diet of their time – especially corn and potatoes, which still show up with amazing regularity in today's cuisine.

In fact, many visitors to Peru are stunned by the number of ways potatoes can be prepared. At the same time, the range of geography and climates in Peru, from the cold highlands and hot, wet jungle to the arid coast and the Pacific waters rich with fish, have handed this South American nation what may be the continent's most extensive and varied menu.

The food not only shows up on the dining table, but it is immortalized in pre-Hispanic pottery, in the centuries-old weavings found in burial grounds and in paintings. In fact, on the arid coast where food was available only after painstaking irrigation and planning by pre-Inca cultures, the priests in those societies had elevated status in the community because they were the ones who studied astral movements and declared when crop planting should take place. Pre-Columbian cultures buried foodstuffs with their dead to sustain them on the journey to the next life. Then, as today, cuisine was based around three main elements – potatoes, corn and hot peppers.

Powerful spices: Hot peppers are found in a number of varieties and are used to add pizzazz to everything from soup to fish. Hot peppers are also the one element that transgresses geography. On the northern coast, where fish is an important part of the diet, sauces of hot peppers and onions are usually heaped on top of the main dish or at least offered in small bowls as self-service condiments. In the jungle, where food in general tends to be less spicy, Amazon residents still routinely dip jungle vegetables and yucca into fiery sauces.

But it is the highland area where *picante* (as the hot spiciness is known), reaches an art form. Dishes are elaborated in a range of degrees of spiciness depending on the type of chile pepper – or *aji* – used. They start with the biting edge that bland food eaters can tolerate and increase to the screamingly torrid *rocoto* peppers whose fire-engine red color is not only decorative but illustrative as a danger signal.

It is believed that South American Indians originally grew about five species of hot peppers which were gradually transported to Central America, the Caribbean and Mexico. Christopher Columbus may be responsible for its misnomer: pepper. He was searching for the black pepper (genus Piper) of the East Indies when he stumbled upon hot chilis. "There is much *axi*, which is their pepper and it is stronger than pepper, and the people won't eat without it for they find it very wholesome," Columbus wrote in his journal in 1493. His cargoes of hot peppers spread like wildfire in Europe, Africa and Asia. In India in particular, they were adopted as irreplaceable in cooking.

Contrary to popular belief, researchers have found that hot spices are not all that hard on the stomach. And, ounce for ounce, they contain double the vitamin C of oranges. However, those unaccustomed to hot peppers should take it easy on the spicing since chili over-indulgence can cause a form of diarrhoea known as *jaloproctitis*. Peruvians generally do not serve *picante* to small children, nursing mothers or the infirm.

Home of a world staple: Hot peppers are often used to spice up the mainstay plate in Peru – potatoes. Known as *papas*, they come in at least 200 varieties (some small farmers have up to three dozen different varieties in a single field) and are served in nearly as many different dishes. Those who think po-

Left, seafood smorgasbord.

tatoes came from Ireland are mistaken – they were taken to Europe from the Peruvian Andes and even today new varieties of the tuber are being exported from South America. Those varieties include the yellow *Limeña* potato, the purple potatoes whose color describes both the peel and the vegetable, and the freeze-dried *chuno* potato that is grown in the high plain surrounding Lake Titicaca. Chuno is a generic term for the frost-resistant potatoes that can be stored for up to four years. They are also known as *papa seca* and show up in a dish called *carapulcra* in which the potatoes (which look like hard stones) are boiled until soft in a stew of meat and spices.

Aymará Indians at Titicaca still ritually

Potatoes are also served alone. *Papa Ocopa* is sliced, boiled potatoes smothered in a spicy peanut sauce, served over a bed of rice and garnished with hard-boiled eggs and olives. Nearly identical in appearance but very different in flavor is *Papa a la Huancaina* covered in a sauce of cheese and hot peppers. *Causa*, a cold casserole of mashed potatoes mixed with hot peppers and onions (occasionally layered over chicken or fish) is another favorite dish. And *papa rellena* is a fried oblong of mashed potatoes stuffed with a tasty mixture of meat, onions, olives, boiled eggs and raisins.

Ritual food: Found in nearly as many colors and varieties as potatoes is corn, perhaps the

stuff potatoes with coca leaves and bury them as a tribute to the earth mother, Pacha Mama, in hopes of a bountiful harvest.

Another tuber, *olluco*, ranges in color from red, pink, yellow and orange to white and has a taste much like new potatoes. It is shredded and served with dried llama meat or *charqui* (similar to beef jerky) in another stew dish. In fact, potatoes are an indispensable ingredient in most of the hearty one-pot dishes so common in highland cuisine. They are present in *estofado* (a mild stew of chicken, corn, carrots and tomatoes) and in *lomo saltado*, where French fries are combined with steak strips and tomatoes to make a spicy dish.

most sacred crop of pre-Hispanic times. Corn was used not only as a food but also as a commodity for bartering. Purple corn is converted into a refreshing drink called *chicha morada*, as well as the purple pudding-like dessert known as *mazamorra morada*. These last two dishes are considered so typically products of Lima that when Peruvians speak of someone born in Lima, they say they are "limeño and mazamorrero."

Another type of *chicha*, a thick whitish fermented corn drink, is a sort of poor man's beer and is ceremoniously poured in the earth during harvest and planting ceremonies in the highlands. In ancient times, only the Chosen Women in the Inca court could prepare this drink. *Choclo*, large-grained ears of corn, are sold as snacks, boiling hot with slices of cheese and chili sauce. Large, boiled corn kernels are served with pork in a dish called *chicharron con mote*. Fried corn kernels, *cancha*, are a popular snack while quaffing beer or pisco.

As far as grains go, corn best survived the Spanish Conquest. Other grains such as purple-flowered kiwicha and golden-brown quinoa – forms of amaranth – were banned by the Vatican and for many centuries disappeared from the Peruvian diet although they have resurfaced in recent decades. Prior to the ban, kiwicha and quinoa were not only

potatoes. Also commonplace is *rocoto relleno*, a hot red pepper stuffed with meat, potatoes and eggs.

Another novelty of the Sierra is the *pachamanca* – a combination of meats and vegetables cooked together over heated stones in underground pits. Peruvians, quick with a double entendre (often at the expense of the tourist), may use the word as the verb *pachamanquear* which technically means to hold a *pachamanca* picnic but more commonly means to engage in public displays of affection. If asked, tell them you are going to a *pachamanca*, not that you are going to *pachamanquear*.

For those who shy away from hot peppers,

nourishing food sources high in protein but they were ceremonial foods. Nowadays, they are folded into breads, cookies and soups.

Potatoes and grains are most often found in the cuisine of the highlands where they are grown. This is hearty food, often prepared in one pot, where the greatest amount of elaboration goes into the spicing. Highland dishes include *anticuchos*, shish-kebabs of beef heart; protein-rich *cuy* or guinea pig prepared in a variety of ways ranging from stewed to fried; and *cau cau* – tripe and

Left, street *ceviche* stall. **Above**, *anticuchos*, shish-kebabs of beef heart.

a *sancochado* is a good option. This is a boiled dinner, usually consisting of beer, onions, potatoes, yams, corn and carrots and finished with a cup of consommé. Typically, the servings are generous and one *sancochado* usually is enough for at least two or three people.

Desert dishes: Like the highland cuisine, food prepared on the desert coast may be hearty, accompanied by potatoes or rice – or both – but rather than beef it employs fish, chicken, duck or even goat. A favorite northern coastal dish is *seco de cabrito* – roasted goat (actually, kid) cooked with fermented chicha and served with beans and rice. If lamb is substituted, it is then called *seco de cordero*. Even better is *aji de gallina*, a rich concoction of creamed chicken with a touch of hot peppers served over boiled potatoes. *Arroz con pato a la chiclayana* is a duck and rice plate originating in the port town of Chiclayo.

Undoubtedly the best coastal dishes are those with seafood bases, led by the ever-popular *ceviche*. This plate of white fish in a spicy marinade of lemon juice, onion and hot peppers is found in other coastal countries but it is never prepared quite as well as in Peru. Traditional *ceviche* is made with fish and served with corn – both fried and on-the-cob, potatoes, yucca, sweet potatoes and

sometimes seaweed, but variations of the dish include *ceviche mixta* in which shellfish are added.

Another delicious fish dish is *escabeche de pescado*, cold fried fish covered in a sauce of onions, hot peppers and garlic, then adorned with olives and hard-boiled eggs. (It is also possible to order *escabeche de galli-na*, made with chicken.)

Fish is believed to have rejuvenating powers and *aguadito* – a thick rice and fish soup (although sometimes prepared with chicken) is traditionally what was served to all-night revelers after the three-day wedding celebrations once common along the coast.

An *aguadito* may also be served to remaining guests after a party that goes on into the wee hours of the morning and, at the multitude of informal vendors' kiosks in working-class areas of Lima, a sign promising *Aguadito para recuperar energia* ("Aguadito to recuperate energy") can be found over many of the food booths.

Fruits of the sea: For fish alone, *corvina*, or white sea bass, is an excellent choice, as is trout – *trucha* (especially Lake Titicaca trout). *Camarones* (shrimp), *calamares* (clams) and *choros* (mussels) are prepared in a number of ways – all of them delicious. Any dish listed as *a lo macho* means it is steeped in a shellfish sauce.

Freshwater fish from the Amazon river and its tributaries are the central ingredient in much of the cuisine from Peru's jungle. These fish range from the small, sharp-fanged *piranhas* to the huge, succulent *paiches*. Broiled or grilled, the fish is nearly always accompanied by jungle fruits and vegetables, including *palmito* (ribbons of hearts of palm that look deceptively like mounds of wide pasta), yucca and fried bananas. The fish may be wrapped in banana leaves before being baked in coals in a dish known as *patarashca*.

The best-known of the jungle dishes are *juanes* – a sort of *tamale* stuffed with chicken and rice, turtle soup (*sopa de motelo*), *sajino* (roasted wild boar) and fried bananas. *Masato*, an alcoholic drink made from fermented yucca, is used to wash down the meals.

As evidence of the Peruvian sweet tooth, desserts abound. Favorites include *manjarblanco*, a sweet made from boiled milk and sugar, *cocadas* (coconut macaroons), and *churros* – deep-fried tubes of pastry dough filled with *manjarblanco* or honey.

During October, the streets of Lima are filled with a seasonal special, *turrón*. This shortbread covered in molasses or honey is prepared in conjunction with the Catholic celebrations honoring the Lord of the Miracles (*El Señor de los Milagros*). *Champus*, (pronounced like the product used to wash one's hair), is a pudding-texture sweet made from wheat.

In the summer, cones of crushed ice flavored with fruit syrups (and optionally topped with condensed milk) are sold on nearly every street corner, although it is wise for the foreigner to steer clear of those *raspadillas* since the water used to make the ice may upset travelers' stomachs.

Other sweets include *yuquitas*, deep-fried yucca dough balls rolled in sugar, *picarones*, deep-fried doughnuts slathered in honey; and *arroz con leche* (rice pudding).

One of the oldest traditional desserts is the crunchy cookie known as *revolución caliente*, dating from the independence era. Sellers of these sweets wander through the streets calling out: *"Revolución caliente, música para los dientes. Azúcar, clavo y canela para rechinar las muelas."* ("Hot revolution, music for the teeth. Sugar, cloves and cinnamon to gnash the molars.")

Fruits from the jungle and desert are won-

of beverages beginning with the national cocktail, *pisco sours*. This potent drink made from a clear, grape-based liquor features fresh lemon juice, bitters, egg whites and sugar mixed and topped with ground sugar. Peru also produces Cartavio rum and wine, although it is generally disappointing except for Tacama and Ocucaje labels.

For something less potent, there is *mate de coca*, a tea which is brewed from coca leaves, or *manzanilla* (camomile) tea. Peru produces a small amount of fine coffee although it is increasingly exported and is difficult to find locally. However, you may inquire in restaurants if they serve good *café Chanchamayo*, named for the region where it is

derful and are served plain or in desserts and juices. *Maracuya* – the seedy passion fruit – is best as a juice or to flavor ice cream, but the *tuna*, the fruit of the desert cactus, is delicious alone. *Chirimoya* or custard apples are tasty and *lucuma*, a small brown fruit with a strong, exotic taste similar to maple syrup is one of the favorite ice cream flavors in Peru. It is recognizable by its dark peach color. Papaya and mango are also grown in Peru.

A range of thirst-quenchers: Peruvians don't eat without drinking and there is a mixed bag

grown. For those who cannot live without carbonated beverages – known here as *gaseosas* – the local soft drink is the bright yellow *Inca Kola*.

As for beer, the main brands are *Cristal, Arequipeña* or *Cusqueña*. It is customary for a group of Peruvian men drinking together to ask for only one or two short glasses to accompany their large bottles of beer. One of the drinkers will raise his glass to a friend, toast him by saying *"Salud"* and drink the contents of the glass. The glass is then refilled by the toast-giver and passed to the friend – who repeats the process with the next person.

<u>Far left</u>, elegant dining. <u>Above</u>, a quick *churro* for the road.

ADVENTURE IN THE ANDES

The great Andes mountain chain stretches the length of the South American continent, and is made up of dozens of individual mountain groups known as *cordilleras*. In Peru, these snow-capped peaks have been the source of superstition, frustration and inspiration to mankind for thousands of years.

Pre-Columbian cultures worshipped individual mountains and made ritual offerings to the deities they believed abided within. Mountain worship, in remote areas, is still practiced by Indian groups under the thin veil of Christianity.

The Spanish conquistadors, led by Francisco Pizarro, found the Peruvian Andes daunting. Hernando Pizarro, brother to Francisco, wrote, "...we had to climb another stupendous mountainside. Looking up at it from below, it seemed impossible for birds to scale it by flying through the air, let alone men on horseback climbing by land."

Long after the Spanish Conquest, a new breed of conquistadors came seeking victory over high altitudes rather than indigenous cultures. In the early 1900s, mountaineers "discovered" the Andes of Peru and began the assault, which still continues, on the highest tropical range in the world. More than 30 majestic peaks rise well over 6,000 meters (20,000 feet) in a region that can only be compared to the Himalayas in splendour.

And modern-day outdoor enthusiasts have found that walking around mountains is as much of a thrill as climbing them. For these trekkers, Peru is a paradise.

Mountain cultures: Except for the most remote and rugged areas, the Peruvian Andes offer little in the way of untouched "wilderness." Only 23 percent of Peru's land is arable, and every fertile meter is farmed by local Indians. For most trekkers, then, "getting away" means leaving behind the 20th century and becoming acquainted with an indigenous lifestyle centuries old.

The formidable Peruvian Sierra, or mountainous region, was tamed by the Incas, whose terraced system of agriculture enabled large

Preceding pages: the Colca canyon, near Arequipa. **Left**, camping out in the Sierra near Cuzco. **Right**, on the Inca Trail.

areas of steep yet fertile land to be cultivated. This unique system is still employed in some areas, and countless remains of ancient terracing give an insight into the productivity achieved by this civilization.

The mountain Indians, or *campesinos*, today cultivate numerous small plots of ancestral land. During growing season the hillsides are plowed in a variety of geometric shapes and, as the crops begin to mature, the mountains are carpeted in colors ranging from deep green to warm gold. It is into these

areas that trekkers wander along ancient paths, occasionally pausing to allow a herd of llamas or goats or sheeps to scramble by, crossing high Andean passes at altitudes above 4,000 meters (13,000 feet), and marveling at the glacier-covered peaks which serve as a spectacular backdrop.

It is the very presence of humanity that makes trekking in Peru a unique experience. There is always the opportunity to stop and converse in simple words or hand signals with local inhabitants. Many of the older *campesinos*, especially the women, speak only a little Spanish – Quechua, the language of the Incas, is more often heard. Though the highland people are typically reticent with strangers, curious children or brave adults may initiate a conversation by wanting to know where you're from, what's your name, or do you have any sweets – the last question being the most relevant.

Passing remote, populated areas is like stepping back into the past. One- or two-room huts constructed of crude mud bricks and topped with ichu grass have changed little in design since Inca times.

There is no electricity, and fresh running water is taken from nearby streams. Small courtyards house chickens and *cuy*, or guinea pig (considered a delicacy in the Sierra), and corn along with other grains can often be

ican Explorers Club, a non-profit information network for the continent. The clubhouse, at Avenida Republica de Portugal 146 (Breña), has available an invaluable stock of reports about trails, maps and guidebooks. The friendly staff are more than willing to give advice to both beginners and experts. Written inquiries can be sent to the postal address: Casilla 3714, Lima 100, Peru.

The first thing to realize is that, despite the fact that Peru is in the southern hemisphere, the seasons are not the opposite of those in the northern. Being so close to the Equator, Peru experiences only two climate changes – a rainy and a dry season. Knowing when to trek is as important as knowing where.

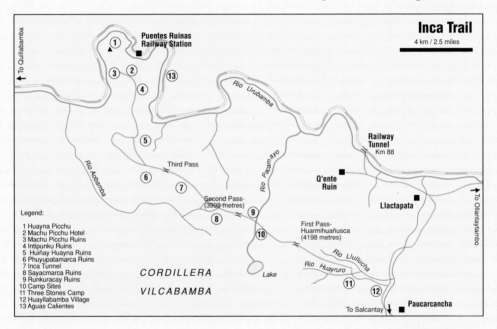

seen drying in the midday sun. This typical scene provides an interesting present-day glimpse of an ancient lifestyle, with the trekker as an anachronism in its midst.

Preparing: Trekking differs from mountain climbing in that it requires little technical skill and the routes are more lateral than vertical. Most treks in the Peruvian Andes are simply extended walks along often steep paths and can be attempted by any reasonably fit and healthy person. Local porters or *arrieros*, *burro* drivers, can be hired to help with a heavy load.

When planning a trek, one of the best places to start is in Lima at the South Amer-

Technically called winter, the months from May through October are the finest for trekking when the weather is clear and dry. During the rainy season, from November through April, skies are often cloudy and rain frequent. Travel during this time can often mean long delays due to washed-out roads and trekking takes on the characteristics of long mud slogs.

Most treks wander through the Andean highlands at an altitude of 3,000 to 5,000 meters (10,000 to 16,000 feet). Days are usually sunny with temperatures of 18–24°C (65–75°F). The equatorial sun is strong and the frequent application of sunscreen is a must. Nights can feel bitterly cold, especially at higher altitudes, so lightweight thermal underwear, a few layers of warm clothes, and a pile or down jacket are necessary. A tent and good sleeping bag are also essential, as well as a dependable stove. White gas, called *bencina*, is usually available, but is often of low-grade quality which can clog up a temperamental cooker. Kerosene and leaded petrol are other choices for use in a multi-fuel stove.

Lightweight hiking boots are suitable for the majority of trails. The best equipment is available in your home country, but if the idea of lugging around an assortment of gear does not appeal, most necessities can be

common symptoms of high-altitude sickness, or *soroche*. By avoiding alcohol and fatty foods in the first few days, and drinking plenty of liquids, the affects of altitude will be minimized. Many find that sucking on hard candies and drinking tea made from the coca leaf, called *mate de coca*, also help to reduce the symptoms.

Food for treks can be easily found in the larger villages, but the freeze-dried variety, along with many Western luxuries, is non-existent. Package soups and dried pastas, as well as dried fruits and grains, are readily available in the markets. Favorite spices brought from home take up little room and add flavor to the evening meals. Take as

hired in the major trekking centers of Huaráz and Cuzco for only a few dollars a day. The quality of hired equipment can vary widely; be sure to check that it is at least adequate. Stoves, especially, have been known to "conk out" after just a few miles into the trek!

Thin mountain air: Before setting off, spend a few days becoming acclimatized to the altitude with short hikes around the area. The thin, high-altitude air can quickly exhaust the unaccustomed and cause physical discomfort. Headaches, mild nausea, shortness of breath and sleeplessness are some of the

<u>**Above**</u>, ruins on the Inca Trail.

much as will be needed for the duration of the trek since it is unlikely that anything will be available on the way other than the occasional piece of bread or fruit in the most populated areas.

A multi-fuel cooker is essential since there is no wood for fires at higher altitudes, and using up the scarce reserves at lower levels only adds to the serious problem of soil erosion that plagues the area.

All drinking water should be treated by using purification tablets, iodine solution or a filtering pump. Iodine works better than chlorine-based purifiers because of its ability to kill more pesky bacteria. The taste of treated water is not especially palatable, but drink-flavoring powder can be bought in most shops, and not only hides the chemical taste but adds energy-boosting sugar.

The Inca Trail to Machu Picchu: Of all the popular treks in South America, the 3- to 5-day Inca Trail is legendary. The adventure begins with a 4-hour train ride along the Urubamba river, known to the Incas as the Sacred Valley. Legions of early-rising *campesinos*, loading and unloading their marketable goods at every station along the way, crowd together in what begins to look more like a cattle car than a passenger train. At **Kilometer 88** the train pauses briefly allowing hikers to disembark. Here at the

looking the valley and often shrouded in morning mist, is the first reward of the Inca Trail. Farther along, the more elaborately-constructed site of **Sayajmarka** (Dominant Town) perches atop a narrow cliff. The fine stonework for which the Incas were famous is apparent. An incredible "paved highway" of neatly-fitted stone snakes along the valley below, masterfully constructed by a culture the Spaniards considered uncivilized.

As the trek progresses, the archaeological sites become more complex. **Puyapatamarka** (Cloud-level Town) is fascinating for its circular walls and finely engineered aquaduct system which still provides spring water to the ancient ceremonial baths. Below,

trailhead, a footbridge temporarily separates the trekker from a rich history dating back more than 400 years.

The first 7 miles (11 km) meander through easy terrain of dusty scrub bushes, low-lying hills, and a few rustic huts. The first barrier is the **Warmiwañusqu pass**. Beyond lies a wealth of Inca ruins, but struggling to the top of this 4,000-meter (13,000-feet) pass is no small challenge. Laboring up the seemingly endless trail, the hiker soon identifies with its name. In English it translates as "Dead Woman's" pass.

From here, Inca history begins to unfold. The small guard-post of **Runkuraqay**, over-

the trail offers up yet another delight to the trekker.

Huge steps, a virtual stone stairway almost a half mile in length, lead down into high jungle vegetation where wild orchids and exotic flowers bloom. Curiously, this section of the trail laid undiscovered until 1984. Until then, a modern footpath connected this interrupted section of the Inca highway.

Tenaciously clinging to the side of a steep ravine, is the last set of ruins, and the most stunning. **Huiñay Hulyna** presents an unbelievable picture when first seen in the distance. The ability of the Incas to construct something so complex in an area so vertical defies comprehension, yet the series of ritual baths, long stretches of terracing and intricate stonework certainly prove what would appear to be impossible.

An hour away lies the jewel in the crown – **Machu Picchu**. From the high pass of **Intipunku**, the Sun Gate, the first glimpse of the fabled city is bestowed. This is the culmination of days of walking; the immersion into an ancient culture complete. Arriving as the Incas did centuries ago, the trekker begins the final descent into Machu Picchu, sharing a path with history.

Other treks from Cuzco: The Cuzco area is rich in superb trekking. Routes around the high mountains of Salcantay and Soray orig-

inate from the small village of Mollepata and provide some exquisite views of the Cordillera Vilcabamba.

With permission from the government, the more adventurous can make a stab at getting into an area called Espíritu Pampa, thought to be the "lost city" of Vilcabamba – a place never visited by the Spaniards, a treasure-house of Inca riches.

Considered by many to be one of the finest hiking areas is the **Auzangate Loop** route around Nevado Auzangate (6,270 meters/

<u>Left</u>, dawn view of Machu Picchu. <u>Above</u>, the quickest way round the mountains.

20,900 feet). A truck from Cuzco is the usual transport, and the village of Tinqui the destination for the start of this 5-day trek. The 8-hour ride is hot and dusty by day, and bitterly cold at night – apt preparation for the days ahead.

The route meanders up and down, through one valley after another, each divided by passes nearing altitudes of 5,000 meters (16,000 feet). Soothing hot springs welcome the hiker on the first day and give a warm goodbye at the finish. Huge moraines, rock and silt deposits left behind by the Ice Age, and glacial lakes, each a stunning yet different shade of blue, provide plenty of visual feasts for the days ahead.

The close-up views of Auzangate are spectacular. At one point the tongue of a glacier extends down within walking distance. A little exploration will reveal a huge ice cave within. It's easy enough to break the few icicles concealing the entrance and roam through the numerous chambers.

Wild vicuña, a cameloid cousin to the llama, are elusive creatures valued for their fine wool. Herds of these skittish beasts are often seen, but only from a distance. Their domesticated relatives, llamas and alpacas, also graze along the route, usually tended by traditionally dressed *campesino* children. The Andean condor, the world's largest bird with a wingspan up to 3 meters (10 feet), may be sighted soaring high above.

Several nights of camping will be near the foot of Auzangate and promised bouts of shivering will last until the early-morning sun drives the cold away. On other nights, campsites are set up near inhabited areas, and the trekker may be rewarded with gifts of boiled potatoes brought around by a generous local. Nothing is asked for in exchange, but a sharing of food is common.

In spite of the strenuous effort this trek requires, the days pass too quickly and in almost no time the final hot spring is reached. The last of the dust is washed away, but not the memories of this marvelous experience.

The Cordillera Blanca: Eight hours by bus north of Lima is one of the most popular trekking areas in Peru. At least for its diversity and large number of mountain peaks clustered so conveniently in one central area, the **Cordillera Blanca** is a trekkers' dream.

The small city of **Huaráz** is the hub for all hiking activity, and frequent rural buses transport enthusiasts to a variety of trailheads. A **Casa de Guias**, located just off the main street, will provide the latest information about routes and mountain conditions, and can provide trekkers with a list of porters and *arrieros*, *burro* drivers, who can help carry gear on the long trek ahead. Along the main street of Luzuriaga, colorful billboard signs lend distinction to an otherwise dull facade of street-front shops. Most of these promote tourism in some form, so finding a comfortable day tour, renting hiking gear, or buying souvenirs is as easy as locating the proper agency by identifying its sign out front. A number of good restaurants (whose status is often elevated to excellent after a long hike)

larly affected was the beautiful circuit around the Cordillera Huayhuash, some 50 km (31 miles) to the south east of the Cordillera Blanca, which was closed to visitors.

The past few years have, however, seen a dramatic improvement in the situation as the center of terrorist activity moved away from the sierra and into the coca growing areas of Peru, most notably the Huallaga Valley.

The highest mountain in Peru, **Huascarán** at 6,768 meters (22,200 feet), and what many consider to be the most beautiful in the world, **Alapmayo** at 5,945 meters (19,500 feet), are just the toppings on an already rich cake. Glacial lakes dot the landscape, and fresh running streams serve up tasty trout.

serve up a variety of food and a couple of lively *peñas*, featuring groups playing the traditional music of the Andes, provide a place to loosen up before or after a strenuous four days' trekking.

The Cordillera Blanca is full of striking views and unique adventures. Hikes from one day to 10 are possible, combinations producing even more possibilities if desired. Here limitations are only the result of a lack of imagination.

In the late 1980s and early 1990s much of the central highlands including the Huaráz area was subjected to a degree of control by Sendero Luminoso (Shining Path). Particu-

The days are warm and scented with eucalyptus. Snow-covered peaks stretch as far as the eye can see.

Trekkers wanting to get the legs and lungs in shape for longer treks can start with a variety of short day hikes in the Huaráz area. Just above the city is **El Mirador**, a scenic lookout marked by a huge white cross. The route heads uphill east along city streets which eventually turn into a footpath beside an irrigation canal lined with eucalyptus trees. Fields of wheat ripening in the sun add a serene, pastoral feel.

At the top, the highest mountain in Peru, Huascarán, dominates the northern horizon, the lower Vallunaraju (5,680 meters/18,600 feet) peeks out over the foothills to the east, and the city of Huaráz sprawls below.

Another choice of many is the **Pitec Trail** to **Laguna Churup**. There is no public transport to this small village 10 km (6 miles) from the center of Huaráz, but often a taxi driver can be persuaded to navigate the terribly rough road to Pitec. Walking is an option, but it's nicer to be fresh at the trailhead and then walk back down to Huaráz afterwards.

The trail begins at the "parking lot" before the actual village of Pitec is reached. A well-worn footpath heads north up a ridgeline and the Churup massif rises just above 5,495 meters (18,000 feet) in the distance. At the

(19,000 feet) and panoramic views abound. Buses frequently leave Huaráz, loaded with an assortment of *campesinos*, their chickens, *cuyes* and children, for the small village of **Yungay**. Here *camionetas*, small pick-up trucks, wait in the plaza to transport hikers and sightseers up the valley to the dazzling, glacier-fed lakes of **Llanganuco**.

The trailhead lies a few kilometers above the lakes, near the **Portachuelo** (high pass) of Llanganuco, and the trek begins with a descent towards the village of **Colcabamba**. Immediately the steep face of **Chopicalqui** (6,350 meters/20,800 feet) towers over the trail like a sentinel and soon a few thatched-roofed houses come into view. A sampling

base of this mountain is the destination of the hike, Laguna Churup, fed by the glacial melt-off and surrounded by huge boulders. A picnic lunch and a midday siesta in the warm sun reward the effort of getting here. A leisurely hike back to Huaráz follows a cobbled road through *campesino* homesteads.

The Llanganuco to Santa Cruz Loop: One of the most frequently hiked trails is the 5-day loop into the Cordillera Blanca which begins at the Llanganuco lakes. The route passes under a dozen peaks over 5,800 meters

Left, camping out in the Cordillera Blanca. **Above**, Climbing Alpamayo in the Cordillera Blanca.

of local cuisine may be possible here.

At this point, the trail begins a steady ascent up the **Huaripampa Quebrada** (narrow valley). The snow-capped peaks of **Chacraraju** (6,110 meters/20,000 feet) and **Pirámide** (5,880 meters/19,285 feet) provide splendid photo opportunities, and a chance to rest, as the trekker labors up the steepening trail towards the high pass of **Punta Unión**. In the last hour before sunset, as camp is set up, the mountains are cast in the silver and pink of "alpenglow."

At over 4,750 meters (15,500 feet), Punta Unión becomes both literally and figuratively the high point of this journey. **Taulliraju**, over 5,830 meters (19,000 feet), glistens in the midday sun, and a number of glacial lakes lie like scattered jewels in the distance. The valley below opens up to reveal a wide stretch of snow-capped peaks, a mere hint of the magnitude of the Cordillera Blanca, and huge Andean condors can often be seen soaring high above the pass.

As the trail descends toward the village of **Cashapampa**, the scenery changes from dramatic mountain vistas to open, marshy pasture land where herds of llamas and goats graze. Farther along, the trail narrows as it begins to wind through forests of stunted trees and follows the easy meandering of a small stream.

Trekkers generally don't experience anything more than *soroche*, or mild altitude sickness, but at higher altitudes serious complications can occur. *Pulmonary Edema* occurs when the lungs begin to fill with fluid. Early symptoms include a dry, incessant cough, a rattling sound and tightness in the chest. *Cerebral Edema* occurs when fluid collects in the brain. Symptoms include loss of coordination, incoherent speech, confusion, and loss of energy. Both of these illnesses are extremely serious and possibly fatal. The only cure is an immediate descent to a significantly lower altitude. The victim is usually the last one aware of the problem, so it's essential that each person in the group

Mountaineering: For the more adventurous and technically-minded mountain enthusiast, the Cordillera Blanca is unrivaled for the pursuit of mountaineering. With glacier-covered peaks varying in altitudes from 5,495 meters (18,000 feet) to 6,795 meters (20,000 feet), and technical levels from very easy to extremely difficult, there is something for everyone. However, because all climbing here is at high altitude, and any glacier travel requires technical knowledge, climbing in the Cordillera Blanca should be attempted by those with experience. Besides the usual trekking equipment, a rope, ice axe, crampons and ice stakes or screws are necessary.

keep an eye out for symptoms in the others.

Another high-altitude problem is *hypothermia*, or exposure. This occurs when the body loses more heat than it can replace. The symptoms begin with uncontrolled shivering that will eventually cease, though the body is still cold. Lack of coordination, confusion, drowsiness and even a feeling of warmth are other symptoms. A victim suffering from hypothermia will need to be immediately dried-off, placed in a warm sleeping bag, and given warm liquid to drink. In advanced cases, the victim will not be able to generate any body heat and will need the warmth of other bodies to get his tempera-

140

ture back to normal. Hypothermia is prevented by staying warm and dry. Wearing wool or a synthetic insulating material next to the skin will help hold in warmth, even when wet. Cotton has no insulating properties and will actually draw off body heat when wet. Layering clothes is an effective way to regulate body temperature during times of exertion and rest. Food also helps stove the internal generators, so eating quickly assimilated food like chocolate will help keep the system functioning.

Many climbers feel that acclimatization comes with activity – getting the legs in shape for the more demanding climbs is as important as having the lungs working at

raine, which unfortunately must be negotiated the next day. Some groups choose to continue on past the base camp, tackle the difficult moraine the same day, and continue on up to the high camp just below the glacier.

An early-morning start from here allows climbers to make the summit and be back in camp for afternoon tea. The next day descent is quick and climbers are usually back in Huaráz by evening.

Peru's highest peaks: When the acclimatization to altitude is adequate, and climbers are ready for some real work, they'll often head for the highest mountain in Peru, **Huascarán**. There are two huge summits separated by a lower saddle giving a sort of double-

capacity. To this end, several short warm-up climbs are favored. **Nevado Pisco**, just over 5,800 meters (19,000 feet), is popular for its steep, yet quick ascent, and the views from the saddle are some of the finest anywhere in the Cordillera Blanca.

The approach to base camp begins just above the Llanganuco lakes. The 5-km (3-mile) hike follows a footpath along the crest of a lateral moraine and gains 750 meters (2,460 feet) in altitude. Camping is in a flat, grassy area below an incredibly steep mo-

humped camel look. The south summit at 6,768 meters (22,205 feet), is 113 meters (370 feet) higher than its north sister, and the most frequently climbed.

The hike into base camp begins at the small village of **Musho**, where *arrieros* can be hired to help carry the heavy load of climbing gear and food provisions to the first camp. The trail wanders through farmland and eucalyptus groves for the first few hours, and then a sharp ascent above treeline finally leads to a flat, grassy area known as Huascarán base camp.

Another two hours up a very steep ridge lies the moraine camp and some climbers opt

Left, mule transport is available. **Above**, scaling Huascarán, Peru's highest peak.

to make it to this point in one day. The load-relieving *burros*, however, can't make it up this section of the trail, so it means donning the heavy weight and sallying forth.

It's usually on the second or third day when climbers pack up at moraine camp and head for Camp One on the glacier. The hike starts with a scrambling across rock slabs, the path marked with stone carins. At the glacier's edge it's a question of finding the best access to the snow through sometimes massive icefalls.

Once on the glacier, the route up to the next camp will often be "wanded" by previous climbing parties. Small flags are placed at regular intervals for an easy descent after-

wards and to avoid getting lost on the glacier during a "whiteout" when clouds obscure everything. The climb up to Camp One is unforgettable. Wide crevasses, icy cracks and massive pillars of tumbled ice are constant reminders that glaciers are anything but static piles of snow.

Camp One at about 5,200 meters (17,000 feet) is a welcome relief after five to seven hours of traversing the lower glacier, but the pleasure is short-lived as the sun goes down and temperatures drop to well below freezing. It is in this bone-chilling cold that climbers rise early the next morning and prepare to set off for the final high camp at **La Gargan-**

ta (the throat) at 5,790 meters (19,000 feet).

This section is probably the most interesting of the entire climb. About an hour after leaving camp and crossing a wide crevasse, the first technical part of the route appears. A 30-foot, 70 degree ice wall must be climbed, and quickly because it is a natural avalanche chute. Early morning is the best time as the snow pack is still frozen and likely to stay in place. Above the chute, the route remains steep and prone to avalanche activity. It's important, but extremely strenuous, to move as quickly as possible, leaving little chance to rest the aching lungs and reeling head.

At La Garganta Camp it's difficult to do any more than set up camp and melt and boil snow for a hot drink. Nightfall brings a dazzling array of stars, but the intense cold quickly drives everyone into tents to nestle in warm sleeping bags. At this altitude sleep can be elusive; it's a long night of tossing and turning and trying to stay warm.

Another early morning finds climbers preparing for the summit attempt. Stiff fingers attempt to sort out gear and groggy minds work out the plan ahead. A small blessing is that the heavy equipment can be left behind in camp. All that's needed are spare warm clothes, food, water and a camera for those magnificent summit photos.

The summit route heads up across the saddle between the two peaks of Huascarán, and the climber is treated to a view of distant mountains set ablaze in the early morning sun. Shifting south the climb ascends several steep snow slopes and the first few hours involve zig-zag traverses up and up until the final approach is reached.

Here the abstract concept of "forever" seems to become tangible. Rather than being just one long, gradual slope to the summit, the climber encounters a series of gentle inclines. From the high-point of one, all that is seen is yet another. Each time, the climber summons what strength, both mental and physical, is left and trudges on, and each time he finds only another long slog, and no sign of a summit. At this altitude, about 6,700 meters (22,000 feet), breathing becomes so labored that three or four breaths are needed for each step taken. Finally the tricks play out, "forever" is ended, and the summit of the highest mountain in Peru is conquered.

Left, scaling the heights.

RIDING THE RAPIDS

Highin the Peruvian Sierra, where icy waters churn and boil over huge boulders and rush through narrow canyons, river travel has never been practical. Not, at least, until the sport of white-water rafting was introduced. With the astonishing number of rivers in Peru – the Andes having been at work for thousands of years forcing new waterways to carry their glacial melt-off – choices for river adventures are unlimited.

The Cuzco area is well-suited for river rafting. The **Urubamba river** winds through the Sacred Valley of the Incas, and floating along its waters gives a unique perspective to one of the most culturally-rich areas in all of Peru. Remains of ancient terracing are evident on the hillsides and simple mud huts with thatched roofs dot the riverbank. Women can be seen washing clothes in the shallows, children herding cattle and sheep, and men working the fields – all of whom will pause briefly to watch with surprise as the floating rubber dinghy makes it way down river. The tranquility lulls you into a peaceful daydream until the next set of rapids brings you to life and starts you paddling for all you're worth.

Trips on the **Apurimac river**, just a few hours from Cuzco, are for those looking for a longer and rougher ride. Superb white water is found in a spectacular, mile-deep tropical canyon on this source river of the Amazon. When not occupied with immediate survival in the challenging rapids, rafters have time to enjoy steep waterfalls cascading down the canyon walls, and search for wildlife including otters, deer, puma, and, of course, the ever-present Andean condor. Afternoons are spent relaxing in camp on a sandy beach, trying a hand at fishing, or hiking along goat trails. The last remaining Inca bridge stretches across the Apurimac just above the common take-out point.

Several hours from the city of Arequipa is the spectacular **Colca canyon**, thought to be the

Above, tackling the Urubamba river.

deepest in the world, with the crystalline waters of the **Colca river** snaking along its bottom. It wasn't until 1981 that a complete exploration of the river was undertaken by the CanoAndes Polish Expedition. Many sections of the river are technically difficult – enough to test the limits of experts. This, along with a setting devoid of vegetation, a lunar landscape of rocks and volcanic lava, makes a trip along the Colca one of the most impressive. Excursions to this zone must be arranged in advance.

For the Huckleberry Finn-type, a completely different sort of rafting trip is possible. This one requires a spirit of adventure, the ability to swim, and an itinerary flexible enough to go with the flow (literally!) of things. The first step is to take the train from Cuzco to the end of the line and start of the jungle at **Quillabamba**. From here, it's an 11-hour truck ride to the village of **Kiteni** on the upper Urubamba river, where a boatman is hired for a six-hour trip to an even smaller village called **San Iriate**.

Here the fun begins. In San Iriate you can hire someone to build a balsa raft in about 4 hours, or sit by the riverbank and wait for an abandoned one to float by. These average about one a day. Also, be sure to buy a good-quality paddle from one of the villagers since balsa paddles are not strong enough. When the raft is ready, and before the journey can begin, another boatman must be located to ferry the passenger and drag the raft down through a stretch of the river known as the **Pongo de Manique**. Below the Pongo, the raft is loaded with passenger and possessions for a four-day (or longer) float down the Urubamba. Gear should be tied securely to the raft, and a plastic sheet helps for waterproofing.

The river is not dangerous, but unexpected rapids have been known to dump the unsuspecting. It's easy enough, however, to swim after the raft and climb back on. Little food is necessary because of the communities situated all along the way – someone will always offer a meal and a place to sleep. The larger village of **Sepahua** has a mission and landing strip with sporadic flights available. Farther along is the town of **Atalaya** with real hotels, ice-cold beer and a lift back to civilization. ∎

The Andes of Peru have been heavily populated by wildlife for thousands of years. In Inca times all types of Andean wildlife enjoyed a form of protection, and although periodic hunts occurred, these were few and the privilege of the ruling class. After the Spanish Conquest and the breakdown of the Inca infrastructure, wild animals were hunted indiscriminately and consequently suffered a population decline which was further advanced by the cutting of high Andean woodlands, which provide essential cover for many animals. Today the persecution of wild animals continues, in some cases because of damage caused by animals to crops, in most cases because of misconceptions. The careful observer, however, can still find a wide variety of Peruvian fauna while traveling in the Andes.

Endangered species: The most conspicuous animals encountered by a visitor to the Peruvian Andes are the cameloids. There are two wild cameloids in Peru, the vicuña and the guanaco. The vicuña, reputed to have the finest wool of any animal, has been brought back from the verge of extinction by the establishment of reserved areas for the species, such as the Pampas Galeras reserve in south-central Peru. They are now to be found in quite large numbers in many areas but are still considered vulnerable. In Inca times, vicuña wool was obtained by running the animal to the ground, picking its fleece by hand and then releasing it. This not only assured a regular supply of wool each year, it also maintained population levels.

The modern-day illegal hunter resorts to firearms, the primary cause of the vicuña's demise. Prosecution is difficult, however, since the people who possess guns are often influential or otherwise immune. Fortunately, due to the concerted conservation efforts, the vicuña is making a welcome comeback in the Peruvian highlands.

The other wild cameloid of the Andes is the guanaco. This species reaches its northernmost limit in the highlands of central Peru, and from here extends down the Andean chain to the southern tip of South America – Tierra del Fuego. In Peru the guanaco is most likely to be seen in the departments of Tacna, Moquegua, Arequipa and Puno and is to be found in isolated rocky ravines with bunch grass. Guanacos are wild relatives of the llama and alpaca but are at once distinguishable from their domesticated cousins by their bright tawny coloration, similar to that of the vicuña. The exact relationship between domestic llamas and alpacas and the wild guanacos and vicuñas is not clear. All possible crosses of the four cameloids mentioned have been accomplished and the offspring of all crosses are fertile. Most tax-

onomists now agree that the domestic llamas and alpacas are a product of the cross-breeding of the guanacos and vicuñas. Whatever the exact relationships, the domesticated cameloids are to be found throughout the Peruvian highlands.

The only natural enemy of the cameloids is the puma or mountain lion. This large tawny, unspotted cat was much revered by the Incas as a symbol of power and elegance. Unfortunately, since the conquest, Andean man has lost the conservationist outlook of the Incas, and the puma has suffered dramatically as a result of indiscriminate hunting. The habit of picking off an unwary llama has not endeared the puma to the Quechua peoples, and now it is only possible to catch a fleeting glimpse of this magnificent cat as it crosses remote Andean valleys or stalks mountain viscachas. Two smaller members of the cat family are also to be found in the high Andes. Both species are shy and little is known of their status and habits. The pampas cat (*Felis colocolo*) is typically an animal of the intermontane Andean valleys, although it does occur close to the coast in northern Peru and in the high cloud forest of the eastern slopes of the Andes. The Andean cat (*Felis jacobita*) is rarer still and in Peru is limited to the southern highlands. This is a high-altitude species, mostly nocturnal, and seems to prey

Andean woodlands which provides essential cover. The white-tailed deer is still relatively abundant in remoter areas where hunting pressure is low since this species shows a remarkable adaptability to various habitat types. It occurs from the coastal plain (in zones of sufficient vegetation) to 4,000 meters (13,000 feet) above sea level and then into the cloud forest of the eastern slopes of the Andes, down almost to the Amazon basin at 600 meters (2,000 feet). This animal is commonly encountered while hiking in the Andes. Its much rarer relative, the Andean huemal (or taruka as it is known in Peru), is much harder to see. The taruka is a species in danger of extinction and is found at extreme-

on mountain viscachas. Tracks of this species can be seen at snow line nearly 5,000 meters (16,000 feet) above sea level, but for the short-term visitor to the Andes, an encounter with any of the Peruvian wild cats is a rare event indeed.

Woodland creatures: More conspicuous and more commonly seen by backpackers in the highlands are the two species of deer. Both species were once more common than they are now, and the principal cause of their demise is hunting and the cutting of high

ly high altitudes. Its presence is governed by the availability of cover, mostly small isolated patches of woodland. This type of woodland is disappearing at an alarming rate as it is a primary source of fuel at high altitudes. Consequently, the barrel-chested, short legged taruka is sadly on the decline. If encountered, it is easily distinguished from the white-tailed deer by its two pronged antlers (the white-tailed deer has one prong only). It is still possible to find this species on the Inca trail to Machu Picchu.

Easier still to see while hiking through the highlands of Peru are the rodents and omnivores. The Andean fox is ubiquitous in all

<u>Left</u>, an ungainly llama. <u>Above</u>, Andean white-tailed deer in mid-flight.

parts of the Andean region, and can be found at all altitudes up to 4,500 meters (14,800 feet). This species of fox is larger and longer legged than its North American and European counterparts and commonly investigates any empty cans or leftover food left outside tents. The Andean fox is everywhere regarded as a dangerous stock killer, especially of sheep. The stomachs of this animal often contain quantities of vicuña wool, but it is not known whether it is a predator of this species or only a carrion eater. Whenever possible, this animal is killed by the local people, yet it remains common.

While walking along stream banks or drystone walls, the observant will notice a large black-chested buzzard-eagle, and aplomado falcon. The guinea pig, or *cuy* as it is known in Peru, is domesticated extensively in the Andes, and the wild version is also not uncommon along stony banks and drystone walls, where it lives in colonies. Any Quechua household will have its colony of guinea pigs living in the kitchen area, and the cooked animal is regarded as a delicacy to be eaten on special occasions.

The last two conspicuous animals of the Andes are the hog-nosed skunk and the mountain viscacha. The former, which should be familiar to visitors from North America, is mostly nocturnal and can often be picked up in car headlights. The latter is a very sociable

number of small rodents, ranging from the typical house mouse type familiar to all of us, to mice with a striking combination of chocolate brown and white. It is not that there are a greater number of mice-like creatures in the Andes, but simply that because of very low temperatures at night, most Andean rodents are diurnal. These diurnal rodents are the principal food source of a variety of predators including the Andean weasel (*Mustela frenata*), a vicious mustelid that will tackle prey twice its size. The abundance of diurnal rodents also accounts for the high density of birds of prey, such as the red-backed and puna hawks, cinereous harrier, creature commonly found in rock screes and boulder fields. Very well camouflaged, it often betrays its presence with a high-pitched whistle. Looking like a cross between a chinchilla and a rabbit, the mountain viscacha can often be seen sunning itself on the top of boulders in the early morning and late afternoon. Mountain viscacha colonies often attract the larger carnivores previously mentioned.

The cloud forest: On the eastern slope of the Andes the environment is dominated by humid temperate forest. Where left undisturbed by man, the forest continues from 3,600 meters (11,800 feet) down to the tropical rainforest of the Amazon basin. The type of forest above 2,500 meters (8,200 feet) is commonly known as "cloud forest", a name derived from the fact that for most of the year the trees are shrouded in mist. Indeed most of the moisture needed by the forest is captured from the enveloping clouds. The cloud forest grades into high grassland at about 3,400 meters (11,200 feet) and harbors some exotic animals that will not be forgotten if once glimpsed.

The spectacled bear is perhaps the most impressive animal of the zone. About the size of a North American black bear, this animal is a true omnivore, eating a wide variety of foods such as fruits and berries, large insects, succulent plants and, at high elevations, the lush hearts of terrestrial bromeliads. The spectacled bear will also eat small mammals and rodents when given the opportunity. An important animal in Andean folklore, the bear has a poor reputation among small farmers due to its habit of raiding maize crops at the edge of hill forests. A bear can cause significant economic damage to the smallholder: farmers complain bitterly of the killing of livestock by the spectacled bear. These habits and attributed habits have not boded well for the bear, and it is extensively hunted to the point where population levels are dangerously low.

Other shy inhabitants of the cloud forest include two species of small deer. The larger of the two is the dwarf brocket deer. About half the size of the white-tailed deer, it is found to a height of 3,300 meters (10,800 feet) in the southern departments of Puno and Cuzco. The other is the pudu, a deer the size of a small dog, difficult to see and mostly nocturnal. It is relentlessly hunted with guns and dogs and must be considered vulnerable at present. Occupying the same habitat as the pudu is the wooly monkey (*Logothrix cana*), which is found in small family groups where hunting pressure is low. A large primate, the wooly monkey can still be found fairly commonly in the cloud forest beyond the town of Paucartambo on the road to Shintuya in the department of Cuzco.

Bird diversity: The Andes are not just the home of mammals, and it is true to say that south-east Peru has the greatest diversity of bird life of any place on the planet. The majority of these species occur in the cloud forests and lowland rainforests of the eastern Andean slopes, but a wide variety can be seen right up to the snowline.

The bird that first comes to mind when writing of the Andean peaks is of course, the Andean condor. This very large member of the vulture family is a carrion feeder but is not adverse to starting his meal a little prematurely. The condor is not a hunter and is incapable of grasping or carrying prey, having feet not unlike those of a chicken. (Reports in newspapers of condors carrying off unattended babies must therefore be dismissed.) The classic sight of a condor sailing effortlessly against the backdrop of ice-capped

Andean peaks will not quickly be forgotten.

The condor is still a common sight when hiking through the high country, but much more commonly seen are the smaller songbirds such as sierra-finches, cinclodes, miners and seedsnipes. Once one reaches the limit of the cloud forest, the number of species increase dramatically and birds become much more brightly colored. Anyone taking a stroll here in the morning will notice mixed-species flocks of colorful mountain-tanagers, flycatchers and furnarids moving amongst the moss-festooned branches. Here birds of a different feather actually do flock together.

<u>Left</u>, majestic flight. <u>Right</u>, the puma.

BAHÍA DE
CARÁQUEZ

Quito

COLOMBIA

Pto. Leguizamo

Ambato

Nuevo Rocafuerte

AMAZONAS

6310
Chimborazo ▲ **ECUADOR**

Santa María

El Encanto

La Pedrera

Guayaquil

Riobamba

5230
Volcán Sangay ▲

Napo

Sta. Clotilde

Pebas

Cuenca

Morana

Andoas

Mazán

Amazonas

PLANICIE AMAZONICA

GOLFO DE
GUAYAQUIL

Marchala

Tigre

Iquitos

Leticia

Tumbes

Orellana

LORETO

Marañón

Benjamin
Constant

Sullana

Barranca

PERU

Ucayali

Boa Vista

Piura

Jaén

Moyobamba

Acuracay

Nauta

Olmos

CORDILLERA

Chachapoyas

Orellana

Sta. Cruz

Chiclayo

Cajamarca

Tierra Blanca

BRAZIL

SAN
MARTÍN

Cruzeiro

ORIENTAL

Trujillo

Tocache Nuevo

Tarauaca

Nevado Huascarán ▲

Pucallpa

6768

Purus

Chimbote

CENTRAL

Sena Madureira

Huarmey

6634

Huanuco

Ucayali

CORDILLERA

▲
Nevado
Yerupaja

Cerro de Pasco

Bolognesi

Xapuri

Paramonga

Alto Purus

Huacho

DE

MADRE

Iberia

Cobija

Callao

Huancayo

DE DIOS

Lima

MANU
NATIONAL PARK

Pto. Maldonado

San Vicente
de Cañete

OCCIDENTAL

Huancavelica

Ruins of
Machu Picchu ■

CORDILLERA

Chincha Alta

Ayacucho

Abancay

6384

BOLIVIA

Ica

LOS

Cuzco

▲
Nevado
Auzangate

ORIENTAL

Nazca

A N D E S

Cailloma

Ayaviri

Lomas

Juliaca

Puno

Lago

Pto. Chala

Nevado Coropuna
6425

Puno

Volcán
Tutupaca
5806 ▲

Titicaca

Pacific Ocean

Camaná

Matarani

Arequipa

Mollendo

Moquegua

Ilo

Tacna

Charaña

Arica

Peru

320 km / 200 miles

Pisagua

PLACES

Mapping out an itinerary for Peru might seem a daunting prospect. The country is three times as large as California and many times more varied, with the Andean mountain range and Amazon jungle creating some imposing barriers to travel. Yet journeys that were all but impossible 50 years ago are now everyday events: each of Peru's major cities is linked by safe, modern jet flights; regular coach services run to lesser urban centers; and even tiny mountain villages can be reached on a rattling ancient bus or in the back of one of the ubiquitous Peruvian trucks. These days, too, the threat from Sendero guerrillas has dramatically receded.

Most travelers to Peru begin their journeys in Lima. As the former center of Spanish South America, it boasts some of the continent's finest colonial architecture as well as Peru's most impressive museums.

A strong contrast is the ancient Inca capital of Cuzco, and for many people this mountain city is the highlight of their visit. A half-hour flight from Lima – one of the most spectacular on earth – takes travelers straight into the heart of the Andes. Apart from its own attractions, Cuzco serves as a base to visit the Urubamba Valley and what is perhaps the most famous sight in the continent: Machu Picchu. No matter how many times you have seen these ruins in photographs, nothing will quite prepare you for the reality. Nobody comes away disappointed.

Also in the Andes, Arequipa is one of Peru's most elegant colonial cities set in the shadow of the snow-capped volcano Misti and renowned for its intellectual life. From Cuzco and Arequipa, many travelers fly or take a popular railway journey to Puno, by the shores of Lake Titicaca. The world's highest navigable lake is populated by fascinating Indian communities, who still ply its waters in totora reed canoes.

Increasing numbers of travelers are visiting an area that takes up over half of Peru's land mass: the Amazon basin. In the northern Amazon, the city of Iquitos is the traditional center for beginning tours. And in the south, Puerto Maldonado (reached by flights via Cuzco) has become the gateway to the Manu National Park, possibly the purest section of rainforest in South America.

South of Lima, the Pan-American highway runs along the barren coastal desert to Nazca, whose plains are etched with gigantic drawings made by a mysterious pre-Inca culture, and only visible from the air. Meanwhile, Peru's north has its own distinctive character, with relaxed coastal cities like Trujillo and the beautiful Andean market town of Cajamarca. Then, in the mountains north of Lima, is the region of Huaráz, considered by experts to have Peru's most impressive mountain scenery – quite an accolade in a land full of breathtaking views.

Preceding pages: dawn over the Sierra; La Compañia Church, Cuzco; putting out to sea near Trujillo; slow afternoon on Taquile Island.

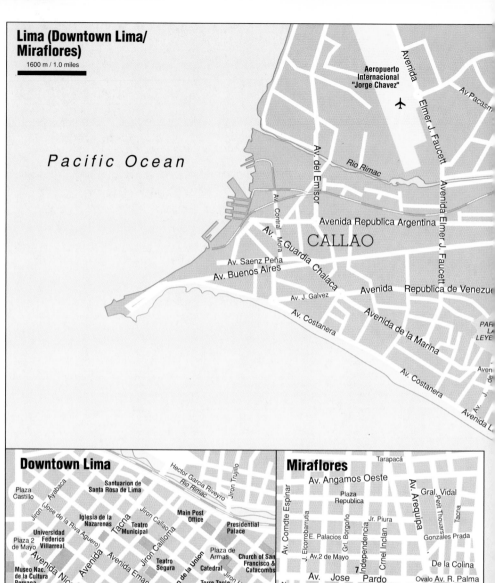

Lima (Downtown Lima/ Miraflores)

1600 m / 1.0 miles

Pacific Ocean

Aeropuerto Internacional "Jorge Chavez"

Av. del Emisor

Av. Contral Mora

Av. Guardia Chalaca

Rio Rimac

Avenida Elmer J. Faucett

Elmer J. Faucett

Av. Pacasm

Avenida

Avenida Republica Argentina

CALLAO

Av. Saenz Peña

Av. Buenos Aires

Av. J. Galvez

Avenida   Republica de Venezue

Av. Costanera

Avenida de la Marina

PAF
LA
LEYE

Av. Costanera

Aven

Avenida L

Avenida

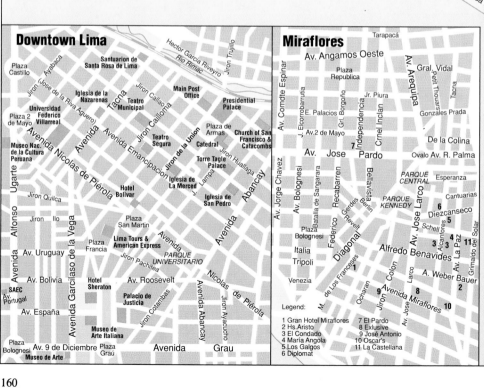

Downtown Lima

Plaza Castillo

Ayabaca

Jiron (Jose de la Riva Aguero)

Santuarion de Santa Rosa de Lima

Hector Garcia Riveyro

Rio Rimac

Jiron Trujillo

Jiron Callao

Iglesia de la Nazarenas

Tacna

Teatro Municipal

Main Post Office

Presidential Palace

Universidad Federico Villarreal

Plaza 2 de Mayo

Avenida Nicolas de Piérola

Avenida Emancipacion

Jiron Cailloma

Jiron de la Union

Plaza de Armas

Church of San Francisco & Catacombs

Museo Nac. de la Cultura Peruana

Teatro Segura

Catedral

Jiron Huallaga

Torre Tagle Palace

Jiron Lampa

Iglesia de La Merced

Avenida Abancay

Ugarte

Jiron Quilca

Hotel Bolivar

Iglesia de San Pedro

Alfonso

Jiron   Ilo

Avenida Garcilaso de la Vega

Plaza San Martin

Plaza Francia

Lima Tours & American Express

Avenida Francia

Jiron Pachitea

PARQUE UNIVERSITARIO

Avenida

Av. Uruguay

Av. Bolivia

Hotel Sheraton

Av. Roosevelt

Nicolas   de   Piérola

SAEC

Av. Portugal

Av. España

Palacio de Justicia

Jiron Cotambas

Avenida Abancay

Jiron Ayacucho

Plaza Bolognesi

Av. 9 de Diciembre

Museo de Arte Italiana

Plaza Graú

Avenida   Grau

Museo de Arte

Miraflores

Tarapacá

Av. Angamos Oeste

Av. Comdte Espinar

Plaza Republica

Av. Arequipa

Gral. Vidal

Petit Thouars

Tacna

J. Elcorrobarrutia

E. Palacios

Grl. Borgoño

Jr. Piura

Independencia

Crnel Inclan

Gonzales Prada

Av. 2 de Mayo

7

Av.   Jose   Pardo

De la Colina

Ovalo Av. R. Palma

Av. Jorge Chavez

Av. Bolognesi

Batalla de Sangarara

Recabarren

Bellavista

Berlin

PARQUE CENTRAL

Esperanza

Federico Gerdes

PARQUE KENNEDY

Alcanfores

Schell

Diezcanseco

Cantuarias

Revett

6

5

Plaza Bolognesi

Italia

Diagonal

M. de Los Franceses

Alfredo Benavides

Larco

Av. Jose Larco

Colon

3

4

Av. La Paz

11

Grimaldo del Solar

Tripoli

A. Weber Bauer

Venezia

Ocharan

José

Avenida   Miraflores

8

2

10

Legend:

1 Gran Hotel Miraflores
2 Hs.Aristo
3 El Condado
4 María Angola
5 Los Galgos
6 Diplomat

7 El Pardo
8 Exlusive
9 José Antonio
10 Oscar's
11 La Castellana

arra de L.Velarde

da Toma Valle

Panamericana Norte

Avenida Tupac Amaru

Cerro
la Milla ▲

Cerro
Arrastre Bajo ▲

SAN JUAN DE
LURIGANCHO

Cerro
Lurigancho ▲

ÁN MARTIN
E PORRAS

/. Peru

Av. E. de Habich

A. Pizarro

Av. Zarumilla

Av. Mayor Elespuru

Av. S. Alcazar

Cerro Attilo ▲

de la Independencia

RIMAC

Museo
Virreynal

Av. Tacna

Av. Malecon M. Checa Eguifuren

Río Rimac

Río Rimac

venida Republica Argentina

(Avenida Colonial)

H. Garcia Riveyro

Plaza de Toros
(Achos)

Av. Proceres

Río Rimac

Jirón Ancash

ida Republica

de Venezuela

Av. Tingo Maria

Av. Arica

Av. Caqueta

Av. A. Ugarte

Av. G. de la Vega

Av. Abancay

Catedral
(Cathedral)

Jirón

Ancash

EL AGUSTINO

Cerro El
Agustino ▲

Vía de Evitamiento

Río Surco

o Arqueolog.
Herrera

Avenida Brasil

Inset
Downtown
Lima

Avenida   Grau

Avenida 28 de Julio

Autopista
a Chosica

Museo
lógico y
eologico

Av. Sucre

Museo Nacional
de Historia

PARQUE
JAPONES

Av. Aviacion

Mercado
Mayorista

Av. Chosica

Av. Chosica

Av. San Nicolas Arriola

Av. Marina

Av. Sucre

Hospital
Central No.2

Av. Mariategui

Avenida Arequipa

Paseo

PARQUE DE
LA RESERVA

Av. San Luis

Río Surco

Avenida Brasil Av. F.S. Carrion

Bolivar

Salaverty

Museo de Historia
Natural J. Prado

Av. Canada

de   la

Avenida Mexico

PARQUE UNION
PANAMERICANA

Av. Canada

SAN LUIS

Avenida   Javier Prado

Avenida

Av. Nicolas Arriola

Av. Canada

Museo de la Nación

Avenida Javier Prado

GOLF
CLUB

Av. del Aire

erez Aranibar

Av. Perez Aranibar

CAMPO DE
GOLF

Jac. Lara

Av. los Conquistadores

Avenida Arequipa

Paseo   de la   Republica

Av. del Aire

Avenida San Luis

Avenida Aviacion

Av. Principal

Ministerio de
Guerra

Avenida Panamericana Sur

Hippodromo
de Monterrico

Av. Wilica Umo

Av. Velasco Astete

POTA
CLUB

PARQUE
TAHUANTINSUYO

Av. Jose Pardo

Avenida

Avenida Panama

Avenida Tomas Marzano

Angamos

Av. Caminos del Inca

Avenida Angamos

Cerro San
Francisco ▲

Av. Larco

Av. M. Benavides

Avenida

Benavides

Av. Benavides

Río Surco

Avenida Tomas Marzano

Av. Reynaldo Vivanco

Av. Panamericana   Sur

Inset Miraflores

Pacific Ocean

Avenida Panama

Av. Baita

Río Surco

SURCO

Avenida Pachacutec

161

LIMA

Herman Melville called **Lima** "the saddest city on earth". Many visitors agree with him, while residents have been even less complimentary – "Lima the horrible", was how writer Sebastian Salazar Bondy described his native city in the early 1960s. But the tourist who is tempted to take such descriptions – and his or her own first impressions – at face value risks missing out on a city of rare fascination and unexpected pleasures. And while locals may gripe, most have an enduring love-hate relationship with their paradoxical city. Lima has both decaying colonial splendor and the teeming vitality of an oriental bazaar; melancholy cloudy winters and warm breezy summers; impoverished urban sprawl and quiet, elegant corners among ancient buildings where the night air is scented with jasmine.

The City of Kings: Lima was founded by the Spanish *conquistador* Francisco Pizarro on January 5, 1535, the eve of the Epiphany of the Magi – from which it derived its evocative original name of La Ciudad de los Reyes or "The City of Kings." Pizarro traced a grid of 13 streets by nine to form 117 city blocks on the site of an existing indigenous settlement beside the southern bank of the River Rimac (from which the name Lima seems subsequently to have been derived). But he had no great army of workers: the city's first inhabitants numbered fewer than 100 *conquistadores.*

Pizarro had originally made his capital at Jauja, in the Andes. The rapid switch was determined by his strategic need to be close to his ships – his only lifeline in a rebellious country that was still largely unconquered. The Rimac Valley provides the best line of communication through the Andean peaks to the interior of central Peru while the rivers Chillón and Lurín also reach the sea within the present-day boundaries of the city, making the site one of the best-watered in the coastal desert. Several *huacas*, or funeral mounds, along with other pre-Columbian ruins, sur-

vive in greater Lima as testimony that the area was populated before the Conquest. Indeed, the most important pre-Inca religous site in coastal Peru was nearby at Pachacamac.

The only drawback was the future city's micro-climate. Because of a meteorological phenomenon known as thermal inversion, Lima is draped in a damp blanket of low cloud from May to October, though the summers are agreeable. And though the visitor may often forget the fact, seeing exuberant gardens of yellow amancaes or purple bougainvillaea (the product of careful irrigation), rainfall rarely amounts to more than a few nights of winter drizzle, insufficient to wash the desert dust from the facades of buildings that require frequent repainting.

Capital of the New World: For two centuries after its foundation, Lima was the political, commercial and ecclesiastical capital of Spanish South America, the seat of the Inquisition as well as of the Viceroys. But its beginnings were modest, and gave little clue to its later splendour. The *mestizo* chronicler Garcilaso de la Vega described it as having "very broad and very straight streets, so that from any of its crossroads the countryside can be seen in all four directions", adding that the houses were roofed with reeds rather than tiles.

But by the early 17th century, Lima's population had risen to about 25,000, the majority of them Indian servants and artisans or African slaves. In the 1680s a protective wall with 12 gateways was built around the city, because of fears of raids by English privateers. (The wall was demolished in the 1870s, although fragments can still be seen beside the railway line in Barrios Altos.) Despite being frequently damaged by earthquakes, the city was rich as well as powerful. Palaces and churches, mansions and monasteries were rebuilt and expanded while across the river pleasure gardens for the aristocracy were carefully laid out.

Lima's gradual decline from pre-eminence began in the late 18th century, as new viceroyalties were created in Bogotá and Buenos Aires and the city's

Preceding pages: dusk at the Plaza San Martín, Lima. **Left**, a guard outside the Archbishop's Palace on the Plaza de Armas.

monopoly on trade between Europe and South America was broken. As befitted a royalist city, independence from Spain came from outside, as expeditionary forces, first from Argentina under José de San Martín and subsequently from Colombia under Simón Bolívar, occupied the city. Installed as republican Peru's dictator in the suburb of Magdalena, even the stern Bolívar was affected by Lima's sybaritic elegance. It was at a ball in Lima that Bolívar met and fell in love with Manuela Saenz, the Ecuadorean wife of a British doctor who was to become the lifelong companion of "the Liberator."

Bursting its boundaries: After a period of stagnation immediately after independence, the city's development resumed in the mid-19th century. The first railway in South America opened between Lima and its port of Callao in 1854, followed swiftly by further lines to connect the city with the growing coastal villages of Miraflores and Chorillos. But setbacks followed, as Lima was occupied and partially sacked by Chilean troops in 1881 during the disastrous War of the Pacific. It was only early in the 20th century that the city burst its 17th-century Spanish limits and embarked on a process of change and growth that has lasted to the present day, the product both of massive migration from the Andean hinterland and the decline of the aristocracy as Peru moved falteringly towards democracy. The outline of the modern city dates from the beginning of this period. Industry began to spread westwards along the Callao railway, and up the central highway to Vitarte in the east.

The building of Paseo Colón and Avenida Nicolas de Piérola or La Colmena (beginning in 1898) and of the Plaza San Martín (1921) created new arteries and a new central focus to the south of Pizarro's Plaza de Armas. The rising urban upper middle class moved away from the crowded center to the spacious south, towards Miraflores and the new district of San Isidro, laid out as a leafy garden suburb. Working-class suburbs sprung up over the river in **Mall in the Correo Central.**

Rimac, in El Agustino to the east and in La Victoria to the southeast. By 1931, Lima's population had reached 280,000, having doubled in little more than two decades.

In the years since then, two trends have given Lima its present urban structure. Infill development of middle-class suburbs has completed a triangle enclosing the area between the city centre, Callao and Chorillos. Outside this triangle, Andean migrants made their homes in sprawling, self-built shantytowns stretching north, south and northeast, occupying the vacant desert sands in the shadow of the Andean foothills. The shanty towns now contain perhaps half the city's estimated population of 8 million. Starting as squatter land invasions of rush-matting huts, decades of hard work have turned some into pleasant districts. Many others remain desperately poor, lacking electricity, piped water or paved streets. But the migrants and their children have changed the character of the city irrevocably. They may be poor, but they are not idle. In the face of massive unemployment, many have created their own jobs as street vendors, thronging the streets of the city center. In turn, the business elite has moved its offices out from the center to San Isidro, and the wealthy have created new residential districts in the Andean foothills in Monterrico and La Molina.

The colonial heart: The usual starting point for exploring Lima is the **Plaza de Armas**. Stand in the middle of this spacious and handsome square, by the 17th-century bronze fountain, and you are at the historic heart of the city. Though most of the buildings are later reconstructions, the spirit of Pizarro permeates the square. On the north side is the **Government Palace**, on the site of Pizarro's own house. The present building (which is not open to the public) was completed in 1938, and suffers from the taste of Peru's dictators of the time for grandiose French baroque. But much of the ground plan at the rear remains the same as in Pizarro's day. On weekdays at 12.45pm, you can catch the changing of the guard, performed in the

The Plaza de Armas.

front courtyard by goose-stepping troops from the Hussares de Junín regiment, dressed in the red and blue ceremonial uniforms and ornamental helmets of the independence period.

The eastern side of the square is dominated by the **cathedral**, again on the site chosen by Pizarro, but reconstructed several times after earthquakes. The present building was begun in the 18th century. Much of the exterior was painted in yellow-ochre in the mid-1980s, as part of a successful policy to brighten up dusty facades with colors used in the colonial period.

Inside, the cathedral is large and unusually austere. Notable are the 17th-century wooden choir stalls. To the right of the entrance is a small side-chapel dedicated to Pizarro. His skeleton is here in a sealed wooden coffin. It was found in 1977 during excavations in the cathedral crypt and put on display in 1985, to mark Lima's 450th anniversary. (It replaced the remains of an anonymous *conquistador*, long mistakenly thought to have been Pizarro.)

Next door to the cathedral is the **Archbishop's Palace**, rebuilt in the 1920s with an impressive wooden balcony.

Opposite the cathedral is the **Municipalidad de Lima,** or town hall, built in the 1940s after fire destroyed its predecessor. The pleasant interior includes a fine library. Next to it on the square is the headquarters of the **Club de la Unión,** a lunchtime haunt of politicians and professionals. Between them at the mouth of Pasaje Santa Rosa is a monument, in the form of a large chunk of rough-hewn stone, to Taulichusco El Viejo, the last *cacique* (chief) of pre-Conquest Lima, unveiled in 1985 as a belated antidote to the ghost of Pizarro. The fourth, southern side of the Plaza de Armas contains shops and offices.

To the left of the palace, in a small side-square, stands an equestrian statue of the ubiquitous Pizarro. Behind him, the building topped with antennae houses an office of Peru's National Intelligence Service; to the left is the Café Conquistador, with tables on the pavement – a good place for a coffee and a

Bones in the San Francisco catacombs.

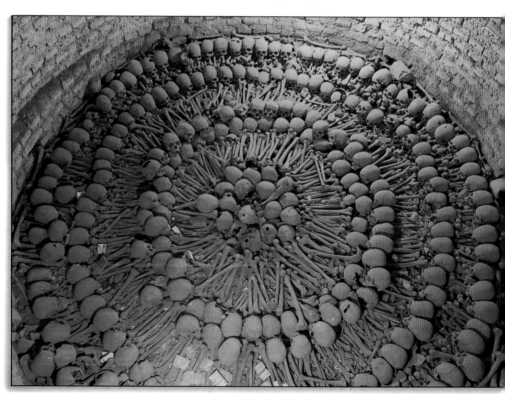

rest while sightseeing. Nearby stands the **Central Post Office**, its offices grouped around a handsome neo-classical arcade, whose roof is sadly missing most of its glass.

Further up towards the river are a couple of splendid old hat shops, where you can acquire a felt stetson or a Panama for around US$12–15. Round the corner lies a taste of Lima's modern social reality – the booming contraband market of **Polvos Azules**, selling Chilean wine, Scotch whisky, watches and cigarettes much cheaper than in the shops (it also sells handcrafts). It is usually packed with shoppers. Thieves abound, and tourists should take great care of their valuables. (This warning goes for the whole of the city center. Until you become accustomed to Lima, you would also be best advised not to wander alone in the center by night.)

Doubling back into the Plaza de Armas again, to the right of the Presidential Palace is a charming street corner (the intersection of Jirón Carabaya and Jr. Junín) that contains the oldest buildings in the square (dating from the early 18th century), with the wooden balconies in the form of enclosed galleries projecting on the first floor that were colonial Lima's most graceful feature. Further up Carabaya, past several shoe shops (hand-stitched cowboy boots made to measure) is the **Desamparados Station**, the terminal for the Central Railway to Huancayo, a neo-classical building dating from 1908. Opposite the station, on the corner of Jr. Ancash, is the **Cordano restaurant** – tasty Peruvian food served in an old-fashioned dining room. There are several cheap hotels for backpackers in this area.

Books and bones: Walk along Jr. Ancash and you come to the **San Francisco Monastery**, the jewel of colonial Lima. Even if you are not a fan of colonial churches, don't miss this one. The monastery faces a small paved square, full of pigeons and portrait photographers. The outside is attractively painted in colonial yellow, but it is the interior that is fascinating; much of it is decorated in the geometrical Mudejar

Visiting the new Museo de la Nación.

(Andalusian Moorish) style. Founded soon after Lima, its outstanding features include the 17th-century library, with 25,000 leather-bound volumes and 6,000 parchments dating from the 15th to the 18th century. The cupola has a superb Mudejar carved wooden ceiling of Panamanian cedar, dating from 1625. In a gallery above the nave of the church are 130 choir stalls and 71 panels with carvings of Franciscan saints, made of the same wood. Recent work has exposed (under eight layers of paint) 17th-century murals in the cloister and adjacent chambers.

The monastery's collection of religious art includes paintings by the Rubens and Zurbaran workshops and a *Last Supper* attributed to Van Dyck. San Francisco has survived more recent earthquakes because of its catacombs, used as Lima's cemetery until 1810. A network of underground chambers open to the public contain hundreds of skulls and bones, stored in racks according to type. A secret passage (now bricked up) led from here to the government palace.

There are half a dozen other colonial churches in the center, but most will be mainly of interest to the specialist. **Santo Domingo Monastery** (on the corner of Jirón Camana and Conde de Superunda, just past the Post Office) has a pleasant cloister with Sevillian tiling. Its church contains an urn with the ashes of Santa Rosa of Lima, the patron saint of the New World and the Philippines. **San Pedro Church** (Jirón Azangaro) is for lovers of baroque and gold leaf altars. The **Sanctuary of Santa Rosa** (Av. Tacna) contains relics of Santa Rosa, the patron saint of Lima.

Las Nazarenas (also Av. Tacna) houses the image of El Señor de los Milagros (The Lord of Miracles), the black Christ painted by a freed Negro slave which has become the most important focus of popular religiosity in Lima. On three occasions in October, the image is borne around the streets of the city center on a one-ton litter by teams of men wearing the purple robes of the brotherhood of El Señor de los Milagros. Hundreds of thousands of

Left, colonial altar. **Below**, mansion door.

people turn out to accompany the image in what is one of the largest public gatherings in South America.

Colonial mansions: The city center also contains several fine examples of secular colonial architecture. Outstanding is the **Torre Tagle Palace**, completed in 1735. It houses the Foreign Ministry, but tourists are allowed into the courtyard and can see the finely carved wooden balconies. It gives a good idea of the opulence of Lima in its colonial prime. Opposite, in another colonial mansion, is the **L'Eau Vive Restaurant**, run by French-speaking nuns. They serve excellent and reasonably-priced French cooking; customers are encouraged to join them in singing the Ave Maria at 10pm each evening. Also worth visiting is the **Casa de Osambela**, in Jr. Conde Superunda, a late 18th-century mansion with an ornamental cupola, beautifully restored between 1982 and 1984. It houses a small art gallery and the offices of various cultural institutions and is open to the public. Conde de Superunda is one of several streets in the center with good colonial balconies. Many others are in a sad state of decay. Other colonial buildings include the **Casona de San Marcos**, in Parque Universitario, the original site of San Marcos University, founded in 1551 and the oldest university in the Western hemisphere. The Casona contains a library and is used for meetings and seminars. (Most of the university's activities moved in the 1940s to a large campus on Av. Venezuela.) Visits to other colonial houses in the center can be arranged through the Lima Tours travel agency.

The **Puente de Piedra** or stone bridge behind the Presidential Palace, built in Roman style in 1610 (its mortar reputedly bound with thousands of egg whites for strength), leads over the river to **Rimac**, once the playground of the aristocracy and now a lively working-class district. The **Hatuchay peña** (nightclub with Peruvian music and dancing), popular with both tourists and locals, is in Jr. Trujillo.

At the **Plaza de Acho** is the **bullring**, the oldest in the Americas and with a

City girls.

small museum including some Goya prints. The bullfight season is in October and November. Behind the large Backus and Johnston brewery (founded 1879) and at the foot of the **San Cristóbal hill** is the **Alameda de los Descalzos**, laid out in 1610 as a pleasure garden with statues and wrought iron railings, but now tatty. It leads to the **Monastery of the Descalzos** (barefoot friars), recently restored. To the right is the **Paseo de Aguas**, another pleasure garden created in the 18th century by Viceroy Amat for his famous mistress La Perrichola, but also in need of repair. Nearby is the **Quinta de Presa**, a mansion in 18th-century French rococo style, now the Museum of the Viceroyalty.

Republican Lima: Six blocks south of the Plaza de Armas is the **Plaza San Martín**, the hub of the modern city center. The two squares are linked by the pedestrianised **Jirón de la Unión**, once Lima's most elegant shopping street. As recently as the 1940s it was considered scandalous for women to stroll along Jirón de la Unión without wearing a hat. Now it is a teeming mass of street vendors, shoppers, and fast-food joints. All human life is here, including an Andean version of *tombola* in which prizes are decided by a guinea pig scuttling at random into one of a number of small cardboard arches set up on the pavement. From time to time the police clear the street of vendors, but these attempts to repress reality never last for very long.

The colonnaded Plaza San Martín, its buildings painted red several years ago, is an important gathering place used for political meetings. In the center is an equestrian statue of José de San Martín, Peru's Argentine independence hero. The square is shabby but lively, thronged with clowns, storytellers and, at weekends, by courting couples or domestic servants or soldiers on their day off. On its west side is the **Hotel Bolívar**, built in the 1920s. Though now it often seems to have more elderly waiters and bellboys than guests, the hotel retains much of its former atmosphere. A Palm Court trio serenades afternoon tea in the domed

The Bridge of Sighs in Barranco.

lobby, while its giant Pisco Sours (called "Cathedrals") remain justly famous. Even if you are not staying here, the Bolívar is the perfect place to stop and rest during a city tour.

Next to the Bolívar is **Jirón Ocoña**, the center of Lima's street foreign exchange market, where moneychangers buy or sell dollars round the clock. The market is sophisticated – in times of high inflation, rates change hourly and are communicated by walkie-talkie throughout the city. Across La Colmena from the Bolívar is the **Club Nacional**. The watering hole of Peru's once all-powerful oligarchy, it has become an anachronism since business and the elite abandoned the city center. On the opposite side of the square, above a fast-food bakery, is the **Phoenix Club**, a British businessmen's club, while a third club, the **Circulo Militar**, is on the north side. Next door is a small shop of the **Instituto Geográfico Militar**, selling good maps of Peru.

A city of museums: Lima has more than a score of museums and visitors will want to make their own selection. But don't miss the **Museum of Anthropology and Archaeology** in the Plaza Bolívar in the suburb of Pueblo Libre. It is one of the most interesting museums in South America, with a superb collection of pottery and textiles from all the main cultures of ancient Peru, as well as stone idols from Chavín. It is well laid out, in chronological order, and the curators have resisted the temptation to swamp visitors with too many exhibits.

While you're in the area, next door is the **Museum of the Republic** or National History Museum, in a mansion Bolívar lived in during his stay in Lima, with exhibits from the colonial and independence periods.

Second on the list of the best is the **National Museum**, opened in 1990 in a neo-brutalist mausoleum on Av. Javier Prado Oeste in San Borja. It was built in the 1970s as the Fisheries Ministry and subsequently used as the National Bank. The museum contains impressive mock-ups of pre-Columbian archaeological sites, and an ingenious replica of the

La Rosa
Nautica
restaurant at
Costa Verde,
Miraflores.

LIMA'S OASIS OF HOPE

Villa El Salvador is a microcosm of Peru's past, present and future. Tucked behind the sand dunes not far from the Inca shrine of Pachacamac, about 30km (19 miles) south of Lima, it is more than just another shanty town formed by homeless Andean migrants in search of the Big City.

Villa El Salvador was founded in May 1971 by an initial wave of 10,000 migrants who had fled from the mountain areas around Huaráz in the wake of an earthquake, and today it is home to around 350,000 people. Named after Christ the Savior, it is a fiery prototype of self-determination by Peru's marginalized Andean Indian majority.

Villa El Salvador's success has enjoyed international recognition. It has been nominated for the Nobel Peace Prize, won Spain's prestigious Prince of Asturias award for social achievement, and has been designated by the United Nations as a Messenger of Peace. Its key is the Andean tradition of community organization centered on the family unit.

Each block of houses or *manzana* comprises 24 families; 16 blocks make up a residential group and 22 of these form a sector. Health centers, communal kitchens and sports grounds bond each group together. Each group also takes an active interest in its members' educa-

tion, and illiteracy in Villa El Salvador is minimal, unlike in other such shanty towns. Most of the houses are built of adobe bricks or concrete. Most have drainage and are connected to mains water and electricity. The community is criss-crossed by roads and dotted generously with shady poplar, eucalyptus, pomegranate and banana trees.

Little by little, clever irrigation, its ingenuity worthy of the inhabitants' Inca forebears, has converted hundreds of hectares of sandy desert into arable land, using the community's own sewage. Sewage ponds, which have been built with foreign grants, are perfumed off by a curtain of eucalyptus trees. Fruit and cotton are grown in the fields, as are corn and fodder crops for the thousands of privately and communally-owned cattle whose milk and cheese are sold locally.

Villa El Salvador's first martyr was Edilberto Ramos, who was shot dead resisting police attempts to expel the original settlers. It was his death that forced the government to hand over the desert.

However, the powerful sense of local identity, forged by such heroism and collective action in combating poverty with no expectations of help from central government, was shaken by terrorist infiltration in the early 1990s. In 1992, popular community leader and deputy mayor María Elena Moyano was shot dead in front of her children by Sendero Luminoso, and later in the same year, a former mayor was wounded in a terrorist attack on his home, after criticizing Moyano's killers. Since then, and particularly following the capture of Sendero leader Abimael Guzman, terrorist influence has been very much reduced in an era of increasing stability.

Villa El Salvador's libraries, community radio station and all kinds of written bulletins demonstrate the determination to communicate and the belief that education genuinely harvests self-advancement and change.

Carnival (in February), which is profoundly perceived as a rite of the renovation of life, features the Yunsa fiesta in which presents hanging from a tree fall to the ground while the tree trunk is struck in turn by the participants' axes. He whose axe finally fells the tree must provide a new one for the following year.

A cultural museum opened in 1991 tells the history of the nearby pre-Columbian ruin of Pachacamac as well as that of the settlement of Villa El Salvador itself. Meanwhile, its industrial park, created in 1987, goes from strength to strength, providing much-needed local employment and exporting wooden goods and other products all over the world.

Villa continues to flourish despite underemployment and malnutrition. It is an oasis which has tapped a spring of hope from deep beneath the desert floor. ∎

Chavín *stela*, a massive carved stone idol. The museum's large models of Machu Picchu and other Inca sites are a good preparation for Cuzco. See also the exhibition of Peruvian costume on the ground floor.

The **Gold Museum** (Av. Alonso de Molina in Monterrico) contains a private collection with some fine items but suffers from overcrowding of exhibits and poor labelling. There is also a collection of armaments. The **Rafael Larco Herrera Museum** (Av. Bolívar, Pueblo Libre) has good pre-Columbian pottery and textiles, but also suffers from overcrowded layout. A small annexe holds a fascinating and amusing collection of erotic pottery.

The **Museum of the Inquisition** (Plaza Bolívar, next to Congress in the city center) is in the building where generations of supposed heretics were tortured and tried. See the main hall (a fine 18th-century wooden ceiling) and the underground dungeons and torture chambers. The stocks are original, while there are mock-ups of other torture techniques.

It's a grim and macabre reminder that the torments inflicted by recent Latin American military dictatorships have a long history.

The modern capital: Two main arteries, the Avenida Arequipa and the Paseo de la Republica expressway, connect the city center with the business district of **San Isidro** (pause at the **Bosque del Olivar**, an attractive olive grove reputedly planted in Pizarro's day and now a park) and **Miraflores**, the main area for shopping, restaurants, cafés and theatres. Av. Larco is the main shopping street. Good, though expensive handicrafts are sold in Av. La Paz (cheaper are the handicraft markets on Avenida La Marina, on the way to the airport). At the top end of Av. Larco is the **Parque Kennedy**, where artists sell paintings at the weekend. Here next to the Pacifico cinema is the **Café Haiti**, a prime spot for people-watching. Round the corner in Ricardo Palma, is the more upmarket **Vivaldi Café**. Walking down Diagonal you will find firstly great imported export-quality Peruvian coffee in the highly

Below, Lima money-changers. Right, a skyscraper in Miraflores.

trendy **Café Café** and a little further on is a pedestrianised side street crammed with pizzerias with open-air tables, a haunt of upper middle-class teenagers. Continue down the Diagonal and you reach the cliffs overlooking the Pacific, laid out with gardens – a lovely place to watch the sunset. A cobbled road leads down a gully to the **Costa Verde**, as the sweep of beaches is called. Though Limeños flock here in thousands to bathe on summer Sundays, the sea is polluted – the resorts to the south are better for swimming. But the Costa Verde is an attractive place, for the coast road sweeps on round (with fine views of the city) to the isolated beach of **La Herradura**, a popular spot to eat *ceviche* (fish marinaded in lemon juice with onion and hot pepper) while watching the Pacific breakers. Closer to Miraflores are two superb fish restaurants (international prices) – the Costa Verde on the beach, and the Rosa Nautica, built on a pier surrounded by the ocean.

From La Herradura, the road doubles back through a tunnel to **Chorillos**, an interesting area of mixed social composition high on the sandy cliffs. Down on the beach is a fishing wharf, where small boats can be hired. Moving back towards Miraflores we come to **Barranco**, a beautiful district of colonial and 19th-century housing, much of it recently restored.

This romantic neighborhood is the home of many bohemians, writers and artists and is celebrated in Peruvian waltzes. It has recently become the center of the city's nightlife, with a score or more of *peñas* and bars where music of all kinds is played. Opposite the attractive main square is the wooden **Puente de Los Suspiros** or Bridge of Sighs, a traditional meeting place for lovers set among gardens overlooking the Pacific. This is also a traditional spot to try *anticuchos*, or marinated beef-heart kebabs at any one of the stalls sitting outside the church.

The Pacific port: Now joined to Lima, the port of **Callao** was originally a settlement apart, 9.5 km (6 miles) west of the city on a low-lying bay. Though Callao is now poor and tatty, it has several points of interest. Permission is required to enter the docks, but at the wharf next door launches take passengers for trips round the bay. Along the shore is the **Yacht Club**, with a good restaurant open to visitors for lunches. Behind the docks, there is an area of colonial housing with balconies, though in poor repair. Nearby is the 18th-century **Real Felipe Fort**, the last royalist redoubt in Peru. It was captured by Bolívar's forces in 1826 after a year-long seige. It now contains an interesting **Military Museum**.

On the outskirts of Lima, 32 km (20 miles) south, are the ruins of **Pachacamac**, once the largest pre-Columbian settlement on the Peruvian coast. The cult surrounding its idol was so important that Pizarro sent his brother Hernando on a lengthy detour to destroy it in 1533. The ruins of the original pre-Inca temple occupy a large site on a low sandhill overlooking the ocean. The complex was expanded under the Incas and there is an interesting reconstruction of the Inca Temple of the Virgins.

Left, Pedro Osma Museum. **Right**, summer swimming on the Costa Verde.

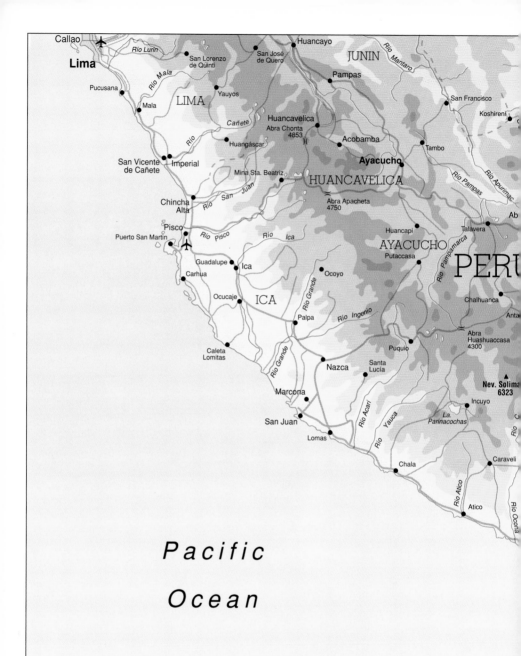

Callao ✈
Río Lurín
Lima
Pucusana
Mala
LIMA
Yauyos
San Lorenzo de Quinti
San José de Quero
Huancayo
JUNIN
Río Mantaro
Pampas
San Francisco
Koshireni
Río Mala
Cañete
Huancavelica
Abra Chonta 4853
Acobamba
Tambo
Huangáscar
San Vicente de Cañete
Imperial
Río
Mina Sta. Beatriz
Ayacucho
HUANCAVELICA
Río Pampas
Río Apurímac
Chincha Alta
Río San Juan
Abra Apacheta 4750
Ab
Pisco
Puerto San Martín ✈
Río Pisco
Río Ica
Huancapi
Talavera
Guadalupe
Ica
Ocoyo
AYACUCHO
Putaccasa
PERU
Carhua
Ocucaje
ICA
Río Grande
Palpa
Río Ingenio
Chalhuanca
Anta
Caleta Lomitas
Río Grande
Puquio
Abra Huashuaccasa 4300
Nazca
Santa Lucía
Nev. Solima 6323
Marcona
San Juan
Río Acarí
Río Yauca
La. Parinacochas
Incuyo
Río Pampamarca
Lomas
Chala
Caraveli
Río Atico
Atico
Río Ocoña

Pacific

Ocean

South of Peru
120 km / 75 miles

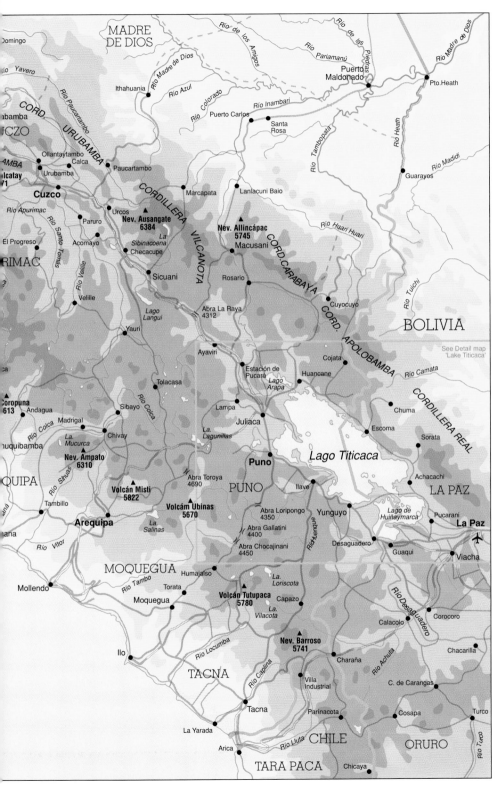

MADRE
DE DIOS

Domingo

Rio Yavero

CORD. abamba

ICZO

AMBA
lcatay
71

Rio Paucartambo

CORD. URUBAMBA

Ollantaytambo
Calca

Urubamba

Cuzco

Ithahuania

Rio Azul

Rio Madre de Dios

Rio Colorado

Puerto Carlos

Rio de los Amigos

Rio Pariamanú

Rio de las Piedras

Puerto
Maldonado

Rio Madre de Dios

Pto.Heath

Rio Inambari

Santa
Rosa

Rio Tambopata

Rio Heath

Rio Madidi

Guarayos

Paucartambo

Paruro

El Progreso

Rio Apurimac

RIMAC

Urcos

Nev. Ausangate
6384

La
Sibinacoena
Checacupe

Sicuani

Marcapata

CORDILLERA VILCANOTA

Nev. Allincápac
5745

Macusani

Lanlacuni Baio

Rio Huari Huari

CORD. CARABAYA

Rosario

Cuyocuyo

Rio Tuichi

BOLIVIA

Acomayo

Rio Santo Tomás

Rio Velille

Velille

Yauri

Lago
Langui

Abra La Raya
4312

CORD. APOLOBAMBA

See Detail map
'Lake Titicaca'

oropuna
613

Andagua

Rio Colca

Sibayo

Madrigal

Rio Colca

Tolacasa

Rio Colca

Ayaviri

Estación de
Pucará

Lago
Arapa

Huancane

Cojata

Rio Camata

Chuma

CORDILLERA REAL

Escoma

Sorata

Achacachi

huquibamba

La.
Mucurca

Chivay

Nev. Ampato
6310

Lampa

La.
Lagunillas

Juliaca

Puno

Lago Titicaca

LA PAZ

QUIPA

Rio Shuca

Tambillo

Arequipa

La.
Salinas

Abra Toroya
4690

Volcán Misti
5822

Volcám Ubinas
5670

PUNO

Ilave

Abra Loripongo
4350

Abra Gallatini
4400

Abra Chocajinani
4450

Yunguyo

Rio Desaguadero

Lago de
Huiñaymarca

Desaguadero

Guaqui

Pucarani

La Paz

Viacha

MOQUEGUA

Humajalso

La.
Loriscota

Mollendo

Rio Vitor

Rio Tambo

Torata

Moquegua

Volcán Tutupaca
5780

Capazo

La.
Vilacota

Calacolo

Corocoro

Rio Desaguadero

Ilo

Rio Locumba

Nev. Barroso
5741

Charaña

Rio Achuta

C. de Carangas

Chacarilla

TACNA

Rio Caplina

Villa
Industrial

Cosapa

Turco

ORURO

Rio Turco

La Yarada

Tacna

Parinacota

Arica

Rio Lluta

CHILE

Chicaya

TARA PACA

CUZCO AND THE VALLEY OF THE INCAS

Indian vendors speak Spanish to tourists and Quechua to each other. Catholic nuns live in buildings once inhabited by Inca vestal virgins. The cathedral's painting of the Last Supper shows Christ and his apostles dining on Andean cheese, hot peppers and guinea pig. **Cuzco** is a city where past and present collide in an uneasy mix.

The Cuzco of today is dramatically different from the city that confronted Francisco Pizarro and his soldiers 500 years ago. Then, the capital of the Inca empire served as home to an estimated 15,000 nobles, priests and servants. Where now daily rail, plane and bus services connect this city to the rest of the country, long-distance Indian runners called *chasquis* once linked the rest of Tahuantinsuyo, as the empire was called. Today, local residents have attempted to recall those glory days, confusingly relabeling streets in this city of 250,000 with their original Quechua names and even calling the city Qosqo, a pronunciation closer to its original Inca name.

Center of the world: For the Incas, Qosqo meant "belly button of the world" and they believed their splendid city was the source of life. Legend has it Cuzco was founded by Manco Capac and his sister-consort Mama Ocllo sent by the sun god Inti. With a gold staff in hand, they began the divine task of finding a spot where the staff would sink easily into the ground. That place was Cuzco and there Manco Capac taught the men to farm and Mama Ocllo taught the women to weave.

The Inca dynasty started regionally here with the empire coming into being during the reign of Inca Pachacutec Yupanqui, who began a great expansion, imposing Quechua as the common language, conquering other Indian nations, creating a state religion and turning Cuzco into a glittering capital as large as any European city (*see "The Incas" on page 45*).

Pachacutec's reign stemmed not from his desire to conquer but from his valiant effort to save the city. His father, Viracocha Inca, was in power when the fierce Chancas Indians began an assault on the Inca kingdom and Viracocha and his eldest son gave up the fight as futile. However, the younger son – who later took the name Pachacutec – triumphantly led his troops to victory over the invading forces and declared himself the new Inca leader.

A modern stone statue of Pachacutec on the south side of Cuzco pays tribute to the Inca King who ruled for 40 years and was one of the empire's greatest warriors, innovators and unifiers of Andean civilizations.

Pachacutec's son Topa Inca continued his father's work, expanding even further the empire's boundaries. But Cuzco's advances do not mean it was always ruled by wise and competent leaders. One Inca chief, Urco, was behind such atrocities that his name later was banned from being mentioned. Another ruler hanged his enemies along

Preceding pages: Inca terraces at Pisac; the Plaza de Armas, Cuzco. **Left,** Cuzco's narrow streets. **Right,** home-brewed chicha.

the roadsides in the empire's cities – a gruesome message for the disloyal. Yet another had the entire population of a nearby city executed for the rape of a chosen woman who had dedicated her life to the sun cult. However, these excesses fail to overshadow the magnificence of a civilization that left an indelible culture.

Some of the best-loved Inca legends have been transferred to the Peruvian theater. Among them is *Ollantay* – the story of Pachacutec's most famous general. Under Ollantay's military leadership, the empire was extended into what is now Ecuador, Bolivia, Colombia, Chile and portions of Argentina. A grateful Pachacutec asked his general what he would like in compensation, agreeing to grant any wish. Ollantay boldly asked for the hand of Kusi Kuyur, the monarch's daughter.

But the Inca, the son of the Sun, could not allow a member of the monarchy to marry a common person even though the daughter professed her love for the military leader. Ollantay rebelled against

Pachacutec and was eventually ordered to be imprisoned for the remainder of his life. Kusi Kuyur refused to marry anyone else and was sent to be a chosen woman, dedicating her life to serving the sun god.

The story does not end here, however, because years later an unforeseen occurrence brought the couple together again for a happy ending. The play is staged frequently in Cuzco and Lima and is worth seeing by those who understand some Spanish.

A brief moment of glory: At its peak, Cuzco was a city with sophisticated water systems, paved streets and no poverty. But it had been an imposing urban center for only about 70 years before the Spanish arrived. It was Pachacutec who turned Cuzco from a city of clay and straw into a thriving metropolis with grand stone buildings in the second half of the 15th century.

Even so, Cuzco was very different from the city shown by early European cartographers, including the German Sebastien Munster who drew it as a

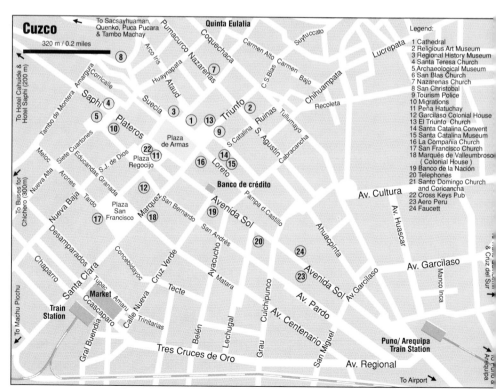

Cuzco

320 m / 0.2 miles

Legend:

1 Cathedral
2 Religious Art Museum
3 Regional History Museum
4 Santa Teresa Church
5 Archaeological Museum
6 San Blas Church
7 Nazarenas Church
8 San Christobal
9 Tourism Police
10 Migrations
11 Peña Hatuchay
12 Garcilaso Colonial House
13 El Triunfo Church
14 Santa Catalina Convent
15 Santa Catalina Museum
16 La Compañia Church
17 San Francisco Church
18 Marqués de Valleumbroso (Colonial House)
19 Banco de la Nación
20 Telephones
21 Santo Domingo Church and Coricancha
22 Cross Keys Pub
23 Aero Peru
24 Faucett

walled city, laid out in a grid, surrounded by featherly trees. In actuality, there was no wall and the housing blocks were irregular. That was in part owing to the design of the city – which reputedly followed the shape of a puma, a religious power symbol, with the fortress of Sacsayhuaman outside Cuzco as the head and the Tullumayo river as the spine of the animal.

Of course, since the Incas left no written records and the Spanish explanations of what they found are contradictory, theories about Cuzco's design are numerous. One specialist in archaeology and astronomy even speculates that one city boundary was warped to make it coincide with the mid-point in the Milky Way, reflecting the Indian sensitivity to astronomy and movements of the heavenly bodies.

Many other details of how the Inca capital looked must be drawn from the often unreliable memoirs of the conquistadors. Pizarro and his men did not set off for Cuzco, the city of wonders, until they executed Atahualpa in Ca-

jamarca. Entering for the first time the fertile valley where Cuzco is located, the Europeans found rain-washed countryside of green, patchworked with barley, alfalfa, corn, and gold and purple fields of *kiwicha* and *quinua* – varieties of amaranth grain.

The Spaniards were certainly impressed by the order and magnificence of Cuzco, and wrote back to Spain that it was the most marvelous city of the New World. But the Incas' cultural achievements were merely a minor distraction in comparison with the lure of their treasures: conquistadors greedily pushed their way into ancient temples, seized their gold and silver artworks to promptly melt into portable bars.

In addition to palaces and gold-filled temples, indestructible buildings, and advanced medical techniques, the Spanish soldiers found the Inca society full of skilled artisans. In Cuzco a storehouse of delicate, bright-colored feathers from tropical birds was used solely for the weaving of fine capes for the Inca and his priests. Rescued examples

of the capes or *mantas*, which may reflect the most extreme test of patience and handiwork, are found in museums in Lima. These survived because the Spanish thirst for gold was so great that they overlooked many of the empire's other treasures.

Although the Inca reign is certainly what most intrigues visitors to this city, Cuzco retained a level of importance for the first few decades after the Spanish Conquest. It was here that Diego de Almagro's faction of Spanish soldiers attempted to wrest control from Pizarro; in fact, de Almagro was executed on Cuzco's main plaza. Also in this city, the Spanish struggled against Manco Inca as the Indian made a fated attempt to stop the European conquest. But by 1535 the capital of this new Spanish colony had been set up in Lima, Cuzco's wealth had been stripped, and silver from Bolivia had turned attention away from this valley.

After centuries of provincial oblivion, Hiram Bingham's discovery of Machu Picchu and the subsequent construction of a roadway to that mountaintop citadel in 1948 transformed Cuzco into the jumping-off point for visits to one of South America's best known tourist attractions.

Walking into the past: The most startling and curious characteristic of Cuzco at first glance is its architecture. Huge walls of intricately laid stone pay testimony to the civilization that 500 years ago controlled much of the South American continent. The Spaniards' attempts to eradicate every trace of the "pagan" Inca civilization proved too ambitious a task; the Europeans ended up putting their own buildings on the mammoth foundations of the Inca ones, often using the same stones that had been finely cut and rounded by the Indian masons. When earthquakes shook the city, the colonial walls came crashing down but the Inca foundations remained intact.

To explore this intriguing city, the **Plaza de Armas** is a perfect place to start. In Inca times it was not only the exact center of the empire known as

The Inca masonry of Calle Loreto

Tahuantinsuyo – or The Four Quarters of the Earth – but was twice as large as it is now. A sample of soil from each of the conquered areas of the empire was joined at this spot and the plaza itself, flanked by Inca palaces, was surfaced with white sand mixed with tiny shells, bits of gold, silver and coral.

This was the spot where important Inca religious and military ceremonies were staged. Some claim the section that remains today was a portion of Aucaypata, the Square of War, featuring a stone covered in sheets of gold where offerings were made before military actions. However, other experts disagree, and suggest it was called Huacaypata – or Weeping Square – because it was here that deceased Incas were mourned.

During the days of Spanish control, the plaza was the scene of much bloodletting, such as the execution of Indian rebel leader Tupac Amaru II in a successful effort by the Spanish to stop an uprising. Captured while trying to flee with his pregnant wife, Tupac Amaru – a *mestizo* whose real name was José Gabriel Condorcanqui – was ordered to be drawn and quartered in the square. Spanish chronicles say the young leader was so strong that the horses tied to his arms and legs failed to dismember him on the first try, so the conquistadors beheaded him – after forcing him to watch the decapitations of his four children and strangulation of his wife.

Festival focus: Nowadays, crowds assemble in Cuzco's Plaza de Armas for festivities, both modern and ancient, solemn and colorful. Annually, on International Workers' Day, the parade of workers through the square continues for hours with each group lined up behind its respective banners – from the organization of transportation workers to the union of informal street vendors (*ambulantes*), which is made up mostly of women with their babies strapped to their backs.

This, like many ceremonies in Cuzco, opens with the raising of the red and white Peruvian flag and the rainbow-colored standard of the Inca empire.

Distant view of Plaza de Armas.

Solemnity marks the beginning of celebrations for Corpus Christi Day, a movable feast usually held in June at which statues and silver are paraded through the streets. But that ceremony ends on a festive note as increasingly generous quantities of alcoholic beverages are imbibed and masked devil dancers frolic among the shrubberies.

By day on the plaza, tourists peruse the handicrafts for sale as insistent Indian women sitting under blankets under the archways chant *"cómprame,"* or "buy from me." Quality varies, but good bargains can be found. However, don't believe it when vendors claim their rugs and weavings are antique. As one traveler said, "They smell like they've been around a hundred campfires, but I think the fires were lit in my lifetime."

Besides, wool does not endure indefinitely in the damp highlands. The centuries-old textiles displayed in Peru's museums were rescued from the arid coast. The most spectacular view of the plaza comes after nightfall when dramatic lighting transforms the square.

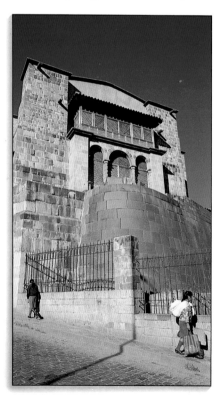

Although the night is best for outside photos, the interior of Cuzco's magnificent **cathedral** can only be seen during the day – and it shouldn't be missed. Built on what once was the palace of Viracocha Inca and made in part from stones hauled from the fortress of Sacsayhuaman outside the city, the cathedral mixes Spanish renaissance architecture with the stoneworking skills of the Indians; it took a century to build and an equally awesome investment of money. The altar is solid silver. In the corner next to the sacristy is a painting of the Last Supper with Christ and his apostles dining on roast guinea pig and Andean cheese. Another painting of Christ's Crucifixion in the church is believed to be the work of Flemish painter Sir Anthony Van Dyck. The third side-altar from the left contains a curious painting of a pregnant Virgin Mary.

Locally, the cathedral's most venerated statue is the crucified Christ known as *El Señor de los Temblores* – or Lord of the Earthquakes. Depicted in a painting in another Cuzco church, El Triunfo, this is the statue that was paraded around the city during the 1650 earthquake. After the tremors eventually stopped, the statue was credited with miraculously bringing about the end of seismic activity. Borne on a silver litter, this gift to the New World from the Spanish King Charles V, is still paraded around Cuzco on feast days. Inside the cathedral, candles are perpetually lit to this icon; it is their smoke that has blackened the statue.

The cathedral's María Angola bell in the north tower can be heard up to 25 miles (40 km) away. Made of a ton of gold, silver and bronze, the more than 300-year-old bell is reportedly the continent's largest. But when it was cast, it had a partner – the Magdalena, which was dropped by workers during a storm at the edge of Lake Titicaca, where the bells were made. Indians in Cuzco now say that the echoes from the first peals of the María Angola each morning are actually the tolling of the Magdalena on the bottom of the lake.

Cuzco's first Christian church: **El Triunfo** – literally "the triumph" – is the

The Inca temple Koricancha, at the base of Santo Domingo Church.

church to the right of the cathedral, up Triunfo Street off the plaza. It was built in honor of the Spanish victory over the Indians in the great rebellion of 1536, when Cuzco was under siege for many months. The uprising was led by Manco Inca, a descendent of an Inca leader whom the Spaniards assumed would be their political puppet. They were surprised, then, to find Manco surrounding the city with some 200,000 followers – against the Spaniards' 200 men and loyal Indians.

The turning point of the siege was a great attack on the city, with Manco's men slinging red hot stones to set the thatched roofs alight. The Spaniards were gathered in the old Inca armory of Suntur Huasi when it was pelted with fiery rocks. When the building did not catch fire, priests declared that the Virgin of the Assumption had appeared to put out the flames and inspire the Spaniards on to defend the city. El Triunfo – the city's first Christian church – was built on the site.

Entering El Triunfo church today, the painting to the right of the entrance shows the 1650 earthquake which shook down the Spanish-built structures but left nary a stone out of place in the Inca buildings. Also in this church is the grave of chronicler Garcilaso de la Vega, who died in Spain in 1616 but whose remains were returned to Cuzco a few years ago. On the other side of the cathedral is the Church of the Holy Family, or Jesus María. At nearly 260 years old, it is one of Cuzco's "newer" structures.

In a city with so many churches, it is an honor to be dubbed the "most beautiful". That distinction belongs to **La Compañía**, sitting in the main plaza where once stood Huayna Inca's Capac palace. The church, with its intricate interior, finely carved balconies and altars covered in gold leaf, was started in 1571 and took nearly 100 years to complete, in part because of damage in the 1650 earthquake.

During its construction, this splendid building drew so much attention that the Bishop of Cuzco complained it out-

Crafts in the Plaza de Armas.

shone the cathedral. But by the time the Pope was called into the spat and ruled in favor of the cathedral, La Compañía's construction was far too advanced to turn back.

The Sun God Temple: The street to the side of El Triunfo led to what was the most important place of worship in the Inca empire. Now the **Santo Domingo Church**, this was Koricancha – Temple of the Sun – to the Incas and was the most magnificent complex in Cuzco. Walls there were covered in 700 sheets of gold studded with emeralds and turquoise, and windows were constructed so the sun would enter and cast a near blinding reflection off the precious metals inside.

The mummified bodies of deceased Inca leaders, dressed in fine clothing and adornments, were kept on thrones of gold here, tended by women selected for that honor. In that same room, a huge gold disk representing the sun covered one full wall while a sister disk of silver, supposedly to reflect the moonlight, was positioned on another wall.

Spanish chronicles recall the Europeans' astonishment when they saw Koricancha's patio filled with life-sized gold and silver statues of llamas, trees, fruits, flowers and even delicately hand-crafted butterflies. Legend has it that Atahualpa's ransom included 20 of Koricancha's life-sized golden statues of beautiful women.

The Spanish historian Pedro de Cieza de Leon wrote a description of the patio "in which the earth was lumps of fine gold… with stalks of corn that were of gold-stalks, leaves and ears… so well planted that no matter how hard the wind blew it could not uproot them. Aside from this there were more than 20 sheep of gold with their lambs and the shepherds who guarded them, with their slings and staffs, all of this metal."

Although the temple's wealth can only be imagined with the aid of such descriptions, its Inca architecture is still left standing to appreciate. Visible from inside Koricancha is the perfectly fitted curved stone wall that has survived at least two major earthquakes.

Left, exampl of the Cuzco school of colonial art. **Below**, ancient stree

Spanish chronicles also described a fabulous Hall of the Sun in Koricancha and four chapels dedicated to lesser gods, including the moon, stars, thunder and the rainbow.

The rainbow had special significance for the Incas and it remains a good omen for the Indians today. Any Peruvian child asked to draw a picture of the *sierra* or highlands almost always will sketch a house with mountains in the background and a rainbow arching the sky. It was in honor of the rainbow that the Inca flag displayed all the colors of the *arco iris*.

Chosen women: In modern Cuzco, yet another Christian enclave was formerly used as an Inca holy place. This is the **Santa Catalina Convent** that centuries ago housed a different group of cloistered females, some 3,000 Chosen Women who dedicated their lives to the sun god. Foremost among these were the *mamacunas*, consecrated women who taught religion to selected virgins called *acllas*. The *acllas* were taught to prepare the alcoholic beverage *chicha* for use in religious ceremonies, to weave and to pray. They made the fine robes that the Inca wore – only once – out of vicuña, alpaca and even a silky fabric that was made from bat skins.

An important contribution to the art world grew out of Cuzco's mixing of the Indian and Spanish cultures and the latter's failure to erase all brushings of gold. In the often violent and bloody paintings known as "School of Cuzco" style, are archangels dressed as Spaniards and carrying European guns, but surrounded by cherubs with Indian faces, or Christ appearing with Indian-looking apostles. The Virgin Mary wears Indian clothes and, in scenes of the crucifixion, Christ is hung on a cross decorated with Indian symbols.

A fine collection of this art, which flourished from the 16th through 18th centuries is found at the **Museum of Religious Art** on Calle Palacio at the corner of Hatunrumiyoc (heading downhill from the Plaza de Armas). Once the palace of Roca Inca, under whose rule Cuzco's schools were started, this now

nca wall nside the lostal oreto.

Moorish building has complicated carvings on its doors and balconies. Just outside is the famous **Twelve Angled Stone**. Called Hatunrumiyoc by the Indians, this masonry masterpiece was left by Inca architects who proved no piece of granite was too irregular to be fitted without mortar.

Heading straight up Hatunrumiyoc Street is the church of **San Blas** with its carved pulpit, said to be one of the world's finest pieces of woodwork. Made of a solid piece of wood, there is some dispute about the craftsman who produced the ornate masterpiece: some say it was an Indian leper who initiated the work after he was miraculously cured of his illness.

The streets around San Blas form Cuzco's artists' neighborhood, with galleries, studios and small shops. Heading straight back down the same street and past the Plaza de Armas takes you to **La Merced**, another important church tucked behind the Trattoria Adriano Italian restaurant and a bookstore. Destroyed by the massive earthquake in 1650, this church was erected a second time four years later. Today, it contains the remains of Francisco Pizarro's brother Gonzalo and *conquistador* Diego de Almagro, who returned to Peru after an unsuccessful search for riches in Chile. Its connected **Museum of Religious Art** contains several fine paintings, including a Rubens, and gold and silver altarpieces. The most ostentatious of these is a jewel-studded, solid gold monstrance.

Garden Square: Continuing down the same street away from the Plaza de Armas lies the **Plaza San Francisco**. This square has been planted entirely with Andean flora, including the once-outlawed amaranth grain. Here, too, is Cuzco's coat of arms featuring a castle surrounded by eight condors. The castle represents Sacsayhuaman and the emblem refers to the bitter and bloody battle fought there in 1536 as the Indians tried futilely to cast off the Spanish conquerors. The condors flying over the coat-of-arms castle vividly recall the scores of flesh-eating birds that circled

Left, Andean pipes. Below, blind musician on Calle Loreto.

192

over the Inca fort as the bodies of the dead piled up.

Plaza San Francisco is named for the 16th-century church and monastery banking one side. Simple in comparison to other houses of worship in the city, it has an extensive collection of colonial art, including a painting showing St Francis de Assisi's family tree and reportedly one of the largest canvases in South America.

Continuing down Marquéz Street past the plaza, you will find **Santa Clara Church**. Although this is part of a convent closed to the public, it is possible to enter the church for the 6am Mass. The cloistered nuns at this 16th-century religious chapel sit at the back of the church, behind a floor to ceiling metal grille, and form the church's choir. The most impressive part of this building, are the tiny mirrors covering its interior.

Returning to the Plaza de Armas and over to the corner of Tucumán and Ataud is the **Admiral's Palace**, once the home of Admiral Francisco Aldrete Maldonado and now the Regional Historical

Museum. A coat of arms over its doorway belongs to a subsequent owner, the arrogant and self-important Count of Laguna who died under mysterious circumstances. His body was found hanging in the mansion's courtyards shortly after he mistreated a priest who had complained about the count's behaviour. In that same courtyard are miniature profiles of Pizarro and Spain's Queen Isabel. An optical illusion at this house is found in a corner window column which looks like a bearded man from inside and like a nude woman from outside.

Before heading for landmarks outside the city, stop by the **Cross Keys Pub**, two blocks from the Plaza de Armas. In this city of contrasts, what could be more natural than a British-owned watering hole for offbeat travelers, cartographers, self-styled pioneers, eccentric scientists and some of the world's most famous birdwatchers. Cozy up to the bar to hear an exchange of their latest adventures and consult them on out-of-the-way tourist stops.

csayhuaman.

Post-cocktail entertainment can be found at the restaurants from which lively Andean music emanates. One of the finest floor shows takes place nightly at El Truco, where the pisco sours pack a hefty punch and the musicians and dancers are first-rate.

Eating a plate of *anticuchos*, a delicious shish-kebab of beef heart, and watching the traditionally-garbed performers singing in Quechua and playing reed flutes will make visitors temporarily forget that the Incas lost their showdown with the Spanish.

But eventually the foot-stomping dance songs will be replaced by quieter mountain music. Locals will tell how when the Spanish came and killed the last Inca, the sun god turned his back on his children – and Andean songs became melancholy.

Monolithic fortress: The best known of the ruins outside Cuzco is the overwhelming fortress of **Sacsayhuaman**, a bold showing of ancient construction skills. Made of massive stones weighing up to 17,000 kg (125 tons) apiece, this military complex overlooking Cuzco has a double wall in a zigzag shape – some say to imitate the teeth of the puma figure, whose head the fort may have formed. Sacsayhuaman also once had at least three fabulous huge towers and a labyrinth of rooms large enough to garrison 5,000 Inca soldiers. It marks the birthplace of the river that runs under Cuzco, channeled through stone conduits cut by ancient Indians to give the city an invisible water supply.

This fortress served as the focus of the Great Rebellion led by Manco Inca against the Spanish in 1536. From here, the Incas besieged Cuzco for 10 months. Historians say if Manco Inca had been able to defeat the Spanish in Cuzco, he may effectively have saved the empire. But, no matter how valiantly his troops fought and died, the Spanish responded in a desperate manner and eventually wrestled back control of the fort, Cuzco, and ultimately all Peru.

Archaeologists estimate tens of thousands of workers labored on this massive structure for up to seven decades,

The Urubamba Valley.

hauling the immense stone blocks that make up its double outside walls and erecting the near indestructible buildings that transformed the complex into one of the most wondrous in all the empire. Although the outer walls remain intact, the buildings in the complex have been destroyed – in part to provide building stones for many of the structures in Cuzco. Still, visitors to the fortress can see the so-called **Inca's Throne** from which parading troops were reviewed.

Hardy travelers reach Sacsayhuaman after a half-hour hike from Cuzco; there are also cabs available and they will wait at the summit. This is one of the area's most spectacular spots to take photos at dawn and, like much of Cuzco, provides a startling contrast of the Indian and Christian cultures. Beside this complex built during the reign of Pachacutec Inca is a giant white statue of Christ, his arms outstretched over Cuzco in the valley below.

Those seeking a quiet place for a picnic lunch or for reading will also find

it at Sacsayhuaman. Visitors perched on almost any stone there have an amazing view of the red tile roofs of Cuzco and the lush fields of the surrounding valley. The ribbon- and yarn-decorated llamas wandering through the ruins are smelly but harmless, and giggling children tending them will almost certainly ask you to take a photograph – be sure to give them a tip.

Peruvian archaeologists and Inca scholars say Sacsayhuaman is not out of danger, although it lies in ruins. They claim that the 100,000 tourists and Peruvians that annually attend the colorful Inti Raymi festival to celebrate the winter solstice – a re-enactment of one of the Incas' most important festivities – damage the fort, not only with their litter but by moving and defacing stones. There is an effort to move the festival from Sacsayhuaman but that has been met by resistance from those who insist Cuzco's largest celebration each year must be held in the Inca stronghold. Since 1944, when the outlawed June 24 celebration was publicly revived, this

Market day in Pisac.

festival has become the area's main producer of tourism revenues.

The Sacred Valley of the Incas: Fewer than 7 km (4½ miles) from Sacsayhuaman is **Quenko**, an Inca shrine with a circular amphitheater and a 5-meter (18-foot) high stone block that locals claim looks like a puma.

Its name means labyrinth and this ceremonial center – dedicated to the worship of the mother earth – includes water canals cut into solid rock and a subterranean room. Unlike Sacsayhuaman, which is a complex made up of huge stone blocks transported to the spot and assembled, Quenko was honed from a huge limestone formation found at the site. Into its walls were carved typical Inca-style niches and alcoves used to display gold and holy items in pre-Hispanic times. The shrine also contains drawings etched laboriously into its stone, among them a puma, a condor and a llama.

Farther along the road to Pisac is a smaller fortress, **Puka Pukara**, believed to have guarded the road and the Sacred Valley of the Incas. Like Machu Picchu, this pink stone complex has hillside terraces, stairways, tunnels and towers. And to the north is **Tambomachay**, the sacred bathing place for the Inca rulers and their royal women. A hydraulic engineering marvel, its aqueduct system still feeds crystalline water into a series of showers where once water rituals were held by worshippers of the sun. The ruins now consist of three massive walls of Inca stonework tucked into a hillside.

There are Peruvian historians who say this was used by Yupanqui Inca as a hunting lodge in addition to being a shrine. Some claim it was the place where the Inca leader Pachacutec received a prophetic vision of the Incas as conquerors. Others say the water running through the aqueduct came from a holy spring and this may have been one of the rare spots where sacrifices of children were made.

From Tambomachay, the journey plunges down some 400 meters (1,500 feet) into a valley on the curvy road

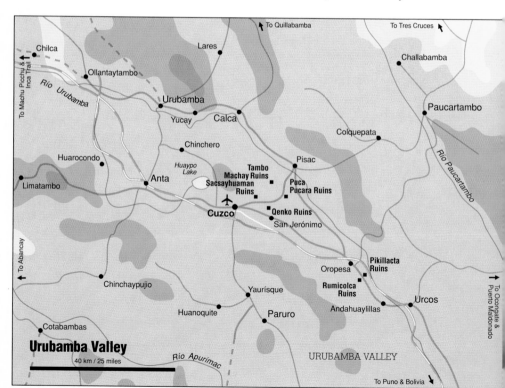

Urubamba Valley

leading to **Pisac**, a friendly village known for its good fishing, Sunday market and the ruins above the town. The ruins can be reached by climbing past the mountainside terraces (Indian children will serve as guides for a small fee). At this high altitude, even the most fit travelers find themselves winded and their hearts pounding, increasing the likelihood that they will be grateful when they round the bend on an isolated trail only to find themselves face to face with one of the many eager Inca Kola drinks vendors who are widely scattered throughout the site.

The steep farming terraces and dramatic architecture mark this one-time fortress city whose many features include ritual baths fed by aqueducts and one of the largest known Inca cemeteries. The stones making up Pisac's buildings are smaller than those at Sacsayhuaman but the precision with which they are cut and fit is amazing, as is the lovely view.

In fact, in some respects, this is more awesome stonemasonry than that of the more famous ruins at Machu Picchu. There are residential buildings and towers that some scientists say may have been astronomical observation spots. Higher up, there is a second set of ruins. Owing to the style – smaller stones more haphazardly arranged – a number of theories have arisen to explain the origin of this section. Some say it was used by servants or other community members with low social standing; another theory says it predates the main part of the complex.

Sunday festivities: Pisac's Sunday market is a riotous affair in a town where the people work hard and – apparently – play hard. The beer tent is the favorite haunt of the motley brass band that adds an increasingly out-of-tune touch to the town's festivities.

Sometimes it seems that the beer tent is the favorite stop for most of the other villagers, too. For that reason, the later in the day visitors arrive, the better their chances for some congenial bargaining for the fine alpaca blankets and sweaters available. (Although, of course, the

Pisac crafts (left) and ruins (right).

biggest selection is to be found earlier in the morning.)

Those unable to make it to Pisac should consider a trip to **Chincheros**, another spot to catch the action at a weekend market. Once again, the Indians use it as a place to buy and barter over goods as much as a spot to socialize. This "town of the rainbow", as it was known in pre-Hispanic days, has kept many of its ancient traditions and its inhabitants live in centuries-old houses, wear traditional clothing and locate their outdoor market in a plaza banked by a massive Inca wall.

It is said that Chincheros was one of the favorite spots of Tupac Inca Yupanqui, who built a palace and had farming terraces cultivated here at the mouth of the Vilcanota river. Other historians say it was an important population center in Inca times and Topa Inca, the son of Pachacutec, had an estate here. If the Inca royalty were lured to Chincheros, it might have been by the commanding view of snowcapped mountains and the river below.

To do a full circuit of the valley, it is necessary to continue on to **Urubamba** and the great fortress of **Ollantaytambo**, 72 km (45 miles) from Cuzco. Urubamba lies at the center of the valley and has a number of simple lodging houses for travelers who want to spend more than a day in this area. This is a peaceful village of flowering trees and has a strong Indian flavor.

The coat of arms on the city hall is sufficient evidence of this; no Spanish symbols are found in the emblem bearing pumas, snakes and trees. It was the beauty and calm of this village that prompted the 18th-century naturalist, Antonio de Leon Pinelo, to expound on his theory that Urubamba was actually the biblical Eden.

Fortress village: At Ollantaytambo, travelers find themselves facing an elegant and intricate walled complex containing seven rose-colored granite monoliths which puzzle scientists, who say the stone is not mined in the valley. A steep stairway enters the grouping of buildings, among which the best known

Boys at Chincheros.

is the **Temple of the Sun** – an unfinished construction in front of a wall of enormous boulders.

Portions of the original carvings on these huge worn stones can still be seen although it is unclear if they really are pumas, as some authorities claim.

Specialists say the unfinished condition of the temple has less to do with Spanish destruction of Ollantaytambo than with the fact that it was simply never completed. They point to huge boulders found at the stone quarry 6 km (3.6 miles) away, at the same time they marvel that the Indians were able to haul the massive stones over the Urubamba river and up steep grades.

Ollantaytambo, strategically placed at the northern end of the Sacred Valley, also has plazas with sacred niches, shrines, an area of stone stocks where prisoners were tied by their hands, and ritual shower areas, including the **Princess's Bath**, or Baño de la Nusta.

The village's military fortification was so well planned that it took the Spanish by surprise when they arrived in search of Manco Inca during the 1536 Indian uprising. Hernando Pizarro led a contingent of about 100 men and a number of Indian assistants to the fort with the intention of capturing and executing the rebel Indian. Chronicles say that as the Spaniards sneaked up to the fort just before dawn, they looked up to see the silhouettes of multitudes of Indian warriors ready and willing to take them on. It is even said they saw Manco Inca himself, directing troops from inside the Ollantaytambo complex while mounted on a captured horse.

In fact Manco Inca's men had diverted the Patacaucha river through some water canals and now they opened barriers that allowed the water to rush out and flood the plain the Europeans were crossing. However, the Spaniards managed to escape to Cuzco, where they recruited a force of 300 soldiers to return to confront Manco Inca. The Indian noble, outnumbered, abandoned the walled city and fled to Vilcabamba, where he was eventually killed by Spanish treachery.

Below, jewelry stall near Urubamba. Right, Ollantaytambo.

FIESTAS IN CUZCO

The dry season (May through September) is the main fiesta season throughout southern Peru, although there are some wonderful celebrations throughout the year. The good news for travelers is that there are several fiestas you can attend right in Cuzco.

Cuzco was the political and ceremonial center of the Inca empire with a major festival celebrated in the city every month. On the theory that if you can't beat them, co-opt with them, the Spanish attempted to transform Andean feast days and sacred sites into Catholic events and shrines. Building the church of Santo Domingo on top of the Temple of the Sun, Koricancha, is a perfect example of this tactic.

The wrath of God: On March 31, 1650, Cuzco was devastated by a violent earthquake, which the clergy attributed to sin and idolatry. To commemorate the disaster they hauled out an image of Christ on the cross dating from about 1560 and called it *Nuestro Señor de los Temblores* (Our Lord of the Earthquakes). The *indigenas* dubbed him Taitacha (Little Father) Temblores and credited him with saving the city from complete destruction. Every year on March 31 Taitacha was paraded through the streets of Cuzco, followed by penitents begging for protection from earthquakes. Eventually Taitacha's feast day was moved to Monday afternoon during Holy Week, the week before Easter – when it is still celebrated today. Taitacha, on a silver litter, is carried on a three-hour circuit of the city, while red flower petals are thrown in his wake, symbolizing the blood of Christ. He always stops at the church of Santa Teresa, which customarily provides his litter bearers. Thousands of Cuzqueños turn out along with the civic, religious and military hierarchies of the city.

When a severe earthquake battered Cuzco in 1950, Taitacha was set up in the Plaza de Armas for three days while

<u>Left</u>, Festival of the Sun, Sacsayhuaman.

the populace implored him to make the earth stop trembling. Shortly after Easter in 1986 another earthquake hit the city, killing several dozen residents and damaging many buildings. The word around Cuzco was that Taitacha was angry because, unlike former times, many people did not prostrate themselves during his procession. If you're in Cuzco on the Monday of Holy Week, you might put in a good word with Taitacha for all of us.

Parading mummies and saints: In June the major Inca festivals included the celebration of the rise of the Pleiades, called Collca (storehouse), about June 8 and the winter solstice festival, Inti Raymi, on June 21. At important Inca celebrations, the mummies of the dead Inca rulers and their queens were carried on litters to visit one another (presumably to gossip and consult on matters of import) and then to the Cusipata (now the Plaza de Armas) where they sat in state. If you're in Cuzco during the Corpus Christi fiesta, you will see vestiges of this tradition.

Corpus Christi (in honor of the Eucharist) is a moveable feast, held on the Thursday after Trinity Sunday. It usually falls in early to mid-June. On Wednesday, the vespers of the fiesta, 13 statues of saints and of the Virgin are brought into Cuzco from their churches in Cuzco's *barrios* and suburbs. Effigies of San Sebastián and San Gerónimo race into Cuzco from the little towns of those names, borne on enormous litters by their devotees and led by a brass band and the faithful of the parish carrying banners and candles. San Sebastián and San Gerónimo and eight or nine other statues pay an overnight visit to the Virgen of Belén in Santa Clara Church in Cuzco, where presumably they all catch up on the news of the year just like the Inca mummies.

On Corpus Christi the Plaza de Armas comes alive. Large altars decorated with flowers, tin, mirrors, crosses and images of the sun are erected on three sides of the plaza and vendors set up booths with food prepared especially for Corpus. These treats, well worth sampling, in-

Twirling in the square.

202

clude *chiriuchu*, made with guinea pig, chicken, corn, cheese, eggs and peppers; and baked *achira*, a rhizome that resembles the sweet potato.

Precious metals: After high Mass, the statues are paraded around the plaza, stopping to bow at each altar – no mean feat when some of the gilded and silver-covered palequins weigh up to a ton. It's an honor to be a litter-bearer and some of the men wear traditional carrying-cloths on their backs, a symbol of humility since Inca times. Each parish has its own brass band, costumed dance groups and devotees, and the plaza is a melange of color and sound. At the end of the procession comes the priest bearing the Eucharist, almost forgotten in the crush.

Slip inside the cathedral if you can because some of the old women remain there to sing Quechua hymns before their patron saint in the high, bird-like voices typical of traditional music.

A week later, the statues are again paraded around the Plaza de Armas and then taken home. If you're in Cuzco in

June, the sound of music or fireworks coming from the center of town should bring you to the Plaza on the run.

Most travelers come to Cuzco for Inti Raymi (the Festival of the Sun) on June 24 and miss Corpus Christi, which is a shame, since Corpus is an authentic local celebration. Still, Inti Raymi isn't just for tourists. If you want to see Inti Raymi be sure to make hotel reservations and arrive by June 20 because the city is mobbed.

Bringing back the sun: Inti Raymi was the Inca winter solstice celebration, held on June 21 or 22. Conveniently for the Spanish, the Catholic feast of Saint John the Baptist (San Juan Bautista) falls on June 24, so the solstice events could be transferred to an ostensibly Christian fiesta. The fires that burn throughout the night of June 23 don't have much to do with John the Baptist. They're lit to bring back the sun during the longest nights and shortest days of the year.

In the 1940s residents of Cuzco revived Inti Raymi, basing their fiesta on colonial accounts of the Inca festival. On June 24, *campesinos*, townspeople and travelers all head to the fortress of Sacsayhuaman for a pageant that combines the hokey and the authentic in a slightly surreal manner. In comes the Inca-for-a-day on a litter, dressed in tin foil and cheap cloth, with a palace guard consisting of costumed Peruvian army troops. Off go the dancers from the mountains beyond Ollantaytambo, in hand-woven clothes that would have made the Inca Pachacuti proud.

The pageant, in which the fires of the empire are ceremonially relit, a llama is "sacrificed" to the sun, and music and dance groups perform, lasts about three hours, but the city becomes a giant fair for the entire week. It's irresistible, but do watch for pickpockets in the crowd.

On Christmas Eve there is a beautiful festival in Cuzco's Plaza de Armas and side streets called Santo Rantikuy (Saint Buying). People come into Cuzco to buy and sell *nacimientos* (Nativity sets). You will see crafts for sale that are available only that day, including locally made statues of the holy family and the three kings.

ie band.

AYACUCHO

In common with much of the central highlands, **Ayacucho** has found itself isolated from the rest of the country for long intervals. The gentle city had no link to the Pacific coast until a road was built in the 1920s and, as late as the 1960s, car and truck traffic between the highland town and Lima was limited. Then, in the 1980s, terrorism made Ayacucho a pariah once again.

The periods of isolation mean the city has not seen the modernization of other areas. For local residents, this translates into many homes without electricity or running water. For visitors, it means the city has maintained its colonial architecture without encroachment, like a spot lost in time.

Terrorism: Celebrated for centuries as a city of churches and handicrafts, Ayacucho's reputation took a plunge in the 1980s when it became the stronghold of Sendero Luminoso (Shining Path) terrorists. Abimael Guzman, the mastermind in the terrorist organization (and now serving a life sentence in prison), launched his violent revolution from the University of Huamanga, where he taught philosophy. In the years to follow, frightened Ayacuchanos, as local are known, fled the region, the government declared the city under military control and tourism became a thing of the past.

But, by late 1993, the terrorist activity in the lovely city with a temperate climate had all but disappeared and families and visitors began returning. It would be a shame to visit Peru and miss this peaceful, place of 150,000 people, with its outstanding crafts traditions and its colonial mansions – especially since there are now daily flights to Ayacucho from Lima and thrice-weekly flights direct from Cuzco.

Ayacucho, founded in 1540 and first named Huamanga after the alabaster used in its handicrafts, is a town to explore on foot. Its reputation as a city with "a church on every street corner" is exaggerated, but only just, for it boasts 33 *iglesias,* the majority of which are still in use. Among the most impressive is the **cathedral** on Plaza Sucre. Built in 1612 with superb gilt altars, a silver tabernacle and a carved pulpit, the cathedral contains Stations of the Cross paintings brought from Rome. During Holy Week, for which Ayacucho's religious processions and ceremonies are legendary, this is one of the most visited churches in Peru. The faithful gather at the cathedral on the eve of Palm Sunday for a dramatic candlelight procession with a Christ statue transported on the back of a white donkey.

Another outstanding church, **La Compañia**, was built in 1605, and boasts an unusual carved facade of orange-red stone and a lovely gold-covered main altar. The interior bursts with carved wood and a good collection of colonial religious art.

A few blocks away, **Iglesia Santo Domingo** features an altar covered in golf leaf, but it is this church's historical role that is most significant. Bells in its small towers rang out the first peals of Peru's independence following the Battle of Ayacucho, which brought Spanish rule to an end. At the corner of Calle Garcilaso de la Vega and Jirón Callao, the **Iglesia San Francisco de Paula**, constructed in 1674, is home to the finest carved pulpit in the city and a series of Flemish paintings.

Although Spanish colonial architecture marks Ayacucho, this was an important spot for several pre-Hispanic cultures. Five hundred years before the Incas, the Wari empire dominated the highlands here and traces of that culture's influence can be seen at the **Hipólito Unanue Anthropology and Archaeology Museum**.

The museum's collection ranges from 1500 BC stone carvings – early evidence of the stoneworking excellence that would become synonymous with the region – to Wari ceremonial cups, Huarpa culture decorative pieces, Chancay textiles and Inca stone and ceramic items. Displays also include artifacts from the Moche, Nazca, Chimú and Ica cultures. The museum awaits funding – not likely in the near future – so it can display its

eceding
ges:
elcoming
ces. Left,
lonial
trance arch
Ayacucho.

colonial and republican-era holdings now in storage.

Mansions: Despite their rich pre-Inca past, Ayacucho residents are proudest of their *casonas históricas*, centuries-old mansions constructed during Peru's colonial years of the 1600s and 1700s. **Casona Vivanco**, one of the best preserved, houses the **Museo Andrés A. Cáceres**. It contains the uniforms, personal papers, furniture, paintings and other effects of Cáceres, an Ayacuchano whose ascent through the military ranks stemmed from his successful organization of *campesinos* in the Andean resistance during Peru's otherwise disastrous performance in the War of the Pacific with Chile. He became president of Peru in 1886.

The patio of the Cáceres mansion displays the sculpture/gravestone known as **Checo Pacheco**, an early 1700s representation of Spanish *conquistador* Alfares Real Juan Gutiérrez de Quintanilla. (Checo refers to the type of stone used and Pacheco is the surname of the sculptor.) A small gallery in the house exhibits modern paintings, folk art and handicrafts.

The city's **Prefecture** is tucked within another colonial house, a two-story mansion erected in 1748. In addition to a lovely interior patio, the structure contains a room used as the cell of María Parado de Bellido, a local independence-era heroine held prisoner until she was executed by a firing squad in 1822.

Crafts abound in Ayacucho and a good spot for purchases is the Santa Ana neighborhood where family workshops are crowded with filigree and silverwork, little painted portable altars known as *retablos*, carvings in Huamanga stone and carved dried gourds.

Shopping is also a lively experience at the city's labyrinth-like market a block south of Avenida San Martín. Here, highland men and women hawk everything from sweaters and handicrafts to rubber boots and hot peppers. Delicious hot bread, spiced with cinnamon and anise, is sold fresh from cloth-covered baskets, as are the various herbal drinks called *emolientes*. You can safely try

Ayacucho is famed for its churches.

the bread, but leave the drinks to the locals; the glasses usually are not properly washed.

The list of regional cuisine, while flavorful, is a short one led by *puca picante*, a spicy Ayacucho stew of pork, potatoes and toasted peanuts served with rice and parsley. This city is also the spot to try *ponche*, a hot milk-based cocktail flavored with peanut, sesame, clove, cinnamon, walnuts and sugar and spiked with pisco. These regional dishes emerge in full force during the city's multiple holidays, led by Holy Week, where each day is marked by agricultural fairs, colorful religious festivals, folk dancing contests and art shows. On the first three days of November, meanwhile, Ayacuchanos congregate at cemeteries to remember their deceased. Locals meet at the grave sites with big baskets of food, including sweet bread loafs shaped like horses and babies.

Battle site: In the rolling hills outside town sits **Quinua**, 37 km (22 miles) northeast of Ayacucho. This was the site of the decisive Battle of Ayacucho

on December 9, 1824. A white obelisk on a plain near the village indicates the site of the skirmish, which brought colonial rule to an end. The event is marked by an eight-day extravaganza each December. Merrymaking, folk dancing and craft exhibitions are central to the celebrations, which include the rollicking Scissors Dance in which leaping men in colorful Spanish-style garb dance with comically oversized scissors in their hands.

Most of the roofs of Quinua's houses are topped with good luck symbols: small ceramic churches decorated with painted flowers or ears of corn. This pottery town, famed for its brown-toned miniature churches, also turns out handmade guitars, figurines in Huamanga stone and fat ceramic bulls with small heads and strong legs. Made originally for festivals coinciding with the branding of cattle, the bulls are a throwback to a turbulent time. Peruvian author José María Arguedas, in his moving novel *Yawar Fiesta*, took a vivid look at an Indian community near Ayacucho in the 1920s, when land battles between small farmers and big cattle ranchers touched off violent uprisings of indigenous people.

Minibuses commute at regular intervals between Ayacucho and Quinua; Morocucho Tours at Portal Constitución 14 in Ayacucho offers Quinua tours with English-speaking guides. Morocucho Tours also operates outings to **Vilcashuamán**, once an Inca administrative center and now a hybrid village with Spanish constructions atop Inca architecture southeast of Ayacucho.

Outside the town, the ruins of **Intihuatana** (a 30-minute walk from the highway) are located beside an Inca-built lagoon. The complex consists of an Inca palace, tower, Temple of the Sun, sacrificial stone and a boulder with 17 angles.

This area is a good spot for fishing; no licenses are necessary but there are seasons for different fish. It is also in this valley that *puya raymondi* thrives. This odd-looking plant lives to be 100 years old but dramatically flowers only after 80 years of growth.

elebrating oly Week ith local iigree.

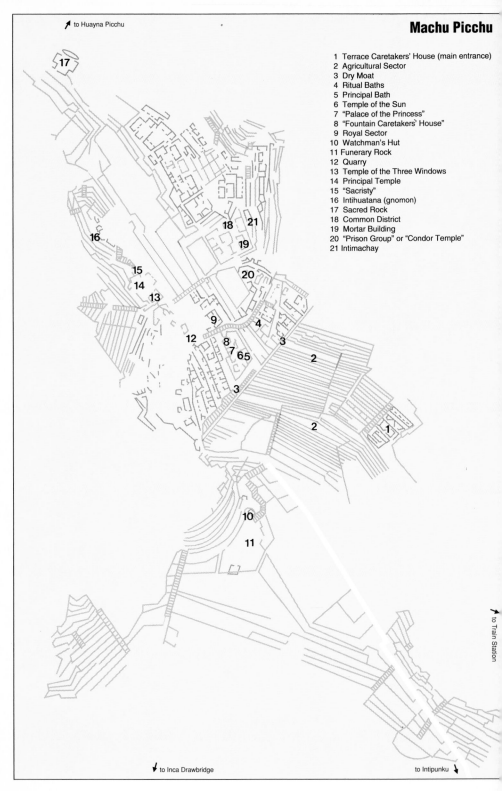

to Huayna Picchu

Machu Picchu

1 Terrace Caretakers' House (main entrance)
2 Agricultural Sector
3 Dry Moat
4 Ritual Baths
5 Principal Bath
6 Temple of the Sun
7 "Palace of the Princess"
8 "Fountain Caretakers' House"
9 Royal Sector
10 Watchman's Hut
11 Funerary Rock
12 Quarry
13 Temple of the Three Windows
14 Principal Temple
15 "Sacristy"
16 Intihuatana (gnomon)
17 Sacred Rock
18 Common District
19 Mortar Building
20 "Prison Group" or "Condor Temple"
21 Intimachay

to Train Station

to Inca Drawbridge

to Intipunku

MACHU PICCHU

When Hiram Bingham stumbled across **Machu Picchu** in July 1911, he was actually searching for the ruins of Vilcabamba, the remote stronghold of the last Incas. Today we know that he almost certainly found Vilcabamba without realizing it, when he visited the jungle-covered ruins of Espíritu Pampa, some 100 km (620 miles) west of Machu Picchu, two months before his spectacular find on the Urubamba gorge. But Bingham saw only a small part of Espíritu Pampa, and dismissed it as insignificant. Considering what he found later, who can blame him?

Bingham was a Yale graduate, later a US Senator, who became fascinated with Inca archaeology in 1909, while in Peru studying Bolívar's independence struggle. He returned with the Yale Peruvian expedition in 1911, and took the narrow mule trail down the Urubamba gorge in July of that year. Melchor Arteaga, a local *campesino* whom he met by chance while camping on the river banks, led him to the jungle-covered ruins.

The locals called the mountain above the saddle-ridge where the ruins were located Machu Picchu – Ancient Peak; and its sister mountain was Huayna Picchu – Young Peak. But Bingham felt that the real name of these ruins should be Vilcabamba. He believed he had discovered the last refuge of the Incas. More than that, he also speculated this was Tampu Tocco, the mythical birthplace of the Ayar brothers, founding ancestors of the Incas.

Bingham's mistake in thinking he had found the location of Vilcabamba is understandable. Who would imagine there was not one, but two lost cities in the jungle north of Cuzco? But today there is overwhelming evidence against the Machu Picchu-as-Vilcabamba hypothesis. So Bingham presented us with an enigma even deeper than he imagined. If Machu Picchu was not Vilcabamba, then what was it?

Outpost in a "lost" province: Bingham had carried out further explorations between 1911 and 1915, discovering a string of other ruins and a major Inca highway (now known as the Inca Trail) to the south of Machu Picchu. Later still, in 1941, the Viking Fund expedition led by Paul Fejos discovered the important ruins of Huiñay Huayna above the Urubamba gorge, about 4½ km (3 miles) due south of Machu Picchu. Thus, Machu Picchu was not merely a lost city, but part of an entire lost region – a fact generally ignored by popular histories. The usual account portrays Machu Picchu as some secret refuge known only to a select few, and concealed from the Spaniards. But this would have been impossible; the location of an entire active and populated region could not have been concealed from the Spaniards, who had many Indian allies.

And yet the Spaniards did *not* know of Machu Picchu's existence. How? The only possible conclusion is that the Incas did not know of it either. Somehow the city and its region were abandoned and depopulated before the Conquest, and the memory lost even to the Incas themselves. Perhaps the area was devastated by plague, or overrun by the Antis, the fierce jungle tribesmen. But then, why the total amnesia concerning its location? This cannot have been accidental. The Incas had a caste of *quipucamayocs* – oral history recorders – who kept detailed accounts of the Inca past. But this was *official* history, and the Incas are notorious among modern historians for wiping inconvenient details off the record. Perhaps this was Machu Picchu's fate: a province that rebelled and was dealt with so ruthlessly that its existence was erased from official memory.

Well, the foregoing is simply one theory that fits the known facts. Here is another: according to new evidence unearthed from Spanish colonial archives, and recently presented by the archaeologist J.H. Rowe, there was a "royal estate" (sort of a Western concept, but how else to put it?) of the emperor Pachacuti at a place called "Picchu," north of Cuzco. This leads to an interpretation that Machu Picchu was built and populated by the *panaca* (royal house) of Pachacuti, and that the eventual disappearance of the *panaca*, a generation or so after Pachacuti's death, led to the depopulation and abandonment of the region.

Signs of a pre-Inca occupation at Machu Picchu, going back 2,000 years, have recently been discovered, but there was certainly no pre-Inca city of any consequence here. If we accept that Machu Picchu was built for Pachacuti, we can speak of the construction dates of Machu Picchu with reasonable confidence. According to a widely accepted chronology, the Inca expansion began in the year 1438, after Pachacuti's defeat of the Chanca invasion from the north. Various chronicles tell us that for strategic reasons (to keep the retreating Chancas out) this mountainous area was the first to be settled in the headlong rush toward empire.

The building style of Machu Picchu is "late imperial Inca," which supports this thesis, and there are no signs of post-Conquest occupation. So Machu Picchu was built, occupied and abandoned in the space of less than 100 years. The rest is speculation. And who can resist speculating when faced with something as affecting and impenetrable as the mystery of these silent stones?

Piecing together the past: What kind of settlement was Machu Picchu? John Hemming states that the site has only 200 habitation structures, leading him to estimate a permanent population of about 1,000 people. It is interesting that the agricultural output of the area would have greatly exceeded the needs of the population; for, besides the large extension of agricultural terracing at Machu Picchu itself, there were also much larger terraced areas at Inti Pata (just behind Machu Picchu peak to the southwest), and Huiñay Huayna along the Inca Trail. More than one archaeologist has lately proposed that the principal material function of the Machu Picchu region was to create a reliable supply of coca leaves for the priests and royals of Cuzco.

Hiram Bingham called the ruin a "citadel," existing for strategic and defensive purposes. But besides its outer walls

A guide explains the ruins.

and moat, Machu Picchu contains an unusually high proportion and quality of religious architecture. Modern opinion leans more to the view that Machu Picchu was essentially a site of spiritual and ceremonial significance, with important agricultural functions. Its strategic purposes, if any, were secondary.

Bingham's fortress idea did not prevent him from speculating that the city was a refuge of Cuzco's Virgins of the Sun, an idea inspired by the revelation that more than 75 percent of the skeletal remains found there were from females. This exciting piece of news has been on the lips of tour guides ever since. Yet there is a difficulty with the argument. The Yale expedition found only skulls, the other bones having disintegrated in the humid climate. It is extremely hard to pronounce on the gender of a skull, particularly if, like the expedition's medical authority Dr Eaton, you are not very familiar with bones of the racial sub-group it comes from. Dr Eaton pronounced most of the skulls "gracile," and therefore, he assumed, female. But

they could as easily have been young or small men. The skulls still exist, and could be studied again by modern experts, but so far no-one has done it.

Allegedly, the terms of Bingham's permission to excavate at Machu Picchu were unclear. This led to vague accusations of smuggling after he shipped all his relics back to Yale University, where most of them remain to this day. There were no precious metals, however, and it is not a visually spectacular collection, so the dispute is mainly for scholars.

Breakthroughs in archaeology: Since 1985 an astonishing number of new discoveries have been made around Machu Picchu. Taken as a whole they support and expand the emerging view of Machu Picchu as the ceremonial and possibly administrative center of a huge and quite populous region. The alluring myth of Machu Picchu as some kind of Andean Shangri-la perched alone on its remote crag must now be laid to rest.

The most extensive finds have been made across the river to the northeast,

ca
rraces.

on a sloping plateau known as Mandor-pampa about 100 meters (328 feet) above the railroad. Its outstanding feature is an enormous wall about 3.5 meters high by 2.5 meters wide (11.5 by 8.2 feet), and more than a kilometer long, which runs straight up the mountainside, toward a pointy peak known as Yanantin. It was apparently built to protect the adjacent agricultural terraces from erosion, and may also have served to demarcate two areas with separate functions.

A road running along its top heads off northeast into densely forested mountains towards Amaybamba, or perhaps some other Inca settlement yet undiscovered. Other finds on the pampa include quarries, circular buildings, a large number of stone mortars, and a large observation platform.

Closer to Machu Picchu itself, the sector on the north slope of Huayna Picchu known as the "Temple of the Moon" has been cleared to reveal a subterranean temple, a fine wall with an imposing gateway, and an observatory directed toward the aforementioned Yanantin peak.

Farther upriver two important burial sites known as Killipata and Ch'askapata have been discovered, and the ruins of Choquesuysuy, just upstream from the hydroelectric project, now appear to be much larger than had been previously believed. Of all these sites only the Temple of the Moon has been opened to the public so far.

In the years following Bingham's discovery the ruins were cleared of vegetation, excavations were made, and later a railroad was blasted out of the sheer granite cliffs of the imposing canyon. Visitors began to arrive. Pablo Neruda came in 1942, and was inspired to write his most famous poem. In 1948 a sinuous 12-km (7-mile) road from the river banks to the ruins was inaugurated by Hiram Bingham himself.

A walking tour of the ruins: Bingham classified the ruins into sectors, naming some of the buildings, and so on. But some of his conclusions appear wide of the mark to modern archaeologists; others seem too arbitrary, resting on minimal evidence. However, for the sake of clear directions we need to name different sectors, and since nobody has come up with a better system than Bingham's, here we go:

You enter the ruins through the **"House of the Terrace Caretakers"** (1), (see map) which flank the **Agricultural Sector** (2). This great area of terracing was undoubtedly for agricultural purposes, and made the city self-sufficient in crops. The terraces end in a **Dry Moat** (3), beyond which lies the city itself.

If you continue straight ahead you come to the **Fountains** (4), which are actually small waterfalls, in a chain of 16 little "baths," varying in the quality of their construction. These were probably for ritual, religious purposes relating to the worship of water. Bingham speculated that Machu Picchu might have been abandoned because this water supply dried up, or became inadequate to irrigate the terraces. The hotel consumes most of this spring water today. The **Main Fountain** (5) is so called because it has the finest stonework and the most important location; it is just above you to the left as you arrive from the terraces.

Here, too, is the **Temple of the Sun** (6). This round tapering tower features the most perfect stonework found in Machu Picchu. It contains sacred niches for holding idols or offerings, and the centerpiece is a great rock, part of the actual outcrop on to which the temple is built. The base of this rock forms a grotto which is casually referred to as the Royal Tomb, although no bones were found there.

Recent archaeo-astronomical studies have shown how this temple served as an astronomical observatory. The rock in the center of the tower has a straight edge cut into it. This is precisely aligned through the adjacent window to the rising point of the sun on the morning of the June solstice. The pegs on the outside of the window may have been used to support a shadow-casting device, which would have made observation simpler.

The temple's entranceway has holes drilled about the jamb, less complex

View through a trapezoid window.

than a similar doorway at the Korican-cha in Cuzco. The adjacent building (7) has two stories and was obviously the house of someone important. Bingham named it the **Palace of the Princess.**

Next to the Sun Temple, just above the main fountain, is a three-walled house (8), which has been restored and its roof thatched as an example of how these structures looked in Inca times. It is usually called the **Fountain Caretaker's House** – but it's unlikely to have been a house at all, since it is open to the elements on one side. The thick stone pegs fixed high up in the wall are thought to have served as hangers for heavy objects.

Students of the more esoteric aspects of the Inca culture have suggested that this complex of adjacent structures forms a temple to the four elements: the Temple of the Sun (Fire); the "Royal Tomb" (Earth); the open-fronted "Fountain Caretaker's House" (Air); the Principal Fountain (Water).

The structures directly opposite the Sun Temple, across the staircase, have been classified as the **Royal Sector** (9), because of the roominess of the buildings, and also for the huge rock lintels (weighing up to 3 tons) which generally characterized the homes of the mighty in Inca architecture.

At the top of the agricultural terraces, high above the city, stands a lone hut (10) that backs on to a gently-sloping area known as the cemetery. Bingham found many bones and mummies at this spot. This is a great place for an overall view of the ruins. A few meters from the hut lies a curiously-shaped carved rock (11), called the **Funeral Rock.** Bingham speculated that this rock was used as a place of lying-in-state for the dead, or as a kind of mortician's slab, on which bodies were eviscerated and dried by the sun for mummification.

Mysterious stone: At the top of the staircase leading up from the fountains you come to a great jumble of rocks (12) that served as a quarry for the Inca masons. There is a fascinating discovery in this sector – a partially-split rock that seems to show precisely how the builders cut stone from the quarry. The

rock bears a line of wedge-shaped cuts where tools were hammered in to form a crack. The problem with this rock, though, is that it was reportedly cut by a 20th-century archaeologist, Dr Manuel Chavez Ballon!

Follow the ridge away from the quarry with your back to the staircase, and you come to one of the most interesting areas of the city. Here is the **Temple of the Three Windows** (13). Its east wall is built on a single huge rock; the trapezoidal windows are partly cut into it. On the empty side of this three-walled building stands a stone pillar which once supported the roof. On the ground by this pillar is a rock bearing the sacred step-motif common to many other Inca and pre-Inca temples.

Next to this site stands the **Principal Temple** (14), another three-walled building with immense foundation rocks and artfully-cut masonry. It is named for its size and quality, and also because it is the only temple with a kind of sub-temple attached to it. This is generally called the **Sacristy** (15), because it seems

The trail to Huayna Picchu.

218

a suitable place for the priests to have prepared themselves before sacred rites. The stone which forms part of the left-hand door-jamb has no fewer than 32 corners in its separate faces.

Ascending the mound beyond this temple leads you to what was probably the most important of all the many shrines at Machu Picchu, the **Intihuatana** (16), the so-called "Hitching Post of the Sun." This term was popularized by the American traveler Squier in the 19th century. But nobody has ever unraveled the mystery of how this stone and others like it were used. Every major Inca center had one. It seems likely that the stones somehow served for making astronomical observations and calculating the passing seasons. There was at least one other "Intihuatana" in the vicinity, located near the hydro-electric power station in the valley below, to the west. The second stone was probably situated to make a specific astronomical alignment with the main one. The main Intihuatana is a sculpture of surpassing beauty. It is the only one in all Peru to have escaped the diligent attention of the Spanish "extirpators of idolatry" and luckily survive in its original condition.

The group of buildings across the large grassy plaza below comprises another, more utilitarian sector of the city. At the north end, farthest from the entrance to the ruins, you find two three-sided buildings opening onto a small plaza, which is backed by a huge rock (17) generally called the **Sacred Rock**. An intriguing aspect of this plaza is that the outline of the great flat rock erected at the northeast edge is shaped to form a visual tracing of the mountain skyline behind it. Then, if you step behind the masma (three-sided hut) on the southeast edge and look northwest, you find another rock that echoes the skyline of the small outcrop named **Uña Huayna Picchu** in the same way.

Walking back towards the main entrance along the east flank of the ridge you pass through a large district of cruder constructions that has been labeled the **Common District** (18). At the end of this sector you come to a building with two curious disc-shapes cut into the stone of the floor (19). Each is about two feet in diameter, flat, with a low rim carved around the edge. Bingham called these mortars for grinding corn, but this is doubtful. True, he did find some pestle stones in the same building, but the normal mortar used by the Quechua Indians today is much deeper and more rounded within; also it is portable, not fixed in one spot. These "mortars" would not have served well for that function. However, to date nobody has suggested a more plausible explanation than Bingham's for these enigmatic carvings.

Just across the next staircase you come to a deep hollow surrounded by walls and niches, which is known as the **Temple of the Condor** (20). Bingham called this the Prison Group, because there are vaults below ground, and man-sized niches with holes that might have been used for binding wrists. But the concept of "prison" probably did not exist in Inca society; punishments tended to involve loss of privileges, or physical suffering, or death. Some early Span-

he view om Huayna icchu.

iards reported pits full of snakes or pumas into which offenders were dropped to see if they would survive, but this is hardly a prison. The complex was probably a temple. A rock at the bottom of this hollow bears a stylized carving, apparently a condor, with the shape of the head and the ruff at the neck clearly discernible.

There is a small cave known as Intimachay (21) above and to the east of the Condor Temple. It has been identified as a solar observatory for marking the December solstice. The cave is faced with coursed masonry and features a window carved out of a boulder that forms part of the front wall. This window is precisely aligned with the winter solstice sunrise, so that morning light falls on the back wall of the cave for 10 days before and after that date.

Further explorations: Having seen the Machu Picchu ruins proper, there are three short walks worth attempting.

Firstly, above the ruins to the southeast you can see a pass scooped out of the ridge, with a small ruin at the center. This is **Intipunku**, the Sun Gate. You can actually see the sun rise in this gateway from the western heights of the ruins at certain times of year. The trail that you can see traversing the mountainside from this point was the main Inca highway from Huiñay Huayna and other sites farther south. It is well preserved, and makes for a fairly easy climb, taking about an hour and a half there and back. The view of Machu Picchu from Intipunku is magnificent.

The second walk is to the **Inca Drawbridge.** A trail winds back from the heights of the ruins, by the cemetery, leading along the west flank of the mountain behind Machu Picchu. This trail grows narrower, until it is cut into the side of a sheer precipice, and you find yourself taking each step with care. Follow it until you come to a spot so abrupt that the ancients had to build a huge stone buttress to create a ledge for the path to cross. They left a strategic gap in the middle of the buttress, bridged by logs which could be withdrawn. Beyond this point the trail quickly peters out, becoming unstable and extremely dangerous. The path has been fenced off shortly before the bridge, ever since a man tried to hike beyond it and fell to his death. To the bridge and back is an exciting one-hour walk demanding a cool head for heights.

Hardy visitors also like to climb **Huayna Picchu**, the towering granite peak that overlooks Machu Picchu from the north. The path is very steep; it's the original Inca path, stepped in places. Approach it with caution – but don't be put off by the peak's fearsome appearance. You don't have to be a mountaineer. If you are reasonably active and healthy you will get to the top – and back. Everyone planning to climb Huayna Picchu must sign in at the control point along the trail leaving the principal ruins. Start before 1pm, as visitors are barred from starting the climb after that time.

As you near the top of Huayna Picchu you pass through ancient terraces so inaccessible and so narrow that their value for agricultural purposes would have been negligible. Hence, it's thought that these were probably ornamental gardens, to be admired from the city below. About one to one and a half hours gets the average person to the peak for a stupendous view.

The **Temple of the Moon** stands inside a cavern halfway down the north face of Huayna Picchu. It was discovered as recently as 1936, and contains some of the finest stonework of the entire Machu Picchu complex. The Inca pathway which leads to the temple forks off the main trail to the left about one third of the way up to the peak of Huayna Picchu.

Physically active people staying overnight at Machu Picchu can also consider taking the **Inca Trail** to **Huiñay Huayna**. The round-trip takes about four hours, including some time to look at the ruins. (Note: they charge the Inca Trail fee, minus entrance fee to Machu Picchu, for this hike.) The journey itself is rewarding, since the trail passes through exotic tropical forest, and is worth the effort. It is also possible to spend the night at the basic hostel at Huiñay Huayna, and return to Machu Picchu the following morning.

Dawn on the winter solstice at the Temple of the Sun.

LAKE TITICACA

Lake Titicaca is the world's highest navigable lake and the center of a region where thousands of subsistence farmers eke out a living fishing in its icy waters, growing potatoes in the rocky land at its edge or herding llama and alpaca at altitudes that leave Europeans and North Americans gasping for air. It is also where traces of the rich Indian past still stubbornly cling, resisting in past centuries the Spanish conquistadors' aggressive campaign to erase Inca and pre-Inca cultures and, in recent times, the lure of modernization.

When Peruvians talk of turquoise blue Titicaca, they proudly note that it is so large it has waves. This, the most sacred body of water in the Inca empire and now the natural separation between Peru and Bolivia, has a surface area exceeding 8,000 square kilometers (3,100 square miles), not counting its more than 30 islands. At 3,856 meters (12,725 feet) above sea level it has two climates: chilly and rainy or chilly and dry. In the evenings it becomes quite cold, dropping below freezing from June through August. In the day, the sun is intense and sunburn is common.

According to legend, this lake gave birth to the Inca civilization. Before the Incas, the lake and its islands were holy for the Aymará Indians, whose civilization was centered at the Tiahuanaco, now a complex of ruins on the Bolivian side of Titicaca but once a revered temple site with notably advanced irrigation techniques.

Geologically, Titicaca's origins are disputed, although it was likely a glacial lake. Maverick scientists claim it had a volcanic start; a century ago, Titicaca was popularly believed to be an immense mountain-top crater. A few diehards today stick to the notion that the lake was part of a massive river system from the Pacific Ocean.

Indian legend says the sun god had his children, Manco Capac and his sister-consort Mama Ocllo, spring from the frigid waters of the lake to found Cuzco

and the beginning of the Inca dynasty. Later, during the Spanish Conquest, the lake allegedly became a secret depository for the empire's gold. Among the items supposedly buried on the lake's bottom is Inca Huascar's gold chain weighing 2,000 kilos (4,400 lbs) and stored in Koricancha – the Temple of the Sun in Cuzco – until loyal Indians threw it into the lake to prevent it from falling into Spanish hands.

Oceanographer Jacques Yves Cousteau spent eight weeks using mini submarines to explore the depths of the lake but found no gold. (What he did discover, to the amazement of the scientific world, was a 60-centimeter (24-in) long, tri-colored frog that apparently never surfaces!)

Urban base: On the Peruvian side of the lake is **Puno**, an unattractive commercial center settled as a Spanish community in 1668 by the Count of Lemos. Although today Puno seems unappealing, during the Spanish period it was one of the continent's richest cities because of its proximity to the Laykakota

Preceding pages, totora reed raft on Lake Titicaca. **Left**, tapestries for sale on the Uros islands. **Right**, a llama by the lakeside.

silver mines discovered by brothers Gaspar and José Salcedo in 1657. The mining boom drew 10,000 people to an area not far from what is now Puno. It also brought a bloody rivalry that ended only when the iron-handed count traveled to Puno, ordered José Salcedo executed and transferred Laykakota's residents to Puno.

At an altitude of 3,827 meters (12,628 feet), Puno is still the capital Peru's *altiplano* – the harsh highland region much better suited to roaming vicuñas and alpacas than to people. It is also Peru's folklore center with a rich array of handicrafts, costumes, holidays, legends and, most importantly, more than 300 ethnic dances.

Among the latter, the most famous is Devil dance performed during the feast of the Virgin of Candelaria during the first two weeks in February. Dancers fiercely compete to outdo one another in this *Diablada*, notable for its profusion of costly and grotesque masks. The origins of the dance have become confused over the centuries but it is be-lieved to have started with pre-Inca Indian cultures, surviving through the Inca conquest and the Spanish takeover of the country, with the costumes being modified each time.

Dance and wild costumes: As numerous as the dances themselves are the lavish and colorful outfits the dancers wear. They range from multi-hued *polleras* (layered skirts) donned by barefoot female dancers to the short skirts, fringed shawls and bowler hats used in the highland version of the *marinera* dance. For centuries the Indians in the *altiplano* were accustomed to working hard, then celebrating their special days with gusto. In fact, many of the dances incorporate features of the most repressive times for the Indians with dancers dressed as mine overseers or cruel landowners – characters that are mocked during the festivities. It is difficult to find a month in Puno without at least one elaborate festival, which is always accompanied by music and dance.

Within Puno, there remain a handful of buildings worth seeing. The **cathe-**

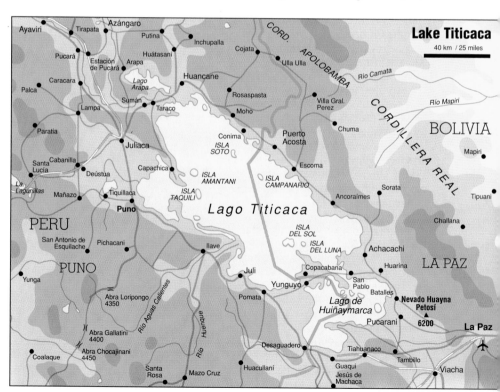

dral is a magnificent stone structure dating back to 1757 with a weather-beaten baroque-style exterior and a surprisingly spartan interior – except for its center altar of carved marble which is plated in silver.

Over a side-altar to the right side of the church is the icon of The Lord of Agony, commonly known as *El Señor de la Bala*. Beside the cathedral is the famous **Balcony of the Count of Lemos** found on an old house on the corners of Deustua and Conde de Lemos streets. It is said that Peru's Viceroy Don Pedro Antonio Fernandez de Castro Andrade y Portugal – the count – stayed here when he first arrived in the city he later named "San Carlos de Puno."

On the **Plaza de Armas** is the **library** and the municipal *pinacoteca*, or **art gallery** and half a block off the plaza is the **Museo Carlos Dreyer**, a collection of Nazca, Tiahuanaco, Paracas, Chimú and Inca artifacts bequeathed to the city upon the death of their owner, for whom the museum is named.

One of the museum's most valuable pieces is an Aymará *arybalo*, the delicate pointed-bottomed pottery whose wide belly curves up to a narrow neck. Throughout the South American continent, the *arybalo* stands as a symbol of the Andean culture.

Views of the Sierra: Three blocks uphill from the plaza is **Huajsapata Park**, actually a hill that figures in the lyrics of local songs and an excellent spot for a panoramic view of Puno. Huajsapata is topped by a huge white statue of Manco Capac gazing down at the lake from which he sprang.

Another lookout point is found beside **Parque Pino** at the city's north side in the plaza four blocks up Calle Lima from the Plaza de Armas. Also called Parque San Juan, it boasts the Arco Deustua, a monument honoring the patriots killed in the battles of Junín and Ayacucho, the decisive battles in the Independence War with Spain.

The "San Juan" moniker for the park comes from the San Juan Bautista Church within its limits; at its main altar is a statue of the patron saint of Puno, the

Procession during the Feast of the Virgin of Candelaria, Puno.

Virgin of Candelaria. Also in the park is the Colegio Nacional de San Carlos, a grade school founded by a decree signed by Venezuelan liberation leader Simón Bolívar in 1825. It was later converted into a university, then subsequently used as a military barracks.

Two blocks down F. Arbulu Street from Parque Pino is the city **market**, a colorful collection of people, goods and food. Tourists should keep their eyes on their money and cameras while here, but it is worth a stop to see the wide collection of products – especially the amazing variety of potatoes, ranging from the hard, freeze-dried *papa seca* that looks like gravel to the purple potatoes and yellow and orange speckled *olluco* tubers.

Woolen goods, colorful blankets and ponchos are on sale here, along with miniature reed boats like those that ply Lake Titicaca. Among the more intriguing trinkets are the Ekekos, the ceramic statues of stout jolly men laden with a indefinite number of good luck charms, ranging from fake money to little bags of coca leaves. Believers say the Ekekos smoke and they are often found with lit cigarettes hanging from their mouths. Those who really believe in the power of these jolly statues claim that they only bring luck if they are received as gifts – not purchased.

Exploring the Lake: Puno is the stepping-off point for exploring Titicaca with its amazing array of islands, Indian inhabitants and colorful traditions. Small motorboats can be hired for lake trips or for catching the 13kg (30lb) lake trout that make it one of Peru's best-known fishing destinations.

Most of the transportation is either by motorized launches or the totora reed boats that Norwegian Thor Heyerdahl studied in preparing for his legendary 4,300-nautical mile (7,970-km) journey from Peru to Polynesia in the reed boat *Kon-Tiki* in the 1940s.

Floating islands: The best-known of the islands dotting Titicaca's surface are the **Uros**, floating islands of reed named after the Indians who inhabited them. Legend has it the Uro Indians had

Navigating in totora reed boats.

black blood that helped them survive the frigid nights on the water and safeguarded them from drowning.

The last full-blooded Uro was a woman who died in 1959. Other Uros had left the group of islands in earlier years – owing to a drought that worsened their poverty – and intermarried with Aymará- and Quechua-speaking Indians. But the Indians who now inhabit this island – a mix of Uro, Aymará and Inca descendants – follow the Uro ways.

The Uros' poverty has prompted more and more of them to move to Puno. That same poverty has caused those who remain to take a hard-sell approach to tourists and, besides pressing visitors to buy their handicrafts, they frequently demand "tips" for having their photographs taken.

Some tourists suggest that bartering with fresh fruit is better than money exchanges. However, there is continued criticism that tourism has not only opened the Uros Islands to the stares of insensitive tourists but has destroyed much of the culture as the Indians modified their handicrafts to appeal to outsiders or abandoned traditional practices to dedicate more time to the influx of outsiders.

The Uros islanders fish, hunt birds and live off lake plants, with the most important element in their life being the lake reeds they use for their houses, boats and even as the base of their five islands – the largest of which are **Toranipata, Huaca Huacani** and **Santa María**. The bottoms of the reed islands decay in the water and are replaced from the top with new layers, making a spongy surface that is a bit difficult to walk on. Even the walls of the schools on the bigger islands are made of totora. The soft roots of the reed are eaten, making it a pretty handy thing to have around.

Another island that lures tourists is **Taquile**, the home of skilled weavers and a spot where travelers can buy well-made woolen and alpaca goods as well as colorful garments whose patterns and designs bear hidden messages about the wearer's social standing or marital status. The residents of this island run their

The Uros Islands, made of reeds.

own tourism operations in the hope that the visits of outsiders will not destroy their delicate culture. There are no hotels on Taquile but the islanders generously open their homes to tourists interested in an overnight stay.

Handicrafts also play an important role in life on **Amantaní,** a lovely and peaceful island even further away from Puno than Taquile. Amantaní was once part of the Inca empire, as attested to by local ruins, before the Spanish invaded and slaughtered the islanders. The Spaniard who was granted a concession to the island used the Indians in forced labor and his descendants were still in control after Peru's independence from Spain. But eventually an island fiesta turned violent and the Indians attacked their landlord with hoes and consequently split up the island into communally-held fields.

Amantaní has opened its doors to outsiders who are willing to live for a few days as the Aymará-speaking islanders do – and that means sleeping on beds made of long hard reeds and eating potatoes for every meal. There is no running water or electricity and night-time temperatures drop to freezing even in the summer. But those happy to rough it catch a glimpse of an Andean agricultural community that has maintained the same traditions for centuries. Some Amantaní residents live and die without ever leaving the island.

Journeys to Amantaní begin at the Puno docks aboard sputtering wooden motorboats operated by the islanders. At the end of the four-hour trip, visitors are registered as guests and assigned to a host family. The family, usually led by a shy patriarch, shows the way to its mud-brick home set around an open courtyard decorated with white pebbles spelling out the family's name.

Prepared visitors usually bring gifts of fruit – a rarity on the isolated island – and the socializing begins when a family member who speaks English offers a guided walk around the island, from where the views are something spectacular. Women wearing traditional black and white lace dresses pass by with

Women on Taquile Island.

slingshots in their hands to kill scavenging birds.

Another island, **Estevés**, is connected to Puno by a bridge and is best known for Turistas Isla Estevés. This luxury hotel is a far cry from what used to be the main construction on the island – a prison that accommodated the patriots captured by the Spanish during Peru's war for independence.

James Orton, a naturalist and explorer who died crossing Titicaca on a steamship in 1877, is buried on Isla Estevés; his memorial sits beside one honoring the liberation fighters who perished in the war with Spain. Orton, a natural history professor from Vassar University, was on his third expedition to explore the Beni river in the Amazon area. The Beni's link to the Mamore river – both crucial conduits during the jungle's rubber boom – was named the Orton river in his honor.

Mysterious burial chambers: Some 35 km (21 miles) from Puno is **Sillustani**, with its circular burial towers or *chullpas* overlooking **Lake Umayo**. The age of the funeral towers, which are up to 12 meters (40 feet) high, remains a puzzle. A Spanish chronicle-keeper described them as "recently finished" in 1549, although some still appear as if they were never completed and the Indians that built them were conquered by the Incas about a century earlier.

The *chullpas* apparently were used as burial chambers for nobles of the Colla civilization; these were Indians who spoke Aymará, had architecture considered more complicated than that of the Incas and who buried their nobility with their entire family.

Not far away is **Chucuito**, a village that sits upon what was once an Inca settlement and which boasts an Inca sundial. Stop by the **Santo Domingo Church** with its small museum in this *altiplano* village; also worth visiting is **La Asunción Church**.

Juli, once the capital of the lake area, has four beautiful colonial churches under reconstruction. Although it now appears a little odd to see so many large churches so close together, at the time

A procession on Taquile.

the Spanish ordered them built they hoped to covert huge masses of Indians to Roman Catholicism.

In addition, the Spanish were accustomed to having one church for the Europeans, one for the mixed-raced Christians and yet another for the Indians. The largest of Juli's churches is **San Juan Bautista** with its colonial paintings tracing the life of its patron, Saint John the Baptist.

From the courtyard of **La Asunción Church** visitors have a captivating view of the lake. The other churches in the city are **San Pedro**, once the city's principal place of worship and the church in which a choir of 400 Indians used to sing each Sunday, and **Santa Cruz**, which is just beside the city's old cemetery. Santa Cruz was originally a Jesuit church upon the front of which Indian stonemasons carved a huge sun – the Inca god – along with more traditional Christian symbols.

It is from Juli that the Transturin hydrofoils leave across the lake for Bolivia. (Information is available from the

Transturin office in Puno, Av. Girón Tacna 201. Tel: 737). There is a catamaran service from Juli and Puno to Copacabana, Bolivia.

Pilgrimage site: Copacabana can also be reached by taking a minibus ride around the side of the lake, passing the reeds waving in the wind, shy but curious children at the bends in the road and always the brilliant blue of Titicaca on the roadway that ends the lake.

This pleasant trip involves a short ferry trip at the **Strait of Tiquina** and the destination is a pleasant one. Copacabana is a friendly little town accustomed to tourists and has a number of modest but clean restaurants and hotels. It is most famous for its cathedral containing a 16th-century carved wood figure of the Virgin of Copacabana, the Christian guardian of the lake.

The statue, finished in 1853, was the work of Indian sculptor Francisco Tito Yupanqui, nephew of Inca Huayna Capac. Except for during Mass, the statue stands with its back to the congregation – but facing the lake so it can keep an eye out for any approaching storms and earthquakes.

One of the loveliest outings in Copacabana is a dawn or dusk walk along the waterfront, watching the sky explode into color with sunrise or slip into the blue black of night at sunset.

It is also possible to reach Bolivia by crossing around the other side of the lake via Desaguadero, but this border town is one of the continent's filthiest and there is no acceptable lodging there in the event buses on the Bolivian side are not running (a common eventuality owing to holidays, strikes or sometimes lack of demand).

From Copacabana, launches can be hired to visit the Bolivian islands which are also on Lake Titicaca – the **Island of the Sun** and the **Island of the Moon**. The Island of the Sun (also accessible via a public ferry) has a sacred Inca rock at one end and the ruins of Pilko Caima with a portal dedicated to the sun god at the other. The Island of the Moon, which is also sometimes called Coati, has ruins of an Inca temple and a cloister for Chosen Women.

Boatman on the lake.

THE WEAVING CO-OPS OF TAQUILE

Taquile, the island of weavers, has a long history. In the 16th century it was awarded by the King of Spain to a man named Pedro Gonzales and became a colonial *hacienda*. After Peru won its independence, Taquile was used as a prison island. Little by little, the Taquile Indians regained ownership of their ancestral lands and, since 1970, they have run their own tourism operations in an attempt to ensure that the old ways are not lost in the effort to bring in visitors. In particular, they have refused to allow the building of any island hotels.

The tourism operations began after enterprising Puno residents began transporting visitors to the island; the Taquile residents wrestled control from the entrepreneurs and began operating their own passenger boats, regulating the number of outsiders that arrive and their activities when they get there.

However, once on the island today, visitors are free to wander to the small Inca ruins dotting the hilltops or take photographs of the farming terraces. The island is narrow, but several kilometers long. The liveliest pictures are to be taken on July 25, St James's Day, when the island explodes into celebration with dancing, music and merrymaking.

Taquile is devoted to weaving, and even men can be seen walking around knitting finely spun sheep's wool into the stocking hats they wear.

The colors and designs also reveal information about the wearer. Certain colors tell marital status or social standing, certain garments are worn only on holidays. Single men wear knitted hats with white tufts on top; married men have red points on their hats. Belts are seasonal and some contain coded calendars, signaling that marriages will take place in one particular month, houses will be roofed in another and crops will be planted in another. Blue and red are the predominant colors.

Samples of these ethnic garments, ranging from delicately embroidered blouses to the belts, hats and jackets that the men use, can be purchased at the island's weaving cooperative store on the main square. Prices can be high (higher than on the mainland), but then the quality is very good. There is also a small museum of antique garments made by the ancestors of the current island residents.

Although there are no hotels on the island, visitors can spend the night in the home of an island family, and the Taquile residents have a reputation for hospitality. Arrangements for such accommodation can be made with the Indians waiting at the top of the steep stone staircase at whose base the boats dock.

Keep in mind that the accommodations are rustic and the blankets offered visitors unaccustomed to the cold nights may be found insufficient. Many overnight guests bring their own sleeping bags, warm clothing, flashlights and food for eating and sharing with their host family; the charge for the lodging is usually less than US$2.

There are some small eating establishments on the island, with fried trout offered as one of the delicacies (from Taquile's own trout farm). Bottled soft drinks are also usually available, although tourists are advised to carry water with them in the event that local refreshments run out. If you have any special dietary needs then you should take food over from the mainland. Fruit and vegetables in particular are in limited supply on Taquile.

If you don't mind spending most of your day on the lake it is possible to take the morning boat trip – a four-hour journey – to Taquile, spend a couple of hours there and return on the early afternoon boat. However, travelers who have roughed it on an overnight stay at Taquile say that watching the moon rising over frigid Lake Titicaca from the island is well worth any minor discomforts. ∎

**weaver with
er loom.**

233

AREQUIPA

Far from Lima, isolated in a fertile valley tucked between desert and mountains and crowned by turquoise skies, **Arequipa** was a key stop on the cargo route linking the abundant silver mines of Bolivia to the coast. Built from the white sillar rock that spewed out from **Misti**, one of a trio of imposing volcanoes looming behind it, this appropriately named "City of White" is Peru's second largest urban area and one of the country's most prosperous. In colonial days it boasted the largest Spanish population and strongest European traditions; the cattle and farming industries that started then remain principal sources of income for the region.

In 1541 the king of Spain granted this oasis at the foot of the snow-capped volcano the title "Most Noble, Most Loyal and Faithful City of the Assumption of Our Lady of the Beautiful Valley of Arequipa." Aymará Indians living here beside the **Chili river** more concisely called it Ariquepa (*sic*), "the place behind the pointed mountain." Another legend has it that one of the Incas, Mayta Capac, was moved by the beauty of the valley during one of his journeys and ordered his entourage to stop. His exact words were said to be "Ari quipay" – or "Yes, stay" in Quechua. Whatever the truth, Arequipa has grown into a magnificent city and the intellectual capital of modern Peru.

The heart of the city: Arequipa's **Plaza de Armas** is one of Peru's most beautiful. One full side is occupied by the massive twin-towered **cathedral**, rebuilt twice in the 1800s after it was destroyed by fire and earthquake. The cathedral's ominous and ornate exterior misleads because the church's interior is unusually bare and simple, except for its elaborate chandelier. The cathedral clock is the city's unofficial timepiece and the place where disputes over punctuality (rare as they are among ever-

Preceding pages: gazing over the Colca canyon. **Left**, Arequipa's Plaza de Armas.

tardy Peruvians) are settled. The church's organ hails from Belgium and its elaborately carved wooden pulpit, the work of French artist Rigot in 1879, was brought to the city a century ago by a local aristocrat's daughter.

Two-story arcades grace the other three sides of the plaza, where palm trees, old gas lamps and a white stone fountain nestled in an English garden attract strollers and those looking for a bench. Outspoken Arequipeños congregate here for political rallies, protests or fiestas. The plaza's thick stone buildings with busily carved portals, their Moorish touches evident, breathe 450 years of history.

This city is full of dignified patricians' homes built in the 18th century and which have withstood the tremors that regularly shake this city. The one-story colonial structures are replete with massive carved wooden doors, grilled French windows and high-ceilinged rooms clustered around spacious central patrios. The best for visiting include **Casa Ricketts**, built as a seminary in 1738 and now used as a bank, the 200-year-old **Casa de la Moneda** or former mint and the **Casa Moral**, named after the venerable mulberry tree on its patio and now a bank with a small museum.

The carvings above the door of Casa Moral depict pumas from whose mouths snakes are slithering – the same designs found on the ceramics and fabrics of the Nazca Indians. Meanwhile, an inscription inside Casa de la Moneda gives visitors an idea of the social status once enjoyed by Arequipa's wealthiest families. When the mint was acquired as a home for the Quiróz family, those patricians had inscribed – in 1738 – their family slogan: *Después de Diós, Quiróz* (After God, Quiroz).

Also worth a stop on **Calle La Merced** is the **Goyeneche palace** with its huge patios, bedroom alcoves and colonial doors and windows. As with most colonial houses, this mansion had a series of patios – one for formal occasions, one for the family and one for the servants and animals. The main patio breaks with the traditional white stone decor; at **The Santa Catalina Convent.**

238

its center is a fountain of black rock.

Indian angels: On the non-secular side, no visit is complete without a stop at **La Compañía**. The frontispiece of this two-story church is a compilation of columns, zigzags, spirals, laurel crowns, flowers, birds and grapevines into which is embroidered in rock the abbreviations of the Masses on Holy Fridays, the city's coat of arms (with the Misti volcano at its center) and the date the massive work was completed: 1698. But a careful look shows that even the European influence had its limits. The angels have Indian faces; one Indian face is even crowned with feathers.

What lies inside La Compañía is equally impressive. The sacristy's ceiling is covered with miniature paintings and carvings of crimson and gold. The view from La Compañía's steeple is fabulous, especially at sunset when the late light casts a pink, then mauve, glow on the city's gracious white buildings.

On the Morán Street side of the church is its cloister, where stark architectural lines are broken by detailed columns, demonstrating the high level stone carving reached during the 17th century.

Nearby sits **San Francisco Church**, the focus of attention every December 8 during the Feast of the Immaculate Conception. From the small chapel of the Sorrowful Virgin found in the church, the devout remove a fairytale-like coach topped with the image of the Virgin Mary surrounded by angels and saints. This is paraded through the streets in a colorful procession of pilgrims carrying flowers and candles.

Secret world: The most astonishing stop in Arequipa is the **Santa Catalina Convent**, opened in 1970 after 400 years as a cloister for nuns. Despite the closed doors, there was little heed paid to the nuns' vows of poverty and silence, at least in the early days. During its heyday this convent's sleeping cells were actually more akin to luxurious European chambers, with English carpets, silk curtains, cambric and lace sheets and tapestry-covered stools. As for silence, French feminist Flora Tristan, visiting the convent in 1832, said the nuns –

elow,
ewspaper
nd a
hoeshine.
ight, an
.requipeña.

daughters of aristocrats – were nearly as good at talking as they were about spending huge quantities of money. Each had her own servants and dined with porcelain plates, damask tablecloths and silver cutlery.

Three blocks from the Plaza de Armas, Santa Catalina takes visitors back to the 16th century. Those who enter the cloister can see the spacious patios, the kitchen and slave quarters and stone wash tubs of this convent where entrance requirements were among the strictest in Peru. Novices had to prove Spanish origin and come up with a dowry of at least 1,000 gold pesos to join the order. The narrow streets, arches and gardens of the convent bear their original names: Córdova Street, its whitewashed walls stark against the pots of bright red geraniums, Zocodovar Square with a granite fountain and Sevilla Street with archways and steps. About 20 nuns still live in a section of the tile-roofed convent, which once housed up to 500.

When the convent opened its doors to the public, its anecdotes and scandals were resurrected. Among them is the story of Sister Dominga, the 16-year-old who entered the convent when her betrothed left her for a rich widow. The religious life did not agree with this beautiful young woman and she staged her own death to escape. Dominga really did place the body of a deceased Indian woman into her bed one night and set the room on fire, but it didn't happen here as some people claim. That scandal belongs to the **Santa Rosa Convent** seven blocks from Arequipa's main square. Santa Rosa's mother superior refused to believe the rumors that the young nun was really alive and living outside the cloister – until Dominga wrote to demand return of the dowry she had paid the convent!

Santa Rosa, which remains cloistered, was founded in 1747 by four nuns from the much larger Santa Catalina; nearly two dozen nuns still reside there.

Even older than Santa Catalina is the ancient colonial church of **San Lázaro**, the oldest neighborhood in Arequipa and possibly the spot where the city's

Left, restful colonial courtyard. Below, Virgin in Santa Catalina Convent.

founding took place. This small hermitage sits in front of a square bearing the same name; the fountain in the middle of the plaza is fed from pre-existing Inca aqueducts.

Seceding from the north: Arequipeños are a proud, even haughty lot and their perennial attempts to secede from the rest of the country are a source of entertainment for Limeños, who jokingly ask Peruvian travelers if they have their passport before heading to Arequipa. In fact, the Arequipeños designed their own passports and flag in one of their futile attempts to separate from the rest of the union. From Arequipa's well-educated and politically passionate ranks have come two of the country's best-known figures, former President Fernando Belaúnde Terry and novelist and failed presidential hopeful Mario Vargas Llosa.

This regionalist passion peaks at annual celebrations marking the anniversary of the city's founding. Every August 15, Arequipeños cut loose with parades, bullfights and night-time revelry highlighted by fireworks. The birthday celebration is accompanied by a weeklong handicrafts and folk festival.

To unwind in Arequipa in the evening, do what the locals do and head to a *picantería* for a cold Arequipeña beer and some spicy food – stuffed peppers, pressed rabbit or marinated pork. If you opt for the peppers (*rocoto relleno*), take care. These red peppers scorch tongue, gullet and bowel of the inexperienced, and tourist reactions to the screamingly spicy pepper are a source of amusement for other diners and concern for restaurant owners. The beer will be accompanied by a dish of *cancha* or salty fried corn for munching.

Restored ruin: Outside Arequipa is **Sabandía** with its flour mill made of volcanic rock that was restored, stone by stone, in 1973. Architect Luís Felipe Calle had, in 1966, restored an old mansion in Arequipa (now functioning as the main branch of the Central Reserve Bank there), when he was given a task he long sought: restoring this old mill in ruins outside the city. He set up a tent

beside the mill and lived there for the two and a half years it took him to finish the project, which he did using old documents and interviews with residents who remembered when the mill last operated nearly a half century ago. After the restoration the bank put the mill up for sale – and Calle himself purchased it.

"Architecture of Arequipa is a fusion. The big *sillar* (stone) houses are humble but at the same time vigorous, a faithful reflection of the spirit of their people," said Calle, whose 18th-century property – open to visitors – is set in some of the area's most beautiful countryside.

A little farther out from the city are the thermal springs of **Yura** in the foothills of the extinct **Chachani volcano**. Crude cement pools fed by the sulfurous waters are open for bathing and lunch is available at the government-run Turistas Hotel at the springs. Two hours from the city on the road to Lima are the **Toro Muerto Petroglyphs**, hundreds of volcanic rocks believed engraved and painted more than 1,000 years ago by Wari Indians living in the region. The petro-glyphs show depictions of llamas, condors, pumas, guanacos, dancers and warriors. A 145-km (90-mile) drive to the coast takes birdwatchers to **Mejía**, where rare and exotic species of the feathered creatures congregate at a series of lagoons.

Deeper than the Grand Canyon: Four hours away from Arequipa and drawing almost as much tourist attention these days is the **Colca canyon**, one of the world's deepest gorges cut 3,182 meters (10,607 feet) into the earth's crust. Twice the depth of the Grand Canyon, the Colca is shadowed by snow-topped peaks – many of them volcanoes – and sliced by the silvery Colca river. The base of this profound canyon is cold and windy and draws only daredevil kayak enthusiasts and researchers. Above, at the brink of the chasm, Indian farmers irrigate narrow terraces of rich volcanic earth much the same way their ancestors did centuries ago.

Though isolated, the Colca was a productive farming area before the Incas claimed it and, even when the Spanish **Waiting for closing time.**

reached the 64-km (40-mile) long valley where this canyon lies, they found terraced fields and thriving herds of lamas and alpacas. When the canyon became part of the route between the silver mines of Bolivia and the coast, the Colca farmers were snatched from their homes and forced to work in the mines. Later, when the railroad reached Arequipa, the Colca Valley was forgotten.

When a multinational consortium began investigating the possibility of diverting the Colca river for a desert irrigation project, eyes once again turned to this valley and its gorge. From a lost chasm trapped in a time warp, the Colca – upon whose basalt sides cactus and brush cling and whose visitors come in jeeps and on mules – has become one of the hottest tourist attractions in southwestern Peru. There has been an modification in the valley's crops as it has more contact with the outside world. Barley is now grown on some terraces for use in the brewery in Arequipa.

The canyon is an average of 900 meters (3,000 feet) deep through most of its journey through the valley. A popular section is the "*Cruz del Condor*" – literally, the "Condor Crossing" – where visitors scan the skies for a glimpse of the majestic birds soaring above in pairs.

A series of canyon trips, usually starting with a bus ride from Arequipa then continuing by foot or by mule, allow travelers to explore this rift full of small towns. Visitors may be puzzled in passing sections of the gorge named "the Polish Canyon" or "John Paul II Canyon." The first in-depth expedition of the chasm's bottom in 1981 was made by Cano Andes, a group of white-water experts from Poland who spent several weeks on the swift Colca river patriotically naming the areas they passed.

Although train travel in Peru has become increasingly difficult, some travelers still use Arequipa as the starting point for rail travel to Lake Titicaca, then on to Cuzco. Inexpensive fares have made trains the Peruvians' most popular way to journey. Thrice-weekly trains leave Arequipa at 9.45pm for the more than 10-hour journey to Puno.

elow, triking a argain. ight, lush erraces of e Colca anyon.

THE PERUVIAN AMAZON

Those who have seen Werner Herzog's 1972 film *Aguirre, Wrath of God*, which opens up with an expedition of armored conquistadors, horses, llamas and manacled Indian slaves making their way over the eastern edge of the Andes and down into the cloud forest, already have a vision of just how dramatic Peru's Upper Amazon can be.

The film, which is based on a true account of a mad conquistador's brutal search for El Dorado, ends appropriately enough with Aguirre and a few survivors drifting on a raft dwarfed by the enormity of the surrounding jungle, the raft circling slowly and infested with marooned monkeys.

Aguirre actually traced the same route of the Amazon and many of its tributaries. The river itself begins at 5,600 meters (18,360 feet) in Peru's snow-capped Andes, then gradually plunges in waterfalls through the cloud forest before broadening and swelling through the immense lowland jungles that stretch over 3,500 km (2,200 miles) to the sea. Although it often surprises the first-time visitor, 60 percent of Peru is actually jungle, even though under six percent of its population lives there.

Because the physical barrier of the Andes has prevented Peru from rapidly integrating the jungle portion of its country and because the Upper Amazon is so distant from the Amazon's mouth and the sea, much of Peru's jungle is still intact. In a nutshell, Peru has some of the best untouched rainforest to be found anywhere in the world.

Jungle from a prehistoric sea: Two hundred million years ago, South America, Africa and the rest of the world's continents were all part of one enormous continent called Gondwanaland. The Amazon basin at that time formed a giant inland sea while much of Gondwanaland was covered in a tropical forest that had no flowering plants but rather tree ferns, cyclads and roaming dinosaurs.

Around 100 million years ago South America broke off from Africa and the continent became an island where evolution continued in isolation. A menage of bizarre animals began to evolve, among them the sloths, the capybara (the world's largest rodent), armadillos and anteaters.

As the eastern edge of the continent began to fold, the inland ocean became a gigantic inland lake where other unusual animals such as freshwater dolphins, piranhas and electric eels began to evolve. Gradually an ancient mountain formation in eastern Brazil was breached and the lake suddenly emptied, exposing an enormous, almost uniformly flat basin below.

Even today the difference in elevation between Iquitos (the most Amazonian town in Peru) and the mouth of the Amazon – a distance of 3,200 km (2,000 miles) – is only 200 meters (660 feet). About 4 million years ago the Andes mountains thrust up and the present contours of the basin were formed. Rivers flowing out of the Andes soon con-

Preceding pages: aerial view in the Madre de Díos region; a jaguar in the wild. **Left,** waterfall in the jungle. **Right,** macaw.

verged on the path of least resistance through a basin as large as the continental United States. After nearly 100 million years of isolation, it wasn't until only a few million years ago that Central America arose, forming a land bridge to the north and allowing such modern animals as jaguars, deer and peccaries to move south.

Because of the characteristics of abundant water, light and heat (straddling as it does the equator) and a continuous growing season (there is little difference between winter and summer), plants flourished in incredible profusion, forming enormous 60-meter (200-foot) canopies.

Unlike other biomes which were wiped out by the massive ice blocks rolling over the southern and northern hemispheres during the ice age, the jungle persisted – it is thus the oldest continuous terrestrial habitat on earth. The plants and animals have had millions of extra years to interact with one another and to evolve into increasingly more specialized forms. It is no wonder, then,

that although the tropical rainforests presently cover less than 4 percent of the earth's surface, they house over 50 percent of all of its species. An estimated 50 percent of those have yet even to be discovered.

It was only within the last 50,000 years that mankind – who had evolved only a few million years before in Africa – was afforded an opportunity to pass into North and hence South America in his modern form. As the polar icecaps grew during the different phases of the ice age, the sea level sank, thus exposing the Bering Strait as a land bridge. Mongol tribes from Asia presumably followed herds of animals over the bridge and roughly 20,000 years ago arrived in the enormous hot-house now called the Amazon. Adapting to the rainforest over a period of thousands of years, the Indians learned to live in harmony with the jungle, using slash and burn methods of agriculture and learning to harvest the jungle's resources well within the limits of what this complex yet surprisingly fragile environment allowed.

Jabiru birds in Manu Park

Dreams of the conquistadors: That balance was immediately disrupted, however, with the arrival of the first Europeans. Far from home and wishing only to stay long enough to gain instant wealth and fame, Europeans viewed the Amazon more as a storehouse of raw materials than as a place to be permanently inhabited. Having found immense Indian empires and plentiful gold in Mexico and the Andes, it was perhaps only natural for the Spaniards to suspect that there might be more golden empires to the east. In 1542 Fransisco de Orellana and his men became the first Europeans to raft down the Amazon. Attacked at one point by bow-and-arrow-bearing warriors wearing grass skirts and with long hair, the surprised Spaniards confused them with women, later christening the river the *Río de las Amazones*, after the Greek myth of a nation of warrior women.

In southern Peru, close to the Incas' capital of Cuzco, the story of glistening cities of gold gave rise to the legend of Paititi, a supposedly lost jungle city where the last Incas had hidden their gold. Various adventurers have sought Paititi – thought to exist somewhere in Peru's southern jungle department of Madre de Díos. (*See "The Quest for Lost Cities" on page 62.*) Thus far only scattered petroglyphs, remote tribes and small Inca ruins have been found.

The search for gold, however, was eventually replaced by other valuable commodities native to the Amazon jungle and found nowhere else in the world: quinine (which allowed British troops to conquer malarial India), cocoa (the basis of the world's huge chocolate industry), mahogany, vanilla, and others. No product made a bigger impact on the world, however, than that which naturally exudes from three species of Amazonian tree: the sticky-white latex called rubber.

The rubber boom: Almost 500 years ago Columbus reported seeing Indians who used strange elastic (rubber) balls for their games. In 1743 the French scientist La Condamine used rubber latex to waterproof his instruments and

caiman.

was the first European to introduce the substance to the Old World. Although an English chemist soon began putting "rubbers" on the end of pencils for erasing purposes, wider commercial use was limited due to the fact that natural rubber grew soft and sticky in hot weather and brittle and hard in cold.

In 1844, however, the process of vulcanization was discovered by Charles Goodyear, thus allowing rubber to stay tough and firm at all temperatures. With Dunlop's later invention of the pneumatic tire, suddenly an enormous demand was created which only the Amazon could satisfy.

The ensuing rubber boom, which lasted roughly from 1880 to 1912, completely transformed the Amazon's economy. Rubber trees in the remotest regions were soon being tapped, the latex gathered in cups, then coagulated into large balls that were cured over a fire. The tappers themselves were bankrolled by entrepreneurs who amassed enormous wealth and lived in luxury in newly-burgeoning jungle cities such as Manaus in Brazil and Iquitos in Peru.

In the midst of the boom, however, an English adventurer named Henry Wickham quietly collected 70,000 rubber seeds and smuggled them out of the Amazon. First planted in Kew gardens in England and then transplanted to tropical Asia where they were safe from indigenous disease, the seeds flourished. By 1912 the Amazon rubber boom was at an end.

Delicate ecology: Viewed from the air, Peru's Amazon looks like an endless sea of lumpy green sponges, stretching in all directions to the horizon. It is this thick umbrella of trees – the jungle's equivalent to an enormous housing project – that creates the millions of homes for animals and specialized plants to live in below.

If you were to enter the upper canopy slowly from the top you would soon discover that the first layer is virtually a desert of sorts. The crowns of the trees are exposed both to the fierce tropical sun and to winds that frequently snap and topple the tallest of trees. To reduce

Dense rainforest.

evaporation, the leaves at this level are quite small. Many of the epiphytes here – plants that live on top of other plants – actually take the form of cacti, to reduce their loss of water.

As you descend through the upper canopy, however, you immediately begin to enter a different world of reduced light. Protected from direct sun and wind, the leaves are thus larger in size than those above and the struggle for light has begun.

Traveling further down towards the jungle floor, leafy plants are much less abundant. Although explorers traveling by river often reported thick and impenetrable jungle, under the canopy away from the rivers one can move quite easily as most branches and leaves are well off the floor.

Like living beneath the sea, even in strong storms the air here is calm, and at other times completely still. The overpowering sound of insects above is enormous as millions call to one another unseen. At the bottom-most level the leaves are very large; less than 5 percent of the sun's light finally reaches the jungle's floor.

It is this enormous variation of light, wind and temperature, and the thousands of different species of plants, that afford a million different homes for animal and plant species. Whole communities of insects, birds and other animals are specialized and adapted to different levels of the rainforest, which not surprisingly contains the highest species diversity in the world.

Manu National Park in southeastern Peru, for example, covering an area roughly half the size of Switzerland, houses over 800 bird species (the same number as found in all of North America), 20 percent of all plant species found in South America, and more than 1,200 species of butterflies (Europe has 400). A recent study of the insects in Manu's upper canopy by the Smithsonian Institute has increased the total number of the world's estimated animal species by 30 million.

Push towards conservation: Although jungles have existed for hundreds of

cautious young puma.

millions of years, it is only within the last 100 years that they have been on the decline. The trend is in direct relation to the population of human beings. A million years ago man had an estimated population of 50,000. That population has now grown to over 4 billion. In the last century humans have destroyed half of the world's rainforests. At the present rate of destruction, most experts agree, the majority of the remaining rainforests will have disappeared within the next 25 years.

In Peru, the largest destructive force on the Amazon has been the unmanaged influx of peasants from the Andes and the coast. Since the 1960s, both military and civilian governments have viewed the eastern Andean slopes and the Amazon basin as an El Dorado of unexploited natural resources, believing that development of the region would provide a politically painless "solution" to land hunger in the Andes, migration of rural poor to coastal cities, and the need to populate remote border regions to defend national sovereignty.

As a result the government financed the construction of a "marginal highway," a road paralleling the Andes to the east which the government hoped would help open up the area to colonization and industry.

The idea of settling the Amazon, however, ignored reality: less than 5 percent of the Peruvian Amazon's soil is suitable for agriculture, and much of the region supports populations of indigenous people and settlers that are already large in relation to the exploitable resources. As a consequence, agriculture that began on a few relatively fertile terraces in the eastern Andes has spread to land ill-suited to continuous exploitation. With inadequate knowledge of better practices, many farmers work the land too long, allowing no time for it to renew. Once the soil has been drained of nutrients, poor farmers unable to buy fertilizer move on, carving yet another plot from the forest.

The result has been extensive deforestation of Peru's cloud forest where incredibly an estimated 50 percent of all

Poison-dart frog in the Manu National Park.

neotropical plant species are found. Thus far over 70,000 square kilometers (27,000 square miles) of the Peruvian Amazon have been deforested; 300,000 hectares (741,300 acres) are deforested every year.

An additional impact on Peru's rainforest has been the illegal, 1.6 billion dollar a year cocaine industry, mostly concentrated in the north-central jungle's Huallaga Valley. Hundreds of thousands of hectares of virgin rainforest have been destroyed in order to grow illegal plantations of coca shrubs – all to support the surprising need of North Americans and Europeans to snort the potent white powder.

In the last few years the US government has pressured Peru to use a major defoliant – Spike – on coca plantations. Protests among local and international conservationists about the effect such a chemical could have on the surrounding jungle, however, has prevented its use. In the meantime, the entry of Shining Path guerrillas into the Huallaga area and the US's offer of military equip-

ment and increasing numbers of advisors, have further complicated the situation.

System of protection: In spite of increasing rainforest destruction, however, a number of encouraging developments have taken place. Peru currently has roughly 5 percent of its territory protected by a system of 24 national parks, reserves, sanctuaries and other designated areas, a process which began only in the 1960s.

In the last 20 years considerable ecological awareness has developed and, as a consequence, a proliferation of conservation organisations has begun. Five of the largest are: The Nature Conservancy Foundation (FPCN, Lima); Ecologia y Conservación (ECCO, Lima); The Conservation Association for the Southern Jungle (ACSS, Cuzco); The Peruvian Association for the Conservation of Nature (APECO, Lima); and the Environmental Development Group (IDMA, Lima). In 1983, with the help of the Canadian government, the US Fish and Wildlife Service and the World Wild-

River transport near Iquitos.

life fund, Lima's La Molina Agrarian University began the only graduate school in the tropical Andean countries to offer advanced degrees in wildlife conservation and management. Also begun at La Molina is the Conservation Data Center (CDC), which is steadily computerizing an inventory of Peru's biological diversity, one of the highest in the world.

In 1990 a giant new 1.5 million hectare "reserved zone" was declared in the Madre de Díos region – Peru's southernmost department which houses some of the richest rainforest found anywhere in the world. This new area – including almost the entire watershed of the Tambopata river – is currently at the forefront of tropical rainforest conservation. The idea is to convert the zone not into a park but rather an "extractive reserve."

The latter is an area of rainforest where renewable yearly harvests of Brazil nuts, rubber and other rainforest products will create more revenue over the long run than the permanent destruction caused by unmanaged farming, logging and cattle-ranching.

Pioneered by the Brazilian rubber tapper Chico Mendez (who was murdered in 1988 by Brazilian cattle ranchers and whose story has recently been made into a film by David Puttnam), the pressure is currently on to see how such extractive reserve ideas fare.

Also developing in Peru's rainforest within the last 10 years is the practice of "eco-tourism," based on the belief that rich natural rainforest can not only be preserved by use as an extractive reserve, but also can act as a lure to attract tourist dollars.

Pumped into local economies and national park infrastructures, tourist dollars may well prove to be one of the few counter-destructive economic forces currently available for preserving the jungle. The more people that travel to virgin rainforest areas, the more people who will become involved in the international fight to save them. And, just as importantly, tourism can prove the monetary value of intact rainforests to the

Calm jungle morning.

256

many hard-pressed, developing nations that can't afford the luxury of the industrialized West's "untouchable" parks and reserves.

The northern jungle: Three thousand two hundred kilometers (1,990 miles) up-river from the Amazon's mouth lies the jungle-locked city of **Iquitos**. It has a population of 350,000, with only rivers linking it to the exterior world. At one time the clearing house for the millions of tons of rubber shipped to Europe, Iquitos still displays the vestiges of its former status as one of the most important rubber capitals in the world. Houses near the main plaza and near the river are still faced with *azuelos* (glazed tiles) which at the height of the rubber boom were originally shipped from Italy and Portugal along with other luxury goods such as turn-of-the-century ironwork from England, glass chandeliers, caviar and fine wines.

On the **main plaza** is an iron house which was designed by Gustav Eiffel for the Paris exhibition in 1898. The house is said to have been transported from Paris by a local rubber baron and is entirely constructed of iron trusses and bolted iron sheets. Also on the plaza is the house of Carlos Fitzcarrald, the Peruvian rubber baron who dragged a steamship over the pass that bears his name thus opening up the department of Madre de Díos. The German film maker Werner Herzog shot part of *Fitzcarraldo* here (he also filmed on the Urubamba river near Camisea) and several of the refurbished steamships that he used are still in port. Hundreds of Iquiteños were used as extras.

Iquitos today is a quiet, colorful, friendly city which seems to have a monopoly not on rubber but on three-wheel taxis (roughly 50 cents a ride), motor scooters, Amazon views and atmosphere. Located some 80 km (50 miles) downriver from where the **Marañon** and **Ucayali** rivers join to create the Amazon river, the local dish here is *Paiche a la Loretana*, a fillet of a huge primitive fish, together with fried manioc and vegetables.

Exotic fruit juices are sold on the

unch by an mazon ributary, Manu Iational Park.

street corners, as are ice-creams which are flavored with mango, papaya, guanabana, granadilla, zapote, pochote, spondia and others.

You can take a taxi or simply walk from the main plaza to the picturesque waterfront district of **Belén**, where many of the houses float on rafts in the water. A Venetian-like labyrinth of canals, canoes and stores, Belén is the center for an incredible variety of Amazon products: exotic fruits, fish, turtles, herbal medicines and water fowl. Plowing the waterways are a plethora of small canoe-taxis paddled by Iquiteños as young as five. A canoe tour costs roughly $3 – it's one of the most unusual waterfronts in the world.

Just south of the city is the beautiful **Lake Quistococha** set in lush tropical jungle. The lake-reserve has a zoo (Parque Zoológico de Quistococha) where animals such as jaguars, ocelots, paiche, parrots and anacondas can be seen (entrance $1, closed Mondays).

Jungle lodges: Due to its character as a stop-over for those going by river to Brazil and for international flights, Iquitos has long been a center for excursions into the surrounding jungle. It should be remembered, however, that because there are a lot of people in this area and this is a main waterway, you must travel well beyond a 60-km (37-mile) radius of the city to see wildlife such as caimen, monkeys, macaws or pink dolphins (the latter are found only on remote tributaries of the upper Amazon and Orinoco rivers).

One way to become quickly acquainted with the jungle is to visit one of a number of lodges which have been set up on nearby rivers. Although many of the two- or three-day lodge tours can be booked through a travel agent in Lima, the tours are much cheaper if booked in Iquitos and are roughly $50 a day. One should avoid the numerous individuals in the airport and city trying to set up a "jungle lodge tour." Since these men are paid a commission, you can buy the same package deal more cheaply by simply walking into a lodge's downtown office, most of which are clustered

Riverboat near Iquitos.

258

around Jirón Putumayo near the Plaza de Armas.

Explorama Tours (Putumayo 150) is one of the largest companies with three different lodges, all well-run and efficient: **Explorama Inn**, 40 km (25 miles; 1½ hrs) from Iquitos and which has hot water, comfortable bungalows, good food and attractive jungle walks, is recommended for those who want to see the jungle (though few large animals) in comfort; **Explorama Lodge** (60 km/37 miles from Iquitos), is at Yanamono, and a little more basic; **Explornapo** (140 km/88 miles from Iquitos) is located on the Napo river and is one of the best lodges for seeing wildlife in the Iquitos area.

Explorama also provide access to their canopy walkway. First opened in 1992, it is now around 500 meters (1,640 feet) in length, and reaching a height of up to 37 meters (121 feet) offers breathtaking views for birdwatching from a unique perspective. One of the most beautiful sights is that of the appearance of mixed feeding flocks of birds in the early morning and late afternoon. Sloths, marmosets and monkeys can also be seen.

Other lodges include the popular **Anaconda Lara Lodge** (Pevas 216), some 40 km (25 miles) upstream from Iquitos, offering trips to the beautiful Yarapa river where river dolphins can be seen. They also offer interesting shamanic tours for the more esoterically-minded travelers; **Amazonia Expeditions** (Arica 432) have conservation-oriented tours; and **Amazon Camp Tourist Service** (Requena 336) which runs a lodge on the Momon river. All lodge routes and prices are controlled by the Ministry of Tourism (Calle Arica) and can be double-checked there.

Slow boats: Another way of seeing the Amazon is to take a commercial riverboat traveling either upriver towards Pucallpa or downriver towards Brazil. Although not much will be seen in the way of wildlife along the way (boats traveling upstream hug the banks, those in the opposite direction travel down the center of the river), the traveler will still see how people live along the Amazon

Paddling near the Belén markets, Iquitos.

as well as enjoy beautiful sunsets and magnificent scenery.

One should be warned that life along the Amazon is slow and leisurely – you should never travel by riverboat if you are in a hurry or have an inflexible schedule. Boats break down, linger sometimes for days in port, and are generally unpredictable. Even so, riverboat travel is an unforgettable experience and well recommended. The best place to look for boats in Iquitos is by actually going down to the docks and asking around or by visiting the following offices: **Menesses** (Jirón Prospero); **Hurtado** (Av. Grau 1223); **Bellavista** (Malecón Tarapaca 596), and **Casa Pinto** (Sargento Lores 164).

A seven- day trip to Pucallpa can cost anywhere from $30–40, and includes food (generally rice, meat and beans cooked in river water – which might prompt you to bring tins and fruits of your own), deckspace for your hammock (you can buy one in Iquitos for $10) and a cabin ticket if you want a berth. Traveling to Manaus in Brazil takes around 10 days and requires a boat change at the border. Both the *Clivie* and *Almirante Monteiro* frequently make this journey, are clean and have reasonable food. If you want to make the trip in style, try the *Juliana*, the refurbished riverboat used in Herzog's film, *Fitzcarraldo*. Travel to the border of Brazil costs around $30.

A third way to see the Amazon, and one highly recommended for those who have a little more time and want to get off the beaten path, is to hire a small boat and guide of your own. In every Amazon port there are boat owners who are willing to rent you their services at only a fraction of the cost paid to a typical jungle lodge. Once with a boat, the entire Amazon suddenly opens up for your exploration. By sharing expenses, for example, a party of four can travel the Amazon daily for as little as $7–10 a person. The best way to locate a boat in Iquitos is simply to ask about on the wharves. Only 100 km (62 miles) from Iquitos, for example, is the biggest national park in Peru, the 5 million-acre **Camping in the jungle.**

(2 million-hectare) **Pacaya-Samiria National Reserve**, a wildlife-packed lowland jungle area that can only be reached by hiring a private boat and staging your own expedition. Permits are needed to enter the park and can be obtained from INRENA in either Iquitos or Lima.

The central jungle: Seven days' travel upriver from Iquitos on the Ucayali river is **Pucallpa**, a rapidly growing city of 90,000 which can be reached from Lima by air. The city was joined to Lima by a highway in the 1960s which has fueled lumbering, oil exploration and also drug trafficking. Most people arriving in Pucallpa, however, prefer to stay on the nearby **Lake Yarinacocha**, a 20-minute bus ride from the city and the main tourist attraction of the area. Both the **Hospital Albert Schweitzer**, which serves the local Indians, and the **Summer Institute of Linguistics**, a nondenominational missionary organization studying many of Peru's jungle Indian languages (visited by appointment only), are based here.

In the small town of Yarinacocha at the edge of the lake is the fascinating artesanal cooperative, **Moroti Shobo**, where extremely high quality ceramics and weavings of the Shipibo Indians are displayed and are sent to museums all over the world. Although several lodges are on the lake, as there is little wildlife to see due to the nearby population, they are more for scenery and relaxation: **Hotel La Cabana**, run by a German, and **La Perla**, run by a Frenchman.

The lodges also arrange jungle excursions. Private excursions by motor canoe into the surrounding jungle and canals are easy to arrange from the port at Yarinacocha. On the canals are numerous piranhas, caimen and occasional monkeys. Trips can also be arranged to the numerous Shipibo villages whose culture has been in the area for at least the last 1,000 years.

The southern jungle: The traditional hopping-off point into Peru's little-explored southern jungle is the city of **Cuzco**, where a variety of trip options are available. A recommended agency

Giant water lilies.

in Cuzco to visit is the Peruvian Conservation Association for the Southern Rainforests (ACSS), a non-profit group dedicated to preserving the rainforests in southern Peru and an excellent source of information on some of the southern jungle's parks.

The adventurous traveler can go from Cuzco by rail and truck to **Quillabamba** and **Kiteni** and from there hire a boat through the **Pongo de Manique**, a narrow gorge surrounded by lush jungle and waterfalls on the upper **Urubamba river**, a journey described in Peter Matthiesson's 1962 classic book, *Cloud Forest*. After visiting the Pongo you can either return to Cuzco or else continue on down the Urubamba past various small missions and Machiguenga Indian settlements.

It should be emphasized that transport is infrequent through this area and you should therefore be extremely flexible. There is a twice-monthly government plane lower down on the Urubamba at the mission town of **Sepahua** which goes to Pucallpa and then Lima, or you can continue all of the way to Pucallpa and points beyond by boat.

The Manu National Park: Also accessible from Cuzco is what has been called the most bio-diverse rainforest park in the world, located in Peru's southernmost jungle department of **Madre de Díos**. At 4½ million acres (1.8 million hectares), **Manu** is one of the best areas for seeing wildlife anywhere in the Amazon rainforest. In many other jungle areas, because of the proximity to humans, you will be lucky to see anything more than birds, insects and the occasional large animal, but in Manu you are guaranteed to see so many monkeys (there are 13 different species) that you may grow tired of them. Besides abundant macaws, turtles and other wildlife, you'll have the best opportunity you'll ever have of seeing giant otters, peccaries, capybaras, tapir and even the occasional jaguar.

The easiest way to visit Manu is with a local tour operator such as **Manu Nature Tours** or **Expediciones Manu**, since all preparations for the trip must

A tropical downpour.

be made in advance and permits are required for entry into the reserve. The tour operator arranges all permits, transport, equipment, gasoline, and food supplies for the trip. It can take two days to reach this isolated area by traveling overland from Cuzco, down through the cloud forest and later transferring to a boat – an unforgettable experience. There is also the option of chartering a small plane which can fly to the junction of the Madre de Díos and Manu rivers. In 1987 Manu Nature Tours built the first tourist lodge in Manu, **Manu Lodge**, which is presently one of the finest Amazon wildlife viewing facilities. Because of the extreme isolation of the area and the fact that it houses only a maximum of 30 visitors at a time, trips to the lodge aren't cheap. However, in terms of seeing wildlife in comfort, it is hard to beat.

Boom town of the south: Linked by road or by air from Cuzco, **Puerto Maldonado** is the capital of the Peruvian department of Madre de Díos. Long cut off from the rest of the world by rapids on

The notorious piranha.

the **Madeira river** and by the Andes, only with the discovery of gold in the 1970s and the building of an airport in the early 1980s has the city developed into a gold rush "boom" town. Nevertheless, Madre de Díos has some of the greatest expanses of pristine jungle that exist anywhere on earth. Not only are there four protected wildlife reserves (including Manu National Park) that rank among the best in the world, but it is also rumored that some of Peru's uncontacted indigenous tribes are hidden here.

Set on a bluff overlooking the Madre de Díos and Tambopata rivers, Puerto Maldonado has a pleasant **town square**, a large government bank (to buy the gold sifted from the river), and numerous hotels for miners on brief trips to town. In 1897 the rubber baron Carlos Fitzcarrald traveled through here after having dragged his steamship, with the help of hundreds of Indians, over the Fitzcarrald pass and down the Manu and Madre de Díos rivers on his way to Iquitos via Brazil. You can make an

excursion about half an hour away from the city to where locals will tell you Fitzcarrald's steamship is located, beached a little way inland. Despite claims, however, this isn't his boat at all; it is the remains of a German hospital ship which plowed the Madre de Díos in mid-century.

Buy a bag or two of Brazil nuts while you're here. These rich, abundant and inexpensive nuts will help encourage the preservation of Madre de Díos' rainforest where 70 percent of the population is involved in nut extraction.

Only an hour south of Puerto Maldonado is **Lake Sandoval**, a beautiful jungle lake which can be reached by boat from Puerto Maldonado's port. Three hours further downriver, and well worth an overnight fishing expedition, is **Lake Valencia** which is quite remote and relatively free of tourists. A several-day expedition can be mounted to the 100,000-hectare (250,000-acre) **Pampas de Río Heath National Reserve**, a wild area of plains and swamps located on the Heath river bordering Bolivia. Guides and their boats can be rented. Travelers wishing to go to Bolivia (about five hours to the border) can easily buy a passage with the weekly cargo boats traveling the Madre de Díos river. Many of the boats stop in small river communities for rubber and Brazil nuts, thus allowing the traveler a privileged view of a way of life that has little changed in the last 100 years.

Tambopata-Candamo Reserve: Created by the Peruvian government in 1989, this 5,500-hectare (13,600-acre) "reserved zone" has been set up both as an extractive reserve (for rubber, Brazil nuts and other products) and for ecotourism. The reserve encompasses the entire watershed of the **Tambopata river**, one of the most beautiful and least disturbed areas in Peru.

The river begins high in the Andean department of Puno; several tour companies lead kayak expeditions down the Tambopata which offers a spectacular transition from the Andes to the low jungle. Recommended amongst them is **Mayuc Tours**; a week and a half expedition runs around $500. Tambopata

Nature Tours also run visits to the area.

Within the same reserve, about a four-hour river journey from Puerto Maldonado on the Tambopata, is the **Explorer's Inn Lodge** owned by Peruvian Safaris. With world record numbers of birds and butterflies, a two day/three night package runs about $160. Tours are led by biology graduate students; yet because there are settlers in the area, large mammals are only occasionally to be seen. The area is beautiful, however, and side-trips are available from the lodge to one of the world's largest macaw coplas (salt-licks), located some four hours further upriver where hundreds of spectacularly colored macaws can be seen everyday.

Closer to the Puerto Maldonado area (and hence in a more disturbed, yet accessible area) are two other jungle lodges: **Cuzco Amazonico** located 45 minutes downriver from Puerto Maldonado on the Madre de Díos river, and **Tambo Lodge**, on the opposite side of the Madre de Díos, only 8 km (5 miles) from town.

Below, ecologist marks a baby caiman. Right, watching from above.

BIRDWATCHING IN THE AMAZON

The forests along the western edge of the Amazon basin, nudging the Andean foothills, contain the highest diversity of bird species of any region on Earth.

The richest, least disturbed part of this unique belt is found in the unlogged, unhunted rainforests of southeast Peru. Here a typical square-mile of forest boasts over 500 species of bird – 40 percent more than a similar area in the central Amazon of Brazil. This species-rich area ranges from the cloud forests of the Andean foothills to the rainforests of the Amazonian lowlands, and offers unmatched opportunities to see rare and fascinating birds. There are many species of birds which only occur at higher elevations. These can be seen in the mountain cloud forests, and include golden-headed quetzals, large green military macaws, and orange-red male cock-of-the-rocks that use elaborate wing displays to attract females.

In the lowland rainforests every level, from darkened forest floor to sun-dappled canopy, supports a variety of insect- and fruit-eating birds. Many of the insect-eating birds gather together in mixed flocks containing dozens of different species. Small antbirds, woodcreepers, gnateaters, and foliage-gleaners all search for insects amongst the leaves and epiphytes in a flurry of activity. Identifying the many constantly moving individuals in these large mixed-species flocks poses one of the real challenges for tropical birders. Other insect-eaters, like the black-spotted bare-eye, specialize in following army ants so as to catch the insects fleeing from the invading ant swarm.

Fruit-eating birds on the other hand are often attracted to the fig tree with its small, soft fruits. Paradise tanagers, euphonias, brilliant blue cotingas, fruitcrows, squawking parrots, and large-billed toucans may all visit the tree, creating a day-long spectacle.

Entry to the jungle: However, to see these birds it is necessary to have a network of trails giving birders access to many types of forest. Such trail systems are provided by lodges located in the protected forests of two huge preserves in southeast Peru.

The largest of these, the **Manu Biosphere Reserve** is one of the few truly pristine regions of the tropics. Its 1.8 million hectares (4½ million acres) harbor over 1,000 species of bird – 300 more species than are found in the US and Canada together. In fact, the world record for the number of species seen and heard in one day was set in Manu in 1982 when 331 species were recorded in just a few square-miles of forest.

The only lodge located in the Manu preserve is **Manu Lodge**, operated by Manu Nature Tours, who offer all-inclusive tours. The lodge overlooks a tranquil rainforest lagoon, and accommodates just 30 visitors. Its expanding trail system provides access to seasonally flooded forest, high ground forest, and patches of bamboo. There are also experienced guides to help visitors find shy bird species, like the Amazonian Antpitta.

eft, macaws
a salt lick.
ight,
xperiencing
e jungle.

Large, rare game-birds such as razor-billed curassows and piping-guans have been hunted out of most areas, but are easy to see at Manu Lodge. Also seen are macaws, pale-winged trumpeters, the tall jabiru storks, roseate spoonbills, and five species of large eagle including the majestic harpy eagle.

New species are continually being discovered along the lodge trails. The extremely rare rufous-fronted ant-thrush, for example, was previously known from only one location but has now also been found at Manu Lodge. Another excellent spot to view birds is the **Parrot Inn Lodge** in the Cultural Zone of Manu, next to a macaw lick on the Madre de Díos river. Parrot Inn is run by ornithologist Barry Walker's **Expediciones Manu**, and provides canoes, floating blinds and planned canopy access for 1996.

Forest for macaws: There are more chances to see birds in the second large reserve: the **Tambopata-Candamo Reserve**. This 5,500-hectare (13,500-acre) preserve protects the largest macaw lick in South America. Here birders can view one of the world's phenomenal avian spectacles.

Hundreds of red, blue, and green parrots and macaws gather at the lick daily. Squawking raucously, they wheel through the air before landing together on the river bank to eat clay. This breathtaking display can only be seen where there is undisturbed rainforest with healthy populations of wild macaws, as in southeast Peru.

Rustic accommodation is provided at the macaw lick by Tambopata Nature Tours, with six days including transportation costing about $500. Trails around the macaw lick offer birding in both floodplain and high ground forest. Orinoco geese and large horned screamers can also be seen along clear streams near the Andean foothills.

Also in the Tambopata Reserve is the **Explorer's Inn** lodge, owned by Peruvian Safaris, with 2 days/3 nights at $160. Up to 500 bird species can be seen around the lodge. These include quetzals, manakins, and many antbirds. The lodge **Searching for rarities...**

trails also provide good access to patches of bamboo with bird specialities like the Peruvian recurve-bill, white-cheeked tobey-flycatcher, and goeldi's antbird.

With all this, the forests of southeast Peru offer the finest birdwatching experience. However, identifying all the different species, and finding elusive birds in the forest undergrowth, can prove overwhelming for an ornithologist inexperienced in tropical forests. An expert guide familiar with the rainforest and its birdlife is invaluable for a rewarding birdwatching trip to southeast Peru. **Manu Nature Tours** at Avenida Sol 627-B, officina 401, in Cuzco provide bilingual guides on their birding tours. High-quality tours with expert guides are also provided to many parts of southeast Peru by **Victor Emmanuel Nature Tours** at P.O. Box 33008, Austin, TX 78764.

Birdwatching tours like these help support many local families who will conserve rainforest birds if their livelihoods depend on it. Local people will not hunt macaws for trade or feathers if they can make more money by taking visitors to see wild macaws at clay licks, as in the Tambopata Reserve. By choosing such tours, visitors can make a positive conservation impact while enjoying the spectacular birdlife. However, the birds cannot survive without the pristine rainforests in which they live. A non-profit group dedicated to preserving these virgin forests is the **Peruvian Conservation Association for the Southern Rainforests** (ACSS), based at Avenida Sol 627-B, oficina 305, in Cuzco. ACSS works to protect the forests upon which this incredible birdlife depends.

Preparations: The most appropriate clothing for a jungle trip is long-sleeved shirts and trousers of a close-woven material. These protect against biting insects. Cotton is more comfortable in tropical climates than synthetic material. Bring a hat as protection. Visits are generally more comfortable during the dry season (May–October) when it may not rain for weeks at a time. The rainy season lasts from November to April.

..in the sky.

CALLEJÓN DE HUAYLAS

Stretching for 160 km (256 miles) and ranging in altitude from a mere 1,800 meters (5,900 feet) to 4,080 meters (13,380 feet), the valley known as the **Callejón de Huaylas** rates as one of the finest areas in all of South America for its superb mountain vistas and a wealth of opportunities for outdoor pursuits. Many dedicated enthusiasts arrive prepared for trekking and climbing to snowboarding, parapenting and skiing, while others are content to spend their days relaxing in a spectacular mountain setting and exploring the villages which sprawl along the hillsides.

The Callejón de Huaylas is bordered on the east by the Cordillera Blanca (white mountains) – a mountain range with the greatest number of 6,000-meter (20,000-feet) peaks outside the Himalayas – and on the west by the more diminutive range known as the Cordillera Negra (black mountains) for their sparseness of vegetation and complete lack of snow. To the north, the valley terminates with the Cañon del Pato, a narrow gorge of a canyon with sheer rock walls, steep precipices and a dirt road winding its way through numerous crudely constructed tunnels down toward the coast. There are daily bus services to Chimbote from Huaráz – go by day for the exciting views. The 40-km (25-mile) wide Callejón de Huaylas is renowned not only for its breathtaking scenery, but for Inca and pre-Inca history, unusual flora and fauna, lively markets and traditional villages.

Regional pride: If one trait was left as a legacy by the early inhabitants of this region, it would be that of independence. Dating from around 1000 BC, the Chavín culture emerged with a highly developed art style and cult whose influence lasted longer than the Roman empire and was so widespread that archaeologists have termed this forma-

Preceding pages: the Cordillera Blanca. **Left,** village in the Cordillera Blanca.

tion period "the Chavín Horizon." The Huaylas culture, occupying the valley during the Inca expansion, was briefly dominated, though not entirely conquered, by this more sophisticated civilization who set up Andean crossroads between the important centers of Cajamarca and Cuzco. When the Spaniards arrived, they were considered liberators of sorts, for the daughter of Kuntar Guacho, the lord of Huaylas, was given as mistress to the *conquistador* Francisco Pizarro himself. In later history, the early 1800s, an Indian uprising against heavy taxation and labor abuses took the Spanish by surprise, requiring several months to crush. Today, the tradition of independence can be sensed in the people who carry themselves with pride, and is evident in the policies of the regional government which maintains a certain distance from the central authorities in Lima only 8 hours away by road.

The Callejón de Huaylas is also well known for a history of natural disasters. Earthquakes and alluvions, floods of water combined with avalanches and landslides have caused considerable damage over the past 300 recorded years. The capital city of Huaráz was severely damaged by an alluvion in 1941 when an avalanche broke loose from a nearby mountain and caused Laguna Palcacocha to overflow. The resulting mixture of water, rock and snow tumbled down the narrow Cojup Valley and inundated the city. Much of the central district was destroyed and nearly 5,000 lives were lost. The most tragic disaster occurred in 1970, when an earthquake measuring 7.7 on the Richter scale devastated the entire region and was responsible for more than 80,000 deaths.

Huaráz again suffered with the loss of more than 30,000 lives and over 80 percent of the city flattened, but hardest hit was the village of Yungay. The entire town and most of its inhabitants completely disappeared under a massive avalanche of rock and snow when part of the Huascarán massif broke loose and plunged down the valley.

In the aftermath of these catastrophes many of the towns and villages have been almost completely rebuilt, but with a dubious eye for design. Progress has been introduced in the form of uninspiring concrete structures with little thought given to preserving an architectural heritage. The colonial charm encountered in other highland areas has been all but lost in the Callejón de Huaylas. Sadly, these natural disasters also took a heavy toll on the archaeology of the region. Notably lacking are many ancient remains, primarily Inca, which did not survive the calamities.

Mountain retreat: The center of most commercial activity and the common destination for visitors to the Callejón de Huaylas is the city of **Huaráz**. As the capital of the department of Ancash and with a population of more than 80,000 inhabitants, this highland mecca is well suited to support the demands of tourism. At first glance, Huaráz appears to be little more than a "one-horse" town, but a closer look proves that all necessities are readily available. Scores of low-cost hostels offer accommodation ranging from very basic to quite comfortable. Edward's Inn is a popular place to stay for its location away from the city center and its warm, family atmosphere. A few higher-priced hotels are available for those who require a bit of luxury during their mountain retreat. Hostal Colomba offers individual bungalows in a lovely garden setting, and the Swiss-run Hostal Andino has great views of the Cordillera Blanca.

Before departing for remote regions or after a long trek in the mountains, you'll find plenty of activity in the bustling town of Huaráz. Along the main street of Luzuriaga, *campesino* street vendors sell a wide selection of woolen goods, pan flutes and ceramic replicas of the Chavín temple. Other traditionally-dressed highlanders sell regional food specialities from wooden carts. Andean cheeses, rich honey and *manjar blanco* (a sweet, milk-based paste used as a topping or filling), are a few tasty edibles that are worth trying. Storefront tour companies set out brightly-colored billboards promoting day trips to popular tourist sites and advertise an assortment of climbing and trekking gear for hire. A wide range of restaurants cater to international tastes. Pizzerias, Chinese food and hamburgers are found along with the more typical dishes of *lomo saltado, pollos a la brasa*, and *cuy*, roasted guinea pig.

Worth a visit is the **Archaeological Museum,** off Ancash on the **Plaza de Armas**. It is a humble affair, yet considered noteworthy for its collection of stone monoliths from the Recuay culture which date from 400 BC to AD600. Also on display are mummies, ceramics and household utensils dating from the same period. The museum is open most days from 9am to 5pm. A modest entrance fee is charged.

Huaráz nightlife also has plenty to offer. Several cinemas show recent American films in English with Spanish subtitles, though the sound system frequently leaves something to be desired. Often the amusement comes more from observing the reaction of the highlanders to the "first-world" dramas and watching the silliness of American films from another perspective. Peñas, or folk-lore nightclubs, entertain with traditional Andean musical groups in the early evening, and switch to disco later on for serious high-altitude dancing. El Tambo Peña is one of the most popular and is packed to capacity on weekends during the high season. Offering a more laid-back atmosphere and a good meeting place is the Tasco Bar, which also serves up some fairly decent Mexican food for being so far south of the border.

The outlying area of Huaráz is replete with many opportunities for day excursions. Footpaths lead to a number of small villages and agricultural areas within walking distance of the city center. Rataquenua, Unchus, Marían and Pitec are just a few of the *pueblos* which can be visited in a few hours.

Ancient remains: Lying about 8 km (5 miles) north of Huaráz and easily reached by foot is the small pre-Inca ruin of **Wilcahuaín**. Little is known about this three-storied structure which stands in the middle of an agricultural valley, but it is thought to date from AD1000 and is a replica in miniature of the temple of

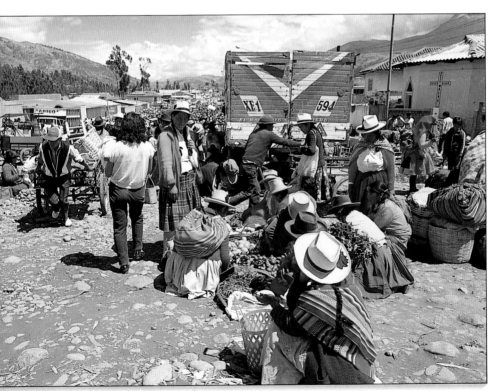

Marketplace Huaráz.

Chavín. The masonry style is typical of the Huari-Tiahuanacu culture which expanded from the coastal region between the 7th and 11th centuries. The windowless inner chambers can be explored with a flashlight, or with candles proffered by any one of the hordes of schoolboys who haunt the site and offer their services as guides. Most of the rooms within the construction are inaccessible from the debris of centuries, but a few have been opened up to reveal a sophisticated ventilation system and skilful stone craftmanship.

Longer excursions to the surrounding countryside are as simple to arrange as locating the proper rural bus to take you there. A major road stretches the length of the Callejón de Huaylas running alongside the Santa river and local transportation is readily available to a variety of villages situated along the route. Quite often the ride can be as fascinating as the destination, when local *campesinos* overcome their shyness and initiate a conversation. A bus ride can turn into a rollicking affair of giggles, stares and laughter as the *gringo*, or foreigner, attempts to answer questions about himself in broken Spanish.

The village of **Monterrey**, just 5 km (3 miles) outside Huaráz, is worth a visit for its *baños termales* (hot springs). Two swimming pools of warm water, and private baths of the steaming variety are extremely inviting, especially after a rigorous trek in the mountains. A few kilometers farther up the valley is the village of **Chancos** which claims to have its own Fountain of Youth – more thermal baths with natural saunas and pools of flowing hot water.

Yungay lies north down the valley and is the turn-off point for the 2-hour ride up to the popular **Llanganuco lakes**, an excellent day excursion from Huaráz. It is this village which was completely destroyed by the 1970 earthquake. In 1962, Yungay was graced with a "near miss" when an avalanche decimated the neighboring village of Ranrahirca. During the most recent rebuilding of Yungay, the village site was shifted a few kilometers north of its original location

Mountain flowers.

276

in the hope that it would now be out of the way of any future disasters. All that remains of the abandoned Yungay is a solitary monument dedicated to those whose lives were lost, and a few battered palm trees that once lined the charming Plaza de Armas.

About an hour by local bus south of Huaráz awaits the small town of **Catac** often visited by those keen to see the giant *Puya Raimondi*. This unusual plant is often referred to as a cactus, but is actually the largest member of the Bromeliad family. It is a rare species, considered to be one of the oldest in the world, and is found in only a few isolated areas of the Andes. At its base, the Puya Raimondi forms a huge rosette of long, spiked, waxy leaves – often reaching a diameter of 2 meters (6½ feet). As it begins to flower, a process which takes its entire lifespan estimated to approach 100 years, it sends up a phallic-like spike which can reach a height of 12 meters (39 feet). As the final flowering begins, usually in the month of May for mature plants, the spike is covered in flowers – as many as 20,000 blooms on a single plant. During this season if you are incredibly lucky groups of Puya Raimondi may bloom together, creating an unbelievable picture set against the backdrop of the snowy peaks of the Cordillera Blanca.

Reserve in the Sierra: Much of the Cordillera Blanca above 4,000 meters (13,000 feet) and the area around Huascarán mountain fall within the confines of **Huascarán National Park**, first conceived in 1958 and finally established in 1972. This, along with other national parks set up at the same time, marked Peru as a frontrunner in Latin America in the area of conservation. Huascarán National Park was formed to protect the indigenous wildlife, archaeological sites, geology and natural beauty of an area threatened by mining and other commercial interests. A small entrance fee is charged to help offset the cost of providing park guardians. Of the more interesting wildlife that you can possibly see, with a little patience and a bit of luck, is the *viscacha*, a small, elusive

irls in the
ordillera
lanca.

squirrel-like animal with characteristics similar to the North American marmot; the vicuña, a cameloid cousin to the llama; and the stealthy puma. On rare occasions, *burros* brought along by travelers for help transporting heavy loads do not finish the trek circuit, having become instead a tasty meal for a hungry puma.

Throughout the Callejón de Huaylas, a lifestyle dating back centuries continues to thrive in the Andean foothills. The traditional dress of the villagers has not changed radically in many years. The women, especially, hold on to their heritage, wearing layers of colorful woolen skirts and embroidered blouses which developed during colonial times. In addition, each wears a hat style which may vary significantly from village to village. The custom of hat-wearing can also be used to indicate marital status, as in the village of Carhuaz. There, a woman wearing a black band around her fedora is a widow, while a rose color would be worn by a single woman and a white band would show that the woman was married.

Agriculture, the mainstay of the valley, has also seen little change over the centuries in either methods or crop variety. Double-yoked oxen still drag crude wooden plows through the black, fertile soil. Honey-colored wheat can be seen ripening throughout the valley and maturing quinoa plants, a high-altitude grain rich in protein, are easily recognized by the rich colors of burnt orange, fiery red and deep purple they blaze along the hillsides.

Corn – the sacred crop of the Incas and one of the earliest foods which took man from hunter-gatherer to farmer – is grown in abundance and is the staple of life along with the ever-present potato. From it, a slightly-fermented maize beer, called *chicha*, is made which is drunk in great quantities, especially during festivals. It was originally the royal drink, suitable only to be consumed by the Inca king and his court.

Festivals play a large part in the lifestyle of the indigenous people who inhabit the Callejón de Huaylas. It is a way to break out of the monotony of the day-to-day existence and reaffirm the traditions which give a continuity to life in the Andes. Since the Spanish Conquest, festivals have assumed a religious veneer and coincided with Catholic feast days, but underneath still lies a thread of meaning left behind by ancient cultures.

Every month of the year sees a celebration, or several, in full swing. Some are particular to one village, while others are observed throughout the region. The festivals of San Juan and San Pedro, celebrated during the last week of June, are particularly lively, especially since they coincide with the national day set aside to honor the *campesino*.

On the eve of San Juan, fires are lit throughout the valley, burning the chaff from the harvest and wild ichu grass on the hillsides. From a high mountain camp, the fires look like starlight brought to earth and the next day the valley is thick with smoke. Semana Santa, or Easter Week, is another widely celebrated festival. Many villages have their own special traditions, but the celebra-

Ice precipice

tions are always colorful and abundant. Processions of finely-adorned religious figures carried on litters, scenes of the resurrection sculpted in flower petals on the ground, and folkloric bands playing music throughout the village are common themes during the festivities of Holy Week.

Jaguar-worshippers' temples: Of the visitors to the Callejón de Huaylas, many not only come for the majestic mountains and typical highland life, but to see one of the oldest archaeological sites designed by one of the most influential cultures in the Americas. The temple complex of **Chavín de Huántar** is actually located across the mountains in the next valley to the east near the village of Chavín, yet transport is most accessible from the city of Huaráz. Here lies the remains of one of the most important cultures that flourished from about 1300 to 400 BC.

Archaeologists have been able to learn very little about the cult whose architecture and sculpture had a strong impact on the artistic and cultural development of a large part of the coast and central Sierra of Peru. Because the culture left no written records, much of what is suggested is based on pure supposition. One thing that has been established is that at the time of the Chavín emergence, man was moving from a hunter-gatherer society to one of agriculture, and subsequently was in a position to devote newly-found leisure time to artful development. The theories that have been put forth about this mysterious culture are based on the study of this 17-acre site containing a temple, plazas, and a multitude of stone carvings and drawings. Based on physical evidence, the temple of Chavín de Huántar is thought to have been a major ceremonial center and the feline, or jaguar, the principal deity of the cult.

What first strikes most visitors upon arrival to Chavín de Huántar is the quality of the stonework found in the temple walls and plaza stairways. The dry stone-masonry construction reflects a sophistication not expected from a culture that produced it more than 3,000 years ago.

oproach to uascarán in e Cordillera lanca.

Added to this are huge stone slabs with highly stylized carvings of jaguars, eagles and anacondas; the designs are intricate and fluid.

The temple sits above a large, sunken plaza where it is believed pilgrims came to worship during certain seasons. On one side sits a large granite slab with seven hewn-out indentations which must have served as an altarstone for group rituals. Two 3-meter (10-feet) high stone portals overlook the plaza and represent the entry way into the interior of the temple. Both feature a finely-etched bird-like figure, one male, one female, which face each other across a stairway, symbolically divided into two halves – one painted black and the other white. Its significance is a mystery, but the effect is striking.

Niches set around the outside of the temple walls originally held protruding sculpted stone heads, human in shape but with the snarling grin of a jaguar. Some suggest that the eyes were originally inset with crystals which would reflect the light of the moon and ward

off evil-doers. Only one of these "keystones" remains in its original place. A few have been stolen and the rest safely stored within the temple.

The interior of the temple is a subterranean labyrinth of passages and galleries set on at least three levels which are connected by a series of ramps and stairs. Though there are no windows, a highly-engineered ventilation system allows the continuous flow of fresh air throughout – another marvel produced by an ancient civilization. Some of the rooms contain what remains of the sculpted heads and intricately-carved slabs which portray a variety of Amazonian and highland animals. These appear to have been originally positioned outside the temple.

Granite god: At the heart of the underground complex, two narrow passageways cross and at their junction stands the crowning glory of the Chavín religion – the Lanzón de Chavín. This 4-meter (13-feet) high granite monolith is thought to be the principal god-image worshipped by this cult. Its Spanish

Left, carving at Sechín. Below, keystone at Chavín de Huántar.

name comes from the lance, or dagger-like shape of the monolith which appears to be stuck in the ground. A mythological image emerges from the elaborate stone carving and its demeanor is in keeping with most of the terrifying god images created by the Chavín people.

The large head of the monolith is square, human-like, yet definite feline characteristics are noted in the grinning mouth, out of which protrudes a long fang from each corner. The nose has two big holes for nostrils and an arm and leg are visible on each side. Round earrings dangle from the creature's ears and long flowing hair is made up of intricately-carved serpents. Carved into the top of the head are thin, grooved canals and some speculate that animals, or even humans, may have been sacrificed to this god.

Above the god image, there was once an opening in the ceiling, now closed to preserve the figure from exposure to the elements. Here it is believed that a sacrificial rock may have positioned and, as animals or people were slaughtered, the blood would flow through the opening in the ceiling and would run down through the canals in the figure. Other archaeologists disclaim the sacrificial theory and suggest that the Lanzón was merely the dominant figure for worship.

Two other monoliths are considered important in the Chavín cult, but both are now housed in the Museum of Anthropology and Archaeology in Lima. The 1.8-meter-high (6-foot) stone "Estela Raimondi" was originally discovered by a *campesino* in 1840, who took the piece home to use as a table. Archaeologist Antonio Raimondi eventually had it transferred to Lima at the end of the last century. It depicts a monstrous feline anthropomorphic god with its arms wide open and holding a large cane. The feet are bird-like claws and serpents represent the hair.

The "Tello Obelisk" was discovered by the anthropologist Julio C. Tello and brought to Lima just after the turn of the century. Again the feline, or jaguar, image is represented in a mixture of jagged teeth and crawling serpents.

arvings at echín.

THE NORTH

The essence of **Trujillo**, Peru's most important northern city, is summed up every year during the flower-strewn Spring Festival. Barefoot women in white lace skirts and blouses, with ornate gold filigree ornaments dangling from their earlobes, whirl and curtsy through the streets in the traditional *marinera* dance. Charming, simple, formal and delicate – all are characteristics of this coastal city, making it the perfect spot to explore Peru's gentle but fiercely patriotic north.

Founded in 1535 and named after Francisco Pizarro's birthplace in Spain, Trujillo was the resting spot along the Spaniards' route between Lima and Quito. It soon merited the title "Lordliest City" and its well-preserved colonial homes with intricate wooden balconies and complicated window grilles pay testimony to an elegant past.

Fiery past: Although European ways were firmly planted here, Trujillanos eschewed blind loyalty to the Spanish crown. In 1820, this became the first Peruvian city to proclaim its independence from Spain, and liberator Simón Bolívar, moving down the coast from Ecuador, set the seat of his revolutionary government here. From Trujillo the Venezuelan leader prepared his campaigns for the decisive battles of Junín, Pichincha and Ayacucho. At the latter battle in the plain bearing the same name, soldiers from Venezuela, Colombia, Peru and Bolivia – under Bolívar's command – turned back the royalist troops once and for all.

A century later, political fervor coursed through Trujillo when the city gave birth to the progressive political party APRA, the Alianza Popular Revolucionária Americana. But the ideas of party founder, Victor Raúl Haya de la Torre, were too radical for the government; the party was outlawed and its militants forced to operate in secret. Government repression and torture of *Apristas* culminated in 1932 in the "Trujillo Massacre" in which a rebellious crowd of party followers attacked an army post and killed the officers in charge. *Apristas* claim close to 6,000 persons were executed by military firing squads in retaliation.

In one of the more bizarre twists of Peru's political history, Haya de la Torre – by then one of the continent's most revered statesmen – was elected president of Peru in 1962 at the age of 67. The military alleged fraud and voided the election. Three decades earlier the military had stepped in to block Haya de la Torre from his first presidential bid, forcing him to seek refuge in the Colombian embassy in Lima – where he remained for a number of years. Haya de la Torre died six years before a 1985 landslide victory finally put the left-of-center party in power under the presidency of Alán García.

Even today, on the anniversaries of Haya de la Torre's birth and death, the statesman's Trujillo grave with its eternal torch and inscription "Here Lies the Light" is piled high with flowers. And the mention of his name sparks perhaps

Preceding pages: rider with Caballo de Pasa, Trujillo. Left, fisherman on the coast near Trujillo. Right, carrying a reed boat.

more outpourings of love – and hatred – than that of any other Peruvian.

Another of Trujillo's militant *Apristas*, Ciro Alegría, was exiled to Chile for his political activity – and there he published the first of the trio of novels that converted him into one of the continent's most acclaimed authors. Although only 22 when he was banned from Peru, repeated jailing and beatings had left Alegría with permanent health problems, compounded later by tuberculosis. He won literary attention with *La Serpiente de Oro* (The Serpent of Gold), but he is best known for *El Mundo Es Ancho y Ajeno* (The World is Wide and Far) – both based on his childhood and rich with material on *campesino* life. When he died in 1967, Alegría was representing Lima in Peru's Congress.

A peaceful present: These tumultuous days of exile, political subterfuge and bloodshed seem distant now in Trujillo, where formality and turn-of-the-century charm hang in the air. The best way to see this city is on foot and the best place to start is the huge and impeccable **Plaza de Armas**, at the center of which is a disarming statue of a running winged figure – Liberty – holding a torch. Part of this landmark's oddness is its disproportionately short legs, designed to appease officials who feared the monument would end up taller than the cathedral facing it.

The plaza is bounded by that newly-renovated **cathedral**, **city hall**, the **archbishop's palace** and the colonial-style **Hotel Turistas**. Travelers who don't overnight at the hotel should consider a breakfast or lunch in its small windowed dining room looking out on to the plaza. From this vantage point one can see the slow-paced comings and goings of the city's elderly men who stake out shady benches to read their morning newspapers, the young mothers carrying their market baskets, toddlers in tow, or the uniformed school girls, huddled together sharing secrets.

Off the main square, dozens of churches, monasteries and convents from the era of viceroys spatter the city. Many are in stages of disrepair or renovation

The Central Club, Trujillo

following earthquakes that shake the northern coast at intervals. But the most intriguing colonial architecture is found in the mansions adorned with the detailed window grilles and intricately carved wooden balconies synonymous with this city. The window grilles are purely decorative; over the centuries their simple designs became increasingly elaborate as the colonial Trujillanos tried to outdo one another. The cathedral, too, once had elaborate metal adornments and railings but they were melted down for armaments during the wars of independence. The balconies, on the other hand, had a practical purpose: they allowed upper-class women to look on to the street but prevented interested menfolk from looking in.

Historial houses: La Casa de la Emancipación is typical of the houses built in the 16th and 17th centuries and is one of the few containing its original furniture. This mansion is open daily to the public and its staff eagerly show visitors where earthquakes and remodeling over the centuries have changed the home's orig-

inal lines. Also worth seeing are **Casa de Mayorazgo, Casa Urquiaga** and **Casa Bracamonte**, as well as **Casa Ganoza**, now an art gallery, and the **Palacio Iturregui** housing the **Central Club**. At the latter, the Marqués of Torre Tagle proclaimed Trujillo's independence from Spain.

Further vestiges of the days of wealth are found on the sugar *haciendas* outside the city. Owing to its warm climate and gentle nighttime temperatures, the Trujillo countryside produces most of Peru's sugar – an important crop in a country where three spoons of the white granules go in each cup of coffee and where every child seems to be born with a sweet tooth. Land reform beginning in 1969 turned most of the sugar *haciendas* into cooperatives but the opulence of the past is still evident. The most impressive *haciendas* are **Casa Grande**, originally owned by a wealthy German immigrant family, and **Hacienda Cartavio**, where the sugar is used to make Cartavio rum.

To step back even further in time,

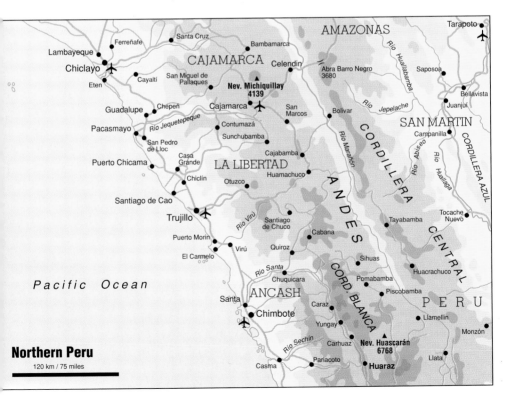

Northern Peru

120 km / 75 miles

Trujillo's pre-Hispanic past is on display at the University of Trujillo **Archaeological Museum**, located a block from the Plaza de Armas. Among the artifacts here are fine pieces of Moche and Chimú pottery found during excavations near the city.

Clay and the Chimús: On the fringe of Trujillo are the ruins of **Chan Chan**, possibly the world's largest adobe city at the time it was discovered by the Spanish nearly five centuries ago. Perched on 20 square kilometers (7.7 square miles) at the edge of the sea, its seven citadels are enclosed by a massive adobe wall. Chan Chan was home to the Chimú Indians, who fished and farmed, worshipped the moon and had no written records – leaving it to archaeologists to unravel their secrets. A hollow silence surrounds visitors to this ancient city where walls bear carvings of fish, sea birds, fishnets and moons and where cash-strapped scientists try to prevent the crumbling of the adobe structures by coating them with a cactus juice varnish.

Aided by sophisticated aqueduct and irrigation systems, the Chimús turned the arid wasteland around them into fertile fields of grains, fruits and vegetables supporting a population that may have reached 700,000. When conquered by the Incas, the Chimús were not forced to change their ways – except for the addition of the sun to their collection of gods; rather, Inca teachers were sent to study the Chimú farming and irrigation systems. It wasn't until the Spanish sabotaged the aqueducts after repeated attempts to invade Chan Chan that the fearless Chimús left the protection of the city – and were conquered.

An entrance ticket to Chan Chan also allows visitors to see the restored **Huaca El Dragón temple** nearby and the **Huaca La Esmeralda** ruins. Licensed guides can be hired at the ticket office at the ruins. Tourists are advised to begin their visit in the morning and avoid going alone; the tourism police at Chan Chan frequently go home mid-afternoon and there have been robberies at the isolated site. Visitors also are cau-

The ruins of Chan Chan.

tioned to steer clear of vendors hawking what they claim is antique pottery. Most of these ceramics are fake. Since Peru is more strictly enforcing laws to halt the trafficking of archaeological pieces, tourists lucky enough to stumble on authentic pottery could find the items confiscated and themselves fined or jailed if they try to take the artifacts out of the country.

Horse hooves and bare feet: Trujillanos are proud of their *Caballos de Paso*, a fine breed of horses with a tripping gait that has made them known worldwide. Another legacy of the Spanish, since there were no horses on the continent at the time of the Inca empire, these horses have been immortalized in Peruvian waltzes. In particular, composer Chabuca Granda, for whom a monument is erected in the bohemian neighborhood of Barranco in Lima, wrote of the *chalanes* or riders in their *jipijapa sombreros* upon their honey-colored mounts. These riders still compete in their own form of the *marinera* dance – smoothly guiding their horses through the steps.

Granda's most famous waltz to the Caballos de Paso is "José Antonio." The best of these trotters are bred in and around Trujillo and buyers from around the world congregate to see them shown at the annual Spring Festival – *Festival de la Primavera.*

The festival spotlight, however, is on the *marinera* dancers who pirouette and twirl as they rigorously vie for the male and female dance titles. The *marinera* is a graceful dance rooted in African and Spanish rhythms and movements; some say its steps mimic the strutting of a cock courting a hen. Shoeless women in ruffled lace skirts seductively flit toward white-garbed men in ponchos before quickly pulling away from the frustrated courter. The men attempt to win back the women's attention, deftly tossing up hats or handkerchiefs, then twirling and snatching them in mid-fall.

The dancers are barefoot and the men's trousers stop just above their ankles – a costume in keeping with this region's proximity to the sea, an area where feet and ankles are routinely dampened by

xamining
ainbow
arving at
:han Chan.

the Pacific ocean. Just 7 km (4 miles) from Trujillo it is possible to watch that unbreakable tie with the ocean in the seaside village of **Huanchaco**. Two centuries ago when the Huanchaco residents paid taxes to the Spanish crown and it was used as the storage city for Trujillo, two leagues away, it was a quiet village of men who fished and women who wove baskets in the sunshine. Little has changed.

Today sun-bronzed fishermen head out each morning with their nets tucked into *caballitos de totora,* literally "little horses" woven of totora reed. The design of these curved, peapod-shaped boats has changed little from the craft used by pre-Inca fishing tribes and the *cabalitos de totora* contrast startlingly to the brightly colored surfboards sharing the Pacific waves.

Excavation and black magic: Three hours to the north of Trujillo is the busy port of **Chiclayo**. This bustling city is a major commercial hub for northern Peru, and is a lively and friendly spot with few pretensions. This vitality is reflected in the architecture of the city center in which the modern happily co-exists with the colonial in the winding streets.

One unmissable sight within the city is the extensive **Mercado de Brojus** (witchcraft market), thought of as one of the most comprehensive in South America. Here one is treated to an overwhelming choice of herbal medicines, potions, charms and San Pedro cacti, from which an hallucinogenic drug is extracted and used by *Curanderos* (curers) in their traditional shamanic healing rituals.

A short distance away is the coastal resort of Pimental, with a good sandy beach – an excellent place to try the local speciality of *pescado seco*, a kind of rayfish known as *la guitarra*, which can often be found hanging out to dry in the sun in Chiclayo's market.

Of course, Chiclayo is also the starting point for visits to two of the continent's most exciting archaeological digs. The greatest attention has been lavished on the Moche Indian burial area at **Sipán** where the Americas' richest document-

Main square Chiclayo.

ed tomb was uncovered. (*See "Discovery and Desecration" on page 39.*) Nearby is the excavation at the **Túcume pyramids** – a project originally directed by Norwegian Thor Heyerdahl (of Kon-Tiki Expedition fame). He still returns to the site from time to time, but is now based in Norway.

Farther north is **Piura**, a hot commercial city best known for its folk dance, the *tondero*, and the black magic practiced by the descendents of black slaves. The *tondero* is a lively, barefoot Afro-Peruvian dance accompanied by strong rhythmic music and sashaying dancers in multicolored outfits. But Peruvian visitors to this part of the country usually come to see more than the dancers. There are Lima business executives who travel to this region every year to consult with the area's *brujos* – witches, folk healers and fortune tellers.

Nearly as famous as its esoteric pursuits is Piura's cuisine, with its sharp flavors and elaborate preparation. The best dishes include *seco de chavelo* (mashed plantains with fried pork), *majado de yucca con chicharrón* (mashed maniocs with fried pork), fried plantain bits known as *chifles*, and the goat milk and sugar cane molasses sweet called *natilla*. It is washed down with *chicha de jora*, a fermented corn drink.

Piura has a proud history, beginning with its founding as a city by the Spanish in 1532 – three years before Lima – and continuing through the War of the Pacific with Chile. That war's most famous hero was Admiral Miguel Grau, born in this oasis in the desert, and his home on Jirón Tacna across from the Centro Cívico has been converted into a museum. Of interest there is the scale model of the British-built *Huascar*, the largest Peruvian warship in that war. Grau was commander of the vessel and used it to keep invading Chilean forces at bay until his death in a battle at sea. During the war he was called "Gentleman Grau" because of his unceasing string of eloquent letters to the Peruvian President, seeking more supplies for his men, and his rescuing of Chilean sailors left in the water after each battle.

Below, northern twins. Right, shopping in Cajamarca.

Atahualpa's last home: Southeast across the dusty desert into the Andean highlands, far from ocean and magic, is **Cajamarca**. Now dotted by cattle herds and dairy farms where Peru's best cheese is made, this was one of the biggest cities in the Inca empire and marks where the Indians and Spaniards had their first showdown. According to Spanish chronicles, it was in Cajamarca that the Inca Atahualpa was kidnapped and later executed.

The heavily-armed Spaniards caught the Inca and his royal soldiers off guard and thousands of unarmed Indians were slain futilely trying to protect their leader in a bloodbath on the Plaza de Armas. Despite the Spaniards' numerical disadvantage, their audacity in kidnapping an Inca threw an already split Indian kingdom into confusion. What followed immediately was a cry across the Inca empire to assemble the outrageous ransom the Spanish requested for Atahualpa's release.

Leading Llamas weighted down by riches, Indians from as far away as Cuzco began the journey to Cajamarca, filling the **Rescue Room** a block from the Plaza de Armas with some of the Incas' most valuable treasures – which the Spanish promptly melted down into bullion. The Rescue Room is still there; a red line on one wall shows where the tall and powerful Atahualpa allegedly drew a mark, agreeing to have his subjects fill the room to that line twice with silver and once with gold. Once most of the treasure had been collected, the conquistadors had the Inca garrotted.

The spot for Atahualpa's execution was the **Plaza de Armas**, still the hub of this slow-paced city of 120,000. Some Peruvians believe the pink grain on a stone slab alleged to be where the Incas was killed is the indelible mark of his blood. What is certain is that in exchange for a promise he would not be burned alive, Atahualpa was baptized "Juan" just before his execution against the backdrop of massive Inca palaces. The palaces are gone and the plaza is now ringed by colonial buildings, the **cathedral** and lovely **San Francisco**

Witchcraft market, Chiclayo.

Church. The plaza's center is graced by a stone fountain frequented by *campesinos* and birds.

No bells toll: The cathedral, opened in 1776, is the most attention-getting building on the plaza. Its carved wood altars are covered in gold leaf and its facade of intricately carved volcanic rock is impressive. But something is conspicuously absent – its bell towers. They were left unfinished in protest against Spain's tax on churches. Next door is the **Hotel Turistas**, a better-than-average lodging with rooms furnished in heavy wooden antiques.

On the opposite side of the plaza is the San Francisco Church, older and more ornate than the cathedral, and home to the **Religious Art Museum** filled with its often violent and bloody colonial era paintings and statues. The guided tour of this storeroom of silver candelabras, gold altar vessels, jeweled vestments and portraits of saints and priests includes entrance to the church's eerie catacombs – precursor to the present city cemetery.

Also on the square is the family-run **Salas Restaurant**, described by one Cajamarquino as the "city's nerve center." Here locals catch up on the latest news and gossip while downing the city's best – and most economical – home cooking. Diners can find anything from crisp salads and thick *chupe verde* (potato and vegetable soup) to hearty beef ribs and spicy guinea pig stew. No meal is complete without *panqueque con manjar blanco*, a sweet, rich dessert consisting of a thick crepe bathed in a condensed milk sauce.

Hung on the restaurant's walls are paintings by local artist Andrés Zavallos, one of the founding fathers of Cajamarca's longstanding community of poets, writers, painters and musicians. Most notable of these was Mario Urteaga, the only Peruvian artist to have his work in the permanent collection at New York's Metropolitan Museum of Art and a person so loved in his hometown that the procession at his funeral in 1957 lasted into the night. Urteaga's oils depict *campesinos*, simple yet human, and the

Cajamarca.

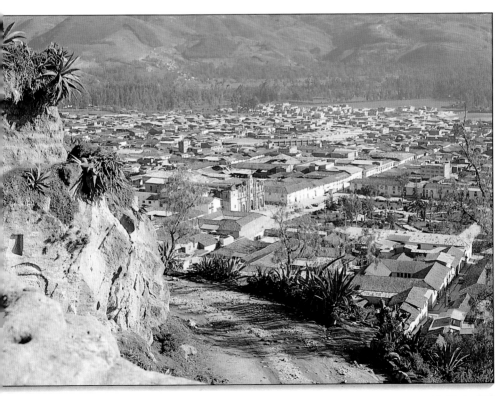

Cajamarca countryside was his studio. Today, Cajamarca photographer Victor Campos Río captures the beauty of the countryside and its people in photos and documentary films.

A few blocks from the plaza is the **Municipal Theater**, rescued by this culture-loving city after being used first as a movie theater then as a storehouse for industrial cleaner. Built by a wealthy German merchant using the architectural plans of a small opera house in his homeland, the theater has an impressive stamped metal ceiling and its seating nearly exactly duplicates the original plans of the theater, although the colors have been changed to add more glitter. The ticket office has listings of cultural events, which range from classical music to folklore dances; ticket prices are intentionally kept low to entice students and less affluent Cajamarquinos, along with city patricians.

Scaling the heights: For the physically fit, the best way to delight in Cajamarca's charms is from above. That means climbing steep **Cerro Apolonia**. Stone steps take climbers as far as a little chapel – a miniature version of Notre Dame Cathedral about halfway up the hillside – and the rest of the journey is on a curvy road bordered by cactus, flowers and benches for the fatigued. Near the top is the **Silla del Inca**, a rock cut into the shape of a throne where, Cajamarquinos say, the Inca sat and looked out over his kingdom. A bronze statue of Atahualpa, and parking for those who arrive by cab or car, top the hill.

The view here is reminiscent of Cuzco with green, rain-fed fields, red tile roofs and whitewashed houses. At night, the Cajamarca skies – which in daytime may switch in minutes from brilliant blue to stormy gray – are clear and star-studded. Early risers are in for a special treat; sunrises in these highlands are joyously beautiful and the show is a long one. It can take the sun up to 45 minutes to switch from a silhouetting blue-black to brilliant red-orange before lightening to a hazy yellow.

An equally spectacular view of the city can be found at Hacienda San

Window in Belén Church Cajamarca.

Vicente, the most intriguing hotel in town. A charming countryside inn perched on a steep rocky hill at the edge of Cajamarca, this lodge was constructed by using Inca techniques – and a few modern twists. The walls are made of packed earth painted with ocher and vegetable dyes. Skylights bring in illumination, fireplaces heat common areas after nightfall and guest rooms are decorated with local handicrafts. San Vicente stands where a real colonial estate house once existed; its original chapel remains next door and on San Vicente's holy day local farmers still take up musical instruments and bouquets of flowers and parade to the tiny church.

Inca bathing place: Looking from the Cerro by day, a white mist can be seen hovering over the edge of the city. This is the steam rising from the **Baños del Inca**, the Inca's bathing spot. These bubbling mineral springs made Cajamarca the Incas' favorite vacation spot; a sign over a huge stone tub at the springs claims that it was here Ata-

hualpa bathed with his family. The springs are so hot at their source that local Indians use them to boil eggs. Whether they are curative as the locals believe or not, they merit a visit. The city has channeled the water from the springs into a lukewarm Olympic-sized outdoor pool, rustic cabanas where families or groups of friends can splash privately and modern "tourist baths" where up to two persons can soak in tiled hot tubs. There is a minimal entrance fee to the facilities.

At the springs, several tourist hostels have sprung up, all of them with bathtubs or swimming pools fed by the springs. The best known and most impressive, despite its rustic appearance, is the **Laguna Seca**, converted *hacienda*, which has a pool, a pungent sauna where eucalyptus is steamed on hot coals, a weight-lifting room, a small bullfight ring, a cockfight arena and "Baños del Inca" water running into the deep bathtubs of every room.

Back in the city, at the base of Cerro Santa Apolonia, is the **Complejo Belén**

Fishing fleet.

housing the Institute of Culture, Cajamarca's most picturesque chapel, a museum and an art gallery. The Belén Church is undoubtedly the city's loveliest with elaborately carved stone and woodwork and brightly-colored statues and side altars. The small, white, carved dove suspended over the pulpit represents the Holy Spirit and allegedly gives those who stand under it the power of eloquence. The chapel's cupola altar depicts the three levels of life – ground level with the common people, an intermediary area with saints and priests and the top level – heaven – with God and the Virgin Mary, represented by the sky-blue dome of the cupola. Many visitors are fooled by the brilliantly painted details on the upper walls and ceiling of the church; these saints and cherubs are not made from painted wood or plaster, they are intricately carved stone. More carving is found on the massive wooden doors in the church, most of them solid pieces of Nicaraguan cedar.

Connected to the church is the **Pinacoteca**, a gallery of local artists' work in what was once the kitchen of a medieval hospital for men. Off the Pinacoteca is the former hospital ward, a room with alcoves along its side walls. The alcoves were the patients' "bedrooms" and the images of saints originally painted above them corresponded to the illnesses of the infirm. The sickest were bedded closest to the altar, conveniently located near the door to the cemetery. A sample alcove with blankets and its preserved saint painting can be seen across the street at the **Ethnographic and Archaeological Museum**, once the maternity hospital of the same era. The only difference was that from the tops of the women's alcoves dangled long scarves, which the patients pulled to help them during births.

The Ethnographic and Archaeological Museum has a collection of ceramics from Indian cultures that dominated this region of Peru, samples of local handicrafts and costumes used during the annual carnival celebrations – the most raucous in the country. Across the street at the **Cultural Institute**, Span-

Country cockfight.

ish-language books and the area's best postcards are on sale. The Institute has details of ongoing archaeological digs that can be visited from October to May, before the highland's rainy season begins. Those excavations include the Huacaloma and Kuntur Wasi digs sponsored by the University of Tokyo.

Ceramic traditions: The Complejo Belén artisan shop and those near the Plaza de Armas are filled with well-made knitted sweaters, pottery, baskets, leather goods and the gilt framed mirrors popular in this northern region. But the most fascinating – and least expensive – spot to buy pottery and ceramics is outside the city at **Aylambo**. Aylambo is a series of ecologically balanced workshops. Sewage at the workshops is processed into natural gas used to generate heat and light. Rather than buy expensive fuel and imported heat-resistent bricks from the kilns that fire the pottery, students collect kindling from the hillside and make their own heat-tolerating kiln tiles – in much the same way as their Indian ancestors did.

Products here range from plates bearing traditional Indian designs to teapots with modern glazes – concocted by the students – and money from pottery sales pays those working in the studios. Aylambo artisans, who range in age from nine to 90, are not charged to learn the crafts but economic necessity would force them to leave the workshop to find paying jobs if study stipends were not available. A long-term goal of the project is to inspire a bevy of environmentally sound workshops providing jobs, reclaiming ancient pottery designs, keeping *Cajamarquinos* living in the countryside and preventing further deforestation of the hills.

Beyond the city: There are many possible excursions outside Cajamarca, although these outings are best accomplished through a travel agency with transportation to the isolated areas. Puzzling and awesome are the **Ventanillas de Otuzco**, the cliffside "windows" that served as ancient Indian burial grounds. Anthropologists and archaeologists still have not unraveled the mystery of how

Cutting sugar cane.

the Indians were able to open the burial holes on the sides of sheer cliffs but they counted the openings to get an idea of the population – and importance – of the area before the conquistadors' arrival.

Equally astonishing is **Cumbemayo**, a valley cut by an Inca irrigation ditch of carved rock. The sophistication and precision of the ditch's angles – hewn by Indians using stone tools – leave modern-day hydraulic engineers marveling. Sharp turns in the ditch prevent the water from rushing too fast, as do imperceptible inclines. In the same valley are Los Frailones, huge rocks that have eroded into the shape of hooded monks, sparking a number of local legends, as well as some primitive Indian worship caves and petroglyphs.

Those who start their countryside ramblings early in the day may have time to reach the **Colpa dairy farm** before cow-calling time. Every day, just before 2pm, the cows at this cooperative are called by name – to the delight of the crowd that gathers to watch their antics. The animals respond by sauntering up to the milking areas bearing their names. Once a *hacienda*, Colpa is an example of the many cooperative dairies outside Cajamarca, famous for its butter, cheese and *manjar blanco* milk sweet. A hostal at Colpa offers travelers a pastoral spot to spend the night.

In the evenings Cajamarca rolls up its sidewalks early as fitting a farm community where work begins at sunrise. But nocturnal souls can listen – and dance – to boisterous local music at the Emperador. Or they can join the camaraderie, and even pick up a guitar if they play, at the more intimate **El Sítio bar** connected to the **Hostal Cajamarca** behind the Belén Complex. Here fans of tunes, ranging from *boleros* to the foot-stomping *huaynos* of the Andean highlands, meet to sing, drink and share their music with tourists.

Hemingway's marlin: Rather than heading inland from Chiclayo, it is also possible to continue along the coast north to Ecuador. Some 135 km (81 miles) north of Chiclayo, **Talara** is a desert oasis and a petroleum producing center with trans-

Building reed boats near Trujillo.

portation to the warm-water beaches of **Mancora**, **Playa Sol** and **La Pena** beach. **Cabo Blanco** is a popular spot for marlin fishing, frequented by Ernest Hemingway in his time, but experts say the marlin have actually now been carried south by the current to Mancora. Seaside seafood restaurants in Mancora are, for obvious reasons, recommended. This is also a popular spot for Brazilian surfers, as Peru's coast has some of the world's most spectacular waves and is frequently the sight of international surfing competitions.

The hotel offerings in Talara are slim and many fill up with visiting oil engineers. Camping is permitted at Cabo Blanco and other nearby beaches. South of Talara are the **Brea tarpits** where the Spanish boiled tar to caulk their ships.

Frontier town: Another 141 km (84 miles) north of Talara is **Tumbes**, a frontier town with a military post and immigration offices for crossing into Ecuador. Although there has been an ongoing effort to give this city of about 40,000 a facelift, there continues to be a problem with theft – particularly affecting tourists who find their suitcases, passports or money snatched most often near the bus offices or at the colorful outdoor market. A few miles outside the city at the actual border, known as **Aguas Verdes** on the Peruvian side, travelers are barraged by unscrupulous money changers, porters and over-friendly individuals with dubious motives.

Police corruption is notorious here, although that usually affects Peruvians more than outsiders and focuses upon the widespread cross-border trafficking in contraband items.

Tumbes is also within spitting distance of the few Peruvian beaches that offer white sand beaches and warm water for swimming all year round. **Caleta La Cruz** can be reached by cab or in collectivos, as can **Zorritos** and **Puerto Pizarro**. The latter has intriguing mangroves; boat rentals can be arranged with fishermen. Offshore here has become increasingly popular among deep-sea fishing enthusiasts drawn by the big fish that follow the Humboldt current.

atching a wave.

HUALLAGA, VALLEY OF COCA

The eastward-flowing Andean rivers have carved out over millennia a distinct ecological region where the mountain flanks meet Peru's Amazon basin. Here in what Peruvians call *la ceja de la selva* (the eyebrow of the jungle) are broad tropical valleys. The largest is the valley of the 935-km (580-mile) long **Huallaga river** in the northeast.

Opened up for colonisation with the extension of the Central Highway from Lima as far as Pucallpa in the 1940s, Huallaga Valley has been nurtured by successive governments as a potential larder for the country. In the 1960s a highway (the Carretera Marginal) was built through the valley to connect it with Lima and the north coast (now in very poor condition in many places). But though maize and rice are grown on a large-scale, in the past decade the valley has become known for another product – coca.

Everyday use: To the outside world, the small green coca leaf is best known as the raw material for the drug cocaine. But in the Andean highlands of Peru – as in Bolivia – it has been a part of the traditional Indian culture for over 4,000 years, and still is.

Coca leaves are for sale in any mountain market. Ask at a café for *mate de coca*, and you will receive a cup full of the leaves and hot water for a refreshing drink – normally taken as the best cure for *soroche* or altitude sickness.

Some 3 million South Americans still chew coca, adding a little bicarbonate of soda to get the saliva going, and keeping a wad of the leaf in their cheeks. It gives energy, and dulls the senses against cold and exhaustion. The biggest consumers have always been miners, who use up to half a kilo a day.

Coca is also used at every stage of the Indians' lives. Before giving birth, a woman chews the leaves to hasten labor and ease the pain. When the child is born, relatives celebrate by chewing the

<u>Left</u>, Andean valley, north Peru.

leaf together. When a young man wants to marry a girl, he offers coca to her father. And when somebody dies, *mate de coca* is drunk at the wake and a small pile of leaves is placed in the coffin before burial.

Ancient tradition: Archaeologists say that coca was first cultivated in the Andes around the year 2000 BC, or three millennia before the rise of the Inca dynasty. But it was the Incas who turned its production into a monopoly, as one more means of controlling subject populations. Its use was restricted to royalty, priests, doctors and the empire's messenger runners, known to travel vast distances in a day on the energy gained from chewing the leaves.

By the arrival of the first European explorers, the Incas had relaxed their monopoly on coca and its use had spread beyond their empire. The Catholic Church first tried to ban chewing of the leaf, denouncing it as "the delusion of the devil."

But they quickly changed their tune when it was found that Indians needed it to survive the brutal conditions in the colonial mines and plantations. Realizing that coca was essential to keep the captive labor force under control, the church then went into the coca business itself, establishing its own monopoly.

Back in Europe and the United States, coca was almost unheard of until the mid-1800s, when a chemist in Paris by the name of Angelo Mariani marketed a wine made from the leaf. Immensely popular at all levels of society, this Vin Mariani inspired American soft-drink companies to produce other drinks based on coca, such as Coca-Cola. At the same time, cocaine was first being developed. The white substance was quickly taken up by such modern luminaries as Sigmund Freud, who called it a "magical substance."

In the 1970s, cocaine became more popular, especially in the United States. Much of the coca grown in the Andes is now crushed by foot in chemicals, turned into a gummy paste and flown to Colombia. After being refined into powder, the cocaine is then smuggled into **Local transport.**

North American and European cities.

To give some idea of the size of the illicit trade, more than 40 light aircraft being used by *narcotraficantes* (drug-traffickers) to transport the paste to Colombia were shot down over Peruvian airspace in the first 8 months of 1995.

Cautious exploring: Cocaine has brought violence to the Huallaga Valley, in the shape of a complex conflict involving the drug police, backed by United States Drug Enforcement Administration agents, Colombian cocaine traffickers, left-wing guerrillas and the coca farmers themselves. Only the foolhardy tourist will venture into the heart of the valley. But the Huallaga is an area of great natural beauty, and around the fringes there are points that can be visited safely.

Tingo María, surrounded by jungle-clad mountains, is the main center for the Upper Huallaga. Founded in 1936, its population is now about 30,000. Police action has driven the cocaine industry further north, and the town is now generally quiet.

It has little to recommend it architecturally, but it has a pleasant Hotel de Turistas, set in beautiful gardens, on the edge of town. A stiff walk up a nearby mountain, with fine views, will take the visitor to the Cueva de las Lechuzas, a natural cave full of owls and bats.

North of Tingo María, the valley opens out and the river broadens, with huge meanders. Here are the towns of **Uchiza** and **Tocache**, the main centers of the cocaine trade. Full of *cantinas* and brothels, they have a Wild West atmosphere and are dangerous for *gringos* to visit, since they may well be taken for DEA agents. Between the two towns are two large palm oil plantations. Continuing north, there is a thinly-populated stretch, dominated by left-wing guerrillas, as far as Juanjui, a maize-growing center.

Further on, up the side-valley of the River Mayo, is **Tarapoto**, the main commercial center for the Middle Huallaga with a population of about 60,000. It is a pleasant, bustling pioneer town, surrounded by exuberant vegetation. A short walk away from the main square, the streets are of dirt and the back gardens are full of mango trees. There is a good Hotel de Turistas on the edge of town, with a swimming pool and tropical gardens.

An excursion can be made to the **Laguna Azul**, a lake (with hotel) deep in the countryside. Tarapoto has a busy airport, with daily commercial flights to and from Lima and Iquitos, and air-taxis from Tingo Maria.

From Tarapoto the Marginal Highway goes on up the Mayo Valley, a great rice-growing area. A side-road leads to **Lamas**, a small town peopled by jungle Indians who have preserved their traditions. The main road goes on to **Moyobamba** and **Rioja**, both pleasant and peaceful towns that were badly damaged by an earthquake in 1990, before crossing the Andean Cordillera and eventually reaching the coast.

Another road, in poor condition, leads from Tarapoto to the riverport of **Yurimaguas** on the lower Huallaga. From here river boats run to Iquitos, a two-day journey when going downstream (six days upstream).

oca leaves.

SOUTH COAST

Peru's southern desert coast, although inhospitable at first glance, is a historical land mine. It is the geographical encyclopedia of a handful of highly developed pre-Inca cultures known for their masterful pottery, fine weaving, medical advances and, in one case, the mysterious mammoth drawings they left on the desert plain at Nazca.

The south coast is also where ancient Indians proved once again they could, if not tame, then accommodate the harsh physical reality of their environment. This time it was not the imposing Andes mountains that separated the Indian tribes, made agriculture difficult and left the humans subject to the subtle changes in climate. Rather it was the parched and desolate desert, often compared to the deserts of North Africa, that proved the obstacle.

Captivating women: Although the more recent Inca culture has overshadowed much of the pre-Columbian development of this area, the artisan work left by the earlier civilizations prove they were more sophisticated than the Incas in both ceramics and textiles.

They were also renowned, according to Indian legend, for the beauty of their women. It is said that Pachacutec, the Inca responsible for expanding the empire, once sent a mission to the valleys of Chincha to begin work in conquering the Indians there. But Pachacutec's envoys – his brother and son – did not realize they were headed into an area where strong resistance against them was planned.

By chance, after meeting the desert leader Aranvilca in the valley, both men were taken by the beauty of his daughter. The Inca envoys befriended the young woman and she served as a go-between in the peaceful takeover of that Indian group. In appreciation, Pachacutec's men promised to help Aranvilca by ordering 30,000 members of the Inca nation to open a water canal from the Andean highlands into the valley, providing water. The tradition explaining the source of the waterway now known as Achirana, claims the work was completed in only 10 days.

Years later, when Huascar was declared the legitimate heir of Huayna-Capac and before he was killed by his half-brother Atahualpa, this heir received as a present from the Indians near Ica a young consort. Huascar was so awed by the woman's beauty that he called her Kory Koyllur – gold star – and fathered her child. His adoration of her so infuriated his other concubines that they murdered the young woman.

Into the devil's mouth: Heading south from Lima, the first community of note is **Pucusana**. This seaside resort town is also a charming fishing village with panoramic views from its cliffs and good seafood. During the Peruvian summer, from January to April, beaches can get crowded here on weekends. In the mornings, it is possible to hitch a ride on a launch and spend the day fishing or swimming offshore. The arrangements usually involve bargaining with local fishermen anxious to take a day off. Or,

Preceding pages: the **barren coastal desert. Left, sea lions on the Ballestas Islands. Right, Nazca lines seen from the air.**

those tired of the crowds at the Las Ninfas or Pucusana beach can ask for a ride to one of the more isolated stretches of sand (arranging for a pickup later in the day), such as Naplo.

Take the trip via the **Boquerón del Diablo**, literally the Devil's Big Mouth, which is a tunnel carved in the rock. It would be fatal to enter the tunnel, either by foot or in a boat, as the astonishing din coming from the Boquerón suggests. One Peruvian has described the groans from the tunnel as those of "a thousand devils."

Further to the south lies sunny **Chincha**, the city synonymous with wine, fine quality cotton, excellent athletes and ferocious fighting cocks. Its name is believed to be derived from *chinchay* – the Yauyo Indians' word for feline – although when the Spanish named it in 1571 it was more pompously called *Pueblo Alto de Santo Domingo*. Grape and cotton crops flourish here thanks to an elaborate system of irrigation and the re-routing of the Cochas river.

The city's fairly modern coliseum pays tribute to the long sports tradition here. Chincha has turned out a number of Peruvian sports stars, principally in soccer and boxing. Great Peruvian boxer Mauro Mina – from Chincha – defeated a number of North Americans including Floyd Patterson before a detached retina prevented him from going for the middleweight world title.

Another distinguished Chincha athlete, Fernando Acevedo was a Pan American running champion in 100- and 200-meter events. His nickname was "The Harpoon of Chincha."

This is home to much of Peru's black population, descendants of slaves brought to work on coastal plantations, and it is the center for Afro-Peruvian dances, including the energetic and comical *alcatraz* in which a gyrating male dancing with a lit candle in hand attempts to ignite the cloth tail hanging from his teasing partner's bright-hued skirt. Many of these dances are accompanied by rhythms supplied by *cajones*, hollow boxes pounded by open-palmed drummers.

Church in Pisco.

308

Continuing south on the Pan American highway is **Pisco**, a port city that gave its name to the clear white grape alcohol used in Peru's national drink, the *pisco sour*. The invention of pisco was actually a mistake by Spaniards trying to introduce grapes and wine production into the dry coastal area of the New World. However, once they tried this potent, yet smooth, beverage they decided it had merit of its own.

A pisco sour is a cocktail made from pisco, lemon juice, egg white and sugar syrup, whipped and served with a dash of Angostura bitters.

The city, now with 80,000 inhabitants, joined the bandwagon when revolutionary fever overtook the continent in the early 1800s. Half a block from the town's **Plaza de Armas** is the **Club Social Pisco** used as the headquarters for liberation leader General José de San Martín while he was fighting the Spaniards.

A statue to this Argentine hero of the independence war is found on the main plaza – the same square where boat trips to the Ballestas Islands can be arranged.

Originally, Pisco stood in another spot not far away. But an earthquake in 1687 and subsequent pirate attacks badly damaged the structures in the city, prompting the viceroy, Count de la Monclova, to order it moved. Construction of the opulent baroque **cathedral** started shortly thereafter, only ending in 1723.

Pisco's small airport serves as the emergency landing strip when heavy fog prevents planes from descending in Lima; passengers are then bused to the Peruvian capital or wait until the weather clears before flying north again. From 1960 to 1970, small propeller planes of the foreign-owned Consorcio Ballenero buzzed the waters offshore in a now defunct project to localize and count groups of whales that regularly ply Peru's coast.

Then, in late 1988, Peruvian scientists, in conjunction with experts from the Natural History Museum at the Smithsonian Institute in the United States, announced the appearance of a new whale species. Named the Meso-

Llamas gather on the southern coast.

plodon Peruvianus, one of these mammals was inadvertently picked up by fishermen working the waters between Pucusana and Pisco. The 4-meter (13-foot) long whale is one of the smallest members of the whale family.

Poor man's Galápagos: Some 5 km (9 miles) down the coast from Pisco is the **Bay of Paracas**, named after the Paracas winds – blustery sand storms that sweep the coast. Transformed into an ecologically-delicate national park, and a popular spot for New Year's Day camping, Paracas is a wildlife reserve boasting a wide variety of sea mammals and exotic birds, among them the red and white flamingos that allegedly inspired hero General San Martín to design the red and white independence flag for Peru.

The beach is lovely, although craggy for swimming and the waters contain jellyfish. A monument marks where San Martín set foot in Peru on September 8, 1820 after liberating Argentina. (A law passed by the National Congress makes September 8 a provincial holiday.)

Not long after the Argentine's arrival, a shipload of British troops under the command of Lord Cochrane dropped anchor in the same bay and headed to shore to help San Martín plan his strategy against the Spanish. The British motivation was to break Spain's monopoly on trade in the region.

The famous **Candelabro**, a candelabra-shaped drawing scratched on to the highest point of a cliffside overlooking the bay, can be seen from the beach although it is best viewed from a boat. Some scientists link the drawing to the Southern Cross constellation; others say it is actually a stylized drawing of a cactus – a symbol of power from the Chavín culture, which flourished farther north but whose influence has been found great distances from its seat of power. The magic associated with the cactus is related to its hallucinogenic powers and use by high priests in ancient Indian cultures.

Recommended from the Bay of Paracas is a visit to the **Ballestas Islands**, part of a national reserve where sea lions, seals, penguins, guano birds and turtles rarely found at this latitude converge before photo-taking tourists.

Dozens of bird species thrive here, among them albatross, pelicans and seagulls. Also worth a visit in a fishing boat or launch is **Punta Pejerrey**, nearly at the northernmost point of the isthmus and the best spot for seeing the Candelabro.

On the exact opposite side of the isthmus is **Punta Arquillo** and the *mirador de los lobos*, or sea lion lookout point. This rough and rocky place, reachable only after an hour's trek on foot, takes visitors to a spot above a sea lion refuge. Looking down, the adventuresome find themselves nearly face to face with a congregation of noisy sea mammals.

On lucky days, a look skyward is rewarded by the sight of a pair of condors soaring above. These majestic birds sweep down on sea lion carcasses, then use the intense coastal winds to wing themselves up to the high altitudes they normally frequent. So well-known was the Andean birds' presence at Paracas

Candelabra engraved into the Paracas desert.

that, when the nature reserve was being named, one scientist pushed for the moniker "Parque Nacional de los Condores" (Condor National Park).

During the last century, this region was important for its guano – mineral-rich bird droppings used as fertilizers in Europe. Extensive exploration of the peninsula is best done with the help of a guide as paths are not clearly marked and it is easy to become lost. In June and August, Paracas is foggy – a reaction to the heat and extremely sparse precipitation combined with the water-laden ocean winds that caress the coast. A meteorological office here recorded only 36.7 mm (1½ inches) of precipitation during a 20-year period.

Desert burial grounds: Paracas not only refers to the area but also to the ancient Indian civilization living here up to 3,000 years ago, a pre-Columbian culture that was literally uncovered in 1925 when Peruvian archaeologist Julio C. Tello found burial sites under the sand dunes. The sand and the dryness of the desert protected the finely woven textiles around and inside those funeral bundles, buried when the Paracas culture thrived from 1300 BC until AD 200. The best examples of the textiles, as well as examples of the funeral bundles and information about how the burial pits were arranged, can be found in museums in Lima. Recommended are the Museo de la Nación, Museo Nacional de Antropología y Arqueología in Pueblo Libre, and the private Amano collection of textiles in Miraflores.

The **Julio C. Tello site museum**, on the isthmus joining the Paracas peninsula to the mainland, has exhibits about the archaeological find, although part of the collection was lost in a robbery.

The discovery of hundreds of so-called "funeral fards" – or burial cocoons – gave anthropologists and archaeologists yet another tiny clue into this civilization. The fine weaving in cotton and wool still astound modern-day textile experts, particularly those who have studied how the Indians were able to develop permanent dyes with such brilliant tones.

Meanwhile, the elaborately wrapped mummies in the funeral bundles show that the Paracas Indians performed trepanation, or a type of brain surgery in which metal plates were inserted to replace broken skull sections – a common injury among these Indians who fought by slinging rocks at one another. The Paracas culture also practiced the intentional deformation or molding of infants' skulls for aesthetic reasons. The results, akin to a conehead shape, not only were considered attractive but they clearly identified an individual's clan, since the molding significantly differed from tribe to tribe.

Heading some 48 km (29 miles) inland from Pisco is **Tambo Colorado**, among the best pre-Inca ruins on Peru's southern coast. There are wall paintings and buildings still standing at this complex, believed to have been a temple.

Grape stomping: Farther south along the coast is **Ica**, a bustling oasis amid one of the continents' driest deserts and Peru's richest wine-growing region. Every March, the city goes all out with its annual wine festival, featuring every-

Mummy at Chauchilla Cemetery.

thing from grape-stomping beauty queens to home-made wine that the locals swear is better than anything available on sale. The week-long party, called the *Festival International de la Vendimia,* is punctuated by sports events, cock fights, music, drinking, religious ceremonies and general merrymaking.

The wine festival is accompanied by an abundance of dancing, including the energetic *yunza.* Hatchet-carrying men and skirt-flouncing women dance around a tree, drinking the alcoholic beverage derived from newly fermented grapes and stopping at intervals to take swings at the unlucky plant. The dance continues until the tree falls; the couple responsible for the felling is promised a year of good luck. In addition, if the woman is unmarried, she expects to have a mate soon.

Although the festival is the most riotous time of year to investigate the area's wine reputation, it is also a tricky time for accommodation. However, visitors can explore the vineyards and wineries all year round. The **Bodega El Carmel** pisco distillery is open to the public; it has an ancient grape press made from a tree trunk. Tours in Spanish can be taken at the **Vista Alegre** wine and pisco distillery in Ica and its shop is recommended. Peruvian wines tend to be overly sweet although Ocucaje and Tacama are finer. (It is difficult to make arrangements to visit their vineyards but the wines can be purchased all over the country.)

Located on the Ica river, this community's second important festival falls in March when religious devotees to Our Lord of Luren show up for all-night processions in which a wood and plaster image of the crucified Christ is taken from a church and paraded around the city. A second procession in honor of the city's patron saint is held every December.

Christ on a wave: The statue arrived in Ica more than four centuries ago, carried to shore on a wave, then transported to the town. Records from the San Francisco monastery in Lima show that the Christ image was purchased by a friar in 1570. A storm at sea and the fear the ship in which the statue was being transported would sink apparently prompted the ship's captain to toss much of the cargo – including the wooden box containing the statue – overboard. Religious Ica residents took the icon's intact arrival as a miracle.

Churches worth visiting are **La Merced**, with its delicately carved wooden altars, and **San Francisco** with admirable stained-glass windows. Balancing out the Christian importance of Ica is the witchcraft side of the city; it is known across the country as a center for black magic and folk healing.

A flood seriously damaged much of Ica in 1963, explaining why its colonial buildings have been replaced by more modern structures. Still, the city center retains its square-block layout based on a chessboard design. Although Ica was founded by the Spanish in 1536, European attempts to control the city were fraught with problems.

Strong tremors caused damage to the town in 1568 and 1571 before a devastating earthquake in 1664 completely leveled it and left 500 people dead – a phenomenal toll in those days. Later, the city residents resisted the Spanish presence. Ica was never granted a coat of arms, owing to its repudiation of attempts to make it a colonial center, and local residents remain proud of that rebellious image.

One of the city's most famous sons is José de la Torre Ugarte, author of Peru's national anthem. He was born in Ica in 1786 and served as a local judge until he joined the revolutionary troops under General San Martín. After Peru's independence, he turned to politics but found that an even more dangerous line of work than freedom fighter; in a power struggle between factions of the Congress, he was condemned to death. When spared by the colonel commissioned to execute him, Torre Ugarte returned to a career in law.

The first civilian president of Peru was also from Ica, although Domingo Elias's tenure in office was short-lived owing to political upheaval in the newly independent Peru. His attempt in 1854 to start a revolution of his own failed, although he was initially able to take control of Arequipa before fleeing to exile in Chile.

Knotted strings: Today, just a 20-minute walk from Ica's center, this region's role in the revolution is traced in a room at the **Museo Regional**. Even more interesting are exhibits of mummies, ceramics and skulls from the Paracas, Nazca and Inca cultures. On display are *quipus* (also spelled *kipus*), the mysterious knotted strings believed to have been used to keep calculations, records and historical notes for the Incas, who had no system of writing.

Since only selected members of the Inca civilization were permitted to "read" the *quipus*, the meaning of these knotted strings has been lost in intervening centuries, although some experts maintain the strings were a sophisticated accounting system in which colored strings represented commodities and knots showed quantities. The *quipus* may have been crucial in keeping food inventories in the Inca empire.

The regional museum also boasts an excellent collection of Paracas textiles and feather weavings. And it is a rare visitor who does not find his or her curiosity piqued by the rehydrated mummy hand on exhibit – a "must" for those who think they have seen everything. Placed in a saline solution after being buried centuries on the dry desert coast, this hand was part of an experiment by scientists who hoped rehydrating would provide medical information about the deceased individual.

An unmarked private museum on the **Plaza de Armas** (at Bolívar 170) is intriguing for the number and variety of stones it contains, but the scientific community has pooh-poohed its owner's theories that the rocks come from a technologically-advanced Stone Age civilization. Javier Cabrera, the eccentric descendant of city patricians, is happy to have an audience for his offbeat theories and visitors are welcome to see the more than 10,000 rocks in this collection.

Consuls and curers: Outside Ica is **Las Dunas**, a full-scale resort and the most

Bodega near ca.

luxurious hotel complex. With a restaurant, swimming pool, horses for riding, sand surfing and its own airstrip for flights over Nazca, this hotel regularly attracts diplomats and was featured in the US television series "Lifestyles of the Rich and Famous." It is said that several foreign diplomats make an annual pilgrimage to Ica, staying at Las Dunas and consulting with *curanderos* or curers and occult practitioners.

Las Dunas has led the sand-surfing frenzy that recently overtook this dune-covered coastal area. Principally attracting European sports fans, especially from Italy and France, the hotel has sponsored competitive sand surfing events on Cerro Blanco – a massive dune some (14 km/8 miles) north of the town of Nazca.

Also on the outskirts of Ica is **Laguna de Huacachina**, a green lagoon of sulfur waters that Peruvians claim have medicinal value. Since Angela Perotti, an Italian living in Ica, began espousing the curative properties of the waters in the 1930s, this spot has become a fa-

vorite pilgrimage center for people suffering from rheumatism and skin problems. Local residents claim up to 1,000 people daily come to the waters to swim and soak. This peaceful setting just 5 km (3 miles) outside Ica also draws those looking for sun and solitude beside the palm trees and sand dunes that ring the lagoon.

Thanks to irrigation, cotton fields and ribbons of orange trees mark the landscape on the voyage farther south along the coast to **Nazca**, the home of the mysterious lined drawings that have prompted theories ranging from the fanciful to the scientific. (*See "Guardian of the Nazca Lines" on page 319.*)

Desert drawings: Sixty years ago Nazca was like any other small Peruvian town with no special claim to fame, except that it was necessary to cross one of the world's driest deserts to reach it from Lima. But it is that desert – a sketch-pad for ancient Indians – that has since drawn thousands to this sun-bleached colonial town of 30,000 and made the pampa, or plain, north of the city one of the great-

Laguna de Huacachina, an oasis resort near Ica.

est scientific mysteries in the New World.

The Nazca lines are a series of drawings of animals, geometric figures and birds ranging up to 300 meters (1,000 feet) in size, scratched onto the arid crust of the desert and preserved for about 2,000 years owing to a complete lack of rain and special winds that cleaned – but did not erase – the pampa.

It wasn't until 1939 that Paul Kosok, a North American scientist flying over the dry coast in a small plane, noticed the lines, then believed to be part of a pre-Inca irrigation system. A specialist in irrigation, he quickly concluded this had nothing to do with water systems. By chance, the day of the flight coincided with the summer solstice and, making a second pass over the area, Kosok discovered that the lines of the sunset ran tandem to the direction of one of the bird drawings. He immediately dubbed the Nazca pampa "the biggest astronomy book in the world."

But instead of Kosok, it was a young German mathematician who became the expert on the lines and put the backwater on the map. Maria Reiche was 35 when she met Kosok, serving as his translator at a seminar on the lines. Following Kosok's speech, she spoke with the scientist and he encouraged her to study the pampa. She dedicated the next half century to the task (*see "Guardian of the Nazca Lines" on page 319*).

There are, of course, those who do not accept Reiche's theories, denying that the ancient Indians would have drawn something that they themselves could not see. Because the drawings can only be seen from the air, the International Explorers Club set out in 1975 to prove a theory that the Nazca Indians had aircraft. The Explorers Club made a cloth and reed hot-air balloon, the Condor I, and flew it for 60 seconds, reaching an altitude of 100 meters (330 feet). But the flight, 14 minutes shorter than planned, has hardly resolved the issue.

Writing from the planets?: The most damaging theory about the Nazca lines came seven years earlier when Erich von Daniken published his book *Char-*

Relaxing on the beach near Ica.

iots of the Gods, in which he argued that the pampa was part of an extraterrestrial landing strip – an idea that Reiche discards impatiently.

Von Daniken's book drew thousands of visitors to the lines, but the newcomers set out across the pampa in search of the drawings on motorcycles, four-wheel-drive vehicles and even horses – leaving the unerasable marks of their visits. Now it is illegal to walk or drive on the pampa and Reiche uses the profits from sales of her book, *Mystery on the Desert*, to pay four guards to patrol the plain.

Other theorists say the lines marked tracks for running competitions, that they were enlarged designs used in weavings and textiles, or that they are actually an enormous map of the Tiahuanaco civilization which once flourished near Lake Titicaca.

Reiche's last trip to the pampa was in 1987 with Phyllis Pitluga, a US astronomer. There is a free, hour-long talk given at the Hotel de Turistas every evening at 7.15pm. It was originally given by Maria Reiche until her increasing infirmity made it impossible. It is now given by one of her assistants in Spanish and English. Pitluga's initial computer-based research on the Nazca Lines appeared to support their link to the constellations. Other researchers have pointed to the elaborate, vividly-painted Nazca pottery, with its clock-shaped pieces and elaborate solar calendars, as further evidence this civilization was closely linked to the movement of the heavenly bodies.

Some 20 km (12 miles) north of Nazca there is a *mirador* (observation tower) although the only lines which can be seen clearly are the *arbol* (tree) and the *manos* (hands). The best way to capture the impact of the lines is to fly over them in small propeller planes. Aero Condor offers flights from Lima, Ica and the small airport in Nazca. A lunch and a stop in the archaeological museum in downtown Nazca are included in the day-long Lima package. Other flights can be taken on Aeroica from Ica or Nazca. The Nazca flight is about 45 minutes and is best taken in mid-morn-

Maria Reiche writing her memoirs.

ing. Earlier there is sometimes a haze over the pampa; later the winds that buffet the plane leave observers more concerned about their stomachs than about the spectacle. The cost is around $55 but it may be possible to bargain.

Unless visitors take the Aero Condor flight from Lima, the only way to reach Nazca is by bus – a trip that can take up to eight hours from the Peruvian capital. For several years there has been discussion of building an international airport at Nazca but the project has never gone farther than the drawing board.

Red dot in the desert sky: Occasionally, Nazca is deluged with astronomers who find the desert plain an optimal spot for viewing some rare cosmic happenings. On September 23, 1989, the autumn equinox, scientists went to Nazca to view Mars – which appeared as a red light in the desert sky for a 12-hour period. Laden down by telescopes, the astronomers said the unusual phenomena would not present itself again until the year 2005.

Although the perplexing Nazca lines

are what draw tourists to this area, they are by no means the only thing to see. Some 30 km (18 miles) from the city is the fascinating **Cemetery of Chauchilla**, where sun-whitened bones and skulls, pottery shards and mummies litter a plain. The cemetery remains as it is in part to avoid further desecration of the area (most of the mummies were unearthed during tomb looting) and in part because there is no funding to arrange proper storage or exhibition of the mummies and grave artifacts.

Local tours to the cemetery usually stop at the **Paredones ruins** beside the Cantalloc aqueducts, an immense and complicated system built by the Incas and still supplying water to irrigated fields nearby.

Inland from Nazca on a well-paved road, **Camaná** is a popular summer resort for Arequipa residents and the hometown of Peru's chess grand master, Julio Granda Zuñiga. Buses from the city center head to La Punta and the fine, although undeveloped, beach area. Camaná was, in colonial times, the unloading point for cargo headed to Arequipa then on to the silver mines in Potosí, Bolivia.

Mollendo to the south is another summer beach resort, busy with Arequipeños from January to March but sleepy the rest of the year. Mollendo was a principal port before replaced by **Matarani**, about 14 km (8 miles) to the northwest. Now its attractions are three sandy beaches and its closeness to the **Lagunas de Mejía** nature reserve that is temporary home to a number of coastal and migratory birds.

At the spot where the Peruvian coastal desert reaches its driest point lies **Moquegua**, a parched and dusty town on the banks of the Moquegua river. Buildings here – even the cathedral – are roofed with sugar-cane stalks daubed with mud. Its streets are cobblestones and its residents' topiary skills are evident on the **Plaza de Armas** where most of the bushes are trimmed into the form of llamas. Wine and avocados are shipped out of this city and both are worth sampling.

Peru's southernmost coastal city is

Spider etched into the desert.

Tacna, repatriated from Chile in 1929 and separated from that country only by a mined stretch of desert that marks the border between the two nations. The Atacama Desert region from Tacna as far as Antofagasta once belonged to Peru and Bolivia but the nitrate-rich territory was lost to Chile in 1880 at the beginning of the War of the Pacific. A vote more than six decades ago returned it to Peru and, in the 1980s, it was one of the main spots for contraband activity in Peru. Government-subsidized milk and medicines were smuggled into Chile while less expensive clothing and imported cosmetics were brought back into Peru.

Unlike other border cities on the continent, Tacna is fairly well-developed and boasts some of Peru's best schools and medical facilities – perhaps owing to its importance as a military base. The downtown area has been refurbished and its main boulevard is cut by an attractive flower-and-tree-studded promenade. A pedestrian mall passes by the shops and here ice cream or cold drinks such as the popular icy cinnamon-laced soy milk beverage helps offset the intense heat during the Tacna summer. The tree-shaded **Plaza de Armas** is a welcome relief from the unrelenting sun.

The centerpiece of the plaza is the monument to the heroes of the War of the Pacific. The bronze fountain nearby is the work of Gustave Eiffel, of tower fame. He also designed the cathedral, with its onyx high altar and interesting stained glass windows.

The **Museo Ferroviario** at the railway station has turn of the century train engines from the days when the British began constructing the complicated and, in some cases, daredevilish railway system in Peru. The museum also has a collection of railway-theme stamps from around the world.

Visitors should be on the alert in the train and bus station areas, and in the evening should avoid entirely the street with the bus companies in. Pickpockets and thieves work these areas and tourists are an easy mark.

Could it be a hummingbird

GUARDIAN OF THE NAZCA LINES

The lines are like precious parchment, very fragile, that needs to be guarded jealously.
—Maria Reiche

When German mathematician Maria Reiche decided to make Peru her home in the 1930s, they called her a witch, a spy and a fortune hunter. In the six decades that followed, she was awarded the Order of the Sun – the highest honor in the country, found herself the first person ever depicted on a Peruvian stamp while still alive and basked in a celebrity status unprecedented for a foreigner.

Reiche's notoriety came from her role as guardian of the Nazca pampa, a dusty plain covered with enigmatic drawings left by ancient Indians and still debated by scientists today.

Nearly 70 years ago, Nazca was a backwater of cotton workers and fishing families. Then North American scientist Paul Kosok flew over the area in a small plane and spotted the series of lines believed to be part of a pre-Inca irrigation system. Kosok, an irrigation specialist, immediately knew this had nothing to do with water systems. Below him were giant drawings of birds, fish and monkeys.

Reiche was 35 when she met Kosok in Peru, where she was governess to the children of the German consul. The German-born woman was assigned as Kosok's translator during a speech about the pampa and found herself fascinated. With his blessing, in 1946 she began to haunt the plain, measuring, charting, cleaning and studying the drawings that range up to 300 meters (1,000 feet) in size. She befriended Air Force pilots who took her aboard surveillance flights over the plain. She hitchhiked on farm trucks so she could explore all areas of the 50-km (30-mile) sketch-pad between Nazca and Palpa. She supervised construction of a 15-meter (50-ft) high metal platform to get a better vantage point on the drawings.

Reiche concluded the sketchings corresponded to the constellations, dubbing them part of an "astronomical calendar," and said they were designed as messages to gods. She speculated that her favorite drawing, the monkey, was the Indian symbol for the Big Dipper, the ancient constellation linked to rain. When rain was overdue – a common occurrence in this plain that only sees the equivalent of a half hour of precipitation every two years – the Indians sketched the monkey to remind the gods the earth was parched.

Using the Hotel Turistas as her base, Reiche gave daily lectures on the lines, battled bureau-crats contemplating development of the area (part of the Pan American highway crosses the pampa) and rallied townspeople around the legacy left by their forefathers. She also broke the key to the puzzle on how the Indians managed the huge sketches with such symmetry. She determined they used a basic unit of measurement, probably the distance from their elbows to their forefingers. Ropes tied to stakes would have formed the perfect circles.

In 1987, blinded by glaucoma and weakened by Parkinson's Disease, Reiche made her last visit to the pampa. Her attempts to designate a female astronomer from the United States as her successor met with resistance from Peruvian scientists and politicians and, today, a private foundation fueled by corporate and individual donations, as well as profits from Reiche's book *Mystery on the Desert*, pays for guards to patrol the plain.

Propeller planes offering tourism flights over the lines also fold into their ticket prices a small fee that goes to the foundation. Proposals ranging from hotel development to a monorail over the pampa surface sporadically but, so far, all have been quashed and the foundation is intent on keeping it that way.

From the ground, the pampa is a hot, dusty field of sand. But from the air it remains an amazing puzzle waiting to be deciphered. ∎

Maria Reiche on the look out.

INSIGHT GUIDES
Travel Tips

Boxell

FOR THOSE
WITH MORE THAN
A PASSING INTEREST
IN TIME...

Before you put your name down for a Patek Philippe watch *fig. 1,* there are a few basic things you might like to know, without knowing exactly whom to ask. In addressing such issues as accuracy, reliability and value for money, we would like to demonstrate why the watch we will make for you will be quite unlike any other watch currently produced.

"Punctuality", Louis XVIII was fond of saying, "is the politeness of kings."

We believe that in the matter of punctuality, we can rise to the occasion by making you a mechanical timepiece that will keep its rendezvous with the Gregorian calendar at the end of every century, omitting the leap-years in 2100, 2200 and 2300 and recording them in 2000 and 2400 *fig. 2.* Nevertheless, such a watch does need the occasional adjustment. Every 3333 years and 122 days you should remember to set it forward one day to the true time of the celestial clock. We suspect, however, that you are simply content to observe the politeness of kings. Be assured, therefore, that when you order your watch, we will be exploring for you the physical—if not the metaphysical— limits of precision.

Does everything have to depend on how much?

Consider, if you will, the motives of collectors who set record prices at auction to acquire a Patek Philippe. They may be paying for rarity, for looks or for micromechanical ingenuity. But we believe that behind each $500,000-plus

bid is the conviction that a Patek Philippe, even if 50 years old or older, can be expected to work perfectly for future generations.

In case your ambitions to own a Patek Philippe are somewhat discouraged by the scale of the sacrifice involved, may we hasten to point out that the watch we will make for you today will certainly be a technical improvement on the Pateks bought at auction? In keeping with our tradition of inventing new mechanical solutions for greater reliability and better time-keeping, we will bring to your watch innovations *fig. 3* inconceivable to our watchmakers who created the supreme wristwatches of 50 years ago *fig. 4.* At the same time, we will of course do our utmost to avoid placing undue strain on your financial resources.

Can it really be mine?

May we turn your thoughts to the day you take delivery of your watch? Sealed within its case is your watchmaker's tribute to the mysterious process of time. He has decorated each wheel with a chamfer carved into its hub and polished into a shining circle. Delicate ribbing flows over the plates and bridges of gold and rare alloys. Millimetric surfaces are bevelled and burnished to exactitudes measured in microns. Rubies are transformed into jewels that triumph over friction. And after many months—or even years—of work, your watchmaker stamps a small badge into the mainbridge of your watch. The Geneva Seal—the highest possible attestation of fine watchmaking *fig. 5.*

Looks that speak of inner grace *fig. 6.*

When you order your watch, you will no doubt like its outward appearance to reflect the harmony and elegance of the movement within. You may therefore find it helpful to know that we are uniquely able to cater for any special decorative needs you might like to express. For example, our engravers will delight in conjuring a subtle play of light and shadow on the gold case-back of one of our rare pocket-watches *fig. 7.* If you bring us your favourite picture, our enamellers will reproduce it in a brilliant miniature of hair-breadth detail *fig. 8.* The perfect execution of a double hobnail pattern on the bezel of a wristwatch is the pride of our casemakers and the satisfaction of our designers, while our chainsmiths will weave for you a rich brocade in gold *figs. 9 & 10.* May we also recommend the artistry of our goldsmiths and the experience of our lapidaries in the selection and setting of the finest gemstones? *figs. 11 & 12.*

How to enjoy your watch before you own it.

As you will appreciate, the very nature of our watches imposes a limit on the number we can make available. (The four Calibre 89 time-pieces we are now making will take up to nine years to complete). We cannot therefore promise instant gratification, but while you look forward to the day on which you take delivery of your Patek Philippe *fig. 13,* you will have the pleasure of reflecting that time is a universal and everlasting commodity, freely available to be enjoyed by all.

Should you require information on any particular Patek Philippe watch, or even on watchmaking in general, we would be delighted to reply to your letter of enquiry. And if you send us

fig. 1: The classic face of Patek Philippe.

fig. 4: Complicated wristwatches circa 1930 (left) and 1990. The golden age of watchmaking will always be with us.

fig. 6: Your pleasure in owning a Patek Philippe is the purpose of those who made it for you.

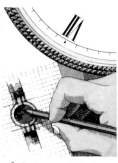

fig. 9: Harmony of design is executed in a work of simplicity and perfection in a lady's Calatrava wristwatch.

fig. 10: The chainsmith's hands impart strength and delicacy to a tracery of gold.

fig. 5: The Geneva Seal is awarded only to watches which achieve the standards of horological purity laid down in the laws of Geneva. These rules define the supreme quality of watchmaking.

fig. 7: Arabesques come to life on a gold case-back.

fig. 11: Circles in gold: symbols of perfection in the making.

fig. 2: One of the 33 complications of the Calibre 89 astronomical clock-watch is a satellite wheel that completes one revolution every 400 years.

fig. 3: Recognized as the most advanced mechanical regulating device to date, Patek Philippe's Gyromax balance wheel demonstrates the equivalence of simplicity and precision.

fig. 8: An artist working six hours a day takes about four months to complete a miniature in enamel on the case of a pocket-watch.

fig. 12: The test of a master lapidary is his ability to express the splendour of precious gemstones.

PATEK PHILIPPE
GENEVE

fig. 13: The discreet sign of those who value their time.

your card marked "book catalogue" we shall post you a catalogue of our publications. Patek Philippe, 41 rue du Rhône, 1204 Geneva, Switzerland, Tel. +41 22/310 03 66.

Reality check. Call home.

—— *AT&T USADirect® and World Connect®. The fast, easy way to call most anywhere.* ——

Take out AT&T Calling Card or your local calling card.** Lift phone. Dial AT&T Access Number for country you're calling from. Connect to English-speaking operator or voice prompt. Reach the States or over 200 countries. Talk. Say goodbye. Hang up. Resume vacation.

Argentina♦	...001-800-200-1111	**Guyana***††	**165**
Belize♦	555	Honduras †	123
Bolivia*	**0-800-1112**	**Mexico**◊◊◊	**95-800-462-4240**
Brazil	**000-8010**	**Nicaragua**	**174**
Chile	**1-23-0-0311**	**Panama**■	**109**
Colombia	**980-11-0010**	Paraguay (Asuncion City)†	0081-800
Costa Rica*■	**0-800-0-114-114**	**Peru**†	**171**
Ecuador*	**999-119**	**Suriname**†	**156**
El Salvador*■	**190**	Uruguay	00-0410
Guatemala*	190	**Venezuela***■	**80-011-120**

AT&T
Your True Choice

You can also call collect or use most U.S. local calling cards. Countries in bold face permit country-to-country calling in addition to calls to the U.S. World Connect® prices consist of USADirect® rates plus an additional charge based on the country you are calling. Collect calling available to the U.S. only. *Public phones require deposit of coin or phone card. †May not be available from every phone. ††Collect calling only. ♦Not available from public phones. ◊◊◊When calling from public phones, use phones marked "Ladatel". ■ **World Connect calls can only be placed *to* this country. ©1995 AT&T.

For a free wallet sized card of all AT&T Access Numbers, call: 1-800-241-5555.

Getting Acquainted
Politics and Economy

When Alberto Fujimori took over as President in 1990, Peru was in despair: guerrillas terrorised the highlands, inflation had risen to extraordinary levels, and cholera raged in the slums of Lima. Fujimori was not squeamish in choosing his methods in dealing with these chaotic problems. He dissolved Parliament and obtained almost dictatorial power through his *autogolpe* (self coup). He succeeded in arresting the leaders of the terrorist groups Sendero Luminoso (Shining Path) and Tupac Amaru.

Today, with the Nuevo-Sol currency in circulation and the cholera epidemic under control, things look as if they are improving. Economic figures promise strong growth. The copper industry, the fishing industry and agriculture are recording high revenues while foreign investors buy into the country with hardly any environmental restrictions or the need to pay social security to their staff. Tourism which came to a near standstill with the cholera outbreak is increasing again.

Fujimori achieved a resounding victory in the elections in April 1995, despite competition from strong candidates such as his trouble-making wife Susana Higuchi and the ex United Nations Secretary-general Javier Perez de Cuellar.

Population

Of a population of 22.6 million, approximately 7 million live in the greater Lima area. The highest density is in the coastal areas (55 percent of the total), 34 percent live in the highlands, most direct descendants of the Inca culture, and 11 percent in the eastern jungle area. About 45 percent of the population are native Indian, 32 percent mestizos (cholos), 12 percent whites (criollos) and 2 percent black and Asians.

The national languages are Spanish as well as Quechua and Aymará, which are spoken by the highland Indians.

Despite the economic upswing achieved through Fujimori's neoliberal politics, the dreadful living conditions of most Peruvians haven't changed. Ten million suffer from the consequences of malnutrition while about the same number have no clean drinking water. The infant mortality rate in Peru is the highest in Latin America.

Time Zones

Lima is five hours behind Greenwich Mean Time and therefore coincides with Eastern Standard Time in the US.

Climate

Peru has wet and dry seasons, although on the coastal desert strip it is, not surprisingly, always dry weather. However, Lima suffers a bizarre weather condition prevailing from April to November called the "garua", a damp cold mist which obliterates the sun and sours everyone's mood. August is the worst month for this with temperatures around 55°F–62°F (13°C–17°C). The rest of the year, Lima enjoys sunshine and moderate temperature from 69°F–79°F (20°C–26°C).

Towns like Nazca on the western slopes of the Andes are dry and hot all year round, but the central Andes do experience distinct wet and dry seasons. The best time to visit the highlands – and for most people, that means the best time to visit Peru generally – is between May and September when views of the mountains are crystal clear. Although the days are clear, nights can be bitterly cold and temperatures fall to 0°C. The rest of the year, weather is warmer but wetter, and the Andes are often obscured.

In the Amazon basin, the wet season lasts from January–April, when landslides and flooding is a constant problem. During the dry season, May–October, it might not rain for weeks at a time (although there might be short showers every day). Daytime temperatures average from 81°F–90°F (23°C–32°C), with nighttime lows averaging 69°F–79°F (20°C–26°C). However unexpected cold fronts called "*friajes*", which come up from the south are unique to the southern rainforests,

and can bring a few days of wind and rain with spring-like daytime temperatures of 55°F–65°F (13°C–18°C) and night lows of 50°F (10°C).

Planning The Trip
What To Bring

What you bring depends on your itinerary, Peru being a country of such diversity. For example, those planning adventure travel will need specific items like tents that other travelers can do without. Bring warm clothes for the Sierra, light clothes for the jungle and a combination for the coastal deserts (which are warm by day and cool at night). See the section on "Climate" for more details.

Items that are difficult to obtain in Peru include: your personal medical supplies, a strong money belt, sunscreen, good books in English and any electronic equipment you use. Bring your camera and plenty of film, as Peruvian stocks are expensive and often outdated.

Electricity

Peru uses 220 volts, 60 cycles AC, except Arequipa which is on 50 cycles. The major hotels provide 110 volt outlets in bathrooms for the use of shavers only.

Maps

The South American Explorer's Club at Av. Portugal 146 (Breña), Lima, is an excellent source for maps, guidebooks and information. For further geographical and aerial maps try the: **Instituto Geographico Nacional**, 1190 Av. Aramburu, Surquillo. Tel: 45-1939. Monday–Friday 8am–12.30pm and 1.30–3.30pm.

What To Wear

Good traveling clothes are comfortable and durable and often made of natural fiber, although one or two synthetics in the form of evening wear won't crush in your suitcase and come in handy for

THOMAS COOK MASTERCARD TRAVELLERS CHEQUES...

...HOLIDAY ESSENTIALS

Travel money from the travel experts

THOMAS COOK MASTERCARD TRAVELLERS CHEQUES ARE
WIDELY AVAILABLE THROUGHOUT THE WORLD.

INSIGHT GUIDES

COLORSET NUMBERS

those formal Latin nightspots. Take some good walking shoes that won't look too out of place in a casual restaurant.

One rarely regrets traveling light, especially in a land where clothes shopping is a dream. Remember all those alpaca sweaters and leather goods – you can buy as many warm clothes as you like when you arrive. But remember it can be difficult to find sizes for tall people because Peruvians are smaller than the average European and American.

The most appropriate clothing for a jungle trip is long-sleeved shirts and trousers of close-woven material. These protect the wearer from most biting insects. A hat gives valuable protection while traveling on the river or birdwatching on the lakes. Mountaineers and hikers should not forget to bring good walking shoes, warm clothes and equipment because there is a shortage of trekking supplies in Peru. Avoid olive green trousers and military style jackets; Peruvians could get the wrong idea!

It is advisable to leave your valuable jewelry at home and not to carry cameras or walkmans in public areas.

Entry Regulations
Visas & Passports

Visas are not required by citizens of South American countries, (other than Chile and Venezuela), western European countries, the United States, Canada or Japan. Australians and citizens of New Zealand do require visas. These can be obtained overnight from Peruvian consulates for a US$10 fee. Note that for a visa, their consulates insist on your showing a ticket out of the country, which can be inconvenient if you plan to travel overland.

All visitors, however, must have a passport and are issued with an entry stamp and tourist card on arrival in Peru. These are valid for 90 days and the card must be surrendered to immigration on departure. These tourist cards can be extended for 60 days at the Ministerio del Interior, Paseo de la Republica at Av. 28 de Julio, Lima.

Health

The most serious illnesses to guard against are yellow fever and malaria, both apparent only in some jungle areas of the north and south Amazon. There have been outbreaks of yellow fever in Puerto Maldonado, so visitors should ensure they are vaccinated. There are drugs which can be used against malaria and visitors are advised to consult their physician before leaving home. Malarial mosquitoes only bite at night so always use a mosquito net when sleeping in jungle towns. Although the South American cholera epidemic claimed many victims, mainly in the slums of Lima, only the poorest people don't have clean water and are threatened by this disease. Tourists risk practically no danger of infection, only if they have direct body contact with acute or chronically infected people. Vaccination against cholera is possible but it can't replace elementary hygiene precautions (See tips concerning eating and drinking, control of flies, avoiding dirty accommodation and public swimming pools below).

Hepatitis A is caused by ingesting contaminated food or water. Never eat raw fish or mussels; stick to bottled drinks, peeled fruit and good quality restaurants, thereby ensuring your standard of hygiene. A gamma globulin injection, taken shortly before your trip, is considered by many doctors to protect against hepatitis.

A less serious and much more common condition for travelers in Peru (or any third world country, for that matter) is upset stomach and diarrhoea – often caused by a change in culture and diet, unclean water or utensils, or simply the change of place. Traveling itself places extra pressure on the immune system, so take it easy until you feel stronger. In most cases, the symptoms will improve after a day or so of fasting and drinking plenty of fluids (hot tea without milk is ideal). If the more serious condition of dysentery develops (i.e. any blood or pus in the stool), you should be treated by a doctor.

Don't be surprised if your exaltation at flying into Andean mountain cities is followed by a less pleasant sensation called "soroche" or altitude sickness. In most cases the symptoms are very mild – fatigue, shortness of breath, slight nausea and headache. The best

prevention and cure is to lie down for a few hours upon arrival at your hotel and then slowly introduce yourself to physical activity. If the symptoms are severe – i.e. vomiting, rapid irregular pulse, insomnia – the immediate treatment is to descend to a lower altitude (although this usually happens only to mountain climbers).

A word about sunburn. The tropical sun can feel very gentle but might burn you to a crisp. Effective sunscreen such as 35+ strength is not available in Peru, so take it with you. It is advisable to take out travel insurance as local medical treatment could work out very expensive. Consult your doctor or hospital about an appropriate first aid kit and necessary vaccinations.

Money Matters

Since 1986 Peru has twice introduced a new currency to stop depreciation. In 1991 the Nuevo Sol (S/.) replaced the shrinking Inti at a ratio of 1 to 1 million. The 1994 annual inflation rate was relatively low at 20 percent. The exchange rate is more or less stable at 2.15 for US$1.

There is certainly no shortage of money changing facilities in Lima, formal and otherwise (i.e if you don't mind haggling on street corners). On the Plaza San Martín, in downtown Lima, hundreds of outdoor bankers run alongside the traffic – the rate is usually a little better than in the banks. It is legal to change with these "cambistas" and usually quite safe – although if you don't feel comfortable with it, there are plenty of alternatives. Banks will change your currency at the slightly inflated "official" rate and good hotels have exchange services or will send a hotel courier to one of the Casas de Cambio for a better rate (give him a tip, though). Travel agents accept payment in some foreign currencies and exchange small amounts.

The Banco de Credito and the Banco de la Nacion are recommended for any international banking business such as receiving US$ or DM from overseas. Ask for a *liquidacion por canje de moneda extranjera*.

Upon arrival in Lima, and especially when traveling in the provinces of Peru, it is convenient to carry some US cash as well as your travelers' checks, credit cards or cash advance card (although the cities of Cuzco, Arequipa and Iquitos, which have large numbers of visiting tourists, boast every money changing facility). It is not always possible to change checks, and cash dollars get a better rate, although you run the risk of theft. American Express will replace lost travelers' checks only in Lima.

The Visa "cash advance" card is quite useful in major cities (the Banco de la Nacion handles these transactions), while credit cards such as Diners Club, Visa, American Express and Mastercharge are accepted by good hotels and restaurants. There are branches of Diner's, Mastercard and Visa in Lima.

Public Holidays

January 1 – New Year's Day (national holiday).

January 15–20 – Lima Foundation Week. Official celebrations of the founding of Lima by the Spaniards on January 18, 1535.

January 24–31 – National Contest of La Mariners - Trujillo. Annual competitions for this traditional dance.

February 1–15 – Cruz de Chalpon – Chiclayo. Handicraft and commercial fair in the nearby prilgrimage center of Motupe.

February 8–14 – Virgen de la Candelaria – Puno. "La Mamita Candicha", the patron of Puno, is honored with continual demonstrations of rich folklore. Thousands participate in the parades, dances, fireworks and music of this important religious event.

February (Every Sunday) – Carnival in Iquitos. Colorful masquerades and dancing the typical "La Pandilla" takes place throughout the city.

February 24–27 – Carnival in Puno and Cajamarca. Carnival is especially celebrated in these two cities with "La Pandilla" dancing and traditional festivities.

March 1–5 – The Vendimia Festival – Ica. The grape harvest of the Ica Valley is celebrated with parades, dances and happy revelry involving the region's most important product, wine.

March/April – Holy Week. Amongst the nationwide commemorations is the spectacular procession in Cuzco in honor of the patron saint "El senor de los Temblores". (Held on Holy Monday

and Thursday.) The people of Tarma make carpets of flowers to cover the streets for their evening processions. Holy Week is solemnly commemorated in many other highland towns. (Half day holiday on Holy Thursday, full day holiday on Good Friday).

April (Third Week) – National Contest of Paso Horses – Lima. This exhibition and contest in Mamacona, 30 km south of Lima, has the participation of breeders from the most important regions of Peru.

May 1 – Labor Day.

May 2 – Cruz Velacuy – Cuzco. The crosses in all the churches of Cuzco are veiled and festivities take place.

May 2–4 – "Las Alasitas" Fair – Puno. Important selling exhibition of miniature handicrafts.

June – Corpus Christi – Cuzco. One of the most beautiful displays of religious folklore, the Procession of the Consecrated Host takes place in the gold monstrance of the Cathedral.

June (First Week) – Mountaineering Week in the Andes – Huaráz. The Callejon de Huaylas and the Cordillera Blanca provide the majestic settings for the National and International Ski Championships, as well as many other adventurous activities.

June 24 – Inti Raymi, or Festival of the Sun – Cuzco. This ancient festival is staged at the Sacsayhuama Fortress overlooking Cuzco and involves authentic Inca rituals,parades, folk dances and contests.

June 29 – St Peter's Day (full day holiday).

July 15–17 – Feast of the Virgen del Carmen – Cuzco. Festivities are held throughout the highlands, especially colorful in Paucartambo, 256 km from Cuzco.

July 28 & 29 – Peru's Independence (public holidays).

August 13–19 – Arequipa Week. This is the most important annual event for this attractive city. Festivities include folkloric dances, handicraft markets and a fireworks display on the 15th.

August 30 – St Rose of Lima Day (full day holiday).

September 18 – Unu Urgo Festival – Cuzco. The Urgo ceremony is conducted with Andean music, dancing and parades in the towns of Urco and Calca near Cuzco.

October 7–20 – Lord of Luren – Ica. Thousands of pilgrims pay homage to

the patron of Ica, with the main procession on the 17th.

October 8 – Battle of Angamos (national holiday).

October 18, 19 & 28 – Lord of the Miracles – Lima. A massive procession in honor of Lima's patron saint takes place on the 18th.

November – Bullfighting Season. An internatioal competition is held at Rimac, Lima, in the oldest bullring in America.

November 1 – All Saint's Day (national holiday).

November 1–7 – Puno Jubilee Week. Puno celebrates its founding by Spaniards, followed by a fascinating re-enactment of the emergence of the legendary founders of the Inca Empire, Manco Capac and Mama Ocllo, from the waters of Lake Titicaca. This week sees the best of Puno's folkloric festivities.

November 29 – Zana Week – Chiclayo. One week of celebrations for the founding of Zana include folklore shows, sporting events and exhibitions of Paso Horses.

December 8 – Immaculate Conception (full day holiday).

December 24 – Festival of Santuranticuy – Cuzco. Native Andean toy fair.

December 24 & 25 – Christmas (half day national holiday on 24th, full day on 25th).

Getting There

By Air

Jorge Chávez airport lies around 16 km outside of the centre of Lima. Minibuses (Airport Express) leave regularly for Miraflores. Guests of bigger hotels can use the hotel shuttle service. There is an international departure tax.

From Europe, direct flights to Lima are available with Lufthansa, Air France, KLM, Iberia, British Airways and Alitalia.

American Airlines and Aero Perú make daily flights from Canada and the US via the South American gateway – Miami. Flying direct is also possible from several major cities including New York and Los Angeles aboard CP Air, Avianca, Aerolineas Argentinas, Air Panama, Varig, Lan Chile and Equatoriana.

There is no shortage of flights to other South American countries. Lloyd

Aero Boliviano now flies between Cuzco and La Paz, Bolivia, twice a week. To and from Mexico use either Aerolineas Argentinas or Aero Perú.

The best route from Australia or New Zealand is probably with the Aerolineas Argentinas direct flight to LA, connecting with Lima. There are also weekly flights from Sydney and Auckland to Santiago in Chile (via Tahiti with Qantas or UTA, connecting with Lan-Chile to Santiago, stopping over at Easter Island). In Santiago, change for Lima. Other travelers go to LA and make a connection there.

By Sea

Few people arrive at Lima's port of Callao by either ocean liner or freight ship. The limited services available are expensive and inconvenient by comparison to flying.

By Land

Peru has borders with five other countries: Chile, Bolivia, Columbia, Brazil and Ecuador. The border crossing with Chile is at Tacna on the Peruvian side, Arica on the Chilean; taxis regularly make the crossing and some long distance buses operate between Lima, Quito, Santiago de Chile and Buenos Aires. Tickets for such marathon journeys sometimes include food and overnight accommodation in resthouses.

From Bolivia, efficient minibus services will take you from La Paz to Puno; alternatively, Crillon Tours in Bolivia offers a hydrofoil across Lake Titicaca via Copacabana and the Island of the Sun – an extremely pleasant way to arrive (*pisco sours* are served en route). The journey from Ecuador is also straight forward: take a bus to the border at Huaquillas and walk through to Tumbes. Other buses operate from there (note that the "international service" advertised in Quito still requires you to change buses at the border, so is actually more expensive and occasionally much less convenient than doing the trip with seperate legs.)

All railway links abroad have been closed due to a lack of profitability.

Useful Addresses
Airline Offices Overseas

Air passes, for cheap domestic travel within Peru, are available from the offices below, as well as from selected specialised South American travel agents such as Journey Latin America in London. Tel: (0181) 747-3108.
Faucett
European office: Haywards Heath, UK. Tel: (01444) 414-116.
In the US: Tel: 1-800-3343556 (Miami).
Aero Perú
European office: London, UK. Tel: (0171) 823-5274.
In the US: Tel: (305) 448-1947 (Miami).
Americana
France: Tel: (1) 4260-7322. Fax: 4260-1454 (Paris).
Italy: Tel: (2) 7202-3196. Fax: (2) 8646-0679 (Milan).
Spain: Tel: (1) 326-6857. Fax: (1) 4260-1454 (Madrid).
UK: Tel: (0171) 734-9354. Fax: (0171) 734-9352 (London).
USA: Tel: (305) 382-6575. Fax: (305) 383-9284 (Miami).

Airline Offices
Aerochasqui, Av. Nicolas de Pierola 611, Of. 301, Lima. Tel: 27-5471/27-5758.
Aero Cóndor, Juan de Arona 781, San Isidro. Tel: 42-5663/41-1354.
Aeroflot, Paseo de le Republica 144, Lima. Tel: 32-1377.
Aerolineas Argentinas, Av. José Pardo 805, 3rd Floor, Miraflores. Tel: 44-0810/45-8845.
Aero Péru, Av. José Pardo 805, 3rd floor Meraflores. Tel: 47-8333.
Air France, Juan de Arona 830, San Isidro. Tel: 70-4870/70-4702.
Alitalia, Camino Real 497, San Isidro. Tel: 42-8507.
Americana, Av. Largo 345. Tel: 47-1919.
American Airlines, Francia 597, Miraflores. Tel: 47-9798.
Avianca, Blvd Los Olivos, Paz Soldan 225, San Isidro. Tel: 70-4435.
British Airways, Camino Real 348, 12th Floor, San Isidro. Tel: 47-1774.
Canadian Airlines, Paseo de la Republica 126, Lima. Tel: 31-9293.
Ecuatoriana, Av. José Pardo 231, Miraflores. Tel: 47-2454.
Expreso Aero, Av. José Paedo 223 Meraflores. Tel: 45-2545.

Faucett, Inca Garcilaso de la Vega 865, Lima. Tel: 64-3322.
Iberia, Nicolas de Pierola 820, Lima. Tel: 28-3833.
KLM, José Pardo 805, 6th Floor, Miraflores. Tel: 47-1277.
Lan Chile, José Pardo 805, 5th Floor, Miraflores. Tel: 47-6682.
Lloyd Aereo Boliviano, José Pardo 805, Of. 201, Miraflores. Tel: 47-3292.
Lufthansa, Av. José Pardo y Aliagra 640. Tel: 442-4455. Fax: 440-5644.
Varig, Nicolas de Pierola 616, Lima. Tel: 24-6060.
Viasa, José Pardo 805, 4th Floor, Miraflores. Tel: 47-8666.

Practical Tips

Emergencies
Security & Crime

As Peru's urban centers have swelled, so has petty crime. Pickpockets and thieves – including senior citizens and children – have become more and more common in Lima and Cuzco. It is recommended that tourists do not wear costly jewelry and that their watches, if worn, be covered by a shirt or sweater sleeve. Thieves have become amazingly adept at slitting open shoulder bags, camera cases and knapsacks; keep an eye on your belongings.

All kind of confidence tricksters pull ever more imaginative ruses; some pose as policemen, others work together with bus and taxi drivers or use diversionary tactics to get hold of the gringos' valuables. Special care is needed at railway stations and airports. Go out at night in small groups if possible. Visits to the slums (Pueblos Jovenes) on the outskirts of the cities are extremely dangerous.

Officials also warn against dealing with anyone calling your hotel room or approaching you in the hotel lobby or on the street, allegedly representing a travel agency or specialty shop. Avoid contact with over-friendly strangers who may want to get you involved in criminal deals. Be aware that dealing with drugs is a crime in Peru and results in a long prison sentence.

Traveling alone and after dusk is not advisable. Don't hitch-hike. For journeys overland choose only well known and established bus companies and take care that you are always able to identify yourself. Carry your passport at all times.

At the height of the Sendero Luminoso terrorist campaign, tourism to Peru plummeted, but the comparative lull in violence following the 1992 arrest of Sendero's leader, Abimael Guzman, sparked interest again. Terrorist attacks have decreased significantly but they haven't stopped completely, targeting the capital Lima during 1993–94 as well as the departments San Martin, Huanaco, Junin and the area around Huaraz in Ancash department. Tourists are seldom attacked directly.

In 1995 the government declared a state of emergency (zonas de emergencia) in several provinces and departments. Before starting your journey it is advisable to check out the areas which are affected because the security situation changes all the time.

Overland journeys in the Andean areas, especially from Lima to Cuzco and from Lima to Lake Titicaca should be avoided as a rule. In contrast, the road link between Cuzco, Puno and La Paz is no problem at all.

Due to the frequent and resurgent border disputes between Peru and Bolivia the provinces of Tambopata and Tahuamana are classified as dangerous. Driving on the Pan-American highway is risky.

Expeditions and trekking tours should only be undertaken in larger groups and accompanied by a local and experienced mountain guide. It a good idea to leave your destination and home address before leaving for a long trekking tour. For more specific inquiries, contact your embassy or the South American Explorer's Club in Lima (Av. Portugal 146, Breña, Lima, Tel: 25-0142).

Police

A special security service for tourists recognisable by white braid worn across the shoulders of their uniform has been created by the Guardia Civil. The tourist police are very helpful if you have a problem and have special English speakers on duty. You can see them in Lima especially in the downtown area. In Cuzco all police have tourist police training.

The tourist police office in Lima is Museo de la Nación, Av. Javier Prado Este 2467, 5th floor, San Borja, Tel: 476 9896.

At police and military controls it is always advisable to ask for the officers' identification to make sure that they are genuine.

In case of an accident, attack, emergencies, etc call:

Radio Patrulla (police radio control and emergency service), Tel. 4-33-3333.

Direccion Contra El Terrorismo (DINCOTE) terrorism and hijacking, Tel: 4-33-3833/4, 4433-9861.

Medical Services

Good hotels will have reliable doctors on call. The following clinics have 24-hour emergency service and an English speaking staff member on duty:

Clinica Anglo-Americana, Defredo Salazar Cuadra 3, San Isidro. Tel: 40-3570.

Clinica Internacional, Washington 1475, Lima. Tel: 28-8060.

Clinica Ricardo Palma, Av. Javier Prado Este 1066, San Isidro. Tel: 41-6064. **Clinica San Borja**, Av. del Aire 333, San Borja. Tel: 41-3141.

One dentist who has been highly recommended is Dr Gerardo Aste. He also speaks English. Tel: 41-7502. Antero Aspillaga 415, of 101, San Isidro.

Travel insurance which covers the cost of an air ambulance should be taken out.

Weights & Measures

Peru uses the metric system for all weights and measures. Translating the Spanish term is fairly obvious. i.e. kilometros, litros etc.

Converting to imperial is not as obvious. Here's a table to help.

To Convert:	Multiply By:
centimeters to inches	0.3937
meters to yards	1.094
kilometers to miles	0.6214
liters to US gallons	0.264
grams to ounces	0.03527
kilograms to pounds	2.205

Business Hours

Most stores are open from 10am to 8pm Monday to Friday with a break for a couple of hours between 1pm and 4pm.

Banks are open only in the morning from 9am–12.30pm during summer (January to March). For the rest of the year there is also afternoon trading between 3pm and 6pm although the hours often change. The casas de cambio (exchange houses) are open from 9am to 6pm, while the money changers are on the footpaths nearly 24 hours a day. These are generally quite safe and are preferred by Peruvians themselves for their convenience, but keep your wits about you.

The central post office in Lima is open from 8am to 6pm, Monday to Saturday and from 8am to noon on Sundays. The Peruvian Telephone Company Office on the Plaza San Martín in Lima is open from 9am to 9pm Monday to Saturday, but can take a lot of waiting before your call goes through.

The Tourist Information Office and the South American Explorers Club are open from around 9am to 5pm, Monday to Friday. Many of the embassies are only open in the mornings. There is very little open on Sundays.

Media

Newspapers

The English newspaper, the Lima Times is published once a month. It is a concise and welcome source of news and information including cultural events in Lima. The major morning newspapers in Lima are El Commercio and Expreso.

Postal Services

The main post office in Lima is beside the Government Palace on the northwest corner of the Plaza de Armas. Here you can collect your mail at the Poste Restante (in Spanish, Lista de Correos) and, after overcoming a bit of "red tape", send certified packages overseas. There are branch offices in other districts of Lima:

Airport office, Monday–Saturday 8am–6pm.

Miraflores office, Libertadores 325, San Isidro.

Miraflores office, Petit Thouars 5201. Tel: 45-0697. Monday–Friday 8am–7.30pm.

San Isidro office, Libertadores 325, San Isidro.

American Express clients can have mail received at: Amex, c/o Lima Tours, Belen 1040, Lima. Bring your passport as identification for this, as well as for the *lista de correos* at the post office. Members of the South American Explorers Club can also have mail held for them at: Casilla 3714, Lima 100, Peru.

Telecoms

Long distance and international calls can be placed either through your hotel desk or by dialing 108 for the international operator with whom collect and trunk calls can be arranged. Peru has recently incorporated direct dialing so check if the service is available in your area. There is a cheaper, more chaotic method at the Peruvian Telephone Company Office located on the Plaza San Martín in Lima. Other cities in Peru are serviced by Entel Offices. International tokens (RIN) are also available from Entel offices which can receive fax messages as well.

Only local telephone calls can be made in telephone boxes. The tokens are sold by many street vendors.

There is a telegram and telex office on the corner of Lampa and Emancipacion in downtown Lima.

The code for Peru is 0051. Below are the codes listed for the most important Peruvian cities.

Arequipa: 054
Cajamarca: 082
Chiclayo: 074
Cuzco (Machu Picchu): 084
Huaráz: 044
Ica: 034
Iquitos: 094
Lima: 014
Pisco: 034
Puno: 054
Trujillo: 044

Tourist Information Offices

Lima, Av. Andrés Reyes 320, Lima 27, San Isidro. Tel: 70-0781. Fax: 42-4195/42-9280.

Also worth visiting is the South American Explorers Club for up-to-date information:
Av. Republica de Portugal 146, Lima.

Tel: 25-0142. Monday–Friday 9.30am–5pm or write to : Casilla 3714, Lima 100, Peru.

Arequipa, La Merced 117 Monday–Friday 8.30am–12.30pm and 2.30–3.30pm. Airport office open daily.

Cajamarca, Direccion de Turismo conjunto Belen (also comprising the colonia church and hospital of Belen).

Casa de Guias (Guide House), Parque Ginebra 28G, Apartado 123, Huaráz–Ancash. Tel: 72-1333.

Chiclayo, Elias Aguirre 830–832, Of. 202. Tel: 22-7776.

Cuzco, Portal Belen 115, Plaza de Armas. Tel: 23-7364. Monday–Friday 8am–5.30pm; Saturday 8.30am–12.30pm. Airport office open until noon daily.

Huaráz, Av. Luzuriaga 459. Tel: 72-1521. Monday–Friday 8.30am–12.30pm and 2.30–3.30pm.

Ica, Cajamarca 179. Monday–Friday 7.30am–3pm.

Nazca, The Hotel Nazca on Av. Lima is the main source of local information.

Puno, Jr. Arequipa 314. Tel: 35-3804. Monday–Friday 8am–12.30pm and 2.15–5.30pm.

Trujillo, Independencia 628. Tel: 24-1936. Airport Office.

Tourist Information overseas is available from Peru's embassies.

Australia: 9th Floor, London Circuit, Canberra: Tel: (62) 257-2953. Fax: (62) 257-5198.

Canada: 130 Albert St, Suite 1901, Ottawa, Ontario. Tel: (613) 238-1777. Fax: (613) 232-3062.

Denmark: Rosenvaengets Alle 20, 2nd Floor, 2100 Copenhagen. Tel: (35) 26-5848. Fax: (35) 25-8406.

France: 50 Avenue Kleber, 75116, Paris. Tel: (1) 4704-3453. Fax: (1) 4755-9830.

Italy: Via Sforza 36, 00184 Rome. Tel: (6) 482-4661. Fax: (6) 482-5235.

Netherlands: Van Alkemadelaan 189, 2597 AE, The Hague. Tel: (70) 328-0506. Fax: (70) 328-2091.

Spain: Principe de Vergara 36, 5 to Derecha, 28001 Madrid. Tel: (1) 431-4242. Fax: (1) 577-6861.

UK: 52 Sloane Street, London SW1X 9SP. Tel: (0171) 235-1917. Fax: (0171) 2354463.

USA: 1700 Massachusetts Av. NW, Washington DC 20036. Tel: (202) 833-9860. Fax: (202) 659-8124.

Embassies & Consulates

Argentina, Pablo Bermudez 143, 2nd Floor, Jesus Maria. Tel: 24-5984/23-8172. 8am–1pm.

Bolivia, Los Castanos 235, San Isidro. Tel: 22-8231. 9am–1pm.

Britain, Washington Building, 12th Floor Plaza Washington, Lima. Tel: 33-5032/28-3830. Monday–Thursday 10am–3pm, Friday 10am–1pm.

Canada (also representing Australian and New Zealand citizens), Libertad 130, Miraflores. Tel: 44-4015/46-3890. 8.30am–11pm.

Chile, Javier Prado Oeste 790, San Isidro. Tel: 40-7965. 8.45am–12.30pm.

Colombia, Natalio Sanchez 125, 4th Floor, Lima. Tel: 31-2074/40-7835.

Ecuador, Las Palmeras 356, San Isidro. Tel: 22-8138 . 9am–1pm.

France, Arequipa 3415, San Isidro. Tel: 70-4968. 9am–noon (Visas 9–11am).

Germany, Av. Arequipa 4210, Miraflores. Tel: 45-7033. 9am–noon.

Ireland, Carlos Povias Osores 410, San Isidro. Tel: 23-0808.

United States, Grimaldo del Solar 346, Miraflores. Tel: 44-3621. Monday–Friday (except Wednesday) 8.15–11am. USA Embassy office on the 1400 block of Garcilaso de le Vega and Av. Espana in the city center. Tel: 28-6000.

Getting Around

Orientation

Lima, the "City of Kings", is Peru's gateway and jumping off point for the rest of the country (although Cuzco and Iquitos have now begun promoting their international airports and direct flights from other countries are planned). If your time is limited, Lima has the facilities to fully organise your itinerary so you can fly directly to any major destination with your reservations or tour confirmed. Machu Picchu and the Sacred Valley might be the one essential destination for many tourists, while others take months in order to appreciate the diversity of cultures between the coastal regions, the Andes and the Amazon.

Lima itself is divided into districts, each with its own distinctive character. Downtown Lima – with its grandiose plazas, mansions and the magnificent Gran Hotel Bolívar – is the oldest, although its streets are now crowded out with street vendors and decidedly chaotic. Many Limeños and visitors prefer to stay in the more glitzy, plastic and international suburbs of Miraflores and San Isidro, where the homes have better security. Their new shopping complexes and landscaped gardens make this a complete contrast. Barranco is a beach suburb with a growing reputation for bohemian lifestyles. Cafes and restaurants have live jazz and creole music while the crumbling old mansions give the streets a relaxed ambience.

Maps & Street-plans

The Touring Club del Perú, Av. Cesar Valllejo 899, Lima 18, Tel: 403270, is the best source for maps and information. Maps and street-plans can be bought at the kiosk, bookshops and at the Instituto Geographico Nacional (1190 Av. Aramburu, Surquillo, Lima, Tel: 451939; Monday to Friday 8am–12.30pm and 1.30–3.30pm. Street-plans can be obtained free of charge at FOPTUR, the Peruvian Tourist office (Av. Andrés Reyes 320, Tel: 700781/424195, Fax: 429280).

From the Airport

Getting to and from Lima airport is easiest in the care of your hotel shuttle or tour organiser. Otherwise there are plenty of taxis but, as ever, be prepared to bargain. Alternatively, Transhotel is a 24-hour shuttle service to and from the airport. They will pick up passengers from any part of town with the fare according to distance. **Transhotel**, Ticardo Palma 280. Tel: 46-9872. Airport Tel: 51-8011. For Cuzco and other cities, taxis into town are very cheap – always agree on a price before you leave.

Public Transportation

Lima's public buses can only really be recommended for a one-time cultural experience. Flagging one down is a feat in itself – then you must survive the jostling crowds and pickpockets. There are thousands of privately-run minibuses stopping and starting every few seconds, but why bother when a taxi from downtown Lima to Miraflores is inexpensive?

Private Transportation

Certain regions are better appreciated with your own mode of transport, such as the Callejón de Huaylas, a 200-km long valley nicknamed the "Peruvian Switzerland" for its glaciers, lakes and snowy peaks. The town of Huaráz is a 6-hour drive from Lima on good surface roads. For quality car rental:
National Car Rental, Av. Espana 449, Lima. Tel: 23-2526. Monday–Friday 8.30am–5.30pm and Saturday 8.30am–12.30pm.
Also at: Diez Canseco 319, or 13 Miraflores. Tel: 44-2333. Monday–Saturday 8am–8pm and Sunday 9am–1pm. Airport Office open 24 hours.
Budget, La Paz 522, Miraflores. Tel: 44-4546. Monday–Saturday 8.30am–7.30pm.
Also at: Corpac 514, San Isidro. Tel: 41-1129. Monday–Saturday 8.30am–7.30pm. Airport office open 24 hours. Tel: 52-8706. An international driving lience and a credit card is needed for renting a car.

Domestic Travel

Most travelers prefer to fly between major destinations, but overland travel in Peru is not always as problematic as often imagined. For example, the coastal Pan-American highway is fully paved and worked by regular, comfortable buses. Unfortunately, highways in the Andes are generally unpaved and the buses range from reasonable to back-breaking – although still popular with young backpackers. The journeys are dirt cheap, colorful and you get to see some amazing scenery, if you have the time and inclination.

By Air

The two major domestic airlines, Aero Perú and Faucett provide daily services to most cities. There is little qualitative or price difference although Aero Perú flies more often to more destinations. Peru's Air Passes offer the possibility of flying to cheaply with both airlines on the domestic flight network. Air Passes have to be booked before you start your holiday and are only valid to transatlantic flight ticket holders. Contact points for Air Passes in Europe and America are given in *Useful Addresses*.

Both airlines are sadly unreliable in meeting their flight schedules. Times are often changed and, in the case of remote destinations, occasionally cancelled due to lack of interest. You often won't find out until you're at the airport. Expreso Aereo, Aero Tumi and Aero Cóndor fly to smaller places and remote jungle airstrips.

It's best to book in person at the reservations office, or through a good travel agent who will confirm your tickets. Don't feel shy about confirming more than once, as tales of travelers being bumped off flights are legion: it is necessary to confirm your confirmed ticket 72 hours in advance and then re-confirm 24 hours ahead of the departure date, otherwise you might simply disappear from the airline computer.

For domestic flights there is a Security Tax and a Municipal Tax at all airports except Lima.
Aerochasqui, Av. Nicolas de Pierda 611 of. 301, Lima. Tel: 27-5471/27-5758. For flights to Trujillo.
Aero Cóndor, Juan de Arona 781, San Isidro. Tel: 42-5663/41-1354. For flights over the Nazca Lines and charter service over the Callejón de Huaylas.
Aero Perú, Plaza San Martín. Tel: 31-7626 (domestic), 32-2995 (international); and Pardo 601, Miraflores. Tel: 47-8900. Reservations, tel: 47-8255.
Faucett, Lima. Tel: 64-3424. Fax: 64-131.

By Rail

Train journeys, however, are very popular with all types of travelers. Rail services run Cuzco-Puno and Puno-Arequipa. The highest rail journey on earth was impassable for a long time; the service should start again in the future (until then you have to take a rented car). Relatively comfortable and well serviced "first-class" carriages are available (book through Lima Tours or other agencies); very cheap seats can also be booked but they can be quite unreliable and slow. The trips provide valuable glimpses of rural life and views of magnificent landscapes. The journey Puno-Cuzco has become a particularly popular leg in recent years.

The Lima-Huancayo journey is no longer open to passengers, although there is talk of privatisation and opening it to tourists.

A modern train, the *Autovagen*, departs from Cuzco early for Machu Picchu and returns in the afternoon. Travel agents in Cuzco sell all-inclusive day tickets for the trip. There are much cheaper, slower trains for budget travelers.

By Bus

Bus companies have morning and evening departures to most cities. Two reliable companies are:

Ormeno, Carlos Zavala 177, Lima. Tel: 27-5679.

Tepsa, P. de la Republica 129, Lima. Tel: 32-1233.

Comfortable buses for the 8-hour ride to Huaráz can be booked at:

Empresa Transportes Rodriquez, *Lima*: Av. Roosevelt 354. Tel: 28-0506. *Huaráz*: Av. Tarapaca 662. Tel: 72-1353.

Expreso Ancash, *Lima*: Av. Zavala 177. Tel: 25-5679. *Huaráz*: Av. Raimondi 861. Tel: 72-1111.

By Boat

Boats can be taken from the beautiful bay of Paracas to the Balletas Islands, home of sea lions, Humboldt penguins and various sea birds.

From Puno, tranquil excursions by boat across Lake Titicaca arrive at the island of Uros, Taquile and Amantani, or a more luxurious cruise is by hydrofoil all the way to Bolivia.

In the Amazon Jungle, motorized canoe down the winding muddy river is the only way to travel.

By Taxi

Taxis in Peru have no meters – you simply bargain on a rate, preferably before even getting in. In many Andean cities you may prefer to walk, but in Lima taxis are often essential and very cheap. Note that your hotel will arrange taxis for you if you ask. This is more expensive, but very secure. If you don't speak much Spanish and don't fancy bargaining on the street, this can be the best option.

Colectivos (shared taxis) are commonly used for traveling south to Ica, Nazca and Paracas. Contact:

Comite 3, Montivideo 561, Lima. Tel: 28-1423.

Comite 4, Leticia 591, La Victoria. Tel: 28-8608.

On Foot

Downtown Lima is definitely best explored by walking. Here amongst throngs of street vendors and money changers you can walk from the government palace to museums to colonial mansions, all in a distance of several blocks. Sit for a while in the Plaza de Armas or San Martín and gain true insights into the Limeño character.

For the more energetic walker, trekking is one of Peru's great attractions. Not all excursions require a high level of expertise. A very famous trek is the Inca Trail to Macchu Pichu. Taking 3 or 4 days, an organised group will include hired carriers who set up camp and cook ahead of your arrival. (See the feature on "Trekking in the Andes" for more information.) Tour operators can arrange shorter and less tiring walking tours.

Where to Stay

Hotels & Motels

Throughout Peru, a government chain called Enturperú owns standard to deluxe category tourist hotels and inns.

Reservations at any **Hotel de Turista** (as they are all called) can be made through a travel agent or by contacting:

Enturperú, Javier Prado Oeste 1358, San Isidro, Lima. Tel: 72-1928.

Lima

DOWNTOWN AREA

Gran Hotel Bolívar☆☆☆☆☆, Plaza San Martín. Tel: 27-2305. Fax: 33-8625. This is the doyen of Peruvian hotels. Even newly-elected Peruvian presidents traditionally occupy one of the Bolívar's 272 graciously maintained rooms on victory night. The stately three room suites overlooking the Plaza San Martín are particularly good value – ask to see one. Even those who are not staying at the Bolívar should make a visit. Tea and cakes at 5pm in the domed vestibule is a luxurious treat, while the grand salon has a competitively priced lunch menu. Dinner comes with a traditional floor show. Ask for a Catedral in the lounge bar and you'll receive the best *pisco sour* in Lima. Like all good hotels, airport shuttle and money exchange service is provided.

Hotel Crillon ☆☆☆☆☆, Colmena 589. Tel: 28-3290 to 28-3295. The hotel's Sky Room, comprising a restaurant, cocktail bar and nightclub, stages the best folkloric show in Lima. Round trip transfer from your hotel is included. Office and Shuttle Service – Tel: 46-6498.

Sheraton Lima Hotel & Towers ☆☆☆☆☆, Paseo de la República 170. Tel: 33-3320. Fax: 33-6344. This more recent deluxe style hotel boasts of 500 guest rooms, 3 restaurants, 2 bars and a swimming pool within its complex.

Hotel Residencial San Francisco ☆☆☆, Jr. Ancash 340. Tel: 28-3643. Very close to the Plaza de Armas and yet quietly situated, here is a great value budget hotel if you decide on the downtown area. The friendly and helpful management keeps the hotel secure, immaculate and efficiently run.

Hostal Esperanza, Av. Esperanza 350, Miraflores. Tel: 4424. Fax: 44-0834. Beautiful hotel of middle price range.

Hostal Torreblanca, Av. José Pardo 1453, Miraflores. Tel: 47-9998. Fax: 47-3363. Friendly, inexpensive tourist hotel.

Renacimiento, Parque Hernan Velarde 52–54. Tel: 31-8461. Secluded colonial style hotel ten minutes' walk from the center.

Miraflores

The newer suburb of Miraflores is the commercial center of Lima and is home to the more affluent Peruvians. Here you will find the fashionable boutiques, restaurants and businesses.

Miraflores Cesar's Hotel ☆☆☆☆☆, La Paz & Diez Canseco. Tel: 44-1212. The most luxurious hotel in Miraflores.

José Antonio Hotel ☆☆☆☆, Av. 28 de Julio 398. Tel: 45-6870/45-7743.

San Isidro

The more residential "garden" suburb of Lima.

El Country Club ☆☆☆☆, Los Eucaliptos 550. Tel: 40-4060.

Hostal Residencial Callacocha ☆☆☆, Andres Reyes 100. Tel: 42-3900/42-4160.

Residencial Los Petirrojos ☆☆, Av. Los Petirrojos 230. Tel: 41-6044. (Av. Javier Prado Este, 9th block). Offers clean spacious rooms with breakfast included.

The South Coast

PISCO

Hotel Paracas ☆☆☆, Rivera del Mar, Paracas-Pisco. Tel: 22-20. Reservations in Lima: 46-5079/46-4865. Bungalows on the beach, tennis courts, swimming pool and excursions to the Peninsula can be arranged.

Las Dunas – Centro Vacacional ☆☆☆, Km. 300 Panamericana Sur, Ica. Tel: 23-1031. Reservations in Lima, tel: 42-4180/42-3092. A holiday resort, complete with horse riding and private airstrip for Nazca flights.

Nazca

Hostal de la Borda ☆☆☆, Panamericana Sur Km. 447, Nazca. Reservations in Lima: 42-6391/40-8430. Located near the airfield, the hotel is a renovated hacienda with garden, swimming pools, hot showers and friendly service.

Arequipa

El Portal Hotel ☆☆☆, Portal de Flores 116, Arequipa. Tel: 21-5530. Reservations in Lima, tel: 40-6447/40-6155. On the Plaza de Armas, with excellent views and roof top swimming pool.

Hostal La Casa de Mi Abuela ☆☆☆, Jerusalem 606, Arequipa. Tel: 22-4582. Receives rave reviews from all

visitors. Behind the huge stone wall is an idyllic garden setting. Breakfast can be taken on the patio or roof terrace. English is spoken and the management is very friendly. A popular spot so reserve well in advance.

Posada del Puente, Av. Bolognesi 101. Tel: 21-7444. Friendly and small.

Turistas, Selva Alegre/Plaza Bolívar. Tel: 21-5110. High standard with pool.

Puno (Lake Titicaca)

Hotel Isla Esteves ☆☆☆☆☆, Isla Esteves, Puno. Tel: 724. Reservations in Lima, tel: 42-8626/42-8633. Fax: 21-588. One of the government owned tourist hotels. Built on a nearby island, a known site of the Tiwanaku period, it is connected to the mainland by a causeway 5 km northeast of Puno. Deluxe services include a discotheque, bar and good restaurant.

Hostal Don Miguel ☆☆☆, Av. La Torre 545, Puno. Tel: 177. Reservations in Lima, tel: 35–1371/35–2873. Fax: 35-1371.

Cuzco

Don't be daunted by the number of hotels in Cuzco. The competition is high and so is the quality.

Hotel El Dorado Inn ☆☆☆☆☆, Av. El Sol 395, Cuzco. Tel: 23-1135/23-3112. Reservations in Lima, tel: 27-6400. Adds a sauna to the list of services.

Hotel Libertador Cuzco ☆☆☆☆☆, Calle San Augustin 400, Cuzco. Tel: 23-1961. Reservations in Lima, tel: 42-0166. Fax: 42-2988. The best of the five stars.

Hotel Marques de Picoaga ☆☆☆☆, Santa Teresa 344, Cuzco. Tel: 22-7251/22-7691. Reservations in Lima, tel: 28-6314/27-9501.

Hostal Royal Inka ☆☆☆, Plaza Regocijo 299, Cuzco. Tel: 22-2284/23-1067. Reservations in Cuzco, tel: 23-4221. Attractively situated on the upper plaza, with good service, though not as new or as expensive as Royal Inka II. Same reservations number for both hotels.

Hotel San Augustin ☆☆☆, Maruri & San Augustin 390, Cuzco. Tel: 23-1001. Reservations in Lima, tel: 23-6006/28-7656.

Hotel de las Marquesas ☆☆, Garcilaso 256, Cuzco. Tel: 23-2512. Colonial ambience is created by a charming inner courtyard.

Hostal Loreto ☆☆, Pasaje Loreto (the famous Inca walled laneway), Cuzco. Very popular with budget travelers, several of the rooms have original Inca walls. Ask for an electric heater.

Machu Picchu

Hotel de Turistas de Machu Picchu, Tel: 31. Reservations in Lima, tel: 42-8626/42-8633. Fax: 21-558. The one and only hotel right next door to the ruins.

Urubamba Valley

EL Albergue (beside Railway Station 1 km from the town center, Ollantaytambo). More adventurous travelers might choose this charming rustic-style hostel managed by a friendly north American family. Trekking groups are accommodated during the June to September season and guided trips arranged. They can be contacted through the Ollantaytambo telephone operator.

Hostal Alhambra III – Plaza, Plaza Manco II 123, Yucay. Tel: 22-4976. Reservations in Lima, tel: 44-1199/47-8776. Situated in the pretty village of Yucay, just 4 km from the town of Urubumba, the hotel was once a beautiful hacienda. It now includes a small museum and as well as a quality restaurant.

Huaráz

Hostal Andino ☆☆☆, Jr. Cochachin 357, Huaráz. Tel: 72-1662. Fax: (044) 72-2830. Reservations in Lima, tel: 45-9230/72-1501. Fax: 72-2830. For the best views of the mountains.

Hostal Colomba ☆☆☆, Jr. Francisco de Zela 210, Huaráz. Tel: 72-1501. Friendly, family run bungalows within pleasant garden.

Edward's Inn ☆☆, Av. Bolognesi 121, Huaráz. Tel: 72-2692. Very popular with trekkers. Edward knows a lot about the region.

El Tumi ☆, Jr. San Martin 1121, Huaráz. Tel: 72-1784. A comfortable place for budget travelers.

Trujillo

Hotel El Golf ☆☆☆☆, Mz. J-1 Urbanizacion E1 Golf, Trujillo, P.O. Box 329. Tel: (044) 24-2592. Fax: (044) 23-2515. Luxury hotel including swimming pools, private parking lot and several suites with direct dial telephones.

Hostería de Sol ☆☆☆, Vallecito de Coina, Coina. Reservations in Trujillo: Los Brillantes 224. Tel: 23-1933. Coina is a village 132 km east of Trujillo, set at 1,500 meters in the Sierra Alto Chicama. The late German Dr Kaufmann gave prominence to the area by building a hospital for the Indians and the Hosteria de Sol. Now managed by Dr Kaufmann's family, the location provides glorious views of the Sierra and full board is offered.

Hotel de Turistas de Trujillo ☆☆☆, Jr. Independencia 485, Plaza de Armas, Trujillo. Tel: 23-2741/23-5741. Reservations in Lima, tel: 42–8626/42–8633. Fax: 21-588. Good value accommodation with an excellent buffet lunch on Sundays.

Cajamarca

Hotel de Turistas de Cajamarca ☆☆☆, Jr. Lima 773, Cajamarca. Tel: 24-70. Reservations in Lima, tel: 42-8626/42-8633. Well located in the center of town and very comfortable.

Hostal Laguna Seca ☆☆☆, Av. Manco Capac, Banos del Inca. Tel: 05. Reservations in Lima, tel: 46–3270. Six km from Cajamarca, you can enjoy hot thermal baths in the privacy of your room at this renovated hacienda.

Chiclayo

Garza Hotel, Av. Bolognesi 756, Chiclayo. Tel: 22-8172/23-8968. Fax: 22-8171.

Hotel de Turistas de Chiclayo, Av. Salaverry (no number). Tel: 23-4911. A short distance from the town center. Includes a swimming pool, car park and car hire services.

Iquitos (Northern Amazon)

Acosta I, Esq. Huallaga & Araujo. Tel: 23-5974. Not quite as prestigious as Acosta II although includes a swimming pool and a very good restaurant.

Acosta II, Ricardo Palma 252. Tel: 23-2904.

Lodges

Amazon Lodge & Safaris, Putumayo 165, Iquitos. Tel: 23-3023. Reservations in Lima, tel: Carmino Real 1106, San Isidro. Tel: 41-9194. Day trips on the powerful "Amazon Explorer" launch. Two day/one night stays.

Amazon Village, Rio Mommon. Reservations in Lima, tel: Alcanfores 285, Miraflores. Tel: 44-1199/47-8776. Excursions to the Amazon jungle are made from this location on the River Mommon, weather conditions permitting. Bungalows are clean and well-ventilated and good food is served. For the more comfort-conscious traveler.

Explorama Lodge & Explornapo Camp, Av. La Marina 340 – Casilla 446, Iquitos. Tel: 23-5471/23-3481. Reservations in Lima, tel: 24–4764. Fax: 23-4968. Also offers two day packages with charges of US$40 for each additional day. Managed by the well-organised Explorama Tours, the Explornapo Camp is better situated than the above two lodges for sighting fauna. It offers a good balance of comfort and penetration of the jungle for those who wish to experience the Amazon with a fairly structured itinerary.

For the more adventurous traveler:
Selva Lodge & Yarapa Lodge, Reservations: Amazon Selva Tours, Putumayo 133. Experienced guides and great food.

Tamshiyacu Lodge, Reservations: Wilderness Expeditions, 310 Washington Av. SW, Roanoke Va. 24016 USA. Tel: (703) 342-5630. Organised trips include Yarapa River Lodge, Tambo Safari Inn Camp and wilderness expeditions.

Yarapa River Camp, Reservations: Amazonia Expeditions, Putumayo 139. Strongly conservationist.

For the conservation-minded:
Albergue Cuzco Amazonico ☆☆☆, Reservations in Lima, tel: 46-2775/46-9777. Fax: 45-5598.
Also at: Procuradores 48, Cuzco. Tel: 50-47. Tambopata-Candamo Reserve.

Explorer's Inn ☆☆☆, c/o Peruvian Safaris, Garcilazo de la Vega 1334, P.O. Box 10088, Lima. Tel: (14) 31-3047. Although not quite as comfortable as the Albergue Cuzco Amazonico, there is a better chance for observing wildlife from this location i.e. a further 2 hours' boat travel away from Puerto Maldonado on the Tambopata River.

ACEER (Amazon Center for Environmental Education and Research), located on the Sucusari River in the 250,000-acre Amazon Biosphere Reserve near Iquitos, not only provides research and study facilities for scientists and educators but also offers guest accommodations in 20 double-occupancy rooms. A unique attraction is a 1,200ft canopy walkway, an environmentally sensitive footbridge suspended among the treetops. Roundtrip fares are available from Miami.
Enquiries: International Expeditions Inc.
Manu Lodge, c/o Manu Nature Tours, Av. Sol 627-B, Oficina 401, Cuzco. Tel/Fax: (084) 23-4793. 15 km from Puerto Maldonado on the Madre de Dios River.

One Environs Park, Helena, Alabama 35080, USA. Tel: (800) 633-4734 or (205) 428-1700. Made De Dios Region (Southern Amazon Basin). Manu Biosphere Reserve.

Also in this area: **Tambopata Macaw Lodge**, c/o Tambopata Tours, Av. Sol 627-B, Oficina 202, Cuzco.

Eating Out

What To Eat

Peru's *criolla* cuisine evolved through the blending of native and European cultures. *A la criolla* is the term used to describe slightly spiced dishes such as *sopa a la criolla*, a wholesome soup containing beef, noodles, milk and vegetables.

Throughout the extensive coastal region, seafood plays a dominant role in the creole diet. The most famous Peruvian dish, *ceviche*, is raw fish or shrimp marinated in lemon juice and traditionally accompanied by corn and sweet potato. Other South American countries have their own version of *ceviche* but many foreigners consider Peru's to be the best. *Corvina* is sea bass, most simply cooked *a la plancha*, while scallops, *conchitas* and mussels, *choros* might be served *a lo mancho*, in a shellfish sauce. *Chupe de Camarones* is a thick and tasty soup, of salt or freshwater shrimp.

A popular appetizer is *palta a la jardinera*, avocado stuffed with a cold vegetable salad or *a la reyna*, chicken salad. *Choclo* is corn on the cob, often sold by street vendors at lunchtime. Other Peruvian "fast food" includes *anticuchos*, shish kebabs of marinated beef heart; and *picarones*, sweet lumps of deep fried batter served with molasses. For *almuerzo* or lunch, the main meal of the day, one of four courses might be *lomo saltado*, a stir-fried beef dish, or *aji de gallina*, chicken in a creamy spiced sauce.

The most traditional of Andean foods is *cuy*, guinea pig, which is roasted and served with a peanut sauce. Another specialty of the Sierra is *Pachamanca*, an assortment of meats and vegetables cooked over heated stones in pits within the ground. Succulent freshwater trout is plentiful in the mountain rivers.

Peruvian sweets might be *suspiro* or *manjar blanco*, both made from sweetened condensed milk, or the ever popular ice-cream and cakes. There are many weird and wonderful fruits available in Lima, notably *chirimoya*, custard apple, *lucuma*, a nut-like fruit, delicious with ice-cream, and *tuna*, which is actually the flesh from a type of cactus.

What To Drink

Peru's national drink is *pisco sour*, which consists of grape brandy, lemon, egg white and a dash of cinnamon. In towns, many Peruvians drink the soft drink *chicha morada*, made with purple maize (different from the *chicha de jora*, the traditional home made alcoholic brew known throughout the Andes). The lime green *Inca Cola* is more popular than it's northern namesake, as well as *Orange Crush, Sprite* and *Seven-up*. The *jugos*, juices, are a delightful alternative to sodas and there are many fruits available. Instant Nescafe is often served up even in good restaurants, although real coffee can be found at a price. Tea drinkers would be advised to order their beverage without milk, to avoid receiving some peculiar concoctions.

The inexpensive beers are of high quality. Try Cusqueña, Cristal or Arequipena. Peruvian vines can't compete with Chilean excellence, but for a price, Tabernero, Tacama, Ocucaje and Vista Alegre are the reliable names. The Peruvian *Pisco Sour* is, however, a strong contender. Try the famous, potent *catedral* at the Gran Hotel Bolívar in Lima.

Where To Eat

Lima

Although Lima offers a huge choice of restaurants in the city area, the following are the most reliable, providing high quality food and service:

INTERNATIONAL CUISINE

Pabellon de Caza, Alonzo de Molina 1100, Monterrico. Tel: 37-9533. Monday–Saturday noon–3pm and 7pm–1am. Brunch on Sunday 10.30am–4pm. Located only a short stroll from the Gold Museum, containing a luxuriant garden and elegant decor.
Carlin, La Paz 646, Miraflores. Tel: 44-4134. Open noon–4pm and 7pm–12am daily. A cozy international style restaurant popular with foreign residents and tourists.
Los Condes de San Isidro, Paz Soldan 290, San Isidro. Tel: 22-2557. Open noon–3pm and 7pm–12am daily. Set in a spectacular San Isidro mansion.
El Alamo, Cnr of La Paz and Diez Canseco, Miraflores. Monday–Saturday 12.30–3pm and 7pm–12am. A cozy spot for imported wines and cheeses. Specializing in fondues.

SEAFOOD RESTAURANTS

La Rosa Nautica, Espigon No. 4, Coasta Verde, Miraflores. Tel: 47-0057. Open 12.30pm–2am daily. Lima's most famous seafood restaurant prestigiously located at the end of an ocean boardwalk.
La Costa Verde, Barrangquito Beach, Barranco. Tel: 67-8218. Open noon–12am daily. Romantic at night under a thatched roof and right on the beach.

CRIOLLA CUISINE

Las Trece Monedas (The Thirteen Coins), Jr. Ancash 536, Lima. Tel: 27-6547. Open noon–4pm and Monday–Saturday 7–11.30pm. Formal presentation within a beautiful 18th-century colonial mansion, including courtyard and antique coach.
Manos Morenos, Av. Conquistadores 887, San Isidro. Tel: 42-6271. Open noon–3.30pm and Tuesday–Sunday 6pm–12am. Criollo Breakfast: Saturday and Sunday 8.30–11am. The best "criollo" fare Lima has to offer, specializing in *anticuchos* (shish kebab of marinated beef heart).

FRENCH CUISINE

L'Eau Vive, Ucayali 370, Lima. Tel: 27-5612. Monday–Saturday noon–2.45pm and 8.15–10.15pm. Fine provincial dishes prepared and served by a French order of nuns. The skylit inner courtyard is one of Lima's most pleasurable settings for luncheon – the perfect place to take a break from sightseeing. (*Ave Maria* is sung nightly at 10pm and dinner guests are invited to join in).

ITALIAN

Valentino, Manuel Banon 215, San Isidro. Tel: 41-6174. Monday–Saturday noon–3pm and 7.30pm–12am. Great Italian food at Lima's best international restaurant.
La Trattoria, Manuel Bonilla 106, Miraflores. Tel: 46-7002. Monday–Saturday 1–3.30pm and 8pm–12am. Authentic Italian fare.

JAPANESE

Matsuei, Canada 236, La Victoria. Tel: 72-2282. Open Monday–Saturday noon–3pm and 7–11pm; Sunday 7–11pm. Excellent quality Japanese food.

STEAK

La Carreta, Rivera Navarrete 740, San Isidro. Tel: 40-5424. Open noon–8.30pm daily. For typically excellent Argentine beef.
The Steak House, La Paz 642, Mezzanine – "El Suche", Miraflores. Tel: 44-3110. noon–3pm and 7pm–12am. Charming setting that has good steaks and salads.

PIZZA

Las Cuatro Estaciones, Vcayali (near cnr Jiron de la Union), Lima. One of the very few great pizza restaurants of South America, also serving exotic local fruit juices. Wholesome and highly recommended for all travelers.
La Pizzeria, Benavides 322, Miraflores. Tel: 46-7793. Open 9.30–12am daily. Nighttime haunt of trendy Miraflores crowd.

"TEX-MEX"

Villa Taxco, Libertad 435 (F. Gerdes), Miraflores. For Reservations: 47-5264. Monday–Thursday noon–11.30pm. The show "Mariachis" on Fridays and Saturdays starts at 9.30pm. Authentic Mexican dishes including Tampiquena Steak, Burritos and Fajitas. Mexican decor throughout with banquet rooms available.

CAFES

La Tiendecita Blanca – Cafe Suisse, Av. Larco 111, Miraflores. Tel: 45-9797. Boasts of 30 different kinds of chocolates, excellent ice-cream and desserts. Popular with shoppers but also serves lunch and dinner.

Arequipa

This attractive city has always maintained a reputation for style and affluence. There are several good restaurants around the Plaza de Armas and cafes can be found in the first block of San Francisco.

La Rueda – Argentine Grill, Mercaders 210. Tel: 21-9330. Barbequed meats and good wine in a cozy ranch style restaurant.

Le Paris, Mercaders 228. French cuisine and other international dishes.

El Fogón, Santa Marta 112. Tel: 21-4594. Specializes in barbequed chicken.

Sol de Mayo, Jerusalem 207 (Yanahuara district). Good lunch time menu of Peruvian specialties such as *rocoto relleno*, stuffed hot peppers, or *ocopa*, potatoes in a spicy sauce with melted cheese. Include a visit to the Mirador de Yanahuara as part of your day's itinerary.

Cuzco

While in Cuzco, sample the succulent pink trout, prepared in many of the Peruvian and international style restaurants. Cuzquenos have also mastered the art of pizza baking and there is always a new establishment to be found within the plaza's portals. Good restaurants will also provide exciting Andean music.

El Ayllu, Portal de Carnes 203 (beside Cathedral). A must to visit for breakfast of ham and egg, toast and fruit juice, or homemade fruit yoghurt, cakes, teas and good coffee.

El Trujo, Plaz Regocijo 247. Catering to most of the large tour groups, this nightly dinner and show is the most elaborate in Cuzco and very good value.

Le Petit Montmarte, Garcilaso 270. Fine French cuisine.

Pizzeria Bella Napoli, Portal Escribanos 177, Plaza Regocijo. Just one of the many restaurants which

serves mouthwatering garlic bread and fresh mixed salads as well as pizzas.

Quinta Zarate, Calle Tortera Paccha. One of the many "quintas", or inns, in the suburbs. The specialty here is roast *cuy*, guinea pig.

Trattoria Adriano, Sol 105, cnr Mantas. Friendly service and excellent pink trout. Try it simply grilled and with a squeeze of lemon.

Cuzco's best two hotels, the **El Dorado Inn** and the **Libertador** have excellent restaurants, with high prices set in US$.

Cafes around the plaza serve *mate de coca*, chocolate mud cake and hot milk with rum on chilly Cuzco nights.

Huaráz

Chalet Suisse, Hostal Andino, Jr. Cochachin 357. International meals.

Creperie Patrick, Av. Luzuriaga 424.

La Familia, Av. Luzuriaga 431. Wide selection of wholesome foods.

Pizzeria Ticino, Av. Luzuriaga 651.

Samuel's, Jr. José de la Mar 626. Good breakfasts.

Trujillo

De Marco, Francisco Pizarro 725. Tel: 23-4251. Peruvian and international cuisine. Popular for ice-creams and desserts.

There is a concentration of restaurants near the market and a number of vegetarian places on Bolívar.

Attractions

Round Trips & Tours

Lima Tours is the main tour organiser in Peru, having branches in every tourist region. They offer tours to every part of the country mentioned in this book – for example, to Cuzco and Machu Picchu of three days and two nights duration inclusive flight; or to Arequipa, the Amazon, the north or Lake Titicaca.

Lima Tours also keeps up-to-date on new events and offer theme trips: for example, they offer tours to the new Sipán archaeological dig; and have

exclusive rights on visits to some colonial houses in Lima (even including evening dinners in 17th-century mansions etc.). It's worth dropping by their modern offices in Calle Belen and asking for one of their brochures:

Lima Tours, Belen 1040. Tel: 27-6624. Monday–Friday 8.30am–5.15pm and Saturday–Sunday 8.30am–3pm.

Also at: 4 Pardo 392, Miraflores. Tel: 43-1948; and Juan de Arona 883, San Isidro. Tel: 72-3559.

Trekking

Preparation: The countryside looks most beautiful in the dry season from May to September when the weather is good. Trekking is best done with three or more people for security reasons and also because it is more fun. Assembling a group in Cuzco is easy using the notice board hanging in the tourist office on the Plaza de Armas. The same service is offered in Huaráz in the Casa de Guias which is just a stroll away from the main road.

Equipment: Essential for trekking tours are: backpack, strong walking shoes, sleeping bag, thermal mat, tent and cooker. Some adventure travel agencies rent all the equipment and these places are quite easy to find. The gear is inexpensive but the quality is often bad. You should check your equipment carefully before starting. The nights tend to be very cold but it is easy to get sunburnt during the day in the Andes. Don't forget a hat and take your own high factor sunscreen, as you won't be able to find it in Peru. If you wish you can hire a porter to carry your luggage up the Inca trail. Mule guides (*arrieros*) can be found everywhere in the Cordillera Blanca and their service is not expensive.

Food: Buy your food in the larger towns because there is not a great choice in small villages. A chain of *supermercados, bodegas* and street markets sell food like dry fruit, cheese, fruit, instant soup and tinned fish in these places. Drinking water should be treated with iodine. Disguise the unpleasant flavour with instant seaweed powder.

Altitude sickness: The onset of altitude sickness can be diminished by sticking to a few rules. Avoid alcohol, excessive eating and getting physically tired out in the first few days. Drinking lots of liquid helps the body adjust. Sugar, for example from sweets and glucose mixtures, stimulates the metabolism and aspirin helps headaches. Mate de coca, a coca leaf tea, is supposed to be the best universal remedy.

Apart from Lima Tours, recommended specialist adventure travel companies for river running, trekking and jungle expeditions include:
Expediciones Mayuc, Conquistadores 199, San Isidro, Tel: 22-5988.
Explorandes, Bolognesi 159, Miraflores, Tel: 45-0532.

Lima

Lima possesses a wealth of tourist attractions in the form of historical landmarks, such as colonial houses and churches, as well excellent museums. Tours can also be taken to nearby archaeological sights located on the central and southern highways leading way from Lima.

The independent traveler can take quite a while seeing all there is to offer or join a city tour if time is limited.

Many travel agencies and tour operators are located on Colmena, the northwest side of Plaza San Martín. For daily sightseeing tours of the city, night excursions including dinner and show, or day trips beyond Lima, the largest and most organized tour company is Vista Peru, providing pick-up from all major hotels, English speaking guides and deluxe motorcoaches. All reservations and enquiries can be made through:
Lima Tours, Belen 1040. Tel: 27-6624. Monday–Friday 8.30am–5.15pm and Saturday–Sunday 8.30am–3pm.
Also at: Pardo 392, Miraflores. Tel: 43-1948; and Juan de Arona 883, San Isidro. Tel: 72-3559.

Reservations for tours or adventure travel throughout Peru can usually be made in Lima. Direct flights from Lima over the Nazca lines can be booked through:
Aero Cóndor, Hotel Sheraton. Tel: 32-9050 ext. 117.

Pisco

Located 235 km south of Lima, Pisco is noted for the wildlife of the Balletas Islands and Paracas Peninsula, as well as the archaeological site of Paracas Necropolis. Boat tours to the Balletas Islands are reserved through the Hostal Pisco and the more expensive Hotel Paracas, which also has tours to the Paracas Peninsula (see "Hotel" section).

Ica

Ica is an oasis surrounded by sand dunes, famous for wine and *pisco*. Tourists visit the distilleries and wineries, particularly Tacama and Ocucaje, as well as the attractive colonial churches and museums. Best time to come is in February, for the grape harvest and Vintage festival.

Nazca

For flights over the Nazca lines in light aircraft, reservations with Aero Condor can be made at either Condor's Nest (across from the airport), at their office opposite the Hotel de Turistas, or at the Hotel Nazca.

The Hotel Nazca will organise ground level viewing of the lines for those who don't want to fly. The Nazca Lines-Mirador Tour includes the observation tower 20 km north of Nazca.

Arequipa

Most attractions in Arequipa are accessible on foot and easily appreciated as an independent traveler, although if you don't have much time, city tours are available to include the Santa Catalina Monastery and other points of interest. Day tours into the mountainous terrain include the Colca Canyon, climbing the volcano – El Misti, viewing the petroglyphs at El Toro and so on.
Lima Tours offer the most comfortable visits. Contact:
Lima Tours, Santa Catalina 120. Tel: 22-4210.

An interesting option is with Holley's Unusual Excursions. The Englishman Anthony Holley knows the surrounding area inside out and runs four–wheel drive excursions of six people. For information write c/o Casilla 77, Arequipa or in Arequipa phone: 22-4452/21-2525. Again, Mayuc Expediciones handles kayak and rafting expeditions in the Colca Canyon. In Arequipa they're located at Apartado 5 96.

Some travelers prefer to drive themselves. National Car Rental in Arequipa rents VW's and Toyota Jeeps at reasonable rates.

Puno (Lake Titicaca)

Tours can be taken around the lake, to the ruins at Sillustani, Chucuito and the town of Juli. Contact:
Turpuno, Jr. Lambayeque 175. Tel: 35-2001. Fax: 35-1431.

Many travelers take the short boat ride across Lake Titicaca to the Floating Islands of the Uros, or to the tranquil islands of Taquile or Amantaní. Simply stroll to the dock area where boats leave every hour.

Hydrofoils to the Island of the Sun, the village of Copacabana and to Bolivia, including lunch, can be booked through **Transturin**:
In Puno: Jiron Tacna 201. Tel: 737. In Cuzco: Portal de Panes 109, Of.1, Plaza de Armas. Tel: 22-2332.
Crillon Tours also operates an all-inclusive bus-hydrofoil-bus journey to La Paz, Bolívia. Expensive but delightful.

Cuzco

The first thing to do is to purchase a "Visitors Ticket", a combination entry pass to all the historic buildings of note. It includes fourteen different sites, many of them "a must", but each site can only be visited once.

Tour operators in Cuzco fall into two categories: those offering standard tours of Cuzco and surrounding ruins or market villages, and those operating adventure tours such as trekking, climbing, river running and jungle expeditions. Recommended for tours are:
Lima Tours, Av. Sol 567, Tel: 22-8431/ 22-1266/22-3791.
Receptour (Hotel Libertador), San Augustin 400. Tel: 22-3981.

Lima Tours offers structured trekking trips (including a "Full Moon on the Inca Trail" trek) and can arrange visits to the Amazon from Cuzco.

There are many other adventure travel companies to choose from. The following also handle jungle expeditions into the Manu National Park from Puerto Maldonado and take reservations for jungle lodges.
Cuzco Maldonado Tour, Portal de Panes 109. Tel: 22-2332.
Expediciones Manu, Procuradores 372. Tel: (08) 22-6671. For the Manu Biosphere Reserve.
Expediciones Mayuc, Procuradores 354. Tel: 23-2666.
Explorandes, Urb. Magisterio N-17. Tel: 22-6599.

Manu & Tambopata Nature Tours, Av. Sol 627-B Of. 401. Tel: 23-4793.

Other specialist adventure companies with guides and equipment for rent include:
APU Expediciones, Portal de Carnes 236, Plaza de Armas. Tel: 23-5408. Recommended for river running.
Dalfi, Plateros 352. Tel: 22-2300. Trips on the Machu Picchu Inca Trail organized and equipment rented.
Peruvian Andean Treks, Pardo 705. Tel: 22-5701. Specialist mountaineering equipment.

Huaráz
For tours to Chavin and other day trips:
Huaráz Chavin Tours, Av. Luzuriaga 740, Huaráz-Ancash. Tel: 72-1922.
Milla Tours, Av. Luzuriaga 515, Huaráz-Ancash. Tel: 72-1742.
Pablo Tours, Av. Luzuriaga 501, Huaráz-Ancash. Tel: 72-1145. Equipment rental for trekking and climbing:
Andean Sport Tours, Av. Luzuriaga 571, Huaráz-Ancash. Tel: 72-1612.

Trujillo
For tours to the five major archaeological sites:
Trujillo Tours, Jr. Gamarra 440-448. Tel: 23-3069/23-3091. Fax: (044) 25-7518.

Chiclayo
Important new archaeological sites such as Sipan can be reached with Lima Tours or the following:
Indiana Tours, M.M. Izaga 774. Tel: 24-0833.

Cajamarca
Tours of the city include numerous colonial churches, thermal baths at Banos del Inca and the Ventaillas de Otuzco. Contact:
Cumbemayo Tours, Jr. Amalia Puga 635. Tel: 92-2938.
Intertours, Jr. Lima (main square). Tel: 92-2777.

Iquitos
There are many interesting sights apart from jungle expeditions. Most tour operators can be found along Calle Putumayo between the plaza and the river.
Explorama Tours, Av. La Marina 340-Casilla 446, Iquitos. Tel: 23-5471/23-

3481. Fax: 23-4968. Reservations in Lima: Camana 851 Of. 1501, Lima. Tel: 24-4764.

Museums

Due to the country's financial situation some cultural sights have been neglected. Nevertheless some museums are worth a visit.

Lima
Amano Museum, Retiro 160 (off 11th of Angamos), Miraflores. Tel: 41-2909. Admission by appointment only, guided tours at: 2pm, 3pm, 4pm and 5pm Monday–Friday. Particularly beautiful is the textile collection from the lesser known Chancay culture.
Museo de Arte, Paseo de Colon 125, Lima. Tel: 23-4732. Tuesday–Sunday 9am–5pm. Grand building containing four centuries of Peruvian artworks, including modern painting. Also houses pre-Columbian artifacts and colonial furniture.
Museo de Ciencias de la Salud (Health Sciences Museum), Junin 270, Lima. Tel: 27-0190. Wednesday–Sunday 10am–4pm. Details pre-Columbian medical practices with English translations. The museum also arranges pre-Columbian banquets for organized groups.
Museo de Historia Natural, Arenales 1256, Jesus Maria. Tel: 71-0117. Monday–Friday 9am–3.30pm; Saturday 9am–1pm. Collection of Peruvian flora and fauna.
Museo de la Nación, Javier Prado Este 2466, San Borja. Tel: 37-7822. Tuesday–Friday 9am–8pm; Saturday–Sunday 10am–9pm. Lima is justly proud of its newest museum, a large modern structure containing many floors of meticulously prepared exhibitions. They include impressive models of new and established archaeological sites as well as a spacious mannequin showroom displaying Peru's magnificent folkloric costumes. Worth at least one long visit.
Museo del Banco Central de Reserva, Ucayali 291, Lima. Tel: 27-6250. Monday–Saturday 10am–5pm; Sunday 10am–1pm. The bank offers a collection of looted pre-Columbian artifacts recently returned to Peru, paintings from the Viceroyalty to the present and also numismatics.
Museo de Oro del Peru (Gold Mu-

seum), Alonso de Molina 100, Monterico. Tel: 35-2917. Noon–6pm daily. There are actually two private museums at this outer suburb address. Apart from Peru's unique collection of Pre-Inca and Inca gold, there is an astonishingly complete Arms Museum which includes a number of highly decorative uniforms.
Museo Etnografico de la Selva, Avenida Tacna (first block). Within the grounds of the Santuario de Santa Rosa de Lima. 9.30am–1pm and 3.30–7pm daily. Dominican missionaries have collected jungle Indian artifacts from south-eastern Peru.
Museo Nacional de Antropologia y Arqueologia, Plaza Bolívar, Pueblo Libre. Tel: 63-5070. 10am–6pm daily. Highly comprehensive exhibitions depicting the prehistory of Peru from the earliest archaeological sites to the arrival of the Spaniards. All the major Peruvian cultures are well represented.
Museo Nacional de la Republica (the National Museum of History), Plaza Bolívar (next door to the Archaeological Museum), Pueblo Libre. Tel: 63-2009. 9am–6pm daily. Both San Martín and Bolívar had lived in this building, now containing the furnishings and artifacts from colonial, republican and independent Peru. A must for those interested in the Peruvian revolution.
Museo Pedro de Osma, Pedro de Osma 501, Barranco. Tel: 67-0915/67-0019. 11am–1pm and 4–6pm. Admission by appointment only. Treasured collection of Viceregal painting, sculpture and silver.
Museo Rafael Larco Herrera, Bolívar 1515, Pueblo Libre. Tel: 61-1312. Monday–Saturday 9am–1pm and 3–6pm. Private collection of over 400,000 well-preserved ceramics, pre-Columbian art and artifacts. Famous erotic "huacos" ceramics from the Moche culture are housed in a separate room beside the gift shop.
Museum of the Inquisition, Junin 548 (right side of the Plaza Bolívar as you face the Congress), Lima. Monday–Friday 9am–7pm; Saturday 9am–2.30pm. Admission free. Explicit representations of torture methods in the Dungeon of this, the headquarters of the Inquisition for all Spanish America from 1570–1820.
Numismatic Museum, Banco Wiese, 2nd Floor Cuzco 245, Lima. Tel: 27-

5060 ext. 553. Monday–Friday 9am–1pm. Admission free. Peruvian coin collection from Colonial times to the present.

PARACAS

J C Tello Museum, Information Center, Paracas Peninsula.

ICA

Regional Museum, Ayabaca, Ica (1.5 km from Plaza de Armas). Best collection in the region of Indian artifacts, including preserved mummies and beautiful Nazca ceramics.

AREQUIPA

Goyeneche Palace, La Merced (two blocks away from plaza).
Casa Moral, Cnr Moral & Bolívar.
Casa Ricketts, San Francisco (near Moral).
Santa Catalina Convent, Av. Santa Catalina 301. Take a few hours to explore this tranquil complex, one of the most fascinating visits in Peru.

PUNO

Carlos Dreyer Museum, Cnr Deusta & Lemos. Monday–Friday 9am–7pm.

CUZCO

A bewildering number of museums and historic sights. Independent travelers can visit them separately with a Visitor's Ticket, available from several of the major attractions. Hours are listed on the ticket and attractions explained in the Cuzco section of this book.

HUARÁZ

Archaeological Museum of Ancash, Plaza de Armas, Huaráz-Ancash.

TRUJILLO

Casa de la Emancipacion, Jr. Pizarro 610 cnr Gamarra.
Casa de Mayorazgo, Jr. Pizarro 314.
Casa Urquiaga & Casa Bracamonte, Plaza de Armas.
Cassinelli Museum, Av. Mansiche (near Av. Espana).
Palacio Iturregui, Jr. Pizarro 688.
Trujillo Archaeological Museum, Jr. Pizarro 349.

CAJAMARCA

Cerro Apolonia, Jr. 2 de Mayo (three blocks from plaza).
Rescue Room, Jr. Amalia Puga 750.
Teatro Municipal, Av. Amazonas.

IQUITOS

The Iron House, Putumayo & Raymondi (cnr of the Plaza de Armas). Supposedly designed by Eiffel and imported piece-by-piece during rubber boom days.

Antique & Art Galleries

LIMA

The best establishments are located in San Isidro, Miraflores and Barranco.
"715", Benavides 216, Miraflores. Tel: 47-2687. Monday–Saturday 4–8pm.
Banco Continental, Tarata 201, Miraflores. Tel: 44-0011. Monday–Friday 2–8.30pm; Saturday 6–8pm.
Borkas, Las Camelias 851, San Isidro. Tel: 40-8415. Monday–Friday 10.30am–8pm; Saturday 5–8pm.
Camino Brent, Burgos 170, San Isidro. Monday–Saturday 4–8pm.
Cosmos, Pasaje los Pinos 173, Miraflores. Monday–Saturday 5–9pm.
El Taller, Los Manzanos 353, San Isidro. Tel: 22-0351.
Equus, Colon 501, Miraflores. Tel: 45-6592. Monday–Saturday 5–9pm.
Forum, Larco 1150, Miraflores. Monday–Friday 11am–1pm and 5–9pm.
Galeria Artesanal Chiwake, Av. Arequipa 4005, Miraflores. Tel: 40-2173.
Peruvian North American Cultural Institute, Arequipa 4798, Miraflores. Tel: 46-0381. Also at: Cuzco 446, Lima. Tel: 28-3530.
Porta 725, Porta 725, Miraflores. Tel: 47-6158. Monday–Saturday 11am–1pm and 4–8pm.
Praxis, San Martín 689, Barranco. Tel: 67-2845. Monday–Saturday 5–9pm.
Sanchez Galeria de Arte Colonial, José Granda 460, San Isidro. Tel: 22-5970.
Sol, Las Lias 150, Lince. Tel: 71-1029. Monday–Saturday 5–9pm.
Trapecio, Larco 143, Miraflores. Tel: 44-0842. Monday–Saturday 5–9pm.

Concerts

In Lima, the Philharmonic Society presents celebrated international orchestras and soloists. For information: Porta 170, Of. 301, Miraflores. Open Monday/Wednesday/Friday 10am–noon. Tel: 45-7395.

Theaters & Music

Teatro Municipal, Ica 300, Lima. Symphony, opera, plays and ballet.

The English troupe – "The Good Companions", which is set up by the British Council, performs different plays each month. These are advertised in the English-language weekly, the *Lima Times*, available at all major hotels. Tel: 47-9760 for information.

Other theater venues in Lima:
Teatro Segura, Huancavelica.
Teatro Arequipa, Av. Arequipa.

Architecture

Many of Lima's architectural jewels from the colonial era are in a catastrophic state of repair. Although the old town was declared a world heritage site by UNESCO, in 1994 the Peruvian civil defence office announced that it would soon demolish 46 buildings due to the danger from decaying walls in the event of an earthquake. It is either too late for restoration or the necessary money is not available.

The following colonial style buildings can be visited:
Casa Aliaga, Unión 224. Beautiful original furniture. The first owner, Jerónimo de Aliaga came with Pizarro's troops to Peru in 1532. Visits have to be booked via travel agencies.
Casa de la Riva, Jirón Ica 426, Tel. 28-2642. Small museum on the second floor.
Casa Pilatos, Jirón Ancash 390. Today a cultural centre.

Nightlife

Live Music

LIMA

In Lima the traveler encounters two types of live music: Folkorica and Criolla. The former is typical of the Andean highlands, while the coastal Criolla style is more popular in Lima.

The best places to see live Peruvian music are "Peñas" – lively nightclubs with colorful performances and enthusiastic audience dancing.
Peña Hatuchay, Trujillo 228, Rimac (across the bridge from the center of town). The best night out for budget-conscious travelers, and anyone else for that matter who is willing to get into the informal spirit. A welcoming interior end a great variety show.

Barranco is Lima's "bohemian" suburb of cafés, bars and live music. A couple of venues offer regular shows:
El Buho Pub, Sucre 315. Creole music.
Karamanduka, Sanchez Carrion 135, Barranco. Tel: 47-3237. Open for lunch and dinner, music every night.
La Estacion de Barranco, Pedro de Osma 112.
Los Balcones, Grau (in front of Municipal Park). For Creole and Negroide music.
Taberna 1900, Grau 268.
For jazz and contemporary music try:
La Casona de Barranco, Grau 329.
La Casa de Edith Barr, Ignacio Merino 250, Miraflores. Tel: 41-0612. A more prestigious ambience presenting creole music.

CUZCO

Cuzco has some of the best peñas in South America, with a range of Andean styles (some of the bands are internationally well-known). They're mostly around the plaza and easy to find because of the blaring music. Two peñas sharing the same staircase on the south-western side of the plaza are probably the best place to start.

Several restaurants around the plaza (such as the Roma and El Truco) also have live music – just stroll around and listen for the playing. Alternatively, many of the larger hotels also stage folkloric shows.

HUARÁZ

El Tambo, José de la Mar 776, Huaráz.
Tasco Bar, Jr. Lucar y Torre 556, Huaráz.
Taberna Imantata, Av. Luzuriaga 407, Huaráz.

Nightclubs

LIMA

Casablanca, 117 P. Fierro, San Isidro. Tel: 40-7751.
La Palizada, Av. del Ejército 800, Miraflores. Tel: 41-0552.
Lions Club, Madrid 338 (by the Plaza Bolognesi). Features live jazz most evenings.
Peña Hatuchay, Trujillo 228. Tel: 24-7779.
Psicosis, Bella Vista, Miraflores.
Satchmo Jazz Bar, 538 La Paz, Miraflores. Tel: 44-1753. Sophisticated New Orleans style jazz and surroundings.

Bars

LIMA

Brenchley Arms, Atahualpa 174. Typical English Pub with wholesome fare and dart board.
Johann Sebastian Bar, Schell 369. Relaxing venue with classical background music.

CUZCO

A favorite hangout for gringos is the Cross Keys Pub, run by British-born ornithologist Barry Walker (who, incidentally, wrote the section on "Wildlife of the Sierra" in this book) and his Peruvian wife. It's very friendly and relaxed – you can even buy English gin and Australian rum if you so desire (although the South American versions are cheaper and just as good). It's on the south-western side of the plaza.

Discos

LIMA

Arizona Colt (below El Pacifico cinema, Miraflores), La Miel, José Pardo 120.
Casa Vieja, San Martín/La Paz, Miraflores.
Faces, Centro Comercial, Camino Real, Level A 68-72 (intersection of Camino Real & Choquehuanca in San Isidro).

Shopping

What To Buy

In Lima as well as the many regional market places, the best quality and value lies in handcrafted products (see chapter on Artesanías). This particularly applies to gold, silver and copper work, as well as Peru's rich textile goods – such as alpaca garments and woven tapestries. Many tourists also take home reproductions of pre-Columbian ceramics, with gourds being a great favorite.

Visitors to the jungle may have the opportunity to purchase traditional handicrafts, including adornments (dance necklaces), utensils (baskets, food bowls, hunting bags), and weapons (bows, arrows, spears). However, visitors should never be tempted to buy skins, live animals, or arrows decorated with colorful parrot feathers. This trade is often illegal and has direct negative consequences in destroying wildlife populations.

The harvesting of wild Brazil-nuts is a major economy of the jungle and is not destructive to the forest. Fresh Brazil-nuts are richer in flavor than processed nuts as they still contain many of their natural oils.

Apart from artesanías, quality shopping goods can only be found in the commercial streets of Miraflores and San Isidro, where suppliers for international brands keep a limited stock at very high prices. For bargains in electronics, you would do better to cross the southern border into northern Chile and its Duty Free Zona Franca complexes.

This is true also for camera supplies, as well as any photo developing. Peruvian standards will often disappoint you, so save your exposed film to be developed when you get home.

If you are looking for books in English, however, there are several possibilities. The South American Explorers Club has a good library for all things South American and relevant guide books are on sales. Members of the club can utilize the free book exchange of paperbacks. There is a chain of ABC bookstores in Lima providing newspapers, magazines, guide books and "coffee table" books in English, French and German. Keep in mind these items will be more expensive than at home. The English language newspaper, *The Lima Times*, also advertises books about Peru which can be obtained from their office in Miraflores at Carabya 928, 3rd Floor.

For paperback fiction try: Libreria El Pacifico, under the cinema "El Pacifico" in Miraflores. There is also a book exchange for used paperbacks at Ocona 211, two blocks from the Plaza San Martín, if you can ignore the money changers.

Shopping Areas

Each region has its own distinctive crafts, however, if your time is limited, you'll find that many cultures are well represented in Lima. There are a number of shops within an attractive courtyard at "1900" Belen 1030, just down from the Plaza San Martín. Two other recognized centers of quality merchandise are at El Alamo, 5th block of La Paz, Miraflores and El Suche, the 6th block of La Paz in Miraflores.

Outdoor markets offer the best bargains although quality varies and one needs to be wary of pickpockets. The best outdoor market, known as the Mercado Indio, takes place on Avenida La Marina from blocks 6 to 10. A relaxed artists' market with varying quality canvasses is on Parque Kennedy in the heart of Miraflores. Here are some other reliable sources for artesanía:

Artesanías del Peru, Av. Jorge Basadre 610, San Isidro.

In Arequipa: Av. General Moran 120.

In Cuzco: There are many outlets facing the main plaza and quite a few more near the major hotels.

In Iquitos: Putomayo 128.

In Lima: **Artisuyo**, Jiron Tacna 460, Miraflores. Tel: 47-2527.

Poco a Poco S.A., Av. Nicolas de Pierola 712, Of. 14, Lima. Also at: Juan de Arona 425–431, San Isidro.

For alpaca, leather and fur products in Lima:

Alpaca 111 S.A. (English spoken), Av. Larco 859, Miraflores. Tel: 47-7163. Also at: Camino Real Shopping Center, Level A, Shop 32-33, San Isidro.

Royal Alpaca, La Paz 646, store 14-15, El Suche commercial center, Miraflores. Monday–Saturday 9.30am–9.30pm; Sunday 11am–7pm.

In Arequipa: **Alpaca 111**, Jerusalem 115. Tel: 21-2347.

Also in Arequipa: **El Zaguan**, Santa Catalina 120A. Tel: 22-3950.

In Cuzco: 4 Ruinas 472. Tel: 23-6322.

For gold objects try in Lima:

Casa Welsch, Jiron Union 498.

Cabuchon, Libertadores 532, San Isidro.

Wako, Jr de la Union 841, Lima. Monday–Saturday 10am–1.30pm and 3–7.30pm.

Ceramics and tapestries are the specialty of **El Artesano**, Jr Diez Canseco 498, Miraflores, Lima.

The major hotels often house exclusive jewelry and artezanía stores such as H. Stern Jewelers, with outlets at the Hotel Gran Bolívar, the Lima Sheraton, Miraflores Cesar's Hotel, the Gold Museum and the International Airport. For clothing printed with Peruvian designs in Lima:

Club Peru, Conquistadores 946, San Isidro.

Silvania Prints, Colmena 714 (between the Gran Bolívar and the Hotel Crillon)

Also at: Conquistadores 905, San Isidro.

Sports

Participant

Lima Tours can arrange visits to El Pueblo Inn, a country club 11 km east of Lima, specifically for sporting activities such as tennis, golf, horse riding and swimming. Another agency to try is:

Sudex Agency, Carabaya 933, Miraflores. Tel: 28-6054.

Ask about other 18 hole golf courses at Country Club de Villa, Granja Azul and La Planicie.

For ten-pin bowling and pool playing, go to the Brunswick Bowl, Balta 135, Miraflores.

Volleyball and polo have a large following in Peru and cricket is played at the Lima Cricket Club.

A great variety of sports are available to tourists outside Lima. Horse riding is popular in the Sierra, where horses can easily be hired. Fly fishing in Andean lakes and streams is a rewarding pastime and there is excellent deep-sea fishing off Ancon, north of Lima.

Spectator

The main spectator sports in South-American countries are football, horse racing and, to a lesser extent, bullfighting.

Association football matches take place at the National Stadium, Paseo de le Republica in downtown Lima, which seats 45,000.

Horse racing takes place most weekends and some summer evenings at the Monterrico Racetrack at the junction of the Pan-American Highway South with Avenida Javier Prado. Take your passport to join the members stand.

The two bullfighting seasons in Lima are October–November and a short one in March. The prestigious bullfighting ring is at Acho in Rimac, where famous international matadors make guest appearances. However, the regular proceedings are often a little sordid, with the bullfighters little more than incompetent butchers and the audience, drunk on beer, throwing bottles and howling in derision.

Further Reading

General

The novels of Peru's high-profile writer Mario Vargas Llosa are another interesting insight into the country's psyche. *Aunt Julia and the Scriptwriter* (the basis for the recent US film "Tune in Tomorrow") and *The Time of the Hero* are probably the most readable. *The Green House* is set in Peru's Amazon basin.

The Conquest of the Incas, by John Hemming. Penguin, 1983. The best modern account of the fall of the Inca empire. Extremely readable style, brings the history of Peru to life.

Hemming has also written a coffee table book called *Monuments of the Incas* with black and white photography by Edward Ranney. Both are classic introductions to understanding Peru.

Cut Stones and Crossroads, by Ronald Wright. Viking Press, 1984 (also in Penguin). Subtitled "A Journey in the Two Worlds of Peru", this is considered the best travel book on the country in recent years. Wright captures the many ups and downs of travel in Peru, with some stimulating insights. Worth reading despite a certain snobbishness in outlook.

Martin Chambi: Photographs of Peru 1920–1950, by Martin Chambi. Banco de la República. A collection of shots by Peru's most famous photographer (and one of Latin America's greats).

The Open Veins of Latin America, by Eduardo Galeano. Monthly Review Press. A vivid account of the region's history from a left-wing perspective.

Peru: Paths to Poverty, by Michael Reid. Latin American Bureau, 1985. Probably the most cogent and readable interpretation of Peru's modern history.

Archaeology & Pre-Inca Cultures

The Adobe Sculptures of Huaca de los Reyes, by Michael E. Moseley and Luis Watanabe. Archaeology 27: 154–161. (1974).

Architecture and Chronology at El Paraíso, Peru, by Jeffrey Quilter. Journal of Field Archaeology 12: 279–297. (1985).

Chan Chan: Peru's Ancient City of Kings, by Michael E. Moseley and Carol J. Mackey. National Geographic 143/3: 318–344. (1973).

Early Ceremonial Architecture in the Andes, Christopher B. Donnan (ed.). Dumbarton Oaks Research Library and Collection, 1985.

An Early Stone Carving from Pampa de las Llamas-Moxeke, Casma Valley, Peru, by Thomas Pozorski and Shelia Pozorski. Journal of Field Archaeology 15/3: 114–119. (1988).

Lines to the Mountain Gods: Nazca and the Mysteries of Peru, by Evan Hadingham. Random House, 1987.

Long Before the Inca. Natural History 2: 66–82. (1989).

Masterworks of Art Reveal a Remarkable Pre-Inca World. National Geographic 177/6: 16–33. (1990).

The Nazca Lines: A New Perspective on their Origins and Meaning, by Johan Reinhard. 4th edition. Editorial Los Pinos, 1988.

Peruvian Prehistory, by Richard W. Keatings (ed.). Cambridge University Press, 1988.

Recent Excavations at Pampa de las Llamas-Moxeke – a Complex Initial Period Site in Peru, by Shelia Pozorski and Thomas Pozorski. Journal of Field Archaeology 13/4: 381–401. (1986).

Tiwanaku and its Hinterland, by Alan L. Kolata. Archaeology 40/1: 36–41. (1987).

Was Wari a State?, by William H. Isbell and Katharina J. Schreiber. American Antiquity 43/4: 372–389. (1976).

Inca Society

Comentarios Reales de los Incas, by Inca Garcilaso De La Vega. Buenos Aires, 1943. Classic 16th-century accounts by mestizo chronicler (in Spanish).

At the Crossroads of the Earth and the Sky, by Gary Urton. . Austin, 1981. A scholarly, well-written and absorbing account of the cosmology of the modern Quechua people, by a field anthropologist. Soon to be reprinted in paperback.

Everyday Life of the Incas, by Ann Kendall. London, 1973. Some useful background information.

Historia del Tahuantinsuyu, by Maria Rostworowski de Diez Canseco. Lima, 1988. Modern, non-imperialist view of the Incas (in Spanish).

Inca Architecture, by Garziano Gaspairini and Louise Margolies. Bloomington, 1980. The most complete book on the subject.

The Incas, by John H. Rowe (section of the *Handbook of South American Indians*). Washington, 1946. A study that set the groove in Inca-ology for three decades. Nowadays its conclusions about Inca history and social organization are challenged by some scholars.

The Inka Road System, by John Hyslop. New York, 1984. Firsthand account of the author's investigations.

Lords of Cuzco, by Burr Cartwright Brundage. Norman, Oklahoma, 1967 and *Empire of the Incas*, by Burr Cartwright Brundage. Norman, Oklahoma, 1963. Two highly tendentious but well written and researched accounts.

Nueva Cronica y Buen Gobierno, by Filipe Guaman Poma De Ayala. Mexico City, 1988. Hard-to-read 16th-century chronicle, with classic illustrations (in Spanish).

Wiracocha y Ayar, by Henrique Urbano. Cuzco, 1981. Summary of Inca origin myths (in Spanish).

Realm of the Incas, by Victor W. Von Hagen. New York, 1957. Still one of the better accounts of Inca daily life.

Colonial History

Daily Life in Colonial Peru, by Jean Descola. Trans. by Michael Hern. George Allen & Unwin, 1968.

Harochiri: An Andean Society under Inca and Spanish Rule, by Karen Spalding. Standford University Press, 1984.

Inca Treasure as Depicted by Spanish Historians, by Samuel K. Lothrop. The Southwest Museum, 1938.

Peru: A Cultural History, by Henry E. Dobyns and Paul L. Doughty. Oxford University Press, 1976.

The Quechua in the Colonial World, by George Kubler. *Handbook of South American Indians* by Julian H. Steward (ed.) Vol 2: 331–410. Smithsonian Institution, 1946.

Vision of the Vanquished: The Spanish Conquest through Indian Eyes, by Nathan Wachtel. The Harvester Press, 1977.

Machu Picchu

Antisuyo, by Gene Savoy. New York, 1970. Fascinating book, long out of print, by a man with an incredible nose for lost cities.

Archaeological Explorations in the Cordillera Vilcabamba, by Paul Fejos. New York, 1944. Hard to find but fascinating record of the first systematic survey of the Inca Trail.

Arqueologia de la America Andina, by Luis G. Lumbreras. Lima, 1981. A search for connections in Andean culture (in Spanish).

Lost City of the Incas, by Hiram Bingham. New York, 1972. Classic account of Bingham's explorations. Outdated theories, but a great read.

Machu Picchu – Enigmatica Ciudad Inka, by Victor Angles. 2nd edition. Lima, 1987. Account of the author's studies and Inca Trail explorations (in Spanish).

Machu Picchu, an Inca Citadel, by Hiram Bingham. New York, 1979. More details of Bingham's discoveries.

Other "Lost Cities"

El Paititi, El Dorado, y las Amzonas, by Roberto Levillier. Buenos Aires, 1976.

The Golden Man: The Quest for El Dorado, by Victor W. von Hagen. Glasgow, 1974.

Mirabilis in altis, by Juan Pérez de Tudela y Bueso. Madrid, 1983.

Operacion Paititi, by Rubén Iwaki Ordóñez. Cuzco, 1975.

Por las rutas del Paititi, by Juan Carlos Polentini Wester. Lima, 1979.

The Search for El Dorado, by John Hemming. London, 1978.

Andean Wildlife

The Distribution and Status of some Peruvian Mammals, by I.R. Grimwood. New York Zoological Society, Special Publication 21, 1968.

Mammals in the Highlands of Southern Peru, by Oliver P. Pearson. Museum of Comparative Zoology, Harvard.

Amazon Jungle

General

The Cloud Forest, by Peter Matthiesson's account of travel on the Amazon and through the cloud forest of Peru.

Jungles, by Ayensu. A good overall account of the world's rainforests.

Lizzie , edited by Tony Morrison. The true story of a young, turn-of-the-century Englishwoman's trip up the Amazon and over the Fitzcarrald pass into Manu, based on her letters.

Tropical Nature, by Adrian Forsyth and Ken Myiata. An excellent introduction to life and death in a New World rainforest.

Wildlife

An Annotated Checklist of Peruvian Birds, by T. Parker.

A Guide to the Birds of Colombia, by Steve Hilty. Princeton Press. The most useful bird identification guidebook.

The Primary Source – Tropical Forests and Our Future, by Norman Myers.

Rainforests: A Guide to Tourist and Research Facilities at Selected Tropical Forest Sites, by James L. Castner. Feline Press.

Tropical Nature, by Adrian and Ken Miyata Forsyth. Charles Scribner's Sons. Entertaining and well written account of rainforest ecology.

Amazon Indians

At Play in the Fields of the Lord , by Peter Matthiesson. Matthiesson's novel of uncontacted tribes and missionaries set in the department of Madre de Dios, Peru.

The Conquest of the Incas – The classic account of the Spanish conquest by the British historian John Hemming. The last few chapters deal with the Inca jungle capital Vilcabamba and its discovery.

Farewell to Eden, by Matthew Huxley. His personal account of the Amahuaca Indians in southeast Peru.

Keep the River on the Right – the true account of a Fulbright scholar who lived with an uncontacted tribe in southeast Peru.

People of the Sacred Waterfall, by Michael Harner. Harner's celebrated ethnography of the head-shrinking Jivaro Indians in northeast Peru.

Shabono, by Florinada Donner. Although this novel is set in Brazil and not Peru, it is one of the best accounts of what it is like to live with an Amazonian tribe, written by an anthropologist who threw away her notes and "went native".

The Wizard of the Upper Amazon, by Ralph Lamb. His true account of a boy captured by Indians in northern Peru and his apprenticeship as a shaman.

ADDITIONAL INFORMATION

Location of Peruvian Amazon Indian agencies:

Antisuyo, Jiron Tacna 460, Miraflores. Tel: 47-2557.

CAAP, Avenida Gonzales Prada 626, Magdalena del Mar (Lima), Peru. Tel: 61-5223. Has small but good Amazon library.

CIPA, 666 Avenida Ricardo Palma, Miraflores (Lima), Peru. Tel: 46-4823. Name of Peruvian Amazon Indian artesanal store in Lima.

COICA, Jiron Almagro 614, Lima 11, Peru. Tel: 63-1983.

Other Insight Guides

Insight Guides cover the world with almost 200 titles, each produced in the Apa Publications' individual style of incisive journalism and stunning photography. Among the titles on South America are Venezuela, Ecuador, Brazil, Rio de Janiero, Argentina, Buenos Aires and Chile.

The whole continent, from Colombia to Tierra del Fuego, is captured between covers in *Insight Guide: South America*, with up-to-date information on all the major countries.

Insight Guide: Amazon Wildlife is one of the series' nature guides. It brings to life the fantastic flora and fauna of this great natural area, and tells you how to seek them out.

Mexico is especially well covered in the series. In addition to *Insight Guides* to *Mexico* and *Mexico City*, there are companion *Insight Pocket Guides* to *Mexico City, Baja Peninsula* and *Yucatán Peninsula*. The Pocket Guides are written by host authors who have designed special itineraries which help visitors get the most from a limited stay, and each includes a full-size fold-out map.

Art/Photo Credits

All photography by Eduardo Gil except for:

Jim Bartle 12/13, 22/23, 138, 139, 272/273, 277
André and Cornelia Bärtschi 109, 244/245, 246/247, 248, 250, 251, 252, 253, 254, 260, 263, 266
Courtesy of Brüning Museum 43
Victor Campos 293, 294
Sue Cunningham cover, 2, 16/17, 82, 91, 95, 137, 140, 168R, 169, 172, 173L, 187, 203, 204/205, 242, 267, 268, 300/301, 302, 320
Mary Dempsey 206, 208
Peter Frost 100, 132, 221, 232
Eco-Expeditions 209
Eduardo Gil/Courtesy of Brüning Museum 40
Eduardo Gil/Courtesy of Gold Museum, Lima 34, 35
Eduardo Gil/Courtesy of Larco Herrera Museum, Lima 32, 33L&R
Eduardo Gil/Courtesy of Museo Nacional de Antropologia y Arqueologia, Lima 112/113
Michael Guntern 103, 182, 217, 228, 229
Adriana von Hagen 98/99, 256, 257
Claire Leimbach 84/85, 202
Lima Times 66, 76, 77
John Maier Jr. 10/11, 14/15, 20/21, 81, 83, 148/149, 167, 175, 192R, 214, 219
Lynn A. Meisch 133, 192L, 233, 291R
Tony Morrison/South American Pictures 316, 319
Tony Perrottet 1, 116, 150/151, 185, 191, 195, 199L, 200/201, 227
Heinz Plenge 38/39, 41, 90, 92R, 101, 102, 111, 115, 118, 145, 146, 147, 152/153, 199L, 238, 259, 261, 262, 264, 265, 280L, 281, 284, 290, 295, 296, 297, 298, 299, 304/305
Heinz Plenge/Courtesy of Brüning Museum 30, 31
Robert Randall 62/63, 65, 136
Rex Features 78
Topham Picturepoint 80, 193
Betsy Wagenhauser 59, 135, 141, 142, 270/271, 276, 278, 279, 280R, 310

Maps Berndtson & Berndtson

Visual Consultant V. Barl

Index